THE CYBERNETIC THEORY
OF DECISION

JOHN D. STEINBRUNER

The Cybernetic Theory
of Decision

New Dimensions of Political Analysis

PRINCETON UNIVERSITY PRESS

Published by Princeton University, Princeton, New Jersey
In the United Kingdom: Princeton University Press, Guildford, Surrey

LCC 74-2479
ISBN 0-691-02175-9 (paperback edn.)
ISBN 0-691-07559-X (hardcover edn.)

First PRINCETON PAPERBACK printing, 1976

This book has been composed in Linotype Janson

Printed in the United States of America
by Princeton University Press, Princeton, New Jersey

For Maureen

Contents

List of Figures

Preface

A BOOK, which presents itself as a reasonably coherent, finished product, actually comes about by a process which is far less orderly. At least that is the case with this one. I offer a brief review of that process for two reasons: to thank those who contributed to it and to lend insight to those who were not involved.

The argument made in the following pages finds its origins in my studies in psychology as an undergraduate at Stanford. There I was sensitized to the empirical and epistemological problems encountered in analyzing the processes of perception and came to appreciate the central importance of these questions in the workings of the human mind. Though they could hardly know or be held responsible for what I would make of their teachings, Jonathan Freedman, Donald Davidson, and Albert Hastorf set me off on the track. I was moved particularly by Professor Hastorf, who imparted some of his enthusiasm for the topic and seriousness about it.

To an anonymous donor acting through Stanford University I am indebted for a year's study at the University of Freiburg, West Germany. That year was not only important in allowing me to effect the transition between psychology and political science, but it also contributed directly to the style of analysis of the book. The philosophy faculty at Freiburg in 1963–1964 was heavily influenced by the writings of its eminent professors of earlier years, Edmund Husserl and Martin Heidegger, who had been influenced themselves, I believe (but cannot prove), by the great developments in modern physics in which German universities played such an important role. In that ambience I learned the utility of analyzing the same events from separate, even contradictory theoretical perspectives and of not trying to impose a resolution of such conflicts when there is no compelling one to be found.

The first and, alas, very imperfect pass at this book was my doctoral dissertation, done for the Department of Political Science at the Massachusetts Institute of Technology. I am indebted to the Operations Research Center at MIT for financial support at the thesis-writing stage and to my thesis committee, Ithiel de Sola Pool, William Kaufmann, and Lincoln Bloomfield. Harold

PREFACE

Isaacs, Lucian Pye, Fred Iklé, and Norman Padelford were helpful to me in more informal capacities. The fact that the analysis
in this book focuses on problems of national defense is due primarily to the influence of William Kaufmann, another of the compelling, inspirational teachers I have encountered.

In the year and a half following the completion of my degree
at MIT, I was given research support by the Arms Control Project, directed by Lincoln Bloomfield under the auspices of the
Center for International Studies at MIT. My work during that
period was not directly on the topic of this book, but in fact it
contributed important refinements of the analysis. I am grateful
to Lincoln Bloomfield and to his colleagues Amy Leiss and Colo-
nel Cornelius Gearin for their help. I also want to thank James
Foster, who was a frequent intellectual confidant at that time,
and Hayward Alker, Jr., for advice offered with infectious
enthusiasm.

In 1969, with the support of the Institute of Politics, John Fitz-
gerald Kennedy School of Government at Harvard University,
I began a second effort, which ultimately produced what follows.
During that period I completely reworked both the theoretical
and the historical analysis. I benefited greatly from the close in-
teraction with a group of colleagues who constituted the Faculty
Seminar on Bureaucracy, Politics, and Policy at the Institute of
Politics: Graham Allison, Francis Bator, Joseph Bower, Frederick
Bohen, William Capron, Barry Carter, Robert Coulam, Michel
Crozier, Thomas Garwin, Morton Halperin, Phillip Heymann,
Henry Jacoby, Doris Kearns, Lance Leibman, Ernest May, Frederick Morris, Mark Moore, David Mundel, Richard Neustadt,
Joseph Nye, Don Price, Richard Smoke, and Samuel Williamson.
I am grateful to them, to the chairman of the group, Ernest May,
to the Institute of Politics, and to the students of my graduate
course at Harvard for support at the critical phase. As connoisseurs will notice, there is a strong resonance in the book with the
work of Graham Allison, and I am grateful to him as a particularly close colleague. I am also particularly indebted to Richard
Neustadt, who lavished intellectual and emotional support and,
again, imparted that essential but elusive element of inspiration.

There is one person who shared the entire odyssey in all its
intellectual and emotional dimensions: my wife, Maureen Steinbruner. Hers was not an easy role to play. As one who understood what I was up to in greater depth than anyone else possi-

bly could, it often fell to her to make the criticisms I did not want to hear or to recapture the point of it all when I was confused or discouraged. She helped in more ways than I can recount.

I cannot look back on the effort without feeling particular gratitude to my parents, Robert and Louise Steinbruner, whose influence was important in ways which defy articulation. I regret that my father did not live to see the product, for I know that he would have enjoyed it and would have been kind enough to be proud of it.

There are many others who gave important support. Many of the participants in the events described consented to be interviewed and were otherwise helpful in establishing what actually happened. As explained below I must thank them anonymously. Susan Lutzker and Susan Ackerman provided research assistance on important details of the study. James Vaupel suggested the label, the analytic paradigm, which I have adopted. Frank Levy supplied a number of corrections and additions to the final manuscript. Raymond Bauer, I. M. Destler, Robert Jervis, John McCarthy, and Henry Owen provided valuable comments on earlier drafts. John Butler, James Baxter, and Elaine Baxter suffered through many therapeutic sessions in which various parts of the argument were rehearsed. A number of the staff members of the Institute of Politics—Susan Ackerman, Sarah Ackerson, Jayne Berry, Diane Chellgren, Mary Lanigan Chenery, Sheila Driscoll, Elizabeth Fainsod, Marcessia Gelowtski, Mary Ellen Gianelloni, Carolyn Hicks, Sabrina Peck, Carole Presser, Judith Randolph, and Rowena Rosen—performed the countless tasks of preparing the manuscript.

I am grateful to all who helped, and I trust that my saying so will not cause anyone to blame them for unfortunate characteristics of the book.

Cambridge, Massachusetts
April 1973

THE CYBERNETIC THEORY
OF DECISION

CHAPTER 1

Introduction

WHEN KARL MARX announced over a century ago that a specter was haunting Europe, few men at the time could have foreseen the momentous consequences which were to unravel. The specter at the time he wrote consisted largely of ideas in the minds of a few men; and, though new modes of thought have regularly had strong impact on history, it is still astonishing to see such power develop from such modest beginnings. Marx developed new assumptions about society, politics, and the critical forces of history, and these evolved ultimately into major political movements and revolutionary changes of government in several countries. It was similar to the ideas of John Locke, which inspired Thomas Jefferson and his colleagues. In times of social change the assumptions which structure a society's understanding of political affairs tend to become unstuck. Men with new perspectives and new modes of analysis are able to shift the basis of common understanding, and widespread consequences flow from that. Few cases, of course, are as dramatic or as consequential as those of Marx or Locke; but the phenomenon also works, and more frequently, at lesser orders of magnitude.

At much more modest levels of significance we seem to be engaged at the moment in such a process of basic intellectual adjustment. There is rapid social change, new problems are unquestionably upon us, and there appears to be a malaise in traditional perspectives. The debates of the past over the form of government and the composition of the ruling class, over the authority of the state and the freedom of individuals, over liberal and conservative social policies remain relevant without a doubt. But it can be argued that these debates and the analytic traditions from which they derive do not capture well some of the most troublesome problems of contemporary society. Crosscutting the distinctions which established intellectual traditions have taught us to make are the new issues of managing the institutional behemoths which modern governments have become, and these are issues which perplex men of every political and intellectual persuasion.

3

INTRODUCTION

Mass bureaucracies generated by mass societies have inherent characteristics which are important in their impact on society but which are not well understood. In search of better comprehension, political analysts are being forced to focus on the managerial and decision-making processes of government and to introduce refinements on the very simple assumptions which were made in this area in the past. Decision making, the topic of this book, is also a topic of the times.

In this context it is significant that new perspectives on decision making are beginning to emerge from the precincts of basic research. These perspectives are far less developed than the established theory of decision which now underlies general understanding of political events; but they promise an interesting challenge to the conventional theory. This book attempts to articulate this impending confrontation, which has remained largely inchoate, and to suggest what the consequences for political understanding might be.

New Issues for Political Analysis

The 1960s have frequently been reviewed in the United States as a decade of disillusionment. And for good reason. The period began with a stirring inaugural by a dynamic young President announcing a new generation of leadership, and calling the nation to service in the cause of peace and world justice. The decade proceeded with the civil rights movement and with the war on poverty. It ended with the bitterness of the Indochina war, with intense social and generational antagonism, with the clear failure of the efforts undertaken to eradicate poverty, hunger, and urban decay. Despite the fact that some of the nation's most talented men held the critical positions of power, despite the fact that they were pursuing some of democracy's most cherished values, the results which they achieved yielded a great deal of anguish and very little satisfaction. The nation by common consensus had fallen far short of reasonable aspirations.

The angry recriminations which have been spawned by this disillusionment are softened in the perspective of history. Though explanation is not tantamount to justification, it does help to understand the evolution of government over the previous decades. The nation during the 1960s was experiencing the con-

4

sequences of very rapid growth; and, whatever the failings of specific individuals might have been, this was an underlying cause of poor government performance.

In 1932, when Franklin Roosevelt assumed the Presidency, the budget of the United States federal government was under $4 billion, and it was still under $10 billion on the eve of World War II. Since Roosevelt's first term, the budget has doubled itself six times, driven first by the massive defense effort of World War II and the ensuing Cold War period, and then by the rise of major domestic programs. From 1940 to 1970 the number of civilian employees of the federal government tripled. Personnel in the armed services went from less than one-half million in 1940 to three-and-one-half million in 1970 (after reaching a high of twelve million in World War II).[1] The basic fact which these figures reflect is that over the past thirty years government has become a large-scale enterprise whose organizational complexities and scope of operations are much greater than before. This drastic expansion in activities has produced problems of management and burdens of decision making for which our society was very imperfectly prepared, both in terms of experience and in terms of basic understanding of the phenomena involved.

As a result of this period of expansion the United States equipped itself with a massive government bureaucracy and came to realize some of the attendant problems. As every experienced citizen is aware, it is difficult to pursue any reasoned, coherent, effective course of action through the disparate and imperfectly responsive institutions of the bureaucracy. Large organizations produce results which regularly defy common notions of national interest, justice, sanity, and human decency. If we consult our history carefully, we know that to be true of earlier and simpler times. The flowering of more bureaucracy than ever before, however, has clearly exacerbated the problem. The sheer scale of activity characteristic of modern government has imposed enormous burdens of managerial capacity, and in doing so has seriously inflamed what has long been recognized as an inherent political problem.

In addition to the problems of scale (or perhaps a multiplica-

[1] Figures are taken from U.S. Bureau of the Census, *Statistical Abstract of the United States: 1969* (Washington: U.S. Government Printing Office, September 1969).

5

tion thereof) are the problems of scope. The increasingly complex and interactive societies which now exist in the United States and in other areas of the world are imposing qualitatively new demands for government service, demands which seem far more esoteric and difficult to meet than those of earlier ages. The familiar parameters of modern society—increased concentration of population in urban complexes; the widespread application of advanced technology; increasing specialization in the labor force; the integrative effects of rapid mass communication; the continuing cycles of poverty, unemployment, and dependency; etc.—all serve to create new occasions for government intervention in the economic and social activities of its citizens. The government is now under political mandate to solve problems that it did not worry about forty years ago, and many of these problems seem decidedly greater in their inherent difficulty.

These new problems of scale and scope present a double bind. At precisely the time when larger government is more difficult to manage, the demands for effective performance have become a great deal more serious. In developing complex urban environments responsive to the necessities of life, in conducting a defense against potentially annihilating attack, in controlling its own capacities for annihilation our society has become dependent upon the output of government and highly vulnerable to its mistakes. The complexities of these problems contribute to the expansion in scale of organizational activity on the principle that it takes more men to do more things. At the same time, in burdening human knowledge well beyond its current capacities, these issues also rob the managers and decision makers of important components of strength. An army general might successfully direct the multiple activities of a division on the battlefield, where the goal is well defined and the factors affecting the outcomes reasonably well understood. Making "war" on poverty is much more complicated business.

These developments have generated new political issues. A society traditionally concerned with constraining government in the interests of avoiding tyranny must now concern itself with effectiveness. Even if it could be fully accomplished, it would no longer be acceptable merely to follow the established principles of democracy and to trust that the outcomes of such a process will be the best attainable, or even acceptable. Even the fairest of elections and the most open and accessible of procedures will not suffice if they do not produce solutions to compelling problems. Achieving effective performance without stumbling into some new form of tyranny is a major issue of coming decades.

These conditions are producing a quiet crisis, if you will, in traditional political perspectives. Government performance is critically affected by the workings of the bureaucracy and in no analytic tradition are these workings adequately understood. We have had long, loud, often humorous lament of this apparition called bureaucracy. We have had capitalist and socialist ideologies, both of which, in different ways, desired and promised to eradicate it. We have had eloquent, well-documented accounts of its dangers, its inadequacies, its failures of performance. We must now have penetrating analysis as to why bureaucracy works as it does. Analysis is almost certainly a necessary condition for achieving more successful government.

The struggle to better understand the workings of large bureaucracy has already focused a great deal of attention on the decision-making process, for conceptions of that process lie at the core of organizational analysis. Since the making and executing of decisions is obviously a major component of what any government does, virtually all political analysis has rested in fact upon assumptions about decision making,[2] but this frequently has not been the main focus of attention. Conditions now force serious analysts to concern themselves with the process of decision, and it is perfectly natural that the social stakes which seem to ride on the topic would stimulate doubts about the adequacy of the established conceptions.

[2] This is particularly true when analysis involves the explanation or prediction of actual events. This focus on concrete events is, of course, what distinguishes policy analysis from other forms of political discourse. Discussions of institutions, such as the Presidency and Congress, of particular voting coalitions, of social class and ethnic cleavages, of broad economic, social, and cultural forces, all provide partial explanations of actual events. These discussions often identify necessary determinants of events, but rarely are sufficient conditions provided within the limits of these special perspectives. If an outcome of some consequence is being analyzed—the outbreak of a war, the state of health in a society, etc.—it is usually necessary to understand the interactions of a variety of men, institutions, and basic social forces. The decision process then assumes unusual importance because it is through such a process that many of the various causal factors exert their influence on an outcome.

7

Paradigms and Prevailing Political Analysis

Though it may seem unlikely at first glance that any interesting assumption could be held in common by the highly diverse perspectives on political events which are to be found in our contemporary culture, the fact is that virtually all analysts use in some way a conception of the decision process derived from the idea of rational choice. In its simplest version the rational thesis holds that a man acts to maximize his values under the constraints he faces. Though there is wide dispute over what values man typically pursues and over the interpretation of constraints, the basic rational thesis is rarely doubted and widely used. Indeed, many theorists would consider the statement an obvious tautology, i.e., they would hold the thesis to be inherent in the definition of what a value is. Even Sigmund Freud, by reputation a theorist of irrational behavior, does not quarrel with this rational thesis, but merely insists that men frequently pursue psychosexual values by means of political behavior. If the result is bizarre in political terms, it is not so within the internal logic of the decision maker, once that is properly understood. Similarly, major theories of government and society, the work of experts in substantive areas of policy, the writings of historians and news columnists, the memorandums of government officials, and the intuitive observations of casual observers—all participate in various ways in the conception of rational choice.[3] It is an impressive phenomenon and an historically important one. Assumptions which so structure a culture's view of its own political affairs are bound to have very real effects on the course of actual events.

The pervasive influence of the assumptions of rational choice is clearly the result of long-building intellectual momentum, and it is instructive to reflect upon the forces which have contributed

---

[3] As is clear from the nature of this proposition, it is difficult to prove quickly and decisively to those who wish to doubt it. A tour through the myriad forms of political analysis to demonstrate that typical writings do indeed rest upon rational assumptions would be an impossibly elaborate digression. The point can be illustrated by noting that analysts as diverse as Marx and Freud, though differing mightily regarding the values they hold to be operative in political life, agree completely on the underlying model of the decision process which structures their respective theories. Both Freud and Marx assume that an actor proceeds rationally once his values are set. Those who have trouble with the proposition are urged to treat it as a working hypothesis. Its meaning and its plausibility will hopefully emerge more strongly at the end of the book.

to this momentum. First, the core logic of rationality has been laid out with clarity and mathematical rigor for simple prototype decision problems, often elementary gambling games. This work has yielded sets of axioms and clear logical inferences which give compelling, if highly abstract, coherence to the idea of rational choice. Second, this basic logic has been developed in disciplines of economics and applied mathematics to provide theories of obvious general significance. Economists have applied conceptions of rational choice to explain and prescribe consumer behavior and the activities of firms in competitive markets. Since these are topics of great interest to industrializing societies, they have been extensively developed. Also, statistical decision theory has been developed in applied mathematics to allow quantitative treatment of decisions under statistical uncertainty, again a topic of obvious concern to a society in increasing need of sophisticated management. Third, the theoretical perspectives of these disciplines have been explicitly applied to actual decision problems in the private and public sectors. The management of production and supply processes in some large industries is now optimized by application of mathematical programing techniques based upon rational assumptions. The procurement of weapons systems for national defense has been analyzed from an explicit rational framework, and in the process abstract theory has been connected to stark reality. The theory of deterrence, a direct embodiment of rational assumptions, has become a central element of United States foreign policy, and upon its principles are staked each year billions of dollars in expenditures and the risk of millions of lives. The common-sense mind has been substantially captured, and intuitive observers who would understand the processes of government have learned to impose rational assumptions on what they see and to work out explanations and expectations along lines required by these assumptions. These developments all have been laborious, consuming many decades and a great many intellectual careers. The result is a heavy investment of the culture in the concepts of rationality.

The historical force exercised by such central, well-articulated, widely shared assumptions has been documented by Thomas Kuhn in his studies of the development of major theories in modern science.[4] In studying seminal scientific developments

[4] Thomas S. Kuhn, *The Copernican Revolution* (New York: Vintage

—the work of Kepler, Copernicus, and Galileo in astronomy; of Lavoisier and Dalton in chemistry; of Newton in physics—Kuhn noted that the impact of these achievements resulted from the fact that they changed the basic working assumptions of their respective fields. Astronomers working before Kepler, Copernicus and Galileo, for example, assumed that the sun and other planets moved about the earth, and all research and argument among astronomers rested on that proposition. The change to a sun-centered system, with the earth in motion, was in itself an esoteric change in the working assumptions of the astronomers. The change provided a new basis for all subsequent theory and research in that field. The remarkable feature of the episode is that an apparently esoteric change could have such profound effect and far-reaching consequences. Not only was a new basis laid for all subsequent theory and research in astronomy, but cascading consequences occurred far beyond the limits of astronomy. Newtonian physics and modern chemistry were logical descendants of the change in astronomers' assumptions. The religious and philosophical basis of society was forced to adjust, and the practical life of nearly every human being has been pervasively affected. The intellectual shifts effected by Copernicus and others somehow struck at the very core of human organization.

What one learns from these experiences, Kuhn points out, is the enormous significance of basic working assumptions in science.[5] These assumptions serve to define problems which receive intellectual attention; they identify what data are pertinent enough to justify the effort required to collect them; they provide coherent explanations for the central phenomena with which a scientific field concerns itself. In short, basic working assumptions provide a coherent intellectual framework which is apparently a necessary ingredient for organized scientific endeavor. "Normal

Books, 1959) and *The Structure of Scientific Revolutions* (Chicago: The University of Chicago Press, 1963).

[5] A central point in this argument is that assumptions which form a paradigm are not necessary in any objective, incorrigible sense. Ptolemaic astronomy formed a paradigm which governed science for many centuries, and men in those centuries held it to be just as compelling as we now hold the governing paradigms of modern science to be. The Ptolemaic paradigm, however, was ultimately discarded as other powerful ones have been, and that experience emphasizes the degree to which even hard science imposes its views on reality rather than receiving instructions from it.

science," Kuhn argues, proceeds within a governing set of assumptions; that is, scientific research does not generally call these into question but, rather, works out their implications with consistency and care. Since there are usually a number of distinguishable assumptions involved in such a basic framework, Kuhn uses the word "paradigm" to refer to these collectively. Ptolemaic astronomy was a paradigm replaced by the new paradigm of Copernicus and others. Euclidian geometry and Newtonian physics are paradigms in other fields, each recently challenged by contrary paradigms.[6]

With appropriate caution and qualification, Kuhn's concept of a paradigm can be usefully applied to the rational theory of decision as it operates in political analysis.[7] Though the paradigm of rational choice is less powerful than those of natural science in rendering its field of endeavor understandable and predictable, it seems to play the same role in organizing human activities. Like paradigms in the natural sciences, the rational theory of decision structures the on-going research, theorizing, and practical analysis of those who seek to explicate political events. Its assumptions are not generally held open to question, but rather provide the basic framework for interpreting evidence.[8] After long years of development, it now provides both sophisticated and more casual analysts with the necessary means for focusing

[6] The word "paradigm" has a residual vagueness resulting from the fact that it is frequently not feasible to list the assumptions of a paradigm exhaustively. The word thus refers to critical assumptions which have been articulated and to others which may be critical but unrecognized.

[7] There are subtle but important differences between the words "paradigm," "theory," and "model." "Paradigm" refers to a set of fundamental and critical assumptions on the basis of which theories and models are developed. Both theories and models are more completely specified. A single paradigm might give rise to a number of theories which have important differences despite being members of the same family. Similarly, a number of different models can be generated which have significant differences despite the fact that they all depend upon the same paradigm assumptions. This is true of the rational tradition in decision theory where, if the argument advanced below is correct, there is a single governing paradigm but a great variety of different models and even different theories.

[8] To be sure, there is a great deal more to political analysis than the assumptions of the rational theory of decision. There are, of course, strong disagreements among political analysts of various kinds, based on their different values and different assessment of the numerous factors which determine events. The point is simply that underlying a great deal of disagreement and difference in perspective are some critical similarities.

their attention and for drawing inferences about inherently ambiguous events.

From history one gains an appreciation that established paradigms are neither lightly nor quickly displaced—even by challengers of clear superiority.[9] If this is true in the natural sciences, it is likely to be all the more true for the theory of decision and political analysis, where the entire field is less structured and clear superiority less likely to occur. Nonetheless, the conditions for a major challenge to the established paradigm of rational decision are unmistakably present. As noted, such challenge is occasioned by increasing concern with complex decision problems and with government performance. These conditions obviously require a more sophisticated understanding of decision processes than that which prevailed in less demanding times. Beyond that, the internal logic of rational theory is under strain, particularly from accumulating experimental evidence on basic decision processes which is difficult to reconcile with central assumptions of the theory.[10] Such internal strain has generally preceded a successful challenge to a paradigm. Most important, however, is the fact that a set of assumptions about the decision process distinctly different from those of rational theory is beginning to emerge from research in a number of disciplines on the fundamental processes of the human mind. These developments are quite unlikely to culminate in anything as dramatic as a scientific revolution in which one dominant paradigm is replaced by another. They do suggest, however, that the theory of decision is in for a major adjustment and that rational assumptions will not continue the degree of dominance they now have.

Assumptions which promise ultimately to compete with rational theory as a basis for policy analysis have been developed by people concerned with the way human beings process information. Critics have long noted that the rational theory assumes such sophisticated processing of information that it strains cre-

[9] This appreciation is an important result of Thomas Kuhn's research. See *The Copernican Revolution* and *The Structure of Scientific Revolutions*.

[10] See Gordon M. Becker and Charles G. McClintock, "Value: Behavioral Decision Theory," in *Annual Review of Psychology*, 18 (1967), pp. 239–286. This reviews a number of experimental studies testing rational assumptions against actual decision-making behavior, usually in gambling games. The models derived from rational assumptions to account for observed behavior are being driven to greater and greater complexity and still do not fully handle observed data.

dulity to impute such procedures to real decision makers. The mind of man, for all its marvels, is a limited instrument. Accordingly, basic research has been directed at discovering how this limited mechanism actually works and how it produces such remarkably adaptive behavior in the normal circumstances of daily life. This inquiry is far from complete, but for very simple decision making a great deal is now known. In fact, a theoretical base fundamentally different from rational theory has been constructed. The pertinent work has taken place in a wide variety of fields—the psychology of learning and of perception, linguistics, logic, epistemology, and information theory, to name the more rigorous of the disciplines involved. What is common to the diverse research of these fields is the logic of cybernetics, and in the discussion below, the emerging new position is labeled the cybernetic paradigm. In brief, cybernetics provides an analysis of extremely simple decision-making mechanisms which are nonetheless highly successful in the proper environments.

The cybernetic paradigm still resides largely in the laboratories of basic research. Though challenging to rational assumptions at the level of simple logic, it is distinctly less developed in application to public policy questions—in significant part, it seems, because the effort to develop it has not yet been made. Nonetheless, there is promise in such an application, for the paradigm is potentially useful in understanding how men and organizations comprised of men actually operate in complex environments. The routine behavior of men in organizational settings— behavior which commonly gives rise to outrage and frustration at the insensitivities of bureaucratic government—often has a very important functional basis when viewed within the perspective of cybernetic logic. That does not make the results more acceptable, but it does promise a more realistic and more appropriate analysis of the requirements for change.

Despite its promise, however, there are two critical problems with cybernetic logic. First, the success of simple cybernetic decision makers depends upon a highly structured, appropriately arranged environment. Within available theories it is unclear how cybernetic decision processes might work for the complex environments of public policy, which are highly interactive and are not rigidly or simply structured. Second, the cybernetic paradigm projects a view of the human mind (clearly the ultimate locus of decision making), which does not account for one of its most critical faculties—the ability to make inductive inferences on its own initiative. Both problems indicate the need to supplement simple cybernetic theories in building a paradigm of the decision process competitive with that operating in rational decision theory. Both problems also suggest the source of supplementation; namely, a set of principles about the operations of the human mind, which is most appropriately labeled cognitive theory.

Cognitive theory as defined below provides principles which analyze how human beings structure their beliefs. Fortunately for purposes of analysis, the structure of human beliefs is far less varied over individuals and cultures than is the fantastically diverse content of those beliefs. Cognitive principles offer an analysis as to how highly complex decision problems are given the stable structure necessary for cybernetic processes to operate—structures very different from those expected by rational theories. In essence, it is cognitive operations of the human mind working in interaction with the organizational structure of the government which set workable limits on highly diffuse decision problems, and it is cybernetic theory, thus supplemented, which offers a base paradigm for political analysis competitive with the rational position.

It is important to note at the outset that the argument being developed is *not* that rational theory is wrong, invalid, or useless. This is certainly not the case. The argument asserts rather that rational theory cannot handle all the observed phenomena of decision making and should not be relied upon, therefore, as the only base theory for political analysis. The various mechanisms used to extend rational theory to complex decision problems—notions of constrained maximization, bounded rationality, etc.—came under severe strain when used to explain certain regularly recurring political events, and we will examine below some interesting examples involving decisions about the sharing of nuclear weapons within the North Atlantic Alliance. It remains true that rational explanations can always be constructed for such events, but the analyst must adopt very strange *ad hoc* assumptions in order to do so. By contrast, the argument runs, the competing cognitive and cybernetic perspectives explain quite naturally and directly precisely those events which are most puzzling when understood within a rational framework.

It is also important to note that a strategy of theoretical confrontation is at work in this argument. In most discussions of decision theory, the basic approach has been to assimilate the dissenting propositions of cybernetic and cognitive theory to the dominant rational position. Again this is done by introducing a number of practical constraints on the ideal rational process—reflecting conceptually such things as the limits of time, the costs of information, and the influence of additional values. The many anomalies which are encountered are taken to reflect the presence of such factors not previously considered, rather than a flaw in the basic model. The understanding of rational theory, however, as a scientific paradigm in Kuhn's sense of the word inevitably suggests the possibility of changing the fundamental logic. And sensitized to this possibility one notices that the core logic of cybernetics and cognitive theory is very different from the logic of rational theory. The strategy of the book derives from this reasoning. It rests on the theses that the natural competition between the separate theoretical perspectives ought to be encouraged rather than compromised and that such competition will drive political analysis deeper than it would otherwise go.

There are two stages involved in developing the argument. The first (Chapters 2–5) works out the theoretical distinctions between rational, cybernetic, and cognitive perspectives. The attempt there is to give these distinctions enough force and clarity to overcome the tendency to obscure them which has been endemic in the literature to date. The second stage of the argument (Chapters 6–9) attempts to demonstrate that the distinctions made are helpful, even necessary, to understand why the policy of United States and governmental action regarding the control of nuclear weapons in the NATO alliance evolved as it did during the early 1960s. The purpose of such an exercise is to show that the theoretical debate within abstract decision theory has practical significance.

THE CONCEPT OF COMPLEXITY

The idea of complexity is central to the discussion of the separate decision paradigms. It is not only that complexity seems to describe both the government and contemporary social conditions; not only that complexity is an underlying cause of poor government performance. In theoretical terms the critical dimensions of complexity provide the focal points of disagreement between the separate paradigms of the decision process. Rational, cybernetic, and cognitive analysis diverge most sharply, it turns out, when analyzing decisions under complexity.

A determination of the critical dimensions of complexity requires in turn some working definition of decision. A decision, let us say, is a choice made by either an individual or a group of individuals (and it matters which) in pursuit of some purpose. The purpose (henceforth called a *value* or *objective* depending upon the degree of generality required by the context) is included in order to distinguish decisions from the larger class of causal occurrences. Some decisions actually have the effect or *outcome* intended; others do not. Some outcomes occur without any recognizable or reasonably imputed decision to produce them. In addition to the presence of values, we will generally assume as basic ingredients of a decision both *options* (i.e., a set of possible actions from which a choice is made) and *information* (i.e., the data and inferential calculations which help determine the choice). For every decision there is a present and future state of the world (or *environment*) which also contributes to the outcome. Most outcomes of interest to political analysts actually emerge over an extended period of time and are affected by a great many distinguishable decisions. The phrase "decision making" thus refers to a process which actually entails a number of discrete decisions.

The complex decision problem then is one in which the following conditions hold:

1. (a) Two or more values are affected by the decision.
   (b) There is a trade-off relationship between the values such that a greater return to one can be obtained only at a loss to the other.
2. There is uncertainty (i.e., imperfect correspondence between information and the environment) of a special character discussed below.
3. The power to make the decision is dispersed over a number of individual actors and/or organizational units.

The trade-off relationships specified in the first condition can arise for two reasons. First, it is a basic fact of the human condition that any significant effort to produce an intended outcome consumes resources—time, money, managerial talent, political opportunity, or whatever. Since resources devoted to one purpose are unavailable for another, any two values which are separate enough to be distinguishable will stand in at least a theoretical trade-off relationship if we assume efficiency in their production. Because that fact is so global, however, it is not very helpful in distinguishing the complex decision problem from other problems. Hence, as a practical matter, informal constraints are usually established whereby some resource-based (or input) trade-offs are considered whereas others are not. The second form of the trade-off relationship is inherently more limited. Under some circumstances the actions taken in pursuit of one value by virtue of their direct effects diminish the return to other values. If one builds roads to facilitate traffic flow in urban areas, the very existence of the road often has disruptive effects on residential neighborhoods. Mercifully, these output trade-offs are not ubiquitous, but when they occur they are particularly troublesome. Without excluding the problem of input trade-offs, it can be said that the clearest and most dramatic cases of a complex decision problem occur when there are significant output trade-offs.

The second condition of the complex problem—the uncertainty condition—requires some specification because of the differing concepts of uncertainty which are available. The development of the theory of games has provided conceptions of uncertainty which refer problems of policy to well-specified games of chance. In this procedure the possible outcomes of a given course of action are arrayed, and the probability of each of the possible outcomes occurring is conceptualized by imagining the actual outcome to be determined by a random process, such as the rolling of a die. Thus, if there are six possible outcomes from a certain action, each might be assigned a number and assumed to occur whenever its number appears on the top of the die, and the probability of each outcome would be one-sixth. In cases where the probabilities of occurrence are known, as in actual games of chance, the decision maker trying to produce a favorable outcome is said to face risk. In cases where the probabilities of occurrence are not precisely known and must be estimated, the decision maker is said to face uncertainty. And some theorists insist that risk and uncertainty so conceived are essentially the same thing.

Though this conception of uncertainty is an exceedingly important one, it is too narrow to capture the meaning of uncertainty for the complex policy problem, for it assumes that a great deal

17

of inferential structure can be imposed on the decision problem with complete confidence. It assumes that the range of possible outcomes is known, and thereby eliminates the possibility that an outcome might occur which was not even visualized in advance. It assumes that the operating characteristics of the game are known—i.e., that its rules are specified and stable. For complex problems neither of these assumptions can be held. Rather, the imposition of enough structure on the situation, so that possible outcomes can be described and their probabilities of occurrence estimated, is itself a matter of uncertainty. The special form of uncertainty can thus be labeled structural uncertainty.

The third condition of complexity is straightforward in its meaning though very difficult in its implication. For complete clarity it should be noted that decision makers are distinguished not merely by physical enumeration but also by the fact that they do not agree among themselves on central characteristics of the decision problem—the values at stake, the weight to be given to them, the resolution of major uncertainties. The complex problem is thus enriched by relationships among the separate, disagreeing actors, who jointly determine the decision and jointly affect the outcome.

It is a fundamental proposition of the current study, then, that most critical issues of government policy are complex in the sense described and that these characteristics of complexity offer important leads into the decision processes which affect the behavior of government. The assertion is that decision making under complexity is the new topic over which rational, cybernetic, and cognitive assumptions will have to contend.

Nuclear Sharing as a Prototype Problem

The ripening of the cognitive and cybernetic perspectives as competitors of established rational assumptions cannot occur through completely general discussion. The ultimate purpose of forcing greater sophistication of decision theory is to yield better understanding of events—events which are important because they affect basic human values. It follows that the utility of the decision paradigms must be evaluated in a context of real issues where there are real stakes. Moreover, a great deal of basic development has already occurred in the rarefied atmosphere of the psychological laboratory, the simple gambling game, the stylized hypothetical problem, etc. Quite apart from the pressure of social needs, it is a reasonable research strategy to seek further theoretical development by turning to the messy world of the complex policy problem. The complexity of actual problems is decidedly inconvenient to the theorist, but is also stimulating. For these reasons, discussions of the separate paradigms of decision are developed in part by analyzing a specific political problem. The problem, though quite interesting in its own right, serves generally as a medium in which to culture specimens of the different forms of analysis.

The prototype of the complex problem which has been chosen is the issue of sharing the control of nuclear weapons among members of the Atlantic Alliance (NATO). That issue, with seeds in World War II, rose to prominence in the wake of the Suez crisis of 1956 and the first Soviet satellites in 1957. The issue caught the United States in a trade-off between its general political purposes in Europe and the military requirements of deterrence strategy. Several options for handling the issue were advanced, reflecting conflicting policy positions. The United States and allied governments developed those options through several points of major decision until a temporary, though probably unstable, resolution was precipitated in December 1964, just prior to the massive American intervention in Indochina. There are major analytic puzzles about the course of events during the 1960–1964 period, and these pose the problems for analysis.

In substantive terms, the decisions concerning nuclear sharing in the 1960–1964 period are interesting because they dealt with central, continuing problems in American foreign policy. The credibility of a United States defense guarantee to smaller but highly advanced nations was one such critical question which stood at the core of the problem, and the stakes attached to that question were high. The American guarantee was seen at the time as an important factor preventing the proliferation of nuclear weapons, and proliferation in turn was seen as a major threat to the stability of deterrence. The nuclear sharing proposals were designed to alleviate allied doubts about the American guarantee and hence to protect the established system of world stability. A preservation of American alliance guarantees, moreover, became a prime justification of the agonizing effort in Vietnam in the period immediately following the episode. The fact that three administrations, in developing American proposals

19

for nuclear sharing, laid down a residuum of intellectual and political commitments on the subject of defense guarantees makes the story one of broad and continuing relevance.

There were other central themes as well. The question of Germany's role in Europe and in the broader Atlantic community was centrally involved in the question. West Germany is at once one of the strongest, most dynamic, most important countries of Europe and the one with the most unhappy past and the greatest potential claims against the *status quo*. It is an axiom of recent history and of current politics that Germany must be taken seriously. It is a virtual certainty that its problems, needs, and political development will be central policy concerns in the decades to come. American proposals on nuclear sharing prior to 1964 were prime mechanisms for dealing with Germany's problems, and that history, therefore, is some part of the current relationship with Germany. Beyond that, broader issues concerning the movement toward European integration and, to a somewhat lesser extent, the question of an East-West détente were also directly raised and dealt with. These dimensions of the period all entail problems of continuing relevance. Both as a microscope on these issues and as an historical element in their current state, the episode is of general significance.

In theoretical terms the episode is a good context for analysis as an excellent embodiment of the complex policy problem defined above. The central trade-off involved competing political and military objectives, and, as a consequence, the issue involved separate State Department and Defense Department jurisdictions. Not only does that trade-off directly pose the theoretical issues discussed, but it also represents an entire class of extremely important policy problems. The intersection of political and military objectives has been a feature of most of the serious foreign policy issues of the last decade or so, and it is clearly an aspect of policy which has given the United States (and others) a great deal of grief. It also seems clear that the nuclear sharing problem fully meets the criterion of uncertainty. It is notoriously difficult to develop credible notions of nuclear war, yet in assessing the military effects of the sharing proposals such conceptions had to be constructed. Similarly, it was difficult to understand the complex political and economic relationships between European states, and yet that also was necessary in coping with the sharing question.

20

It is also theoretically interesting that the nuclear sharing issue extended over a reasonably long period of time and largely did not involve crisis situations. There is no question but that normally operating decision processes are in view in the situation. The issue entailed neither high drama nor marginally significant routine. It was an issue which involved the President and the Cabinet at various times, but in which the bulk of work was done within the policy machinery. There is a sufficient number of points of decision extended enough in time to give some confidence that the processes analyzed are reasonably stable and systematic, and not the sole product of idiosyncratic persons or events.[11]

In general, then, the nuclear sharing issue provides a decent example of the kind of problem which besets the modern age—the problem of making successful decisions under complexity.

[11] The major disadvantage of the MLF issue from a theoretical point of view is that it does not involve an extended implementation phase. The military forces proposed were not in fact established and therefore not turned over to military services for actual operation. This means that some features of the cybernetic paradigm are less pertinent and there is no opportunity to check some of the policy expectations against actual results. The implementation of firm and final policy decision through the organized machinery of government has become a critical problem which remains in important ways beyond the limits of this study. Some problems of implementation do arise, however, in the sense that preliminary decisions made in developing the sharing proposals required some subsequent action of the policy bureaucracy. The major restriction is that routine, repetitive operations on a reasonably large scale were never established.

PART ONE
PARADIGMS OF THE
DECISION PROCESS

CHAPTER 2

The Analytic Paradigm

PRECISELY because they are so pervasively used, rational assumptions appear in a variety of forms, and this complicates the task of providing a clear, manageable characterization of the paradigm. Embodiments of rational analysis can be found in formal axiom systems,[1] in economic analysis,[2] in historical accounts of political events,[3] in discussions of substantive policy,[4] and in common observation. The care taken in articulating the underlying assumptions varies accordingly, from the precise axioms of formal models to the loose, inchoate suppositions of casual observers. Given this variety of embodiments, it presumably would be very difficult to provide an exhaustive list of all the assumptions that are important in structuring rational analysis in all of its many forms. Accordingly, a more limited task is set; namely, the articulation of assumptions which are critical to the paradigm in three senses: (1) they are utilized by most influential models falling in the rational tradition, (2) they provide an account of how decisions are made under complexity, and (3) they are disputed by the contrasting paradigm derived from cybernetic logic and cognitive psychology. These specifications in effect focus the theoretical discussion on the conditions of complexity.

It is natural to begin with formal discussions of rationality. The explicit statements of basic assumptions which formal models provide give the clearest view into the intellectual structure of the paradigm. There are some important specifications which

[1] R. D. Luce and Howard Raiffa, *Games and Decisions* (New York: John Wiley and Sons, Inc., 1957).

[2] Paul A. Samuelson, *Economics* (New York: McGraw-Hill Book Company, Inc., 1970); William J. Baumol, *Economic Theory and Operations Research* (Englewood Cliffs, N.J.: Prentice-Hall, Inc., 1965).

[3] Graham T. Allison, *Essence of Decision* (Boston: Little, Brown and Company, 1971), points out how rational assumptions are ubiquitously used to structure historical interpretation.

[4] Charles Hitch and Roland McKean, *The Economics of Defense in the Nuclear Age* (Cambridge, Mass.: Harvard University Press, 1960); Otto Eckstein, *Water-Resource Development* (Cambridge, Mass.: Harvard University Press, 1961).

must be made, however, and these affect the way in which the critical assumptions are handled. It is important to recognize that the logic of decision theory takes on a different cast depending upon the purpose of the analyst.

Formal versions of the rational theory of decision are frequently advanced as *normative* arguments; that is, as statements of how decisions ought to be made with no necessary implications that they actually are made in that way. Use of the theory to explain actual events, however, requires *positive* assumptions which do purport to explain or predict how actual, empirical decision processes work. The transition from a normative to a positive model is often made by using the critical assumptions tautologously. That is, the decision process is assumed to approximate the formal ideal, and observed data are interpreted in such a way as to make them consistent with the critical assumptions of the paradigm. In this usage the assumptions themselves are not held open to revision or disconfirmation. Finally, it is also possible to treat the central assumptions as positive (that is, empirical) but non-tautological assertions and thus to interpret data on the actual decision process under rules which allow for the possibility that the assumptions are wrong. Though the basic logic of rational theory is highly similar for all these uses, these different rules deeply affect the connection between the theory and evidence from actual events. It is important to note, therefore, that what follows is a positive, non-tautological articulation and application of rational assumptions.[5]

[5] Attempts to challenge rational decision theory as an empirical account of actual decisions are frequently deflected by proponents of the theory by taking refuge in the normative claim. There is in the first place only limited validity in this. If no concrete instances or near approximations of rational decision making could be observed, one would quickly discard the theory as a utopian ideal. Hence the empirical validity and the normative validity of the paradigm are inextricably bound. An empirical defense of the theory, moreover, is entirely possible. Though it is decidedly more convenient to argue in normative terms, the positive non-tautological rule does not preordain the paradigm to rejection as is often casually supposed. Indeed one of the earliest quantitative articulations of the theory was provided by W. Fechner, a psychophysicist concerned with explaining basic processes of sensory discrimination (see Gordon M. Becker and Charles G. McClintock, "Value: Behavioral Decision Theory," in *Annual Review of Psychology*, 18 (1967), pp. 239–286); and contemporary work on sensory detection of signals against background noise has also found empirical validity in a basic

The adaptation of this rule means that care must be taken to state a set of assumptions which might conceivably be verified or refuted by actual observation. One cannot demand that decision makers have perfect information, as did the classical theory of the firm, for actual decision makers never do. One cannot demand that they make impossibly elaborate calculations in making choices. The requirements which the assumptions impose must be scaled to human dimensions. Hence some limits must be imposed on the critical assumptions of rationality as articulated in formal models. In the simplified, often hypothetical problems used by pure theorists to develop axiomatic accounts of rational choice, highly sophisticated processing of information is frequently required. This provides severe problems of scale as the resulting theory is applied to the complex policy problem, and acceptable constraints must be found to preserve the plausibility of the paradigm.

Finally, it must be recognized that the positive, non-tautological orientation promises grief over the use of language. In common discourse the word "rational" is drenched with normative connotations. It means doing that which is "best" under the circumstances, or that which is most worthy of approval. By implication, any decision which is not held to be rational is thereby condemned. Such implication, however, does not follow from a positive definition of rationality. A decision process meeting the assumptions of the paradigm may or may not produce outcomes more beneficial or more worthy of approval than those achieved by other means, and the question as to whether it does or not is more a matter of investigation than of deductive assertion. To avoid confusion, the paradigm stating rational assumptions in the restricted sense intended will be labeled the analytic paradigm, a label which is in fact more suggestive of the internal logic. As the word implies, the picture of decision making presented by this line of thought is one in which the decision problem is broken down into major components, and then a deliberate procedure for aggregation is evoked to achieve a decision.

---

rational model (see J. A. Swets, W. P. Tanner, and T. G. Birdsall, "Decision Processes in Perception," in Ralph N. Haber, ed., *Contemporary Theory and Research in Visual Perception* [New York: Holt, Rinehart & Winston, 1968], pp. 78–101). These sources provide evidence that at least in some circumstances the human mind does indeed work in accord with assumptions of the theory.

THE INTEGRATION OF VALUE TRADE-OFFS

Formal discussions of analytic decisions generally begin with a single decision maker whose values have been aggregated to form a set of preferences regarding alternative states of the world. The decision maker has absolute discretion to define his values, and the only requirement is that his preferences be transitive in some sense.[6] Formal discussion then turns upon the question of assigning value units to each alternative outcome of the decision problem. The concept of utility has been adduced in these discussions to represent conceptually a measure of ultimate value, and various techniques have been worked out for making utility assignments for one person for a simple decision problem.[7] The major postulate of analytic theories of decision holds that decisions will be taken which maximize value (utility) given the constraints of the situation. Without an independent way of establishing utility values (which is virtually always denied), the postulate is tautological.

The concept of utility reflects the fact that many dimensions of value generally recognized in human affairs are logically incommensurate; that is, that there is no generally accepted objective procedure for comparing between them. Each individual needs a variety of objects to satisfy his various desires—food, clothing, housing, etc.—and each object assumes some value for him. In contemporary economies, monetary prices provide a common measure (i.e., money) of the relative value of these various objects, and thus money is taken as a general measure of value. Everyone recognizes, however, that money is inadequate as an ultimate measure, since many valued "objects"—love, honor, sense of dignity, etc.—cannot be effectively included in the pricing arrangements of the marketplace. Indeed, many of the most important ones are quite independent of the pricing system, a fact which has given rise to moral homily and many novels. The concept of utility arose to denote, in the abstract, the ideal measure which would subsume all dimensions of value and would

[6] The simplest and strongest transitive relationship is one which is well ordered in the mathematical sense; that is, for a given ordering of three alternatives, if A is preferred to B and if B is preferred to C, then A must be preferred to C. Since observed preferences frequently violate this criterion, a number of probabilistic conceptions of transivity have been advanced to account for behavior. See Becker and McClintock, "Value."

[7] Luce and Raiffa, *Games*; Becker and McClintock, "Value."

provide a basis for relative assessments between concrete choices. As a practical matter, such a global measure of relative value is beyond accomplishment, but the abstract ideal has inspired formal conceptions of rationality.

Lacking an objective and independent means of establishing utility values, the analytic paradigm leaves to the discretion of the decision maker the matter of determining relative value. The analysis of the paradigm cannot begin until the assignments have been made. By allowing this descretion and assuming the product to be a utility assignment (or a preference ordering, such that a utility assignment can be objectively derived which reflects the ordering), the analytic paradigm assumes that the individual decision maker makes the assessment of relative value. Thus, in the two-value trade-off situation of complex decisions, the analytic paradigm holds that the individual integrates the separate dimensions of value by setting up a tacit metric which gives the worth of one value in terms comparable to the other. This assumption is often graphically displayed by positing a set of indifference curves whereby an individual establishes a set of allocations between the separate dimensions of value which represent equal amounts of overall value. Thus in the traditional example, indifference curves are postulated which establish equally valued procurements of guns and butter.[8]

The assertion that two separate values are related and integrated in this fashion—the competing interests balanced—is a critical assumption of the analytic paradigm. It will be referred to henceforth as the assumption of value integration. This assumption must hold if a given decision or decision process is to qualify as an instance of analytic decision making.

The assumption of value integration clearly demonstrates the need for serviceable limits. Unless the assumption is qualified, every decision observed would constitute negative evidence. Despite the implication of their decisions, given fixed budgets, human beings do not take *all* trade-offs into account when making a decision, and no elaborate study is required to establish that fact. When hospitals are considered, the question of roads is sel-

[8] This is an early lesson in the widely used text on economics by Paul Samuelson (see Samuelson, *Economics*). The widespread acceptance of this text and the fact that Samuelson has been accorded a Nobel prize for his work in economics are strong indications that rational conceptions have achieved the status of a paradigm in Kuhn's sense.

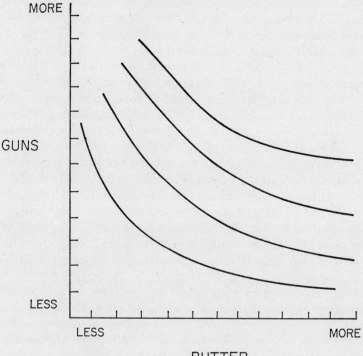

1. Indifference curves, each representing equally
valued allocations of the two valued objects

dom raised. Nor does the effect on crop production become an element in the decisions regarding administration of the space program. If the analytic paradigm is to be taken as a serious, positive framework for understanding decision processes, then the assumption of value integration must be limited.

The overall requirement of value integration has been extended to policy problems by means of cost/benefit or cost/effectiveness calculations. Under this form of analysis, measures of cost to be borne and beneficial output to be achieved are attached to the available alternatives. An analytic choice is then achieved either by holding cost constant for all alternatives and choosing the option producing the greatest benefit, or, equivalently, by holding the expected benefit constant and choosing the least costly option.[9] To the extent that the benefit measure approaches overall utility and that cost assessments are complete, value integration is achieved.

Unquestionably, cost/benefit calculations can be approximated for some policy problems. It is widely recognized, however, that achieving complete cost estimates and a valid benefit measure is extremely difficult, and one can never be sure as a practical matter that it has been accomplished. If analytic conceptions are to have truly broad applications, even this concept must be limited.

The required limitation can be achieved in an intuitively obvious way by demanding merely that immediate outputs involving direct effects of policy actions be constructed as trade-offs in the decision process and that only these separate dimensions of value be related. Thus modified, the critical assumption can be labeled the *assumption of limited value integration*, and that constitutes the first defining characteristic of the analytic process of decision. In concrete terms it means that evidence of an analytic decision process in operation must include some indication that cost/benefit assessments, however informal, are attached to available options and that these include some estimate of the effects for both values. In the mind of the analytic decision maker, in other words, the competing claims of the values directly and immediately presented in an output trade-off relationship are weighed against each other, and some deliberate balance is produced.

As an example one can imagine a decision maker with responsibility for the transportation system of a major urban area. Enough experience has now accumulated to make it apparent that major freeways constructed in developed areas have powerful disruptive effects on the communities which they transverse. The production of more transportation by means of urban freeways involves a direct output trade-off with important values pertaining to community development. Hence a decision maker facing the problem of whether or not to build an urban freeway must give some evidence of having related the costs of social disruption to the value of more transportation if by the defined rules he is to fit the assumptions of the analytic paradigm. This need not be done with quantitative precision, but some direct judgments structured in these terms must be observed.

[9] Hitch and McKean, *The Economics of Defense.*

Uncertainty and the Estimation of Outcomes

Formal models of the decision problem belonging to the analytic paradigm treat uncertainty as a statistical problem. The decision maker, in these formulations, does not know which of a number of possible states of the world will occur, and it is assumed that he will utilize available information—and perhaps procure more —in attempting to make optimal judgments. The clearest conception is provided by the expected value models which posit a decision process of the following character:[10]

1) For each option, a measure of value (v) is estimated for each possible state of the world yielding a series of values (v_1, v_2, v_3 ... v_n).

2) The probability of occurrence of each state of the world is independently estimated, yielding a parallel series of probabilities (p_1, p_2, p_3 ... p_n).

3) The value of each option in each state is then discounted (i.e., multiplied by the probability of that state actually occurring; thus, p_1v_1, p_2v_2, p_3v_3 ... p_nv_n).

4) The expected value (EV) of each option is defined as the sum of the values established in step 3 (i.e., $EV = p_1v_1 + p_2v_2 + p_3v_3 ... + p_nv_n$).

5) The option chosen is the one with the highest expected value.

Though the simple expected value model captures the spirit of analytic assumptions concerning uncertainty, it is generally recognized as inadequate both conceptually and empirically.[11] Perhaps the most fundamental conceptual problem is presented by the measure of value. The expected value model assumes that values are measured on an equal interval scale—that is, that the basic units on the scale are equal over the full range of numbers that can appear on the scale. Though this property would pre-

[10] Howard Raiffa, *Decision Analysis* (Reading, Mass.: Addison-Wesley Publishing Co., 1968); Ward Edwards, "The Theory of Decision-Making," in *Psychological Bulletin*, 51, 4 (1954), pp. 380–417.

[11] As suggested in Chapter 1, it is interesting that empirical work on expected value models has cast extreme doubt on the positive validity of the simple models, and that it has been necessary to develop increasingly elaborate probabilistic models to account for behavior. In the light of Kuhn's work, that is evidence that the paradigm is coming under strain. See Becker and McClintock, "Value."

sumably be possessed by an ultimate measure of utility, practical approximations fall far short. As a consequence, people will regularly treat the twenty-fifth unit of value as different from the third and any negative unit as different from a positive unit. In general, losses are usually feared more than gains are coveted, and the degree to which this is true varies over individuals. Both of these phenomena betray variation in the basic unit of value. The practical consequence for the handling of uncertainty is that the components of the expected value model—measures of value and probability of occurrence—are not independent. Many people (but not all) would prefer a 90 percent chance to win $1,000 to a one-in-a-million chance to win $1 billion, even though the expected value of the latter is greater ($1,000 to $900). Many of the same people would nonetheless prefer a one-in-a-million chance of winning $1 million (EV = $1) to a 90 percent chance of winning $2 (EV = $1.80).

A more subtle problem has to do directly with the measure of probability. In formal discussions of decisions under certainty, examples are generally chosen for which probability assignments are easily made, either because they are intuitively obvious (e.g., that the probability of getting heads from a fair toss of a fair coin is 1/2) or because frequency counts over a large number of trials make it possible. An appealing feature of games with cards, dice, roulette wheels, etc., is that the outcomes they generate can be assigned probability values in advance by either rule. Few real decisions, however, are so nicely structured in this regard as the gambling game, and there are severe conceptual difficulties in assigning probabilities of occurrence to events for which neither of these procedures is applicable. Many critical events affecting complex policy problems occur only once, and many events which decision makers worry about never occur at all. Thus, the problem: If probability assignments do affect important decisions, they must be made on some fashion other than the accepted, objective procedures of probability theory. This theoretical conclusion is supported by experimental studies which indicate that even for gambling games, expected value models using objective probabilities cannot account for observed behavior.[12]

Driven by such considerations, formal discussions of analytic decision making have adduced the concept of subjective probability. The decision maker, faced with complexity, is urged to

[12] Ibid.

make subjective estimates of the probability of occurrences of critical events and to use these as he would objective probabilities in calculating his optimal choice. He is further urged to update these estimates as new information becomes available—in the most sophisticated version, to update according to the calculations of contingent probabilities given in Bayes' theorem.[13] The positive, non-tautological variant of this position holds, therefore, that the decision maker makes intuitive, subjective probability assessments which are then inserted into an intuitive approximation of the expected value calculus.

Again, it is important to place some plausible limit on this formulation since the calculations required by Bayes' theorem for any but the simplest of problems are very laborious. It would strain credulity a great deal to suppose that intuitive probability estimates which people make unconsciously follow the theorem, and the cases in which complex problems have been given enough structure to allow explicit judgments in Bayesian terms are reasonably rare. The required limitation can be achieved by stating two critical assumptions in qualitative terms.

The first of these assumptions holds simply that the analytic decision maker conceptualizes alternative states of the world which would produce differently valued outcomes from the same course of action. This supposition may be called the *assumption of alternative outcomes*. The assumption does not require the decision maker to adduce quantitative assessments of the relative likelihood of future events. It does require him to recognize that events may not follow a single predicted course and that the possible course of events may differ in their desirability. Above all, the assumption requires outcome calculations, a direct attempt to predict the consequences of a given course of action. Thus, a decision maker, in the highway example, might well be required to consider not only whether the highway would better meet current demand and thus ease traffic congestion, but also whether it might stimulate growth in demand and thus re-create congestion at a higher level.

The second qualitative assumption requires that decision makers undergo some intuitive process of updating their outcome calculations as new information becomes available. Without re-

[13] Howard Raiffa, *Decision Analysis*; William Fellner, *Probability and Profit* (Homewood, Ill.: R. D. Irwin, Inc., 1965).

quiring the quantitative manipulations involved in Bayesian statistics, the assumption holds simply that decision makers will pay attention to information pertinent to the alternatives under consideration and that they will adjust their outcome calculations under the impact of new information. Thus, the analytic paradigm would expect a decision maker faced with the highway location problem to be very interested in the trend of property values of the neighborhood affected, its racial and economic composition, the relative scarcity or abundance of neighborhoods of similar character, the ease (and hence cost) of sinking the highway below ground level, typical traffic patterns across the highway route, etc. Major changes in the estimates of such information should have substantial impact on the decision process. This supposition can be labeled the *assumption of sensitivity to pertinent information*.

These qualitative statements—i.e., the assumptions of alternative outcome calculations and of sensitivity to pertinent information—leave a great deal of vagueness, and the specificity necessary for any serious explanation or prediction of an actual event therefore must be worked out *ad hoc* for any given application. Nonetheless, these assumptions generate realistic guidelines, specific enough to be meaningful, yet loose enough to allow application to actual conditions of complexity. Some actual decisions plausibly fit the assumptions and allow reasonable imputation of an analytic process; others rather clearly do not. With such an ability to discriminate actual cases, the analytic paradigm achieves a workable account of the handling of uncertainty in a complex environment.

The two qualitative assumptions also reveal the underlying spirit of the paradigm. The analytic decision process is one which rests upon a causal model on a "blueprint" of the environment, in Herbert Simon's analogy.[14] The quintessential analytic decision maker is one who strains toward as complete an understanding as possible of the causal forces which determine outcomes. He seeks to predict the flow of events and, where he has leverage, to manipulate them to his advantage. The processing of information while making decisions is all done for the purpose of con-

[14] Herbert A. Simon, "The Architecture of Complexity," in Herbert A. Simon, *The Sciences of the Artificial* (Cambridge, Mass.: MIT Press, 1968), pp. 84–118.

structing and improving the blueprint from which the optimal choice emerges.

COLLECTIVE DECISIONS

The assumptions of the analytic paradigm regarding the integration of values and the handling of uncertainty have been worked out in formal presentations at the level of an individual decision maker. This focus has not been arbitrary, for an individual is unquestionably a more highly organized, more coherent behavioral system than is any level of society. The individual, moreover, at least in Western culture, is the unit of greatest moral significance. Information is processed and decisions are made ultimately by individuals; the determination of value resides ultimately in the individual.[15] It is natural, then, that the most carefully articulated models of the decision process apply to individual decision makers. Society, however, can hardly be ignored, for in no case does an individual operate in isolation and in no interesting case does an individual make a policy decision completely by himself. Reflecting this, the third condition of complexity—the existence of multiple actors—requires that any useful paradigm give some account of collective decision processes.

Unfortunately, there are formidable logical barriers to extending the analysis of individual decisions to the collective level. Logical conceptions of utility which are now available do not provide for the comparison of utility values across individuals, and this effectively prevents a process of aggregating the separate calculations of analytic actors under trade-off conditions.[16] Accordingly, there is a logical gap between the individual level and

[15] As those familiar with the history of ethics know, there has long been an attempt to give a compelling logical account of value inferences which would in some sense objectify the determination of value. These attempts have failed and the individual human being has been given irreducible (though not unconstrained) sovereignty over the determination of value.

[16] Many assaults have been made on the problem of constructing a social welfare function which could provide collectively determined indifference curves for a given trade-off relationship. Such attempts have not been successful. The Pareto criterion (that a decision be taken if some people's values will gain and everyone else is at least as well off), which is generally accepted as a guide for public decisions, does not handle the case in which one person's values must be traded off against another's. Unfortunately, nearly every public issue of interest does present such trade-offs.

the collective level of decision making which is decidedly problematic to rigorous analytic models.[17] Similarly, many of the activities of government agencies involve the production of what are labeled public goods—namely, goods or services which automatically accrue to all or to a large number of people, if they are produced at all. This too introduces logical distance between the individual and the collective levels of decision, for it can be shown that an application of analytic logic at the level of individuals produces individual decisions which systematically undervalue and underproduce public goods.[18] Hence, market analysis which provides an account of the collective decisions of the general economy does not work for large areas of governmental activity.

Despite these formal logical barriers, understanding of public decisions based on the analytic paradigm cannot and does not remain trapped solely at the individual level of explanation. If the activities of the government are to be comprehended at all, some conception of the collective decision process, however tacit, must be adduced, and this of course has been done. There are in fact conceptions of the collective decision process in general use by political analysts, and the most prominent and widely used of these derive from the analytic paradigm.

The usual procedure for handling the problem of collective decision is to assume that the decision-making entity, whether a small bureau, a cabinet department, the executive branch, or the entire government, acts as if it were a single person, as if it could assert objectives and calculate strategies in their pursuit with the intellectual coherence of a single human mind. Analytic calculations are then imputed to the individualized entity which plausibly explains its actions. Popular language reflects this procedure: such phrases as "The administration thinks . . . ," "the British feel . . . ," "the military argue . . ." are replete in political discourse of all kinds. Graham Allison has compellingly pointed out both the widespread use of this procedure of reducing a collective entity to an individual and the fact that the decision process generally attributed to such collective entities roughly belongs to the rational tradition.[19]

---

[17] See William J. Baumol, *Welfare Economics and the Theory of the State* (London: Longmans, Green and Company, 1952).

[18] Mancur Olson, Jr., *The Logic of Collective Action* (Cambridge, Mass.: Harvard University Press, 1965).

[19] Allison, *Essence of Decision*.

Despite its widespread acceptance and obvious usefulness, however, the direct reduction of a collective entity to an assumed individual cannot meet the rules established here, for the device is too uncompromisingly tautologous. Since the assumed individual does not exist to be observed, the calculations imputed to him must be tailored to analytic specifications. Indeed, the entire point of this type of analysis is to find a plausible embodiment of the paradigm's demands in terms of the specific facts of the situation. The applicability of the paradigm is assumed from the outset and not questioned.

A non-tautological application of the analytic paradigm at the collective level of decision requires that calculations fitting the assumptions of the paradigm be explicit and observable and that they have a direct effect on decisions made and actions taken. A reasonable approximation of this requirement can be achieved if the public objectives at stake are clearly identified, if their trade-offs are explicitly considered, if some model of the problem allowing estimates of possible outcomes is explicitly worked out, and if the numerous actors involved accept, or at least are constrained by, the estimates. This posits a collective decision process working by consensus in which the multiple actors attempt to evolve by debate and mutual effort a set of calculations which meet the criteria of analytic logic. If a dominant decision emerges from the explicit, shared analysis, then according to the paradigm that should be the one taken. If clear dominance of one alternative does not emerge, then the decision taken should at least be within the range defined by the common calculations if the decision is held to be the result of an analytic process.

This formulation leaves residual vagueness, to be sure, for without examining an actual case the degree of requisite explicitness cannot be made clear, nor can judgments be made as to whether non-dominant decisions can plausibly be said to follow from prior calculations. The formulation does capture the spirit of the paradigm, however, and does provide enough specificity to identify some actual instances.

In 1942, for example, the Allies faced the problem of defending friendly shipping from attack by German submarines in the waters off Great Britain.[20] A certain amount of aircraft were

[20] This illustration is taken from the annals of operations research. The techniques of operations research which came into wide use in government during World War II are, of course, procedures for applying analytic

available for the mission, and the policy question was whether the aircraft ought to be used to bomb German submarine bases, escort the convoys, or hunt down submarines in the Bay of Biscay. Operations analysts were employed, and they succeeded in structuring the questions in analytic terms. The measure of value chosen to assess the problem was the number of friendly ships saved from destruction. Though this measure was far short of ultimate utility, it was judged useful for the limited problem which the decision makers faced. The analysts approached the problem by gathering data from previous months of U-boat warfare. They calculated that a German U-boat on patrol during previous months of the war sank 0.8 ships per month, and this, therefore, was the number of ships assumed saved for every month of patrol by a single U-boat denied to the Germans. They also calculated that German production of U-boats was controlled not by the construction of boats but by the time required (six months) to train crews. Thus, for every U-boat sunk, six months of patrol by a boat was denied the Germans and 4.8 Allied ships were saved.

The analysts also calculated the number of boat/months of patrol denied the enemy by bombing submarine basing facilities during previous months of the war. Using these figures, the analysts computed the number of ships saved per sortie (one flight by a single aircraft). They considered various possible aircraft deployments: (1) escorting only threatened convoys (only 1 out of 10 shipping convoys was attacked), (2) escorting all convoys, (3) general scanning of the Bay of Biscay, and (4) bombing of the submarine docking facilities. The resulting numerical comparisons are presented in the following table:

Ships saved per 100 sorties

(1)	Escort of threatened convoys	30
(2)	Escort of all convoys	3
(3)	Anti-submarine patrols	3–4
(4)	Raids on submarine bases	1

These calculations were given to Royal Air Force commanders, and to the extent that they influenced decisions regarding force

assumptions to problems of public policy. The specific example is from P. M. Morse and G. E. Kimball, *Methods of Operations Research* (Cambridge, Mass.: MIT Press, 1962).

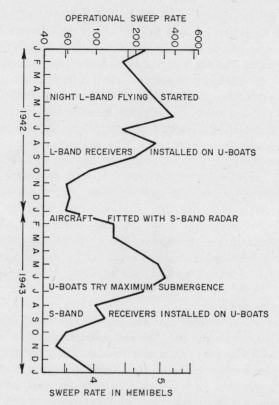

2. Effectiveness of patrols by British aircraft in sighting submarines
(Source: Morse and Kimball, *Methods of Operations Research*, p. 44.)

operations that the commanders actually made, it can plausibly
be said that their decision process was analytic in character.

LEARNING

The operation of a decision process over time poses some special
problems for the logic of the paradigm. Time brings accumulating experience and changes in the environment, both of which by
the assumptions of the paradigm should produce adjustments in
decision calculations. Perhaps the central characteristic of the
analytic decision maker is the construction of careful, explicit,
disaggregated calculations of the possible results of his actions.
By the assumptions of the paradigm, the analytic decision maker
constructs a model of the causal forces controlling the environ-

40

ment in which he acts. As new information becomes available over time, it should be integrated into the working model and the critical causal assumptions of the model should be adjusted whenever the weight of evidence requires it. That is, the assumptions of alternative outcome calculations and sensitivity to pertinent information require a *causal learning* process in which new information is integrated into explicit causal inferences.

The importance of the causal learning process can be appreciated by reflecting further on the anti-submarine warfare example. An analytic decision maker in that example, acting shortly after the completion of the analysis described, might well have chosen option number three—the anti-submarine patrols—after having ascertained that it was not possible to distinguish in advance between convoys that would be attacked and those that would not be. The criteria of the paradigm are all roughly approximated. The alternative missions for the aircraft—search and destroy, bombing bases, convoy escort—were all objectives authoritatively established by military commanders. The devised measure —ships saved per sortie—did achieve a limited integration of these separate missions by imposing a standard measure of value. There was a good deal of sensitivity to pertinent information, and straightforward probability assessments based on available information were made. Also, alternative outcomes were considered —notably, that it would be possible to ascertain in advance which convoys would be threatened with attack and that it would not be.

The calculations presented to British commanders, however, did not include any estimate of possible countermoves by the German submarine force, and that turned out to be a critical question. At the time the calculations noted above were done, British planes had just instituted night search operations utilizing L-band radar.[21] The German submarines could run submerged for only short periods of time, and they were in the habit of surfacing at night when visual contact by searching aircraft was most difficult. The L-band radar enabled the planes to find submarines on the surface at night. In the middle of 1942, the British were reaping the results of their technical innovation, and this was the time period from which data for the analysis of the anti-submarine missions were taken. It is instructive to see the data on search operations for the year following the analysis of anti-

[21] Ibid., p. 44.

submarine warfare missions just presented. Figure 2 presents these data, using the measure of effectiveness of search operations which the British had devised—the operational sweep rate.[22]

As one can see from the figure, the actual success of British search operations varied widely as a function of technical moves and countermoves. The British introduced L-band radar and increased their ability to find German submarines. The Germans then introduced L-band receivers so they could hear the planes coming and submerge before being attacked or even effectively discovered. The sweep rate then declined. Another cycle occurred with S-band radar in 1943. The point is that these fluctuations would clearly affect the outcome of anti-submarine warfare operations, though they were not included in the analysis described. If analytic decision makers chose search and destroy missions (with the preferred option infeasible) based on data from the first six months of 1942, then one would clearly require that they reopen and probably revise their decision as data from the last six months became available.

The example illustrates one important component of causal learning, a process which can be labeled lateral expansion. The possible German response to patrols was a question clearly implied by the original analysis, but excluded under the pressures of time and uncertainty. The subsequent incorporation of this problem into the analysis would be necessary to make the model on which the estimates were based more complete and more accurate. In general terms lateral expansion can be conceived as a process of including in the decision maker's working model critical environmental phenomena which affect the outcome and which were previously excluded.

There is also a second important component of causal learning, a process which can be labeled by contrast upward expansion. A decision to conduct search and destroy operations against the German submarines in the example would be a low-level suboptimization. The integrating measure of value—ships sunk per sortie—is still remote from the greater value of winning the war, to say nothing of still higher conceptions of value. The aircraft not only could have been deployed for this anti-submarine warfare mission which the analysts considered, but could also have

[22] Ibid.

been used for other missions, such as perhaps bombing critical points in the petroleum supply network. As the process proceeds through subsequent points of decision, the analytic paradigm expects and requires some effort to achieve explicit higher-order integration of the separate objectives. The paradigm would require that a broader range of alternative missions for the aircraft be included in the analysis and that the measure of value be expanded from ships saved per sortie to something approaching days of war saved per sortie. This in turn would lead to broader conceptions of the decisions to be made. An upwardly expanding analysis would raise the question as to whether more aircraft should be procured, and if so, how many and of what type.

These concepts of lateral and upward expansion of the decision maker's working model specify critical components of the general notion of iterative cycles of analysis which has been propounded in the literature.[23] The application of these basic notions of analytic decision to complex problems is what has been attempted in systems analysis. It was the realization of such procedures in the actual operations of the United States government which Planning, Programing, Budgeting systems sought to accomplish.[24] The sophisticated concepts of how these procedures were to operate reflect expectations of gradual development of analytic calculations in specific issue areas. Such development proceeds not only by using new information to get better estimation of critical parameters, but also by arriving at new conceptions of the decision problem itself and new alternatives.

One of the most frequently cited examples of such an expanding process of decision analysis is the strategic basing study done by the RAND Corporation for the U.S. Air Force in the early 1950s.[25] At the point of its original conception the study was to address the question as to what overseas bases ought to be developed to solve logistical supply problems for the Strategic Air Command. The study expanded upward to involve a considera-

---

[23] Hitch and McKean, *The Economics of Defense*; E. S. Quade, *Analysis for Military Decisions* (Chicago: Rand McNally and Company, 1964).

[24] Robert H. Haveman and Julius Margolis, eds., *Public Expenditures and Policy Analysis* (Chicago: Markham Publishing Company, 1970).

[25] A. J. Wohlstetter, F. S. Hoffman, R. J. Lutz, and H. S. Rowen, *Selection and Use of Strategic Air Bases*, RAND Corporation paper R-266, 1954. The study is described in Bruce L. R. Smith, *The RAND Corporation* (Cambridge, Mass.: Harvard University Press, 1966).

tion of the overall strategic mission of SAC, and the measure of value utilized was not something like cost of supplies delivered, but rather the cost of destruction of a given Soviet target system. The analysis also expanded laterally to include problems of SAC vulnerability to Soviet attack, problems which by most accounts had not seriously been confronted before the study. The sequence of decisions made in the decade following the study regarding the procurement and deployment of U.S. strategic forces has generally been regarded as a model of the analytic decision process in operation on a complex problem, and there is a good case for this. The process did center at least in part around the developing model.[26] That model gradually evolved reasonably high-level value integrations in adopting an analytic measure which reflected the overall strategic mission. The model coordinated a number of separate and diverse decisions, not only concerning base procurement and location, but also questions of force operations and issues of force procurement and deployment much broader than the bomber questions originally addressed.[27]

Causal learning, then, and the underlying, dynamic model of the environment which generates outcome estimates are hallmarks of the analytic decision process.

SUMMARY

The discussion to this point has developed a specification of that class of problems defined as complex and has derived from that

[26] As early as 1948, analysts at RAND Corporation were developing models of the force interactions between the United States and the Soviet Union. These models, though not widely discussed, have become very important in the analysis of strategic weapons measurement and associated arms control issues. Most of the major debates about weapons procurement have been conducted using calculations derived from these models. The models have hardly resolved these debates, but they have provided a structural context in which they could occur.

[27] Careful students of history will recognize that the actual impact of the RAND study on basing decisions and force deployments is rather problematic. At no point were the conclusions reached simply and directly implemented. The study, however, played a critical role in the deployment of strategic analysis which, a decade or more after the completion of the basing study, did have unmistakable influence over actual decisions. It cannot be said that the basing study was merely a piece of analysis having nothing to do with the making of decisions.

specification three main topics with which any theory of complex decisions will have to deal: (1) the determination of values which are operative in the decision process, (2) the handling of uncertainty in the decision process, and (3) the effects on the decision process of a dispersion of the power of decision over a number of individuals.

The analytic paradigm is defined as a set of assumptions about how the decision process operates in relation to the complex decision problem. A given process of decision is analytic if upon examination one can find evidence that there was at least limited value integration, that alternative outcomes were analyzed and evaluated, and that new information regarding central variables of the problem did produce plausibly appropriate subjective adjustments. In following the process through a sequence of decision points, it can be found analytic if one can observe a causal learning process; that is, an explicit set of calculations which evolve in such a way that higher, more general conceptions of decision objectives came to be included (upward expansion), as well as critical environmental interactions which were previously excluded (lateral expansion). The shift from an individual level of analysis (where most of the intellectual development has occurred) to a collective level of analysis is achieved by requiring that the collective process be constrained by an explicit set of calculations, shared by the individuals involved, which meet the analytic criteria advanced at the individual level. There is a good deal of residual ambiguity in this determination. It does not specify how far and how rapidly expansion must proceed in order for this process to qualify as analytic. Such a specification is not readily made without knowing something about the problem, but this very fact gives leeway for a tautologous use of these notions similar, if more sophisticated, to the tautology involved in the outright reduction of an entire nation to an assumed individual. While this must be conceded, some gain clearly has been made. The assumptions define a notion of analytic procedure for which real examples seem to exist and which thus must be feasible even for limited human beings. The assumptions render the meaning specific enough that it seems clear that examples of decision processes can be found which do not meet the criteria and thus cannot be considered analytic. This indeed will be demonstrated later on. The result is a conception which can be given real empirical content and which still offers scope for a valid normative argument. The conception also allows one to observe degrees of rationality within feasible ranges, and that is a very great benefit for the substantive purposes of understanding the policy problems of the nuclear sharing episode.

The implications of the analytic paradigm conceived as a positive statement are clearly enough defined by these specifications to be put to work in this study. However, their utility becomes even greater, as does our power over the substantive issue, when the analytic paradigm is held in comparison with other paradigms of the decision process. Subsequent chapters thus pursue the idea of a theoretical framework competing with analytic assumptions.

CHAPTER 3

The Cybernetic Paradigm

CRITICISM of analytic assumptions has frequently been motivated by the observation of complex events where unfortunate outcomes are hard to reconcile with those assumptions. For example, a number of apparent failures of deterrence have been noted, episodes where nations acted against what would appear to have been compelling analytic logic. Japan's attack on the United States in 1941 is not easy to reconcile with analytic assumptions. Similarly, British decision makers in 1941 apparently believed estimates about the destructive capacity of the German Luftwaffe which should have made them much more interested in peace terms than they in fact were.[1] The Egyptian Army's mobilization against Israel in May–June of 1967 was a risk whose outcome leaves doubts that the men who chose to take it were operating in accord with analytic logic. In all these cases the events can be rationalized *post hoc*, as some historians have in fact done.[2] There is strain in doing so, however, and events such as these have generated doubts about the dominant paradigm.[3]

Doubts of this sort, though serious and longstanding, have done very little damage to the stature of the analytic paradigm. The rigorous clarity of its articulation, its widespread application, and the long years of indoctrination are protection against simple refutation. As with any well-established position in human thought, it counts for little to offer apparently disconfirming observations without providing at the same time replacements for the critical assumptions which serve important functions in the conduct of daily affairs. Beyond that, observations such as those

[1] George Quester, *Deterrence Before Hiroshima* (New York: John Wiley and Sons, Inc., 1966).

[2] See for example Stephen Pelz, *The Race to Pearl Harbor* (Cambridge, Mass.: Harvard University Press, forthcoming).

[3] Such doubts have been fueled by other considerations as well. In itself, the enormity of the wager which is being staked on the validity of the concepts of deterrence—billions of dollars and the risk of millions of lives—has inspired a great deal of anguish about that particular application of analytic logic. See for example F. C. Iklé, "Can Nuclear Deterrence Last Out the Century?" in *Foreign Affairs*, 51, 2 (January 1973), pp. 267–285.

mentioned do not strike at all at an important element of strength of the theory; namely, the fact that analytic assumptions have an enormous intuitive plausibility when applied to everyday events. The normal human being surviving to adulthood is obviously a very successful decision maker in matters concerning his basic welfare. In a wide variety of environments human beings manage to feed, to clothe, and to house themselves, to raise their young, and to avoid a large number of subtle dangers. In doing so they solve trade-off problems so consistently and reliably that it becomes natural to impute to them the processes of value integration and outcome calculation which analytic logic requires. If rough approximations of these requirements were not being met, the tacit argument runs, how could successful solutions be produced with such regularity? Pointing out apparent failures of rationality in relatively rare and esoteric circumstances does not answer this question.

For these reasons a serious challenge to the hegemony of analytic logic must come from men who have alternative assumptions to offer and who can use them to give an account of routinely successful decision making. Herein lies the promise of cybernetic theories. They are based on a logical structure with a completely different focus than that of the analytic paradigm, and the central assumptions of that structure do provide apparent substitutes for analytic assumptions. Moreover, much of the work in developing these theories has been directed precisely at the problem of explaining highly successful behavior (usually called adaptive) without assuming elaborate decision-making mechanisms. Such accounts provide an important theoretical base from which to develop a treatment of the more demanding problems of complexity.

VARIETY AND THE CYBERNETIC MECHANISM OF DECISION

Men who have studied living organisms have been enormously impressed by the felicitous relationships which they develop with their environment. Numerous studies have probed the matter and we can take the honeybee as but one example.[4] It is a social

4 August Krough, "The Language of the Bees," in *Scientific American*, Vol. 179 (August 1948), pp. 18–21. This reviews the extensive work done by the German scientist Karl von Frisch.

creature whose basic functions, notably the reproductive cycle, require the care and feeding of an entire colony. As with any society, this basic task requires that decisions be made, and researchers have naturally been curious as to how such a limited organism as a bee manages to make successful decisions. How, for instance, does a group of worker bees manage to locate pollen-bearing flowers at a place remote from the hive and focus their efforts on gathering the pollen and bringing it back to the hive? Studies have shown that they use the sun for navigation and a peculiar dance for communicating the location of the pollen source to other workers by giving them instructions regarding the angle and direction of the sun in reference to the field. If seen in analytic terms, the task of locating the field of flowers and of finding their way back to the hive by navigating from the sun would require a very sophisticated set of calculations which no one believes bees are able to perform. Such observations lead the theorist to look for a far simpler decision mechanism of a different character.

Even a careful observation of some human behavior impels one away from the analytic paradigm to account for it. Take the tennis player, for example. Balls fly at him from across the net at different speeds and in different trajectories. Usually, he must move to intercept them and do so in a very short time. The degree to which the skilled player can achieve such interceptions is much greater than would be expected by chance. The moves of the tennis player clearly reflect decisions on his part, a fair number of which are successful in that they enable him to bring his racket in contact with the ball. Given what we know about the pace of the game and the intellectual characteristics of tennis players, it seems intuitively very implausible that the player makes his moves by estimating the speed and trajectory of the ball and by computing the probable intersection point given his own rates of movement. Few, if any, tennis players could provide the proper equations on demand. Even the mathematically inclined player would find such calculations a significant chore if presented the issue as an intellectual problem. One may choose, as we have noted, to engage in tautology and to impute unconscious calculations to the tennis player on the basis of observations that he can, in fact, intercept a great many moving balls. When the elaborate nature of the implied calculations is kept in mind, however, such an imputation seems strikingly implausible, and this phenomenon too leads theorists to look for other mechanisms of decisions which would better explain the intuitive evidence.

What is striking about both of these examples to those who analyze such situations is the enormous intrinsic complexity of the problem which is being solved. Again, consider the tennis player. At the very least, in a given exchange he must decide where to intercept the ball, what stroke to use to hit it, and where in the opposite court he wants to hit it. From where he stands when the ball starts toward his court, he could move forward, backward, right, left, or angle at various degrees. He also could move at various speeds. It is a considerable simplification to attribute to him ten possible directions and two possible speeds and an overall repertory of twenty move vectors. Let us also give him but five possible strokes and seven possible targets in the opposite court. Also, since move, stroke, and target all involve interacting considerations in overall strategy, he must establish some sequence of decisions—e.g., move, stroke, target; or target, move, stroke. As all connoisseurs of the game will recognize, this is a highly stylized and greatly simplified version of tennis. Even so, for each stroke of the ball in this version there are 4,200 different solutions to the problem for the player. The speed at which tennis players can find a solution makes it very unlikely that they examine all the alternatives, establish a preference ordering, and choose the best one.

Already one can sense the appeal to the decision theorist of these examples.[5] They seem to require a very simple decision

[5] The examples used could so clearly be replaced with everyday life experience arbitrarily chosen that one begins to wonder why, if rational assumptions are implausible in this context, they could ever become established in the first place. The answer doubtless lies in part in the ability to lapse into tautology to prevent this everyday experience from becoming compelling evidence *against* the notions. The result is to identify the fact of adaptation with the notion of rationality and to further anchor that notion in our habits of mind. The only evidence against rationality thus becomes behavior which seems obviously maladaptive. Since adaptation is so closely related to survival itself, maladaptive behavior is *perforce* a rare event. The slowness to challenge rational assumptions in any radical way seems clearly related to this association with adaptation. It is only as the notions have been worked out with reference to unusual events (dramatic episodic policy decisions) that we have become willing to challenge the logic. The common aphorism that the fish is the last to discover water seems to reflect the phenomenon here.

mechanism but one with considerable logical power. The mechanism, whatever it might be, clearly solves problems of impressive difficulty and does it with apparently little burden on the decision maker. It is from considerations of this sort that a cybernetic paradigm of the decision process has begun to emerge—organized around notions of short-cycle information feedback and the elimination of uncertainty.

The simple decision mechanism, which the honeybee and the tennis player examples seem to require, can be readily conceptualized in terms of a servomechanism, a central cybernetic idea. Servomechanisms, which have some remarkable properties, are exceedingly simple in conception, and it takes very little imagination to find many examples from everyday life. The thermostat is one of the favorites. It is quiescent only within a reasonably narrow range of temperatures, and the range is set to desirable values. If it records temperatures below the desired range, it closes a connection which activates a heating system; if it records above the desired range, it closes a separate circuit activating a cooling system. The result is that normal environments in proximity of the mechanism are kept within or closely approximating the desired range. Similar principles are used in engine governors, radar homing devices, automatic pilots, etc. In the practical world, servomechanisms are ubiquitous.

One of the famous examples of a servomechanism is the Watt governor devised in the nineteenth century to regulate the speed of a steam engine.[6] The machine involves two steel balls (or any other form of mass) on arms suspended from a central shaft (see Figure 3). The shaft of the governor is attached to the shaft of the engine and rotates as a direct function of the speed of the engine. The swinging arms of the governor are attached to the throttle of the steam engine such that as the arms swing outward they begin to close the throttle and as they swing inward they open it. As the speed of the engine increases, the balls on the governor swing outward by centrifugal force and close the throttle, thus decreasing the speed of the engine. As the engine slows down, the balls swing toward the shaft by gravity, thus increasing the speed of the engine. The overall effect of the governor is to keep engine speed within a particular range, and the relation-

[6] The properties of the Watt governor as a cybernetic mechanism are discussed by Stafford Beer, *Cybernetics and Management* (New York: John Wiley and Sons, Inc., 1959).

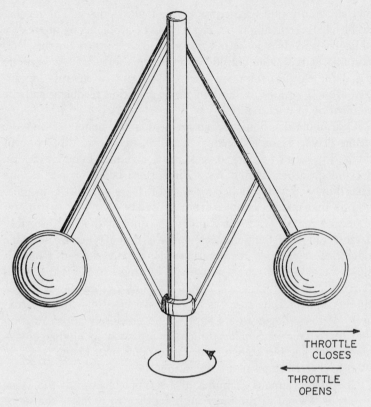

THROTTLE
CLOSES

THROTTLE
OPENS

3. Schematic drawing of Watt governor
for steam engines

ships within the system (mass of the balls, length of the arms, etc.) can be adjusted to insure that this range is the desired one. Once set properly, the Watt governor successfully makes decisions regarding the speed of the engine.

The decision-making capacity of the Watt governor, it has been recognized, exists in the fact that it sets up a structured feedback loop between the speed of the engine and the degree of throttle opening. It serves to focus decisions about throttle openings on a single variable (speed), which is itself a function of the throttle's action. Obviously, in this decision mechanism there is no explicit model calculating the effects of engine speed and relating these to basic preferences to derive an optimal speed. If such calculations are done they are done completely outside the mechanism by an industrial engineer who, seen from a perspective within the system, plays a role often relegated to God in human affairs.[7]

As seen from within the system, the decision process of the servomechanism avoids the preference ordering, the explicit calculations of alternatives and outcomes, and the optimizing process which form the core of the analytic paradigm. The fact that the process of decisions can be embodied in a mechanical device is tribute to the degree to which intelligence functions can be trimmed and still yield successful decisions. The Watt governor is an extreme case of the simple cybernetic decision maker, but as such it illuminates the divergence in assumptions.

A slightly more complicated version of the basic mechanism has been worked out by W. Ross Ashby, who explicitly took on the task of explaining non-purposive adaptation.[8] He articulated his prototypical problem as a cat sleeping by the fire who moves closer to the fire as it grows dimmer, and farther away as it grows hotter. The cat, says Ashby by implication, does not maintain a preference ordering of desirable temperatures and does not calculate the optimal spot by considering the energy output of the fire and heat conduction in the surrounding atmosphere. Rather, Ashby's cat maintains a set of "critical variables" and changes position only as those variables move outside tolerable ranges. When changing position, the cat moves randomly. If it should go toward a growing fire it would not restore the critical variable to its proper range and thus another move would be immediately

---

[7] Many discussions of cybernetics adopt the point of view of the system as a whole and therefore see a servomechanism such as the Watt governor as operating within a completely determined process. If many aspects of the system are unknown, however—both exact values and the parameters themselves (as is the case under complexity)—then this perspective is simply not available and the situation must be viewed from within the decision-making mechanism. This produces a drastic shift in the nature of cybernetic analysis, but it does not affect some of its most important assumptions. The argument here is that such a shift is necessary. It is decidedly inconvenient in that it denies quantitative rigor available in analyzing closed known systems. It is nevertheless necessary because of the importance of complex problems. It is on this point that the discussion here parts with cybernetic-based analyses which adopt the system perspective. See, for example, Karl W. Deutsch, *The Nerves of Government* (New York: The Free Press, 1966).

[8] W. Ross Ashby, *A Design for a Brain* (New York: John Wiley and Sons, Inc., 1952).

required. Eventually in the sequence of moves, one is made which reduces the temperature on the cat's skin and at this point it stays in position until there is another change in the fire.

Ashby developed a concrete model for his process which he embodied in a system of four pointers in a magnetic field. (He called it a homeostat.) He defined stability in terms of ranges on a scale for all four pointers and studied the process whereby such equilibrium is restored once disturbed by some outside force. He discovered that the system, in order to achieve what he called ultrastability, required two feedback loops. The first loop carries simple environmental input and in effect represents the process of perception. Simple programed behavior adjustments are made according to this input—the process of perception required for the cat to be able to move when the fire gets too hot. The second feedback loop monitors the critical variables and their changes. These variables are affected by the behavior of the system and thus are part of a feedback loop, but there need be no knowledge of that fact on the part of the decision maker. If the critical variables are observed to be outside of a defined interval, then a "state" change occurs in the organism. A state change alters the manner in which the primary feedback process operates. This means simply that Ashby's organism carries a repertory of behavior patterns each of which operates in a characteristic way upon receipt of perceptual input. Thus the first feedback loop produces minor (or incremental) adjustments within a given state, and the second produces the major changes of state.

Ashby showed that his sytem, which made completely random moves to restore stability once it was disturbed, was in fact able to achieve such stability quite readily.[9] In other words, he makes completely explicit a very simple decision process and shows how it is able to maintain stability in an environment for which it had no theoretical understanding whatsoever. Moreover, it can be demonstrated that the same principles which govern Ashby's homeostat seem to govern some of the information-processing behavior of humans and animal subjects in psychological laboratories. The homeostat is another extreme case, but it represents a continuum which stretches to man.

Herbert Simon has suggested a simple set of images for catching the distinctions between servomechanisms and analytic calcu-

[9] Ibid., Chapter 8.

lation as mechanisms for decision.[10] Simon notes the difference between a "state" description of reality and a "process" description of reality. The former constructs a "blueprint" or model of the environment as the focus of decision, and specific action is taken in accord with the model. The latter, which he argues is like a recipe rather than a blueprint, details a sequence of operations which when performed do produce the object or actual situation desired, but which works without any clear picture of the actual product. Roughly speaking, the mechanism of decision advanced by the cybernetic paradigm is one which works on the principle of the recipe. The decision maker has a repertory of operations which he performs in sequence while monitoring a few feedback variables. He produces an outcome as a consequence of completing the sequence, but the outcome need not be conceptualized in advance. The cook, in this model, does not construct the relative preference for sweetness or tartness for an average range of customers in baking his pies. Rather, he follows established recipes and watches attendance at the restaurant and the rate at which his pies disappear.

This focus on process gives deep philosophical and logical resonances to the simple cybernetic ideas. Simon makes it quite provocative by citing evidence that DNA in the chromosomes of an organism, which plays the executive role in determining the development of the organism, operates on the recipe principle.[11] This is one of the most delicate production processes known, and it is controlled entirely by microbiological mechanisms whose decision processes can hardly be elaborate. To have such delicate work done by such simple mechanisms constitutes a rather strong suggestion as to the power of the approach. Equally provocative is the relationship which the distinction bears to concepts in fundamental logic. Though this tangent winds too quickly into technical complexities to pursue in the current context, it is clear that the distinction between the concept of a number as an entity in elementary number theory and the recursive definition of a number bears a striking relationship to the sort of distinction sketched out in the blueprint and recipe metaphors.[12]

[10] Herbert A. Simon, "The Architecture of Complexity," in Herbert A. Simon, *The Sciences of the Artificial* (Cambridge, Mass.: MIT Press, 1968), pp. 84–118.

[11] Ibid.

[12] Beer, in *Cybernetics and Management*, reviews the logical roots of

Fortunately, Stafford Beer has provided as provocative a discussion of the connections of cybernetic notions to elementary logic as anyone would wish to have, and there is no need to repeat his effort.[13] His interpretation strains at the limits and doubtless is more suggestive than the cautious logician would care to be. However, the main point is readily accepted. The simple notion of servomechanisms and broader conceptions of decision processes based on the recipe principle are not, even at this early point, simply isolated hypotheses dissenting from the dominant assumptions of the analytic paradigm. There is an underlying coherence to these ideas of considerable significance, and the theoretical issues raised go to the very core of human knowledge. Considerations of this sort suggest that cybernetic ideas represent a major stream of thought whose implications for the understanding of complex decision processes may ultimately be very extensive indeed. One can see a systematic challenge to analytic assumptions as a major possibility, a challenge which might be broadly based enough and theoretically rooted enough to yield in time strong implications for concrete policy in many areas.

Such broad implications, if they are to emerge, will do so, we can be sure, over an extended period of time. For the moment, the cybernetic paradigm yields but a simple claim. The dominant set of assumptions in decision theory—the analytic paradigm—should not rule unchallenged. The central focus of that paradigm—finding an optimal solution under given constraints by direct calculation—is seriously under dispute. The cybernetic paradigm suggests rather that the central focus of the decision process is the business of eliminating the variety inherent in any significant decision problem.

Non-Purposive Adaption and the Phenomenon of Decomposition

A main source of fascination with servomechanisms as decision makers is their ability to produce strikingly adaptive outcomes in very complicated environments. Von Frisch, for example, in

---

cybernetic theory. Stephen Cole Kleene, *Mathematical Logic* (New York: John Wiley and Sons, Inc., 1967), provides a good discussion of logical analysis related to cybernetics.

[13] Beer, *Cybernetics and Management*.

his experiments on the bees once carefully led the workers around a ridge by putting food at successive points. When he finally had them foraging in a place which put the ridge between them and the hive, the bees "discovered" that they could save fifty meters by flying over the ridge instead of around it and they commenced to do so in an impressive display of optimizing behavior.[14] The complicated behavior in which many species engage in order to reproduce—e.g., salmon returning hundreds of miles to their own birthplace to spawn—provide even more dramatic examples. Moreover, as we have seen, these felicitous outcomes are isolated quickly and efficiently from very large sets of theoretically possible outcomes. Since complexity clearly has something to do with variety, it is interesting, to say the least, to see such simple decision-making mechanisms coping so successfully with problems containing enormous variety.

We have seen already the secret of the ability to handle variety. The simplest cybernetic mechanisms do not confront the issue of variety at all, for they make no calculations of the environment. The mechanisms merely track a few feedback variables and beyond that are perfectly blind to the environment. Hence, degrees of complexity in the environment are of no concern within the decision-making mechanism itself, and the burden of calculation which the analytic paradigm seems to impose is not a problem for cybernetic assumptions.

The committed analytic theorist, however, is likely to assert that he finds no challenge in these observations. The successful behavior of which these decision mechanisms are demonstrably capable, he argues, is due to designs created outside of the decision-making system. He can point to Watt, who designed the environment in which the governor which bears his name so successfully operates. He can point to the use of metalanguages in fundamental logic and to the programer in the case of the electronic computer. It is the decisions of the designer, the analytic theorist would claim, that he seeks to understand; once these are known, the rest is determined.

This defense falls in part because, in the more complicated situation, it is very difficult to point to the designer or even conceive of him. Who designed the honeybee? Moreover, even where a designer can be found whose decisions might be discovered (as

[14] Krogh, "The Language of the Bees."

57

with the computer programer), the decision-making system he sets up will produce outcomes in a complicated problem which could not be foreseen, i.e., solutions not inherent in the design alone. Heuristic programing of computers has made this clear, if the point was ever in real doubt. Faced with a problem having great variety, as in the popular example of chess, even a very large computer (say one multiplying a thousandfold or a millionfold, the computers now available) could not solve it by complete calculation as an uncompromised application of the analytic paradigm would require. The conclusion, of course, is overwhelming that the mind cannot do it either. Hence when existing computers are applied to the problem of chess, heuristic procedures allowing for partial approaches to the problem must be used. These produce solutions which cannot be predicted in advance. One must actually run the machine to know what it will do.

This objection of our hypothetical analytic theorist, however, does have one major benefit. It points to the fact that the success of the cybernetic mechanism depends a great deal on the character of the surrounding environment. Ashby concedes the point in his explicit formulation. Though his homeostat was capable of adapting to certain environmental disturbances without understanding in the least what they were, it is clear that "lethal" discontinuities in the environment, such as a change in the nature of electromagnetic forces, would defeat his system.[15] So would improperly timed feedback cycles. Even Ashby's "ultrastable" system, which derives its adaptive power from having a repertory of response patterns and an ability to shift patterns, is dependent upon a fair amount of structure and stability in its environment. If variation is too great along certain dimensions, the ultrastable system cannot adapt.

This raises some difficult questions. Let us assume that for purposes of reaching the issues of public policy we must define complexity not only by theoretical variety but by its practical character. We have seen that great theoretical variety can be imputed to apparently simple problems by calculating all permutations. Under this procedure even very few variables can produce a very large number of possible outcomes. What if we define practical complexity to mean wide ranges for the values of each vari-

[15] Ashby, *A Design for a Brain*, p. 93f.

able or rapid change in the pertinent variables? Must we then reject the cybernetic paradigm as inapplicable to the complex decision problems because of the variation imputed to such problems? Does complexity mean that "lethal" discontinuities are guaranteed?

Herbert Simon has confronted this issue most directly, in pursuing the characteristics of complexity.[16] He argues that in a number of physical and biological systems, which contain a great deal of variety, there is a hierarchical organization which imposes structure on complexity. A complex environment, which may be conceptualized as a system of elements in a relationship, is everywhere in nature and in human affairs divided into subsystems and so on down through many levels of organization. A book is divided into chapters, which are divided into major and minor headings, which are divided into paragraphs, etc., down to elementary letters, punctuation marks, and numerals. A city is divided into a variety of districts, neighborhoods, buildings, rooms, and individual occupants in successive layers of organization. Within such hierarchically organized systems, the interactions and interrelationships among elements of the same subsystem are generally greater than interaction among elements of separate subsystems—a property which renders complex systems in Simon's terms "nearly decomposable."[17] Thus, in a city the members of a family (a subsystem) interact more with one another than they do with members of another family down the block. At a higher level in the hierarchy, residents of the North End in Boston (a subsystem of the city) interact more with one another than they do with residents of the Back Bay.

In a decomposable environment there are hierarchically arranged channels of variation that already provide at an abstract level the conditions for successful adaptation by cybernetic mechanisms of decision. The mechanism can operate within a

[16] Simon, "The Architecture of Complexity."

[17] The concept of near-decomposability is used in quantitative treatments of decision theory which belong to the analytic paradigm, and the notion is implicit in the limits which were imposed on value integration and outcome calculation in Chapter 2 above. Within the analytic tradition, however, it is used as a practical adjustment and the spirit of the paradigm strains against reliance on it. Within cybernetic theory, near-decomposability plays a central role and there is complete reliance on it. See Simon, "The Architecture of Complexity," pp. 99–107.

particular subsystem of such an environment and encounter variation which is a great deal more regular than the environment as a whole and certainly more regular than would be the case were hierarchical organization not present.

Take the case of the tennis stroke. The discussion above focused on the player's problem well down in the hierarchy of the environment in which he operates. What was described was actually an elementary component of a single point. Frequently a player must put together a sequence of stroke, move, and target combinations to win a single point in the game. And, of course, he must win a sequence of points to win the game, a sequence of games to win the set, a sequence of sets to win the match. If each "element" has 4,200 solutions, one can imagine what the variety becomes if one considers the possible outcomes for each successive level of hierarchy. A point requiring five "elements" will have $4,200^5$ (i.e., 1.14×10^{18}) theoretically possible solutions. This would be overwhelming if confronted all at once, but the fact that these stroke/move/target problems come in regular sequence, that there is stable variation hierarchically arranged, makes the game manageable. Each of our "elements" is a subsystem; each point sequence is a higher-order subsystem. The movement of the ball and the two players within a point sequence constitutes the most salient variation in the subsystem, and a decent game of tennis can be played with decision mechanisms concentrating on that variation alone. Other pertinent variations in the environment—changes in the surface characteristics of the court, in the resiliency of the balls, in the angle of the sun, the physiological functions of the players—proceed at lesser rates and the player need not integrate them into his calculations for a given point sequence. At some stage of a match a player is likely to have to pay attention to at least some of these variables, but he can usually focus his attention on one of these other subsystems between points and make whatever decisions are required independently of the stroke/move/target decision in a point sequence. The hierarchical organization of environmental variation allows him to do this and get away with it.[18]

[18] It is to be noted also that our tennis player makes important use of environmental hierarchy subordinate to the situation we have treated as elementary (the single stroke of the ball). The 4,200 different solutions to his elementary problem would number much greater if the game were somehow constituted so that a given elementary action might require any com-

The discussion is pursued to such an extent in order to drive home the point that the cybernetic paradigm, in positing a decision mechanism based on selective feedback and programed operations (the recipe), is building upon the notion of hierarchically organized environments. The adaptive capacity of cybernetic decision mechanisms occurs when the decision maker is operating within a stable environmental subsystem.[19] There may be great complexity in hierarchical levels above and/or below this subsystem, and the consequences of actions taken in these other areas of the environmental hierarchy may be considerable. However, whatever the consequence in the larger environment, decisions according to the paradigm are controlled by events within the subsystems.

This phenomenon of highly focused, highly programed decision is so ubiquitous that the tendency is to treat it as insignificant. Most of our everyday behavior falls readily into the paradigm—walking down the street, making a phone call, writing a speech. That is, most human activity involves decision sequences which run out in close interaction with and are heavily structured by decomposable hierarchies within the environment. Few would care to argue with that point. Much analytic attention goes not to the routine, however, but to the unusual decision of great consequence.[20] The point at issue as a practical matter is not whether the cybernetic paradigm is important in studying routine behavior, but whether it is important in decisions which everyone recognizes as involving higher-order thought processes. Do the mechanisms which seem to dominate immediate behavior —patterned physical movements, basic sensory perception, etc.— also influence and somehow structure more abstract thought

---

bination of three from the sets of strokes, targets, and moves. The number of resolutions in this case would be a great deal larger than 4,200.

[19] Ashby, in recognizing the point, speaks of "joined systems"—the cybernetic mechanism and the environmental subsystems upon which it focuses its activity. See Ashby, *A Design for a Brain*, p. 76.

[20] The routine appears boring only if it goes well. In cases where it is disrupted through sickness, injury, or mental illness, it comes to have rather transcendent consequences for the individuals involved. Multiple sclerosis, for example, disrupts routinely operating feedback channels and renders normally simple problems impossibly difficult. In observing tragic cases of failure, one comes to appreciate the importance and complexity of routine procedures for processing information and for making and executing decisions.

processes? Do they affect high-level policy decisions? The argument of the cybernetic paradigm is that they do, that assumptions derived from cybernetic logic can provide an account of decision making under complexity. Since these assumptions contradict those of the analytic paradigm, the resulting view of decision making under complexity is strikingly different.

CYBERNETIC DECISIONS UNDER COMPLEXITY

Value Trade-offs

Since the cybernetic paradigm is so centrally concerned with the issues of uncertainty and the processing of information, there is some ambiguity in the paradigm as to the handling of values. In one of the leading papers on the subject, Herbert Simon advanced a model of choice in which he adjusted the assumptions of classic rationality.[21] Arguing the importance of uncertainty and of the unsolved problems of aggregating incommensurate values, he suggested that values in the decision problem be represented conceptually by a payoff vector rather than by the scalar function which the notion of utility requires. The separate components of the vector could represent either: (1) payoffs to separate individuals, (2) contingent payoffs for a range of possible outcomes, and/or (3) payoffs to incommensurate dimensions of value. Each component of the payoff function, moreover, is restricted to limited variation. Rather than reflecting degrees of goodness or evil through a range on some numerical scale, they can assume one of a set of but two or three denoting either acceptable/unacceptable or acceptable/irrelevant/unacceptable. The decision process then is one which proceeds sequentially to examine a set of alternative actions until one with an outcome valued as acceptable is found. The model has been dubbed the "satisficing" model.

The result of these adjustments is to weaken the assumption of limited value integration. The construction of close-in trade-offs, which is a major assumption of the analytic paradigm, is eliminated. The separate dimensions of value are held separate in the Simon model. Thus, the limitations introduced are not merely limits on the scope of application, but rather limits on the logic

[21] Herbert A. Simon, "A Behavioral Model of Rational Choice," in Herbert A. Simon, *Models of Man: Social and Rational* (New York: John Wiley and Sons, Inc., 1957), pp. 241–260.

required of the decision maker. In this sense Simon, in a limited fashion, does challenge the analytic paradigm rather than merely adjusting it. It can be argued, however, that the challenge Simon presents is relatively moderate. If he eliminates the construction of trade-offs, he nonetheless seems to imply that separate dimensions of value are held simultaneously relevant. He also requires a focus on the outcome of policy actions and some assessment of payoffs. For the two-value trade-off problem, Simon's model seems to require elements in the payoff vector for both values. Such simultaneous consideration represents some degree of value integration, however limited in logical terms.

A starker challenge to the analytic paradigm is presented by Ashby. Ashby's decision maker is presumed to make no calculation about the outcomes of his action at all and to attach no payoff value in advance to any alternative action. The Ashby decision maker harbors a repertory of behaviors which it performs in some ordered sequence. The sequence is not so much related to the problem at hand as it is to past experience.[22] This decision maker monitors a small set of "critical variables" and his values consist in keeping these variables within tolerable ranges. The effect of any given action on this set of critical values is discovered only after it occurs. As a positive model, Ashby's decision maker (understood in terms of his process rather than the outcome he effects) is neither a maximizer nor a "satisficer." With such a mechanism of decision, the integration of separate dimensions of value, though it may be seen as a *de facto* consequence of the decision process, has nothing to do with the way that process actually works. The assumption of limited value integration of the analytic paradigm is decisively rejected.[23] This is what

[22] This entails accepting assumptions that repertories of behavior are ordered in terms of past reinforcement. With the principle of reinforcement, Ashby's formulation in essence summarizes a main argument of learning theory in psychology. The phenomenon of conditioning, whose characteristics are reasonably well established, and various stimulus-response theories of behavior are all models falling within the spirit of the cybernetic paradigm. See K. W. and J. T. Spence, eds., *The Psychology of Learning and Motivation* (New York: Academic Press, 1967 and 1968), vols. I and II; G. A. Kimble, ed., *Hilgard and Marquis' Conditioning and Learning*, 2nd ed. rev. (New York: Appleton-Century-Crofts, Inc., 1961).

[23] The problem of definitions, essentially that of fixing the scope of analysis, becomes acute here. Cybernetic operations have a distinctly different appearance if one adopts the viewpoint of the designer of the system than

Ashby means when he announces his intention to produce a model of non-purposive adaptation.

The Ashby formulation is too extreme to be strictly tenable. While allegedly banishing all outcome calculation as inherently tainted with purpose,[24] he nevertheless reintroduces a functional equivalent in the notion of "critical variables" which must be kept within certain ranges. The logical nitpicker would presumably have little difficulty in pinning Ashby with a tacit conception of purpose. The important point is not, however, whether the logical extreme can be defended but rather the basic spirit of the analysis. The cybernetic theorist, believing that the decision process must be a simple one, strains to eliminate value calculations, and Ashby provides a clear expression of this spirit. Values in the cybernetic paradigm are minimally articulated, and that formulation is sufficient to reject the assumption of value integration.

When forced to characterize the decision maker in purposive terms, the cybernetic theorist would have to assume a fundamentally conservative purpose. The essential problem for the cybernetic decision maker is not to achieve some result in the external world, not even an acceptable as opposed to an optimal result.

---

they do if one looks at the matter from the viewpoint of the decision-making mechanism within the system. Karl Deutsch, in applying cybernetic models to politics, adopts the viewpoint of the system designer, and in that context he speaks of "goal-seeking feedback" and of a servomechanism which ". . . includes the results of its own information by which it modifies its subsequent behavior." (Deutsch, *The Nerves of Government*, p. 88.)

Such notions are acceptable only in a discussion of the overall system and are clearly absurd if the analytic focus is on a particular servomechanism embedded in one of Deutsch's networks. A goal-seeking radar is performing a set of programed operations which, though drenched in the designer's purpose for operations in a particular environment, are utterly devoid of purpose as an internal matter. It is precisely this reason that "gain" and "lag" must be adjusted with the environment in mind, and if not properly adjusted the system will oscillate out of control. The reason for adopting the lower-order point of view here is that for most interesting applications the overall system cannot be known. That is the meaning of structural uncertainty. The problem is one of understanding how cybernetic decision processes operate when they cannot be set (as by some designer) to produce some desired outcome with complete confidence.

[24] Careful readers will note that the working definition of decision set up in Chapter 1 is similarly tainted. Without a purpose in some form, one might speak of causal events affecting outcomes, but not of a decision as herein understood.

The cybernetic decision criterion is therefore not that which represents maximum value or a convenient approximation. Rather the essential criterion is simply survival as directly reflected in the internal state of the decision-making mechanism, and whatever actions are performed are motivated by that basic value. This by no means posits quiescent behavior, for a cybernetic decision maker might well take strong, aggressive, radical action under certain kinds of environmental provocation. Actual behavior can vary over wide ranges, but the motive force is always assumed to be simple and conservative.

Uncertainty and Information Processing

As articulated above, the analytic paradigm posits that decision makers will consider the range of possible outcomes for any course of action and that they will utilize available information to tune their judgments. Substantial new information regarding the likelihood of major contingencies actually occurring should be integrated into an analytic decision maker's calculations and should affect his behavior. These propositions emerge from analytic assumptions that decision makers operate on the basis of a valid model of their environment. The normative version of the paradigm instructs the decision maker to create such a model, and the positive version assumes that this is in fact done in some fashion, no matter how intuitive the decision process might be.

The logic of the cybernetic paradigm attacks this network of assumptions largely because of the improbable requirements of processing information that it seems to impose on the decision maker. For most interesting applications, inherent capacities and the state of knowledge could not support explicit calculations of the sort required. The simple examples of the tennis player and the bee, cited above, provide instances, and others can be found from the behavior of government policy machinery. The government has recently been considering income maintenance schemes, for example, as potential substitutes for direct categorical aid to low-income citizens. Existing knowledge is insufficient to establish what the effects of such programs would be on the work behavior of low-income citizens, and this sharply limits the degree to which alternative outcomes can be assessed. Though some large-scale experimentation has been undertaken to try to build this knowledge, the results are not conclusive and serve to underscore the difficulty of obtaining requisite knowledge. The knowl-

65

edge of these effects has not been gained in over thirty years of government experience with welfare programs. Still, decisions are being made and have been for some time.

There is a possibility, of course, that the required calculations are done intuitively and that even if the state of basic knowledge is insufficient to support high-grade analytic calculations, intuitive judgments provide a rough approximation. The cybernetic paradigm argues against this possibility by pointing to the great variety which inheres in even such simple problems as the tennis player's decisions. Such variety, it is argued, makes it improbable that information-processing mechanisms in the human mind, the basis of "judgment" or "intuition," operate for complex decisions in the manner projected by the analytic paradigm. The cybernetic theorist doubts that decision makers engage in sophisticated outcome calculations with any degree of regularity or consistency.

The result of this argument is a clear rejection of the central analytic assumptions of alternative outcome calculations and sensitivity to pertinent information. The cybernetic paradigm is based on the contradictory *assumption of uncertainty control*. According to this assumption, the decision maker—primarily and necessarily engaged in buffering himself against the overwhelming variety which inheres in his world—simply avoids direct outcome calculations. Such a decision maker possesses procedures for processing information which in fact generate decisions and outcomes, but psychologically he is not engaged in the pursuit of an explicitly designed result. The psychological effects of uncertainty are therefore held to a minimum.

Cybernetic mechanisms which achieve uncertainty control do so by focusing the decision process on a few incoming variables while eliminating entirely any serious calculation of probable outcomes. The decision maker is assumed to have a small set of "responses" and decision rules which determine the course of action to take once he has received information to which he is sensitive. That is, decision rules associate a given action with a given range of "values" for the critical variables in focus. The "responses" are action with a given range of "values" for the critical variables in focus. The "responses" are action sequences, of the character of a recipe, established by prior experience. They are programs which accept and adjust to very specific and very lim-

66

ited kinds of information. For the tennis player, his responses—
the forehand, the backhand, the overhead slam, etc.—which adjust to the speed and direction of the incoming ball offer examples. In cybernetic understanding, the tennis player tracks the
ball and adjusts his swing in rapid feedback cycles as the ball approaches. He does not calculate in the analytic sense.

The cybernetic thesis then is that the decision mechanisms
screen out information which the established set of responses are
not programed to accept. That is, uncertainty control entails
highly focused sensitivity. Since the response sequences adjust
to a very narrow range of information, most incoming information will be shunted aside, having no effect. This decision maker
is not calculating alternative outcomes and will also not be broadly sensitive to pertinent information. He will not engage in a
process of updating subjective probability estimates about various states of the world. Again, the spirit of cybernetic logic
rejects the analytic assumptions regarding the handling of information and posits a much more limited process. The cybernetic
decision maker is sensitive to information only if it enters
through an established highly focused feedback channel, and
hence many factors which do in fact affect the outcomes have no
effect in his decision process.

But what happens if this occurs in a complex environment? In
the tennis player example, uncertainty control and focused sensitivity cause no difficulty, for as we have seen, the game is so
structured that such screening can occur without serious negative effects. As long as we are concerned with decision-making
mechanisms operating in stable, structured, hierarchical environments, conflict with the analytic paradigm is considerably muted.
Even analytic logic does not require that attention be paid to ir-
relevant variables. The conflict only sharpens when the decision
problem is complex in the sense established above. If the presence of complexity means, as surely it must, that the pertinent
environment is not in fact composed of subsystems which are at
once small, stable, and hierarchically arranged, then formulations
of cybernetic assumptions using highly structured problems such
as the tennis player's must be reconsidered. There are two inter-
related questions: whether the logic of the paradigm is affected
by complexity, and whether the capacity of the paradigm to explain successful behavior is affected.

In terms of processing information, the central principle of the paradigm—that of controlling uncertainty and reducing variety —applies as well for the complex decision problem as it does for the less demanding examples. The highly focused, highly programed cybernetic decision process is no more sensitive to higher orders of complexity than it is to higher orders of simple numerical variety. Information enters the cybernetic process through specific feedback channels, and the complexity of the feedback cycle prior to the actual input of information does not affect the internal logic of the decision maker. Indeed, the simplest cybernetic decision maker is not even aware that information input is in fact the result of a feedback cycle.

What is affected by complexity, however, is the response repertory. Adapting a theorem of Shannon's, Ashby has argued that a successfully adaptive cybernetic mechanism must have variety commensurate with its environment. That is, if "critical variables" are to be held within tolerable ranges, then the decision maker must have responses to match the possible environmental disturbances that might be encountered.[25] Since greater complexity clearly entails greater variety,[26] it follows that under conditions of complexity the cybernetic decision maker must have a more elaborate response repertory if he is to retain adaptive capacity. This logic then poses a fundamental problem. If one attributes to the decision maker an arbitrarily elaborate set of responses in order to account for adaptive capacity under complexity, then it seems clear that the simplicity of the decision process is thereby compromised and along with it a major principle of cybernetic analysis. If, however, simplicity is preserved, then the adaptive capacity of the decision maker is apparently threatened under conditions of complexity. This tension between

[25] Shannon demonstrated that the capacity of a correction channel to remove the noise in a communications network is limited by its channel capacity—i.e., the amount of information it can carry. Ashby's law of requisite variety provides the corresponding argument for decision theory. Though apparently innocuous, the thesis has powerful theoretical implications in mathematical treatments of cybernetics. See W. Ross Ashby, *An Introduction to Cybernetics* (London: Chapman & Hall, Ltd., 1970), p. 211.

[26] The reason, readily demonstrated in mathematic treatments of information theory, is that complexity entails less clearly defined structure, and it is structure which constrains variety. See W. R. Garner, *Uncertainty and Structure as Psychological Concepts* (New York: John Wiley and Sons, Inc., 1962).

adaptive capacity and internal simplicity is in fact a major drama of cybernetic analysis.[27]

Though one embarks at this point into poorly charted seas, there is a natural course for cybernetic logic to follow in confronting the dilemma. Internal simplicity can be preserved under complexity if the number of decision makers concerned with a problem is increased. Each decision maker then can focus on some limited dimension, and the effect which his responses produce in other dimensions will become the concern for other decision makers. Complex problems under such a scheme become fragmented into a large number of very specific problems, each addressed by a separate decision maker.

This, of course, is a plausible description of exactly what happens. Under conditions of complexity, decision-making organizations arise which attempt to match the complexity of their environment by means of an internal complexity which is not the property of a single decision maker, but rather of the collective. This is the natural cybernetic explanation for the rise of mass bureaucracy. According to the cybernetic paradigm, each individual decision maker of such an organization will be a cybernetic operator, a fact which might be expected to yield systematic characteristics of the behavior of the organization as a whole.

A simple example might help to make the point more concrete, and the problem of welfare programs mentioned above will do. The cybernetic theorist finds ready grist for his mill in the development of welfare programs. Such a theorist would note that the programs were first set up under conditions of intense economic crisis (the Depression) constituting, as it were, an obvious wandering of critical variables from their tolerable states. The nation's response in this view was basically simple and direct—give money to those who did not have it. That response, however, pro-

---

[27] Many readers will have long since noticed that the theory of evolution in biology is in fact an embodiment of cybernetic logic. This problem is handled in biology by allowing for very large numbers of unsuccessful adaptations. The surviving species, it is assumed, constitute a very small subset of all the biological forms which have existed at some point in the course of time. With this leeway one can account for very elaborate couplings between organism and environment which enable the organism to be at once simple and yet highly adapted. In decision theory, however, the problem is more severe. One has to account for adaptive decisions and preserve simplicity without allowing for such a drastic failure rate.

duced an immediate secondary problem—a concern for cheating and/or for too liberal application in a culture which did not like the dole. The natural evolution of the program therefore involved a process of setting constraints to define eligibility and to prevent those who were ineligible from receiving benefits. As case loads expanded, a large bureaucracy grew up to carry out and elaborate the eligibility rules. Unfortunately, the problem was not decomposable in terms of eligibility. The welfare program, the product of complex social and economic forces, began producing highly problematic effects; for example, the apparent effect of Aid to Dependent Children in splitting up families, or the incentive for unskilled rural Southern blacks to migrate in large numbers to urban Northern ghettos which were economically and socially unprepared to receive them. When this process reached apparent crisis proportions in the racial disturbances of the mid-1960s, there was another simple and direct response, again to give money directly to the poor—the income maintenance idea. Such would be the summary view of the paradigm, and this rough interpretation would help explain how thirty years might go by with the negative effects of welfare unmeasured, unattended to, and only barely noticed.

Cybernetic analysis of such phenomena provides a coherent account of what in an analytic framework appears to be stupid, absurd, incompetent, incomprehensible, etc. A decision process which controls uncertainty and preserves internal simplicity is very likely to produce outcomes which are unfortunate in many respects, particularly the respects to which it is insensitive. Though the cybernetic paradigm gives no reason to approve of such outcomes, it does promise some understanding of why they occur. If the paradigm is accepted as the framework for analysis, then many unfortunate outcomes appear as the result of a decision process powerfully affected by complexity and fundamentally designed to limit its effects.

Following this logic, then, the handling of uncertainty under complexity leads directly from the cybernetic paradigm to the third component of complexity—the existence of multiple actors and large organizations. But it is well to note that there is a residual question. If the simplicity/adaptability problem is to be solved by proliferating decision makers, how are the individual cybernetic decision makers under such a system to receive the structure which affords necessary focus? This is a clear problem to the paradigm if a decomposable environment cannot be assumed. The answer in part lies in existing organizational machinery, which is in the end a prime means of imposing structure. The answer in part also lies outside the paradigm—in capacities of the mind not envisaged within the framework of cybernetic assumptions. The latter question must await Chapter 4. The question of organizational behavior is the next step.

ORGANIZATIONAL BEHAVIOR

The positing of multiple decision makers (and hence an organized decision process to meet environmental complexity) introduces the third dimension of the complex policy problem. As with the analytic paradigm, the problem encountered is how cybernetic assumptions, which have been worked out for an individual decision-making mechanism, can give an account of an organizational decision process which involves many individuals acting simultaneously. Happily, a great deal of attention has already been devoted to cybernetic accounts of organizational behavior. March and Simon,[28] and Cyert and March[29] have supplied well-articulated arguments as to how the basic mechanisms determine organizational decision making, and it is sufficient for current purposes to state their central propositions.

An organization, the argument runs, is a coalition of separate individuals with diverse goals. The individuals are located in subunits, and their behavior is coordinated within the subunit such that the subunit produces a coherent set of products as a result of the collective individual efforts. The Chevrolet division of General Motors turns out a particular kind of car, and separate subunits within that division provide separate pieces of work which all aggregate to finished cars on a regular basis. The routine operations of organizational units engaged in a productive enterprise are referred to as standard operating procedures (or SOP's).

In government, clusters of SOP's are bound up together to form what are called "programs," which are intended to constitute coherent, useful activity by a well-defined subunit of the or-

[28] James G. March and Herbert A. Simon, *Organizations* (New York: John Wiley and Sons, Inc., 1968).

[29] Richard M. Cyert and James G. March, *A Behavioral Theory of the Firm* (Englewood Cliffs, N.J.: Prentice-Hall, Inc., 1963).

ganization. Thus, there are programs to give money and services to blind persons, programs to vaccinate parts of the population against influenza, programs to insure home mortgages, etc. The activity of each organizational subunit consumes resources and has direct effects of diverse character, some of which may well affect other subunits of the organization. How, the question is, do overall decisions get made?

It is assumed (and is virtually always the case) that the organizational subunits are hierarchically related so that subunits conducting programs are subjected to managerial oversight by subunits whose area of responsibility includes a number of diverse programs. The problem then is to explain the decision process operating over levels of hierarchy. It is particularly important to explain what happens at higher levels of the organizational hierarchy, for that is the likely locus of the sort of integrating calculations imputed by the analytic paradigm. Using cybernetic assumptions, Cyert and March develop a picture of organizational process quite different from the analytic notion. The process of decision in an organization, argue Cyert and March, is one in which the decisions peculiar to individual subunits are held separate. Top management, in their view, focuses in sequential order on the decision issues raised by separate subunits and does not integrate across subunits in its deliberations. Decisions are made wholly within the context of the subunit raising the issue. Complex problems are thus fragmented by organizations into separate components having to do with subunit organization, and the decision process at the highest levels preserves the fragmentation. Such a process is labeled sequential attention to goals, and this is a major hypothesis of the Cyert and March theory.[30] As with uncertainty, the model holds that the problem of aggregating across different individuals who are involved in the decision process is solved by avoiding it.

There are many apparent examples in government organization. The United States, for example, maintains conventional war capabilities justified as preparation in case it must fight again for the defense of Europe, as it has had to do in the past. Toward this end, the Army maintains infantry, tanks, and artillery of various kinds. The Air Force, for its part, operates fighter planes for air superiority, long-range interdiction, and close support of ground forces. Both the Army and the Air Force are clearly en-

---

[30] Ibid., Chapter 6.

gaged in procuring the capacity to concentrate conventional fire power on an invading army. However, the size and character of these separate service programs are not considered in relationship to each other when decisions are made about them. These two organizations maintain essentially separate budgets, and Congressional reviews consider their needs separately. Though some effort has been made by the office of the Secretary of Defense toward bringing these separate programs into explicit relationship, this attempt has not been successful to date.[31] As a consequence, the decision process whereby these force capabilities are bought and maintained proceeds sequentially as Cyert and March have hypothesized. Similarly, separate entities of the government construct river projects to control floods, on one hand, and to provide disaster relief to pay for flood damage on the other.[32] Though the separate programs jointly affect private investment in flood plain areas, they are operated separately and decisions about them are made separately. Jointly over the years, they have produced uneconomic investment in flood-plain areas so that the more flood control projects that have been constructed, the *greater* the national flood losses have become. Since the decision process treated the programs as separate issues, no one noticed the inherent problems until the investment had been made and the paradoxical flood losses began to occur.

The latter example provides a classic case of not only the mechanism of sequential attention to goals, but of other characteristics of the Cyert and March argument as well. In their formulation, the decision process for each subunit proceeds as described by the cybernetic paradigm. The decision makers control uncertainty and do not attempt to calculate outcomes. They monitor feedback variables and discover the effects of their actions only as they register on the feedback variables. In the case of the flood programs, the disaster-relief effort required estimates of flood losses. It thus provided a feedback channel whereby the unfortunate effects of flood programs could be discovered, and this is the way the situation ultimately came to the attention of

[31] U.S. Congress, Joint Economic Committee, Subcommittee on Priorities and Economy in Government, *The Analysis and Evaluation of Public Expenditures: The PPB System*, 91st Congress, 1st Session (Washington: U.S. Government Printing Office, 1969), vol. 3, p. 305.

[32] Charles L. Schultze, *The Politics and Economics of Public Spending* (Washington: Brookings Institution, 1968), p. 107.

government policy makers. The investment which was the result of the programs was not envisaged in advance as a possible outcome, and it was not discovered and related to the programs until flood losses began to increase.

Interwoven with the notion of focused attention—the monitoring of selective feedback channels—by organizational subunits is the idea of acceptable-level objectives. This latter notion is derived from Simon's satisficing model. Cyert and March argue that organizations maintain acceptable-level goals. This means that organizations have to establish measures of performance and act to hold these measures at levels deemed appropriate. As long as acceptable levels of performance are being registered, the organization proceeds routinely, with subunits performing their programed activities without intervention. The occasion for what we would call a decision (a choice between alternatives) arises when an established performance measure fails to achieve the levels defined as acceptable. This failure brings about management review and, if persistent, a decision to change the organization's routine in some way. It is the occurrence of such performance failures which determines the decision sequence within an organization, and Cyert and March label the process "problemistic search."[33]

This concept of search is required by the existence of uncertainty in the decision problem. Given a performance failure, there are grounds for looking for more information (a deeper understanding of the state of the world) and also for more effective alternatives. The analytic paradigm in this situation expects the process of lateral and upward expansion whereby new components are added to the specified sets for values, information, and alternatives. Cyert and March label this the scanning theory of search to reflect the fact that the analytic paradigm posits no particular restrictions on the source and scope of these new components and at least tacitly expects them to be broad-ranging. By contrast, the cybernetic paradigm posits a limited search mechanism. Exclusive focus on established feedback channels limits the scope of new information essentially to the fact of a derivation from acceptable levels of performance, and this is what is meant by "problemistic search."

The generation of new alternatives in the problemistic search

---

[33] Cyert and March, *A Behavioral Theory of the Firm*, pp. 120–122.

process is limited by the existence of response repertories. Paralleling Ashby's notion of a double feedback loop, two possibilities emerge when a failure of performance occurs. The first is to make marginal adjustments on variables of the alternative currently in use. The second is to undergo what Ashby would call a change of state, which entails essentially discarding the alternative in use and taking up the next item in the response repertory. Cyert and March call this latter process "mating," whereby an alternative already in existence (and probably designed in some other context) is applied to the current problem.[34] They provide an example from one of their case studies in which an industrial accident caused a firm to install some new equipment even though the connection between the equipment and the actual cause of the accident was at best remote and probably non-existent.

The basic example provided for the model of the decision process which Cyert and March present is that of the department manager in a retail store.[35] He must make a number of pricing decisions for commodities under his jurisdiction. Cyert and March theorize that such a man will set sales goals closely related to past sales performance for each particular item. If sales of an item slip below the goal that defines a problem for him and attracts his attention, he will tend to adapt a new policy (which will be a close variant of the old one), using a small price adjustment. If sales return to the old level or nearly there, he will leave the situation in its new state and concern himself with other problems. If not, he will take some additional actions—a new price change—and continue to monitor sales. Cyert and March programed a computer to make sales decisions in this fashion and compared it with the actual sales decisions of a department manager. The programed model predicted some 85 percent of the sales manager's price decisions *exactly*, and that counts as impressive evidence in favor of the model. Although the evidence regarding correspondence between the decision process of the model and that of the sales manager is indirect and impressionistic, the very strong correspondence between the decisions independently produced by the two sources lends plausibility to the model as a valid statement of the way decisions in organizations actually proceed.

[34] Ibid., p. 80. [35] Ibid., Chapter 7.

Similar evidence has been provided by other researchers seeking to argue that important public policy decisions are also made in the fashion described by the Cyert and March model. Davis, Dempster, and Wildavsky[36] simulated the process of making decisions for the federal budget with a set of decision mechanisms which are a variant of the Cyert and March model and which belong to the cybernetic paradigm. They compared their results to the actual budget decisions of the Congress over a number of years; and, finding correspondence, they suggest that Congressional decisions proceed as described by this cybernetic model. Crecine simulated municipal budgets with similar results.[37] Crecine[38] also extended the argument to the Defense Department budgets in the late 1950s and early 1960s and found that the evolution of Defense budgets fits the pattern projected by the model, and that direct testimony from participants in the budgetary process indicated that that process did indeed have the character described by the model. Jackson[39] extended the model to a different type of decision and provided evidence that roll call votes in the Senate are determined by a process of decision closely approximating the Cyert and March model and certainly belonging to the cybernetic paradigm. The evidence provided by these studies is not conclusive, if the proposition is that the model provides a complete, valid explanation of how the decision process works in these cases. It is, however, powerfully suggestive. The studies serve to extend the cybernetic paradigm, which is anchored in basic logic, informal observation, and a laboratory experimentation, to the world of actual policy decisions, the world of the complex policy problem.

Graham Allison has applied the same logic to problems which do not benefit from the highly structured conditions of the budget cycle.[40] He is concerned with the explanation of major

[36] O. Davis, M. A. A. Dempster, and A. Wildavsky, *On the Process of Budgeting: An Empirical Study of Congressional Appropriation*, reprint #252, Graduate School of Public Administration, Carnegie-Mellon University, Pittsburgh, 1966.

[37] John P. Crecine, *Governmental Problem Solving* (Chicago: Rand McNally & Company, 1969).

[38] John P. Crecine, "Defense Budgeting," in W. W. Cooper et al., eds., *Studies in Budgeting* (Amsterdam: North Holland, 1971).

[39] John Jackson, "Statistical Models of Senate Roll Call Voting," in *American Political Science Review*, vol. 65 (June 1971), pp. 451–470.

[40] Graham T. Allison, *Essence of Decision* (Boston: Little, Brown and Company, 1971).

events of foreign policy and uses the Cuban missile crisis of 1962 as a prototype for his analysis. In this context the emphasis is on the momentum of organizational routine—the standard operating procedures of organizations guided by the decision mechanisms which Cyert and March describe. In elaborating this analysis for broader ranges of problems, Allison provides a set of concepts and propositions useful for understanding how organizational routines affect the outcomes of government action, and he demonstrates in the case of the Cuban missile crisis that this form of analysis yields a very different understanding of the events than that which emerges from traditional, analytic-based approaches. Moreover, he demonstrates that events which appear anomalous from an analytic-based perspective ("Model I" in his language) are much more readily understood if analyzed with cybernetic ("Model II") assumptions. He provides some striking examples. The Soviets, in putting missiles into Cuba, built the launch pad with the same distinctive design that was used for the missiles on their home soil and which the United States intelligence officials had learned to recognize. This fact was very important in enabling United States officials to identify the Cuban sites from photographs before the missiles were in place, and this early detection played a crucial role in the crisis, to the apparent detriment of the Soviet Union. Under analytic assumptions, the Soviets, if they were going to display missiles in Cuba at all, should have changed the design of the launch pad. The fact that they did not is readily understood if one grasps the power of organizational routine and the difficulties in changing it even under the most compelling of circumstances.

These studies illuminate the consequences of cybernetic decision processes on an organizational level. If the collective decision process is to produce a reasonably adaptive outcome with a reasonably low failure rate, then the separate activities of the individuals involved in the process must be directly coordinated to some degree,[41] for otherwise chaos would be too likely an out-

[41] It is clear that some implicit notion of design with an outcome in mind creeps in at this point and this must be acknowledged. The consequence of being rigid on the point and of positing a freely acting, random operator such as Ashby's homeostat set in an organized network would be the acceptance of a very high failure rate, again an assumption which biology can use in explaining the long evolution of species and which decision theory cannot.

77

come to account for what we observe. "Coordinated" in this sense does not mean analytically integrated, but it does mean that established routines must be rendered consistent. If, in addition, the simplicity of the individual decision-maker mechanism is to be preserved, then coordination must be rather rigid, inflexible, heavily structured. To the cybernetic theorist this is the reason that organizational routines, once established, are not readily changed. This is the reason why large organizations are often observed to persist in activity which appears stupid and damaging in the analytic perspective.

CYBERNETIC LEARNING

The models of organizational behavior discussed above articulate the way in which the basic cybernetic process of decision works out in an organizational setting. The major focus is on processes which remove or avoid uncertainty, thus reducing the burdens of processing information, and which divide problems into segments, thus avoiding conflict within the organization. The consequence is a dissection of complex problems—a decision process which disaggregates values, utilizes information selectively, and does not perform outcome calculations. If this paradigm obtains, it is clear that the processes of lateral and upward expansion posited by the analytic paradigm will not occur, and that the passage of time and the inflow of new information which it brings will have fundamentally different consequences. The cybernetic paradigm, in other words, implies a fundamentally different learning process.

The learning process which would characterize the cybernetically operating organization manifests itself in terms of changes in behavior rather than changes in outcome calculation. The organizational decision-making entity is assumed to have a limited repertory of action patterns (programs). It proceeds with one sequence of actions (which produces a certain product as outcome) until feedback on critical variables forces one of these variables out of its tolerable range. There is then a change in the response patterns which, if it restores the critical variable to its desired range, then persists until another disruption occurs. Learning occurs in the sense that there is a systematic change in the pattern of activity in the organization. Over time, those programs and standard operating procedures persist that are successful in the limited sense which is pertinent; unsuccessful ones drop out. Such learning is of the kind commonly known as *instrumental learning*.[42] The cycle of adjustment in this learning pattern tends to be slow relative to causal learning, and instead of being a consistent process it occurs only sporadically—when the established action sequence is inappropriate enough to result in substantial disruption.

A simple illustration can be taken from informal observations of an army maintenance unit staffed with men who knew next to nothing about the vehicles they were charged with repairing, and hence were decision makers under uncertainty. They responded with a cybernetic decision process. Faced with a broken-down jeep, they replaced the battery and tested to see if it then ran. If that did not work, they would change the spark plugs and test again, then the distributor, then the carburetor. If all these actions failed, they declared the jeep inoperable and junked it. They proceeded thus for a substantial period of time, with the order of the sequence of actions reflecting roughly (by the principle of reinforcement) the frequency with which each action proved successful. The men never did develop more elaborate causal understanding of the operations of jeeps or internal-combustion engines.

Similar phenomena seem to appear regularly in situations where the intrinsic uncertainty is more recalcitrant than in the jeep-repair problem. The navies of the world powers, for example, were centered around battleships until World War II, and arms competition during that period frequently centered on the building of these ships. From the early part of the century on, evidence was available which indicated that these ships were very vulnerable to torpedo attack (or could be made so),[43] and in the wake of World War I, torpedoes delivered from the air became a major threat. Still, battleships were built and operated until the harsh experience at the outset of World War II drove home the point incontrovertibly. In the United States, at any rate, the consequent adjustment was such as to replace the preeminent battleship with the preeminent aircraft carrier, which did better in World War II. By analytic calculations, the carrier has become similarly vulnerable. In the absence of disastrous naval battles

[42] See Kimble, *Hilgard and Marquis' Conditioning and Learning.*

[43] Richard Hough, *The Hunting of Force Z* (London: William Collins Sons & Co., 1963).

79

where aircraft carriers are sunk, however, the carrier remains to-day the central focus of the Navy. The cybernetic theorist would see in this a manifestation of the instrumental learning process.

EVOLUTION OF ORGANIZATIONAL OUTPUT

The analysis of organizational behavior in cybernetic terms has direct implication for the way in which policy outcomes are expected to be affected. Great emphasis has been placed in the pertinent literature on the notion of incremental change.[44] The decision-making process proceeding along cybernetic lines, it has been argued, produces policy outcomes which are closely related to previous outcomes. The tracing of Congressional appropriations and municipal budgets over time in the simulation models cited above is part of this argument. The evolutionary process whereby output in each successive time period represents only a small change from the previous time period is thought to be a primary consequence of a cybernetic process. The limited scope of the cybernetic decision process and the large amount of energy required to change standard operating procedures in a large organization are thought to prevent any dramatic shifts in organizational output. A frequently implicit corollary to the argument has been that the analytic paradigm expects a pattern of outcome change which shows sharper changes—a decisive reallocation process as the marginal advantage shifts. "Incrementalism" has come to be taken as a sign of decision procedures which do not follow the analytic paradigm and have therefore been associated with the cybernetic tradition.

Upon reflection, however, we can see that this marginally adjusting outcome process is not necessarily peculiar to the cybernetic paradigm, nor is it necessarily the only process of outcome change which a cybernetic decision process would produce. Recalling Ashby's articulation of the basic paradigm in his construction of the "homeostat," we note that he provides for a double feedback loop in the operations of his decision maker and a response repertory which is capable of what he calls "state"

[44] Charles Lindblom has been most prominently associated with this idea and is in many ways an expositor of cybernetic logic. See Charles E. Lindblom, *The Intelligence of Democracy* (New York: The Free Press, 1965), and "The Science of Muddling Through," in *Public Administration Review*, 19, 2 (Spring 1959), pp. 79–88.

changes.[45] The primary feedback loop, however, which monitors the "critical variables" (or central values) is capable of changing the basic behavior pattern; and the operations of that mechanism would produce a more substantial shift in the outcome pattern. The cybernetic theorist would likely cite the shift from procurement of battleships to aircraft carriers as an illustrative example of such a "state" change. The change in the outcome pattern in that case was not incremental, but it is fully compatible with the cybernetic paradigm.

A second point is that outcomes which emerge from a decision process operating according to the analytic paradigm may be incremental in character without any contradiction in logic or even natural expectation. The key questions are whether close-in trade-offs are constructed and their competing claims weighed in some fashion, whether outcome calculations occur, and whether information is systematically used to update outcome calculations. A decision process working in this fashion may still proceed by marginal adjustment, and indeed often does. The optimizing techniques used in mathematical economic analysis, for example, often proceed in practical application by a process of successive approximation in reiterated cycles of setting and adjusting constraints.[46]

If the notion of incrementalism is not a reasonable basis for distinguishing between outcomes produced by decision processes fitting the analytic and the cybernetic paradigms respectively, then some other basis must be established if the distinction between the two processes is to be preserved. Clearly, the absence of any systematic difference in outcome would destroy the importance of the distinction between the two paradigms.

If one examines a decision organism capable of only a very rigid form of the cybernetic paradigm, it is reasonably easy to arrive at the conclusion that there will be systematic differences in outcomes. The army ant provides a dramatic example. Like the honeybee, it operates on a rigidly structured feedback mechanism for which one essential variable in focus is the scent left by its species as it moves along the ground. The trail of scent enables

[45] Ashby, *Design for a Brain*, Chapter 7.
[46] Frank Levy has pointed out to me that models of optimal economic growth provide a good example of this process. See Michael D. Intriligator, *Mathematical Optimization and Economic Theory* (Englewood Cliffs, N.J.: Prentice-Hall, Inc., 1971), Chapter 16.

these ants to foray into the jungle and find their way back to the colony, and this simple feedback mechanism enables them to perform remarkable adaptive feats in the complex environment of a lush jungle. These ants have been observed, however, after having been caught in a cloudburst on a flat concrete surface.[47] The effect of the rain was to wash away the trail of scent, and the result on the ants was that they milled in a circle on the concrete surface until they died of exhaustion. An analytic decision process would not have been defeated by so simple a problem.

Far more important is the problem of determining the difference between outcomes produced by analytic and cybernetic processes in human decision makers. The operations of cybernetic mechanisms in men are clearly a great deal more complicated and more flexible than those of insects. The question arises as to whether these mechanisms simply blend into analytic capacity, and whether it is not more appropriate at the outset simply to assume that mechanisms for analytic calculation build upon feedback mechanisms. One might assume, for example, that basic perceptions and information intake operate along cybernetic lines and that the higher mental processes operate along analytic lines. Should this be true, then the two paradigms would simply reflect different stages or different components of the same decision process. Since actual output would reflect the operations of the decision process as a whole, the distinction between separate components would not produce systematic differences in actual outcomes. Rather, outcomes would be jointly determined.

A preliminary reading on this question was provided by a set of experiments directed to the question and reported in detail elsewhere.[48] The experiments were done in the framework of policy games in which graduate students in political science, economics, and related fields were given scenario situations which conformed to the definition given here of the complex decision problem. The students were randomly assigned to one of two experimental situations which respectively did and did not give them an inducement to approach the problem in the manner prescribed by the analytic paradigm. Otherwise, they all were given

[47] T. C. Schneirla and Gerard Piel, "The Army Ant," in *Scientific American*, 178, 6 (June 1948), pp. 17–23.

[48] John D. Steinbruner, "Some Effects of Decision Procedures on Policy Outcomes," Center for International Studies, MIT, 1970.

the same scenario problem and the same information, and because of randomization there were no systematic differences between the two groups in initial attitudes regarding the problems (crises in Vietnam, Korea, and the Middle East respectively for three sets of experiments). Analysis of the decision processes in the games showed that the two groups used distinguishably different decision procedures which approximated the specifications of the analytic and the cybernetic paradigms. The two groups of participants in the games who utilized these separate decision processes did produce significantly different decisions in the games, based upon the same information. Though one set of experiments is far from conclusive, these results lend direct justification to the assumption that the analytic and cybernetic paradigms describe distinct, independently complete, and coherent decision processes which operate at least in some circumstances as substitutes for one another.

To strengthen the argument, these results can be related to the arguments made by the proponents of analytic planning associated with the introduction of Planning, Programing, and Budgeting techniques in the government.[49] The decision procedure advocated by the policy planners belongs, as we have seen, to the analytic paradigm. In introducing their concepts they have emphasized the degree to which they differ from decision procedures practiced routinely in the government bureaucracy. Their arguments, which offer a number of illustrative examples, provide informal evidence drawn from actual policy experience that we are indeed faced with separate decision processes. Though the analytic planners tend to see established processes simply as deviations from their rational ideal, one can see in their observations of established governmental procedures a reflection of the cybernetic paradigm in operation. For example, the tendency of military men to fix on the performance characteristics of weapons systems—which analytically represent very low-level and undesirable suboptimizations—is a completely understandable focus in the logic of the cybernetic paradigm. This sense of the analytic planners that they are propounding an approach to decision very distinct from what goes on normally in the govern-

[49] Schultze, *The Politics and Economics of Public Spending*; Robert H. Haveman and Julius Margolis, eds., *Public Expenditures and Policy Analysis* (Chicago: Markham Publishing Company, 1970), Chapters 18, 20, and 21.

ment can be evoked as informal evidence corroborating the proposition of the experiments that the paradigms do indeed describe separate processes which produce different outcomes.

Support can also be gathered from investigations of decision problems falling outside of government. Architects, for example, face problems of design which readily meet our criterion for the complex policy problem. Indeed, even the most mundane of design problems—fashioning a teakettle, in one author's example— can be shown to involve many more than two important values and to entail high uncertainty of the structural variety.[50] Christopher Alexander has examined the approaches which men have historically taken to the problem of design.[51] He discovers two distinct processes—distinguished by the labels self-conscious and unself-conscious—and these are rough versions of the analytic and the cybernetic processes respectively. Alexander argues that the history of design reflects the separate operation of these two processes. The evaluation over long periods of time of highly adaptive architectural designs in peasant societies is a direct example of the cybernetic paradigm in operation. The introduction of highly self-conscious, highly calculated designs in modern architecture reflects roughly the analytic process. The assumption, then, that the separate paradigms describe separate decision processes is a tenable argument. It remains to ask what implication this has for outcomes.

Though it frequently is reasonably easy to say for a given decision problem how the outcome would differ if an analytic as opposed to a cybernetic decision process were applied to it, it is very difficult to provide general characteristics of such differences over a range of cases. Analytic planners want to assert, of course, that the outcome of their preferred decision process will be better, on the average. At the current state of the art, this is an assertion which is hard to establish. Problems of determining better for whom and in what terms of value are severe enough to force any such assertion into sharp qualification. For the moment, let us continue to use the paradigms in positive or empirical terms and leave aside the question of valuation. Let us ask what the differences are, in fact.

It is clear from what has been said that the cybernetic para-

[50] Christopher Alexander, *Notes on the Synthesis of Form* (Cambridge, Mass.: Harvard University Press, 1968).
[51] Ibid.

digm tends to fragment complex decisions into simpler components treated separately. The outcomes therefore will tend to be very loosely integrated. Payoff will be focused upon very specific dimensions of the problem and will be short-range in character. There should, in other words, be a set of rather specific outcome streams with oscillations in emphasis over time. In particular, the separate values of the trade-off problem will each give rise to separate policy actions directed primarily at that one value. If there are substantial interactions between the separate components of a problem, one would expect this to go unresolved. One would expect further that the system would be prone to gradually evolving crisis in the problem areas.

The analytic paradigm, on the other hand, expects a more integrated policy to evolve—even if gradually. The separate dimensions of the outcome should be brought into explicit relationship and balance. Payoffs should accrue at a medium range of generality. In the defense area, to cite earlier examples, change should be recorded over time, not primarily in performance characteristics of certain weapons systems (though this will happen, of course), but rather in overall capacity to conduct certain missions (e.g., ability to hold the central front in Europe against a specified form of attack). To the extent that the latter depends on factors more diverse than the former, the analytic paradigm should integrate these together gradually over time. An ever-expanding, explicit model of environmental interactions should be produced together with the flow of actual outcomes.

One can readily see traces of this distinction in the recent evolution of defense policy, where there appears to have been a confrontation between organizational decision-making techniques reflecting the two paradigms. Defense analysts, as we have seen, have been in the forefront in articulating the requirements of making defense decisions in analytic terms, and they have been vehemently opposed by military officers who argue that only their long-accumulated professional experience can provide the basis for sound decisions on defense policy. One of the major episodes in this recurring debate has been a set of decisions regarding advanced manned bombers.[52] Air Force officers (pilots by training), having experienced the dramatic aerial combat of

[52] See Alain C. Enthoven and K. Wayne Smith, *How Much Is Enough? Shaping the Defense Program, 1961–1969* (New York: Harper & Row Publishers, 1971), pp. 243–251.

World War II and Korea, quite naturally learned to focus on performance characteristics of the aircraft which potential enemies procure, and they insist upon building planes which fly higher, faster, and farther. Thus, in 1962 they had developed an advanced bomber design, the B-70, which, at great expense, promised greater performance in all these dimensions than the B-52s of the previous generation. The Air Force has vehemently argued the military necessity of procuring the new bomber.

Analytic planners have had great difficulty making sense out of the Air Force argument. In the established models of strategic interactions, the speeds, altitudes, and ranges which aircraft can achieve do not make much difference to the probable outcome of battles; and there is a strong analytic case that the marginal investment in weapons ought to go elsewhere. The cybernetic theorist, however, readily understands what is driving the Air Force. In his terms, the Air Force officers are clearly focusing decisions on a few key variables for which there is information feedback (the concomitant characteristics of the enemy's forces). These single-weapon interactions constitute a simple segment of a very complex problem, and indeed the segment about which there was the greatest information and experience in the Air Force. It does not take much imagination to see in the continuing debate over manned bombers a clash between analytic and cybernetic decision processes.

SUMMARY

In contrasting cybernetic notions with the analytic paradigm, we find that the specific propositions used to define the latter in application to the complex policy problem have all been disputed. The analytic assumption of value integration is rejected. It is replaced with a somewhat vaguely specified conception which posits minimally articulated, preservative values, and which does not yield a coherent perference ordering for alternative states of the world under trade-off conditions. The major theme is that the decision process is organized around the problem of controlling inherent uncertainty by means of highly focused attention and highly programed response. The decision maker in this view does not engage in alternative outcome calculations or in updated probability assessments. The learning process is not causal but, rather, instrumental. At the level of collective decisions the paradigm posits a process in which decisions are fragmented into small segments and the segments treated sequentially. The process is dominated by established procedure.

This challenge to analytic propositions is derived from a logic which outlines a distinct and independently coherent decision process. The set of ideas which have been gathered under the label "cybernetic" merge into a distinct paradigm with roots in diverse traditions of thought. Distinctions made in formal logic and elementary number theory contribute, as does the experimental literature on learning theory in psychology. Careful examination shows that the decision mechanisms involved are used ubiquitously in the natural world by organisms running the range from army ants to man. Also, some informal glances at historical examples of human problem-solving behavior—the design of houses, the procurement of weapons—strongly suggest the operations of the paradigm. While positing a very simple decision mechanism, it can account for highly successful behavior. The cybernetic paradigm, therefore, emerges as something more than a dissent from ideas of rationality. It begins to appear as a fundamental and ubiquitously used process of decision.

If the discussion has given some clarity to the implications of cybernetic notions when applied to complex policy problems, however, it has also pointed out some logical puzzles. The structure of the environment has a great deal of significance for a cybernetic decision process. The determination of structural uncertainty as a characteristic of complex policy problems opens up a critical problem; namely, how do important constraints come to be established? In the case of the complex decision, the constraints required for the cybernetic process to operate are much more stringent than those imposed by the intrinsic nature of the environment. The constraints, which seem clear in the simple prototype problems with respect to which cybernetic notions have been developed, are not so clear for complex environments. In part, of course, organizational arrangements provide such constraints, but that is but a partial answer. Organizational arrangements are susceptible to human manipulation, and the problem is readily removed to the question of how organizational structure becomes established. In seeking a more fundamental answer, one must reach outside of the simple cybernetic paradigm for a more elaborate treatment of the high-level thought processes of the human mind.

CHAPTER 4

Cognitive Processes

IT HAS BEEN argued that much of the power and promise of the cybernetic paradigm as a theory of decision processes is given by the fact that it explains how very simple decision mechanisms produce highly adaptive outcomes in environments which are quite complicated, if not fully complex in the sense herein defined. We have seen that such adaptation seems to depend upon decomposition of the environment into subsystems which are stable over time. In one of the examples mentioned, highly successful designs in peasant architecture have been able to evolve over very long periods of time because the environments in which they evolved were stable and decomposable in critical dimensions. The process of error correction was cumulative, allowing very well-adapted designs to emerge gradually.[1] The definition of a complex problem, however, presents a situation in which interactions between separate dimensions in the environment tend to deny conditions of stable decomposability. Putting 500,000 American troops into South Vietnam in the period 1965–1968 deeply affected the political structures of that country as well as the United States itself. However much decision makers might have longed for it, there does not seem to have been a stable decomposition between political and military dimensions of the Indochina situation. Highly interactive problems of this sort abound in both foreign and domestic policy.

The absence of stable decomposition and the concomitant presence of enormous uncertainty present what would appear to be staggering problems for the decision maker. Virtually everyone has come to recognize that decisions which put large government bureaucracies into motion might well have very widespread and diverse effects on society as a whole. Decision makers can appreciate this fact but are unable to say with any objective certainty what these effects might be. Knowledge is too fragmentary to provide them with reliable analytic calculations. The problem is

[1] Christopher Alexander, *Notes on the Synthesis of Form* (Cambridge, Mass.: Harvard University Press, 1968).

88

not sufficiently structured to yield a coherent cybernetic process. The classic hedge discussed in the literature—that of making "incremental" adjustments and letting experience accumulate[2]—is undermined by the decomposability problem. It is not clear what adjustments would be helpful; it is not clear that any such adjustments would aggregate over time to an adaptive solution. Indeed, if complexity reigns, this is not likely to happen. Burdened with responsibility for the consequences of his actions, the decision maker should under these circumstances find it very difficult to arrive at any action at all. Complexity should breed indecisiveness.

This is not, however, what one observes. Though there are strong tendencies in government to delay difficult decisions, it is not the case that Presidents, for example, faced with actions of great consequence are unable to decide. President Kennedy, faced with Soviet missiles in Cuba in the fall of 1962, was subject to great uncertainty. He did not *know* in any reliable way what the consequences of various actions on his part would be. If he did nothing, he did not know whether it would irrevocably shift the world balance of power; whether it would be a reasonably minor shift in the arms balance, which was inevitable anyway; or whether some unforeseen but major effect might appear. No knowledge available to man could tell him such things, and yet he did in fact form some very strong opinions. He apparently saw his own impeachment as a probable consequence of inaction. He saw the precipitous decline of American power the length and breadth of Latin America. He saw the probable loss of West Berlin.[3] These are exceedingly strong and decidedly non-incremental predictions, and they led him to accept a substantial risk of major war. How could he arrive at such conclusions? How could other men at the time, and subsequently, consider them reasonable? Clearly, great uncertainty does not in every case boggle the human mind or render it incapable of action. Nor is uncertainty in every case controlled or avoided, as in the simple cybernetic process. In this and other dramatic instances of decisions, we ob-

[2] Charles E. Lindblom, *The Intelligence of Democracy* (New York: The Free Press, 1965).

[3] Graham T. Allison, *Essence of Decision* (Boston: Little, Brown & Co., 1971), gives a complete account of the crisis. See also Robert F. Kennedy, *Thirteen Days* (New York: W. W. Norton & Co., 1969).

serve uncertainty being decisively resolved in the minds of men. General structures of belief are set up within which the decision process proceeds quite smoothly.

This decisiveness under conditions of complexity, which is puzzling when viewed from either the analytic or the cybernetic perspective, is readily explained by those who have carefully observed and recorded the fundamental operations of the human mind. To cognitive theorists, the mind reveals itself in all its activity as a mechanism for resolving ambiguity, as an inference machine which actively manipulates the information it receives to create the stuff of conscious experience. In this view, what President Kennedy did in facing the Cuban missile crisis is not as far removed as it might seem from the feats of inference performed constantly by all human beings.

This central thesis of the cognitive theorist and the fundamental distinction between cognitive theory and the cybernetic paradigm has been persuasively stated by linguist Noam Chomsky in his famous attack on B. F. Skinner. Skinner has argued that he can explain the verbal behavior of human beings by simply using the principle of operant conditioning—a model fitting the cybernetic paradigm.[4] If Skinner is correct, then the cybernetic paradigm appropriately worked out would presumably be a sufficient framework for analysis of decision making. Chomsky has argued that the learning mechanism posited by Skinner is not sufficient to account for the acquisition of language, a process which virtually all human beings undergo.[5] Using tacitly the concept of complexity, Chomsky argued that the environment of the child is not sufficiently structured to convey the rules of grammar solely by the principle of reinforcement. Rather, the child, in learning language, constructs the rules of grammar by inductive inference, thereby giving impressive testimony on the inherent capacities of the mind. To the cognitive theorist, this inferential capacity of the mind which is actively involved in imposing structure on otherwise highly ambiguous data is a fundamental force in the decision process.

Is this then a step back into the analytic paradigm, or a resolution of the apparent conflict? The answer, the cognitive theorist

[4] B. F. Skinner, *Verbal Behavior* (New York: Appleton-Century-Crofts, Inc., 1957).

[5] Noam Chomsky, "Review of B. F. Skinner's *Verbal Behavior*," in *Language*, vol. 35 (January–March 1959), pp. 26–58.

would argue, is no. The known principles of cognitive operations suggest a very different response both to uncertainty and to value trade-offs from that projected by the analytic paradigm. Hence the logic of cognitive theory deserves careful attention.

BASIC PRINCIPLES OF COGNITIVE OPERATION

To those intimate with the state of cognitive psychology, an appeal to that discipline for analysis of decision under complexity might appear quixotic at first glance. It is an intensely researched, but loosely ordered field, rich in promising leads, unintegrated experimental results, partial theories, and a great many unresolved arguments. The skeptic is likely to suggest that since so many of the first-order problems are not completely resolved and since cognitive psychology has not reached the level of the more highly developed sciences, we can hardly expect cognitive theory to carry the burdens of complexity. It is wise, in other words, to walk with proficiency before attempting to run.

This counsel, however, is excessively gloomy, rigid, and conservative. The state of cognitive theory necessitates great caution in attempting to extend its basic results, but it does not justify complete neglect. If one looks not at the frontiers of the field but rather at its underlying consensus, there is in fact general agreement on some fundamental propositions about human mental operations. This agreement has weathered decades of rigorous research and intense argument, and that is about as good a criterion of proof as can be found outside of pure mathematics. To researchers in the field, the propositions are so familiar that their rehearsal gives little sense of accomplishment. Within the context of decision theory and the complex policy problem, however, the implications of basic principles of cognitive theory have not been seriously and systematically drawn. As a consequence their impact in this area is potentially significant.

Presumably there is no one who would seriously contest that the human brain is the ultimate locus of decision making. When we speak of such things as organizational process, political bargaining, and rational calculation, we tacitly know that in the final analysis the phenomena involved are based upon human mental operations. Presumably also no one would have much difficulty with the implication that if there are indeed systematic regularities in the way in which the human mind deals with incommensurate values and structural uncertainty, then a knowledge of such regularities is likely to yield an important theoretical hold over the decision process. If one can get that far by common sense, then cognitive theory yields three further claims: (1) that there are such regularities having to do with the structure as opposed to the content of cognitive operations; (2) that the full human mental apparatus is engaged in the simplest of operations such as direct, immediate perception (and hence susceptible to fruitful study by experimental methods); (3) that most of what happens in the human mind is not accessible to direct, conscious experience.

These three claims provide the basis for applying cognitive theory to the analysis of decisions under complexity. Of major importance are the asserted regularities of the first proposition, but the other two play important supportive roles: the second because it defines an applicable method and a body of rigorous evidence, the third because it represents a recent breaking of new ground and a reason to believe that after centuries of inconclusive discussion the analysis of human mental operations may be entering a more advanced phase. Though the main exposition of cognitive theory inevitably focuses on the first claim, it is well to take brief note, in advance, of the other two.

The third proposition reflects a consensus within cognitive theory that *a great deal of information processing is conducted apparently prior to and certainly independently of conscious direction and that in this activity the mind routinely performs logical operations of considerable power.* Consider any everyday event such as the visual perception of an object, say a glass of water sitting on a table. The sensory experience of which the perceiver is conscious is not directly given by the light patterns which strike the retina of the eye. Even in the most elementary situation the eye makes small rapid movements which produce a varying set of patterns.[6] Moreover, as the perceiver moves about the room these mechanisms make automatic adjustments for the varying size of the light stimuli and the varying angles at which they strike the retina. These adjustments, if attempted consciously, would require very sophisticated calculations, and yet

[6] Interesting, readable reviews of the technical literature on perception are provided by Julian E. Hochberg, *Perception* (Englewood Cliffs, N.J.: Prentice-Hall, 1964), and Ulric Neisser, *Cognitive Psychology* (New York: Appleton-Century-Crofts, Inc., 1967).

the perceptual mechanisms perform them automatically and with ease. The ability to build stable, reliable perceptual images out of varying stimulus patterns reveals that the mind is routinely capable of powerful logical operations on inherently ambiguous data.

Outside of psychology the notion of unconscious processing is widely attributed to Sigmund Freud, who did indeed make central use of the thesis in constructing his theory of personality dynamics. It is important to realize, however, that the proposition has a status independent of Freud's formulation, and that it is accepted by theorists who would reject the Freudian theory. Indeed, much of the evidence for it rests upon studies of the physiological sensing mechanisms, rather than on the interpretations of dreams and the esoteric tangles of neurotic behavior.

The proposition is strongly supported, for example, by studies of speech perception.[7] The sound patterns which strike the ear can be analyzed by electronic techniques called spectral analysis, and this reveals that the physical sound patterns associated with speech are continuous, very complex, and enormously varied. A given word or phrase can actually have a large number of different sound-wave patterns. In perceiving speech the mind operates to break the continuous wave stream into recognizable segments and to infer words and other units of meaning. Here the performance far outstrips what can be done by conscious explicit calculation using even the largest and most sophisticated of computers, and, of course, the process proceeds without awareness or conscious direction. It is very important to note in the case of speech perception that the process is one which clearly requires the use of stored information or memory. It takes some time for the human organism to learn to recognize coherent speech, and even the accomplished do so only within a particular language system. The operation of perceptual mechanisms, then, is such as to bring stored information to bear on incoming data in order to build the stable, integrated, meaningful content of conscious perception.

The process of inference, whereby immediate perceptual experience is constructed out of incoming sensory data, also seems to apply to the operations of memory.[8] Rather than storing dis-

---

[7] Neisser, *Cognitive Psychology*, Chapter 7.

[8] This is the view propounded in the famous work by F. C. Bartlett,

crete information or images, memory seems to operate by means of inference mechanisms as well. Even in cases where a person vividly recalls concrete experiences of the past, what actually happens is that the material is synthesized from fragments of information by the same sort of inference mechanisms which are active in immediate perceptual experience. It is also the same sort of inference capacity which Chomsky attributes to the mind in accounting for the learning of grammar.

The same observations which have contributed to the concept of unconscious processing also yield the second basic claim of cognitive theory—that even in the simplest of operations, such as the perception of speech, the full mental apparatus is brought to bear. "Full" in this sense means all the basic functions. Of course, it does not require all the resources of the mind to hear a spoken sentence. Much stored information and learned skills (including reasoning capacity) clearly do not become involved. However, even the simplest of perceptions do apparently require memory capacity and the capacity to perform inductive inferences.[9] Such processes do involve the central nervous system and do entail cortical functioning of the brain. Thus, both physiological and behavioral analyses indicate that there is no basic component of the mind which is exclusively reserved for higher logical operations and does not become involved in basic sensory perception. The capacities involved in perception are the same capacities which perform the higher mental operations.

As suggested, the implications of this thesis have to do with the range of evidence that can be legitimately brought to bear on the question of decision making under complexity. The virtue of the simple processes of perception is that they can be studied—and have been—in highly controlled laboratory settings with the application of experimental methods. Highly controlled experiments, of course, yield much more powerful analytic results than uncontrolled observations of normal behavior, but the very process of controlling the laboratory phenomena generates questions

---

Remembering (Cambridge, England: Cambridge University Press, 1932). There is a great deal of disagreement on the nature of memory, reflecting the fact that knowledge is not very highly developed. Some schools of thought would contest Bartlett's constructivist view. Neisser, *Cognitive Psychology*, Chapter 11, provides a defense based upon recent evidence.

[9] H. Begleiter et al., "Evoked Potential Correlates of Expected Stimulus Intensity," in *Science*, vol. 179 (February 23, 1973), pp. 814–816.

about the validity of the results under uncontrolled conditions (the conditions we really care about). What the basic proposition says is that the validity of laboratory experimentation, however difficult it may be to establish, is not absolutely denied. It is not as if one were dealing with fundamentally different processes. According to this argument, it is likely to be useful to evoke the results of laboratory experimentation in understanding complex policy problems, even though these are apparently remote from the phenomena which have been studied in the laboratory.

These propositions, then, set the context for the major arguments of the cognitive theorist; namely, that there are regularities in cognitive operations, known to a significant extent through laboratory experimentation, which powerfully condition the decision process. These regularities, the proposition holds, are not primarily found in the content of what is processed and stored. Indeed, in terms of substantive content, the perceptions, opinions, attitudes, beliefs, and assumptions of human beings vary so enormously over both individuals and cultural conditions that empirical generalizations are simply overwhelmed. By contrast, the critical propositions of cognitive theory concern themselves with the structure of beliefs; that is, with the way in which the relationships between beliefs are organized and with the manner in which information is processed in reference to existing beliefs. In these terms human beings seem to differ much less markedly. Though one can hardly abstract completely from the bewildering variety which the content of human belief presents, nonetheless some important structural and procedural regularities seem to have emerged gradually and unobtrusively from extended research. These regularities, which are part of the current consensus within the field, essentially promise to explain how decisions under complexity become structured.

Inferential Memory

It is known that there are what we might call both "hierarchical" and "lateral" relationships in memory. If a person is given a series of digits to memorize—9541492—he will establish some overall structure or rhythm to organize the list and will learn the elements as part of the general structure. The fact can be established by observing that memory decays differentially at different points on the list, and by observing a dramatic decline in ability to learn the list if one interferes with the process of establishing a struc-

95

ture.[10] Further evidence comes from visual perception. If a person views a picture such as presented in Figure 4, he is likely to remember either a pedestal or a pair of faces (or a well-known reversible figure). The same elements can fit into one of two overall concepts. If asked to reproduce the picture from memory, the person will draw an approximation. The details will not be remembered exactly, but rather the overall image. If he happened to see only one of the two possible pictures, the person would be very likely to distort in his memory some of the details of the picture to make that interpretation even clearer.

4. Figure susceptible to alternative
patterns of cognitive organization:
a vase or a pair of faces

The relationship between the individual digits and the overall rhythm of the list, 9541492, and between the details of the picture and the image it represents are hierarchical relationships. The content of memory is so organized as a general matter. People remember the overall concept and are very loose with its details, and this holds for the more abstract, loftier ideas of policy as well as the mundane details of everyday life. Thus, if a person is asked to recall the Munich conference, he is very likely to think first of the notion of appeasement and then gradually bring back details

[10] The evidence for this is reviewed by Neisser, *Cognitive Psychology*, Chapter 9.

—the specific issue of Czechoslovakia, the participants, the actual date. At any rate, he will think first of *some* general notion and will be a good bit more confident (justifiably) about that than about his grasp of subordinate detail.

There are also "lateral" associations between hierarchically organized concepts within memory.[11] If one wants to make the recollection of the above string of digits long-lasting, one would do well to make associations, such as the fact that the last four digits give the year of Columbus's voyage. Of course, lateral relationships can be and are subsumed under still higher orders of hierarchy to an arbitrary degree of complexity, but that does not diminish the point of interest. In obviously important, if imperfectly understood ways, the components of memory are related, and the mental process of drawing inferences is affected by these relationships once they are established. This is true of both trivial tasks in the experimental laboratory and of thinking about matters of the greatest consequence.

Consistency

A second principle of cognitive theory holds that the inference mechanisms of the mind are constrained by a principle of consistency. This simply means that the mind operates in such a way as to keep internal belief relationships (both hierarchical and lateral) consistent with one another, a constraint which affects both the organization of memory and the processing of new information. As with many fundamental concepts, it is exceedingly difficult to give a precise definition as to what is meant by consistency, and this has plagued psychology. The meanings intended for the purposes of this study emerge in the discussion which follows, but it should be noted that consistency in formal logic and the psychological principle of consistency addressed here are related but different notions. The fact of a difference is critical.

It is well to note briefly some of the basic evidence upon which the principle of consistency is based. Some of the most striking experimental work has been done by Adelbert Ames, who was

[11] Jack Adams, *Human Memory* (New York: McGraw-Hill Book Company, Inc., 1967), reviews some of the traditional mnemonic literature as well as recent experimental work. It is clear from both sources that anchoring information in a meaningful structure is a frequently used method of memorizing.

concerned with separating out the hypothesis that perceptual experience simply reflects directly what happens in the external world from hypotheses ascribing perceptual experience to the information-processing mechanisms of the mind. Ames and his associates constructed situations in which apparently clear and compelling sensory information was inherently ambiguous, thereby raising what is, in terms used here, a low-order version of the problem of uncertainty. Ames constructed a trapezoidal room which, when viewed from a certain point along the one wall, presents to the eye essentially the same stimulus pattern which would result from a normal square room.[12] Subjects, even when consciously aware of the true state of affairs, tend very strongly to see a square room, since past experience, and hence the information stored in memory, all support such an assumption. Ames then demonstrated the striking fact that when another person walks across such a room, he appears to the perceiving subject to grow and/or to shrink in size, depending upon the direction in which he is walking. This apparent size change in the individual traversing the room is an automatically operating inference necessary to make the information about the individual received from the retina of the eye consistent with the assumption that the room is square. Ames also demonstrated that when the normal inference that a person does not change size when he walks across a square room is particularly strong—e.g., when the perceiving subject is married to the person walking across the room, and thus has a great deal of stored information about him or her—there is a greater tendency to maintain this assumption and to change instead the inference that the room is rectangular. In such cases the marriage partner tends to a greater degree to see the room in its true dimensions, i.e., as trapezoidal.

In another striking experiment showing inference manipulations to maintain consistency, Ames constructed a trapezoidal window frame which rotated in front of perceiving subjects. Again, the strong inference based on stored information is that window frames are square, and hence subjects tend to see it as a square. In order to make the inferred shape consistent with the

[12] The work of the Ames group is briefly reviewed by W. P. Ittleson and F. P. Kilpatrick, "Experiments in Perception," in *Scientific American*, vol. 185 (August 1951), pp. 50–55. It is more extensively discussed in F. P. Kilpatrick, ed., *Explorations in Transactional Psychology* (New York: New York University Press, 1961).

perceived motion, subjects perceive the window frame not as rotating but as oscillating. This inference is established easily and is highly stable, since there is little or no evidence from past experience to suggest that window frames must rotate rather than oscillate when hanging from a wire. When Ames then inserted a solid bar through one of the panels of the window frame, however, a consistency problem was established because the appearance of the rotating bar cannot be readily rendered compatible with the inference of oscillating motion. In order to maintain the existing set of beliefs—i.e., a square window frame oscillating—the subjects must either establish the inference that the solid bar passes through the solid window frame, or that it bends and contorts. Subjects do adopt one of these latter inferences and thus "see" the bar doing some rather strange things. All these inference manipulations, Ames demonstrated, occur without conscious awareness on the part of the perceiver. The resulting appearances occur as normal perceptual experience, even when the true state of affairs is consciously known, and the operations of the consistency principle in these phenomena are striking and highly predictable.

The effects of the consistency principle have also been demonstrated with respect to attitudinal phenomena not tied to direct and immediate perception. Heider,[13] Osgood and Tannenbaum,[14] Abelson and Rosenberg,[15] and Festinger[16] all have theorized that the receipt of information inconsistent with existing attitudes will generate attitude change such as to remove or reduce the inconsistency or to bring about some other behavior to produce this effect.[17] Rosenberg and Abelson provide some especially com-

[13] Fritz Heider, "Attitudes and Cognitive Organization," in *Journal of Psychology*, vol. 21 (January 1946), pp. 107–112.

[14] Charles E. Osgood and Percy H. Tannenbaum, "The Principle of Congruity and the Prediction of Attitude Change," in *Psychological Review*, vol. 62 (January 1955), pp. 42–55.

[15] Robert P. Abelson and Milton J. Rosenberg, "Symbolic Psycho-logic: A Model of Attitudinal Cognition," in *Behavioral Science*, vol. 3 (January 1958), pp. 1–13.

[16] L. Festinger, *A Theory of Cognitive Dissonance* (Evanston, Ill.: Row, Peterson & Company, 1957).

[17] The literature on the social psychological effects of consistency is reviewed in Robert P. Abelson et al., eds., *Theories of Cognitive Consistency* (Chicago: Rand McNally & Company, 1968), and by S. Feldman, *Cognitive Consistency* (New York: Academic Press, 1966).

pelling evidence in a study in which they used hypnosis to change a fundamental evaluative inference.[18] Through hypnotic suggestion, they reversed a value inference which was a fundamental component of their subjects' beliefs relating to social issues. (In essence, they reversed established attitudes towards race.) As a result of this change, they observed a number of concomitant changes in factual or "instrumental" inferences, as the subjects generated factual rationalizations for their temporarily established bigotry or liberalism. These changes were in the direction of greater consistency with the new evaluative inferences. The subjects were not conscious of the inference manipulation until their normal attitudes were restored at the end of the experiment. This experiment again reveals the existence of a set of cognitive processing mechanisms *unconsciously* operating to restore disturbed consistency in a person's inference structure. These results corroborate those of the Ames experiments, but with the important distinction that here "secondary" or higher-order mental processes not tied to immediate perception were very clearly the ones engaged.

A large body of evidence on the effects of belief inconsistencies in motivating behavior to reduce inconsistency has been provided by Festinger and his associates in relation to his formulation of the most general of the consistency theories.[19] It is typical of these studies that the effects of inconsistency in a person's inference structure do not appear to be as powerful or as predictable as those of the Ames experiments, or even as the effects discovered by Rosenberg using hypnosis. However, the weight of this evidence, consisting of a large number of separate studies, leaves little doubt that consistency, somehow defined, is a major principle in cognitive processing.

Reality

The third principle is what Freud called the reality principle.[20] It simply asserts that the human mind is in contact with its envi-

[18] Milton J. Rosenberg and Robert P. Abelson, "An Analysis of Cognitive Balancing," in M. J. Rosenberg, et al., *Attitude Organization and Change* (New Haven: Yale University Press, 1960).

[19] Abelson et al., *Theories of Cognitive Consistency.*

[20] Sigmund Freud, *A General Introduction to Psychoanalysis* (New York: Liveright Publishing Corp., 1963), Lecture 22, or Calvin S. Hall, *A Primer of Freudian Psychology* (New York: Mentor Books, 1954).

ronment, that stable, important features of the environment impose themselves quite reliably on the mind. In other words, the operations of the mind are in important ways constrained by reality. This thesis has very complicated philosophical overtones; for, as the long history of epistemology makes clear, it is very difficult indeed to give a coherent logical account of this proposition.[21] But however difficult it might be to analyze the notion of reality and the process by which it is recorded, it is quite clear that it happens. The human mind does perceive things and in many instances gets it right. However it happens, many features of the environment are clearly enough presented that virtually any given individual will perceive them in substantially the same way. The reality principle is certainly not all one needs to know about the mind, but it is an indispensable element of any analysis.

Principles of Economy: Simplicity and Stability

The cognitive decision maker, while maintaining a complicated, interacting set of beliefs and while constrained by external reality and internal consistency, clearly is in need of principles of economy. The world—"reality"—is enormously varied and constantly in a process of change. If everything in it were recorded and if the abstractions of cognitive operations were kept perfectly consistent, the burden of information processing would far exceed even the remarkable capacities of the mind. As it is, we know that the mind is highly selective about the information to which it attends and that which it uses. The mind remembers some things of importance but forgets a great deal and never even attends to most of the information it physically receives. This fact—that perception and attention are selective—is in accord with a fundamental proposition of the cybernetic paradigm. Cognitive theory adds to that analysis two principles which govern the process of selection; namely, simplicity and stability.

The principle of simplicity asserts that cognitive inference mechanisms work to keep the structure of belief as simple as possible. This has been demonstrated in various ways, perhaps most notably by the work of the Gestalt school on visual perception.[22]

[21] A. J. Ayer, *The Problem of Knowledge* (Baltimore: Penguin Books Inc., 1966).

[22] See K. Koffka, *Principles of Gestalt Psychology* (New York: Harcourt, Brace, 1935), for the basic statement of the Gestalt position. Hochberg,

101

Their experiments have demonstrated that human beings have an observable tendency, other things being equal, to regularize complex figures; that is, to make circles, triangles, squares, etc., out of irregular figures and in general to establish simple belief structures rather than elaborate ones. Just as in the case of the reality principle, the principle of simplicity does not apply absolutely. (The simplest belief structure obviously would be one without any content.) But even though a man's beliefs may undergo extensive elaboration under the stimulation of a complex environment, the principle of simplicity is expected to obtain for the core structure of beliefs. A high degree of organization of perceptions and beliefs will be maintained and that organization will be as simple as possible. Ptolemaic astronomy, for example, became quite complicated in the years just prior to the Copernican revolution as various *ad hoc* calculating procedures proliferated. At the core, however, was a single idea: that the sun and other heavenly bodies revolved around the earth.

The principle of stability asserts that cognitive inference mechanisms resist change in the core structure of beliefs. Because of extensive lateral and hierarchical relationships within a system of beliefs—each of which must be held to some level of consistency—a major restructuring of beliefs is likely to set off a chain reaction, imposing severe burdens upon the information-processing system. Economy thus requires a bias against change in major components of belief structure once they have been established.[23] The point is well established by observation. Psychologists are generally agreed that the basic structure of attitudes, once established, is very resistant to change, and the effects of this fact play themselves out in everyday life. It is commonly recognized that characteristics of personality and life-style are stable for most in-

---

Perception, provides a short summary. See particularly in Hochberg p. 86, the Gestalt "laws of organization." The Gestalt theory of perception is, of course, far more elaborate than can be acknowledged here. It is referenced because it provides a very rich research tradition in which the operations of the mind to organize perceptions are repeatedly and compelling demonstrated.

[23] This point overlaps with motivational analysis which sees stability or, if one wishes, rigidity in the belief system as a function of the motivational connections of attitudes which anchor them against empirical evidence. The pure cognitive theorist, however, leaves the latter point aside and deals with the necessity for economy in information processing.

dividuals over their entire adult lives. Voters display stable party loyalties throughout their lives, and in many cases these appear before adolescence. Mathematicians tend to form their major ideas at a very early age. Once they have matured, their minds become less flexible. They are able to work out the implications of their early insights, but generally they do not strike out in completely new directions.

In summary, then, these five general principles—inferential memory, consistency, reality, simplicity, and stability—provide enough basis for a discussion of how the human mind, as we know it through logical analysis and empirical study, handles the complex decision problem.

THE COGNITIVE ANALYSIS OF COMPLEXITY: SEPARATION OF VALUES

The complex decision problem has been defined in part as a problem of trade-offs involving two or more values. The first task, then, in extending cognitive processing principles to policy questions is that of specifying how the mind, operating in the manner described, goes about handling incommensurate values. The applicable assumption of the analytic paradigm holds that a process of limited value integration occurs whereby one value is weighed in relation to another, even if this cannot be done explicitly or made logically compelling. For cognitive theory, the question is whether the inference mechanisms which compromise the information-processing system of the mind operate in such a fashion. Given the fact that much of the human information-processing system operates outside of consciousness, it is possible that value integration occurs even when the decision maker is unaware of it and does not consciously try to do it.

There is evidence to be found for this latter proposition. Some of the earliest empirical studies of the sensory mechanisms done by the German psychologist Fechner generated a constant utility model which properly belongs to the analytic paradigm.[24] Recent research on signal detection—the ability of visual or auditory perceptual mechanisms to recognize a signal against background noise—has followed this lead with explicit reference to statistical

[24] Gordon M. Becker and Charles G. McClintock, "Value: Behavioral Decision Theory," in *Annual Review of Psychology*, vol. 18 (1967), pp. 239–286.

decision theory. Swets, Tanner, and Birdsall[25] have shown that for signal-detection problems (which are binary-choice decisions), actual performance follows closely the predictions of expected value models belonging to the analytic paradigm. They have shown in their work that changing the payoffs for detecting the signal changes the actual perceptual performance in the way that expected value models would predict. In other words, the perceptual mechanisms, which are not themselves under conscious direction, nonetheless respond in the predicted manner to payoff values consciously introduced. This constitutes evidence that at least in some situations the information-processing operations of the mind do in fact construct and weigh trade-offs, in this case between type I and type II errors in detecting the signal.

There is no difficulty, at any rate, in appreciating that *some* higher-order, conscious thought processes construct and resolve trade-offs. The very existence of the discussion of the analytic paradigm here, and the intellectual tradition from which this discussion derives is sufficient to establish the conclusion that this pattern of thinking *can* occur. Those who would wish to see it in operation in actual decision problems, as opposed to abstract theory, need only observe an engineer at work. A ship designer is aware of the characteristics of water which make it necessary for him to increase the power he designs into his ship as a cube of the increase in its speed he might desire. This involves him in trade-offs with cost, range, fuel consumption, displacement, etc., which he constantly juggles with the aid of very explicit calculations. So also the captain who commands the ship once it is designed and constructed. He is aware of the distinction between cruising speed and top speed and the consequence for fuel consumption and range. He will switch from one to the other as conditions in his environment, such as the location of enemy ships or the presence of an epidemic on board, cause him to change his values. The point in question is not whether the mind *can* operate in this fashion; the issue rather is whether that is the only pattern of thought one need worry about.

The results of cognitive research clearly indicate that value integration is *not* the only pattern of human inference in trade-off

[25] J. A. Swets, W. P. Tanner, and T. G. Birdsall, "Decision Processes in Perception," in Ralph N. Haber, ed., *Contemporary Theory and Research in Visual Perception* (New York: Holt, Rinehart & Winston, 1968).

situations and that value integration tends not to occur under conditions of intense uncertainty. Cognitive theory suggests, in other words, that analytic decision processes are highly sensitive to uncertainty and that under high uncertainty a different pattern of mental operations appears. Specifically, it has been discovered that the trade-off relationship violates the principle of consistency and that under complexity, cognitive inference mechanisms tend to eliminate trade-offs from a belief system. In doing so, of course, they prevent the analytic process from occurring. This is obviously a crucial point, and in order to get it clear it is helpful to review some of the underlying experimental work.

The two-value trade-off situation can be depicted very clearly in the simple model of cognitive structure developed by Rosenberg and Abelson in the work cited above.[26] Each of the two values can be conceived as a hierarchically organized set of inferences stored in memory; that is, factual information arranged under a governing value assertion. Thus Shakespeare's Richard III, who offered his kingdom for a horse, was expressing a single-minded will to survive. He so valued a horse because he saw that his life depended on it. The horse, as his expressed objective, belonged to a set of hierarchically related inferences comprising a single value. In Rosenberg and Abelson's terms, the trade-off situation is conceived as a triadic structure involving the lateral relationships between two such values, separately defined, and the decision maker himself. Each of the three components is assumed to have an overall value, as is each of the lateral relationships. Thus in diagrammatic terms:

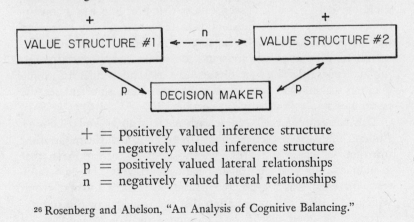

+ = positively valued inference structure
− = negatively valued inference structure
p = positively valued lateral relationships
n = negatively valued lateral relationships

[26] Rosenberg and Abelson, "An Analysis of Cognitive Balancing."

If the separate values are to be objectives for the decision process, they each must be positively valued (+) and each must stand in a positive relationship to the decision maker in the sense that he must believe his decisions generally promote his values. The negative relationship between the two values reflects the trade-off—i.e., that as an empirical matter they counteract one another.

The principle of consistency, as articulated by Rosenberg and Abelson to account for their data and other results of attitudinal research, holds that the above attitudinal structure for the two-value trade-off problem is inconsistent. The relationship, + n +, which expresses the trade-off between the two values, violates psychological consistency and renders the entire structure unstable. Though there is a general problem in cognitive theory in establishing which of the many mechanisms available for reestablishing consistency will actually be used, in this case the prediction is rather clear. Rosenberg and Abelson, following the principles of economy (i.e., simplicity and stability), have posited a tendency for the mind's inference mechanisms to make the least change necessary to eliminate inconsistency. In the triadic structure of the two-value trade-off decision problem, a unique solution is achieved by changing the + n + bond, either by asserting the opposite of the trade-off relationship (thus + p +) or by denying that a relationship between the two values exists, thus breaking the triadic structure. Since the presence of uncertainty means in essence that the reality constraint will be relatively weak (i.e., the trade-off is a matter of some subtlety and therefore hard to see), it seems clear that breaking the inconsistent relationship should predominate under complexity. Decision makers by this logic can be expected primarily to deny the trade-off relationship in their minds and to assume that they are pursuing the separate values simultaneously and independently. Some decision makers will actually reverse the relationship and see the two objectives as mutually supportive.

This pattern emerged very clearly in Rosenberg and Abelson's studies. They gave their subjects hypothetical department store management cases and arranged the initial information so that it induced inconsistent (or imbalanced) triads. The two-value trade-off triad was represented in the experiment by one group which was given the information that the manager of the rug department (a good man) was planning a display of modern art

106

(which the subjects liked) in order to promote sales (the goal of the organization). They were also given data indicating that modern-art displays actually hurt rug sales rather than helped them. This establishes an imbalanced triad corresponding to the two-value trade-off problem. Having assimilated this information, the subjects, as hypothetical store managers, were given three additional arguments, indicating respectively: (1) that modern-art displays helped sales after all, (2) that the rug department manager could be dissuaded from his plans for an art display, or (3) that the rug department manager was not such a good man as originally thought. The subjects who had been exposed to the two-value trade-off triad displayed a strong tendency to accept argument number 1 and to reject the other two arguments (as opposed to subjects who were initially exposed to different kinds of imbalanced structures). This is exactly the pattern predicted; the subjects accepted the argument which removed the trade-off relationship.[27]

It is easy to find apparent examples of this phenomenon working in actual decision-making processes. It is widely recognized that trade-off relationships are painful. Indeed, systems analysts, who have made a career of applying to complex decision problems the logic of the analytic paradigm, have recognized the psychological pain that they thereby inflict and have counseled avoiding it whenever possible. Rather than decide between "agonizing" trade-offs, Kahn and Mann counsel, better figure out ways to make trade-offs less agonizing.[28] Decision makers constantly try to do this. Friendship with Arab states hurts relations with Israel and vice versa, but American policy makers often announce their intentions to aid one without offending the other. The United States sent American troops to aid the South Vietnamese government under military attack and at the same time sought ways to make it more acceptable politically to the South Vietnamese people. Military operations which aided the one purpose hurt the other, but at least one participant in the pertinent decisions reports that U.S. policy attempted to pursue both goals

[27] In this experimental situation the subjects were tested on the strongest resolution of inconsistency—asserting a positive rather than a negative bond —thus leaving the triadic structure intact. Under complexity there is reason to expect the weaker resolution—a dissolution of the structure.

[28] H. Kahn and I. Mann, "Ten Common Pitfalls," RAND Corporation paper RM-1937, 1957.

independently and at the same time, without constructing the trade-off:

> Vietnam shows this problem quite clearly. Examples abound where we have destroyed with the left hand what we were building up with the right. For instance, one of our basic goals in Vietnam is to establish strong armed forces and an honest civil service. Yet the heavy development of American forces has contributed directly to the great inflation which has eroded the economic position of both the Vietnamese officer corps and civil servants, making them more susceptible to corruption and disunity.[29]

To reiterate and summarize, in analyzing higher-order cognitive operations under uncertainty, cognitive theory directly contradicts the assumption of value integration advanced by the analytic paradigm. For the two-value trade-off problems, the cognitive structure required to make the trade-off explicit violates the principle of consistency. Under the assumptions of cognitive theory, the information-processing mechanisms of the mind operate to deny the trade-off relationship unless compelled to recognize it by a highly structured external situation (the reality constraint). Under uncertainty, the reality constraint is weakened, and the cognitive criterion of consistency forces a mental dissolution of the trade-off. Cognitive principles thus suggest the contrary *assumption of value separation.* According to this assumption, the two values of a complex problem will not be related to one another in the mind of the decision maker, but divided and pursued separately, as if they were independent considerations. The information-processing operations of the human mind strain to set up single-value decision problems.

This hypothesis of value separation has strong implications for the cybernetic paradigm. It will be recalled that one of the problems encountered in applying cybernetic ideas to complex decision problems was that of understanding how, under uncertainty, the necessary problem decompositions could come about. The inference processes just analyzed suggest one way in which this happens. By its own internal logic, the mind severs under uncer-

[29] U. S. Congress, Joint Economic Committee, Subcommittee on Priorities and Economy in Government, *The Analysis and Evaluation of Public Expenditures: The PPB System,* vol. 3, 91st Congress, 1st Session (Washington: U.S. Government Printing Office, 1969), p. 969.

tainty the lateral relationship between the separate values and sets up separate decision problems, each governed by a single value or a set of values hierarchically arranged. This psychologically based decomposition can quite clearly provide part of the structure required for the operation of cybernetic mechanisms. It also suggests an underlying mechanism contributing to the decomposition of a decision problem within an organization. Cyert and March, for example, have posited in their formulation that each organization subunit has operational objectives different from other subunits.[30] Principles of cognitive operation provide an apparent basis for such breakdowns and indicate the sort of internal cognitive structure which would accompany the sequential decision-making process of the Cyert and March model.

COGNITIVE ANALYSIS OF COMPLEXITY: THE SUBJECTIVE RESOLUTION OF UNCERTAINTY

Uncertainty, in simple terms, refers to the discrepancy between the actual state of the world at any time and the information available to the decision maker. It was argued in previous chapters that the analytic and the cybernetic paradigms presented different decision processes for handling uncertainty. The analytic paradigm pictures a decision process using (via probabilistic calculations) whatever information is available to build a model of critical environmental relationships. The model is upgraded as experience accumulates. The cybernetic paradigm, emphasizing that decision makers seek to control uncertainty, pictures a decision maker who makes no calculations of outcome and simply monitors certain information channels, tying his behavior to what is received in those channels via some decision rule. The question introduced at the beginning of this chapter— how beliefs become established under uncertainty—implies a set of considerations differing in important ways from both paradigms. If, despite uncertainty, the mind operates so as to establish strong beliefs and to act upon them, then neither the analytic nor the cybernetic paradigm can accurately reflect the implications of uncertainty for the decision process. The principles of cognitive processing assert that this is exactly what happens, thus introducing new factors thought to shape the decision process.

[30] Richard M. Cyert and James G. March, *A Behavioral Theory of the Firm* (Englewood Cliffs, N.J.: Prentice-Hall, Inc., 1963).

The analytic paradigm is identified with the reality principle. It assumes that the mind constructs a reasonably accurate model of reality and treats unknowns by means of probabilistic inferences. This phenomenon of a firm belief becoming established on the basis of meager or even contradictory evidence is alien to that paradigm. Thus President Kennedy's statement—that he expected his own impeachment would result from a failure to take strong action in Cuba—would be interpreted by an analytic theorist as a judgment that there was, say, 1 chance out of 10 that this would occur. Following the assumption of alternative outcomes, the analytic theorist would then probe to find what outcomes Kennedy identified with the other 9 chances. That Kennedy might have taken his impeachment quite seriously as *the* outcome of his following a conciliatory course in the crisis is much harder to imagine within the analytic paradigm. It would appear as a rare limiting case (all other outcomes each assigned a probability of zero).

By contrast, cognitive theory readily accounts for the existence of firm, categorical, non-probabilistic beliefs in the presence of intense uncertainty. The cognitive processing mechanisms of the mind provide a number of ways in which beliefs become established, independent of the weight of objective evidence. Careful experiment has shown that the mind at all levels of experience, even the simplest, is exceedingly active in processing information. There is no situation so simple, so structured, so certain, that the mind operates in it simply as a recording device. At higher orders of complexity, when the reality constraint is weakened, the internal inference-mechanisms of the mind are likely to become even more important. To the cognitive theorist it becomes quite readily conceivable that Kennedy meant exactly what he said about his impeachment—as he said it. As a general matter, cognitive theory makes the assumption that structure will be imposed on uncertain situations, and uncertainty thereby resolved, not by probabilistic judgments, but by categorical inferences.

Take, for example, the famous phenomenon of probability matching in a binary choice situation.[31] The phenomenon appears in experiments in which the subject decides between two alternatives, with alternative A rewarded on a certain percentage of

[31] This is discussed by H. Simon, "Theories of Decision-Making in Economics," in *American Economic Review*, vol. 49 (June 1959), pp. 253–283.

trials and alternative B rewarded on the remainder. In this task if choice A is rewarded two-thirds of the time and choice B one-third of the time, the decision pattern which maximizes reward picks A on every trial. Actual subjects, however, show a strong tendency to distribute their decisions between A and B in the same two thirds–one third proportion, thus reducing their reward and violating the direct expectations of the analytic paradigm. The analytic theorist recognizes in such behavior a failure of the most straightforward expected value calculations (which can be corrected with some tutoring of the subject on decision analysis), but he is likely to take heart in the distribution of choice. Since that distribution matches the actual probabilities (which the experimenter determines), the analytic theorist finds evidence that the subject is in fact making probabilistic judgments even if he then uses them "incorrectly."

Cognitive theory explains the phenomenon very differently. In that view, the fact that the subject is able to observe the frequency of occurrence of reward for A and B does not mean that he treats this as the result of a random process. Nor does it mean that the correspondence between the subject's guesses and the objective probabilities reflects a probability judgment on his part. Cognitive theory expects the subject to seek to impose some overall meaning on the sequence of reward (which, if adduced correctly, would achieve reward on every trial and thus dominate the expected value solution).[32] The cognitive theorist would point out that many subjects in such experiments find it difficult to believe that they are dealing with a random process, and persist in trying to infer some single clear, knowable pattern to the sequence of rewards. If the experimental situation is elaborated so as to reduce its similarity to a gambling game, then the tendency to infer a single, non-probabilistic pattern is even stronger.[33]

[32] Even in gambling games, where the randomness of the outcome-generating process is very difficult to deny, there are always people with a "system" to beat the game.

[33] Some experiments done at Stanford and informally reported to the author presented subjects with slides of healthy and diseased cells. The subjects were naive as to the difference, which only an expert could detect systematically. Upon being shown each slide the subjects guessed whether it was diseased or not and then were told what it "really" was. There was a reward for guessing "right." For some of the subjects the feedback given was probabilistic—i.e., it was not in every case the truth. Nonetheless, they

111

According to cognitive theory this is the main pattern of operation of the mind. The mind constantly struggles to impose clear, coherent meaning on events, uses categorical rather than probabilistic judgments in doing so, and thus expects to anticipate outcomes exactly rather than having to assign probabilities to a range of outcomes. This tendency is the natural result of built-in, unconsciously operating inference mechanisms which are highly functional in everyday life. Under complexity, where the decision maker does not encounter highly structured and obviously random processes, the tendency is even stronger. This process of resolving uncertainty by imposing an inferential structure is a critical assumption of cognitive theory.

The subjective imposition of structure entails different assumptions than the process of uncertainty control set forth by the cybernetic paradigm, but the underlying argument is similar. The central problem of decision for the cognitive theorist, as for the proponents' simple cybernetic assumptions, is the management of uncertainty, the process whereby the great variety of the environment is brought within tolerable limits. In well-structured, decomposable environments, where cognitive operations are highly constrained by reality, cognitive analysis is in accord with the simple cybernetic paradigm in expecting uncertainty control to work by focusing decisions on a few, obvious information channels given by the immediate situation. The subjective imposition of structure is a more elaborate process evoked by the more complex environment.

In order to reflect this argument in the subsequent language of the study, let us refer to the cognitive paradigm to mean cybernetic assumptions supplemented by cognitive theory (i.e., value separation and the subjective resolution of uncertainty) and the cybernetic paradigm to refer to the more restricted set of assumptions.

Mechanisms for the Subjective Resolution of Uncertainty

How, then, does the subjective resolution of uncertainty occur? This question is of considerable significance to the analysis of

---

did not develop probabilistic judgments associating characteristics of the cell with disease with some probability. Rather, they developed single theories about the characteristics of diseased cells and persisted in these even after the structure of the experiment was explained.

complexity, since it is clear that in advancing this assumption, cognitive theory is suggesting a very different process of outcome calculation than that assumed by the analytic paradigm. The essential assertion of the cognitive paradigm is that human beliefs are given strength from sources other than the weight of objective evidence and that these partially independent sources of belief are important in imposing structure on complexity (and thereby resolving uncertainty). Cognitive theory suggests three ways in which uncertainty is subjectively resolved:

(1) by the principle of reinforcement and the weight of information in memory,

(2) by the operation of inconsistency-management mechanisms,

(3) by the effects of small-group interactions.

REINFORCEMENT

The first of these cognitive determinants of belief derives from the noted discrepancy between cognitive operations and cybernetic processes. It is a major principle of psychology that the strength of a belief is a function of past reinforcement—i.e., the number of times its use has been followed by reward in terms important to some value. The familiar example is the slot machine, which entices many people despite the well-known fact that it takes in a good deal more than it pays out. The slot machine embodies the principle of intermittent reinforcement and capitalizes on its effects—occasional reward is sufficient to induce people to participate in behavior despite a great deal of frustration.[34] In cognitive operations this means that if a decision maker attaches very general beliefs to the information which he receives in the decision process, intermittent success with specific decisions will tend to give strength to the general beliefs, quite apart from the validity of the connection in strict logical terms. This effect enables beliefs to become established and maintain themselves despite weak connections to reality or even contradictions of it.

Clearly allied to the principle of reinforcement is the principle taken from attitudinal research that the amount of stored information organized under a given belief will determine in part its

[34] G. A. Kimble, ed., *Hilgard and Marquis' Conditioning and Learning*, 2nd ed. rev. (New York: Appleton-Century-Crofts, Inc., 1961).

propensity to change with new information.[35] Stability is a function of the age of a belief and the frequency of its use as an organizing concept, even if particular reinforcement is difficult to observe. Experimental evidence as well as survey studies of mass-media effects and of attitudes on public issues indicate that the amount of adjustment which an attitude will undergo with new information is in some sense a function of the proportion of the new information to the old. This is a phenomenon which people who have run political campaigns, for example, have learned to recognize. A candidate, by focusing on well-chosen topics, can increase his support through favorable messages about himself presented to the voters. He also evokes established attitudes, however, and any increase is relative to that base. In many cases the established attitudes will determine the vote regardless of a marginal change the campaign message might produce. Thus, by campaigning in certain areas, a candidate, by increasing the salience of the election (and thus turnout), can actually produce a decrease in the critical variable—his percentage of the actual vote. Sophisticated campaign strategies are based on calculations about the established propensities of the voters.[36]

INCONSISTENCY MANAGEMENT

A second set of cognitive determinants of belief strength derive from the structural configurations in which they appear. That is, the strength of some beliefs depends not upon any direct evidence but rather upon inferential logic connecting them to other established beliefs. In part this can refer to the familiar processes of deductive inference, as in the famous example in which the existence and location of the planet Uranus was deduced in order to account for the orbital behavior of other planets. Some people came to believe in its existence even before it was observed em-

---

[35] This point, which is generally assumed as obvious, is ironically difficult to extract from the technical literature. The effect shows up in a number of experiments primarily designed to show what produces rather than what retards attitude change. See A. R. Cohen, *Attitude Change and Social Influence* (New York: Basic Books, 1964), Chapter 1; C. I. Hovland, A. A. Lumsdaine, and F. D. Sheffield, *Experiments on Mass Communications* (Princeton, N.J.: Princeton University Press, 1949); and R. A. Bauer, I. Pool, and L. A. Dexter, *American Business and Public Policy* (New York: Atherton Press, 1963), p. 466f.

[36] See Penn Kimball, *The Disconnected* (New York: Columbia University Press, 1972), p. 150f., for an example of such calculations.

pirically. What is not so familiar is the fact that some beliefs are established and supported not on the basis of substantive deductions, but, rather, because of cognitive processing requirements— the need to maintain at least a minimal level of consistency in the complex storage system that is the human memory. Substantive beliefs can play critical roles in maintaining the coherence of existing patterns of belief in memory, and they appear to draw their strength in part from this role. Dramatic examples are provided, at the level of primary perceptions, by the Ames experiments noted above in which the solid bar is "seen" to pass through the solid window frame or to undergo physically impossible distortions. This distortion apparently spares the mind the more difficult process of constructing an image of the rotating trapezoid—a bizarre configuration in terms of established perceptual habits.

There are reasons to expect the structural determinants of belief strength to be of considerable importance in the handling of complex decision problems. As noted, the presence of uncertainty means that the burden of establishing a stable pattern of beliefs falls to a greater than usual extent upon the imagination of the decision maker. In processing new information against the established pattern, a policy official will be prone to inconsistency and to a proliferating complexity of beliefs matching the complexity of the environment. If the principles of consistency, simplicity, and stability within memory are to be maintained, there must be reasonably effective mechanisms for managing the inconsistency which new information constantly brings. Four important mechanisms of inconsistency management can be documented.

Images and Arguments from Analogy

One means of anchoring a set of beliefs when direct evidence is weak or contradictory is to utilize a structure well established in some simpler situation. Simple images and analogies, widely used in high-level policy processes as well as in everyday life, seem to perform this service, not only summarizing and clarifying complex ideas, but anchoring their inferential logic. There are many famous and infamous examples. Churchill used a notion of three circles intersecting uniquely in Britain to conceive of the British world position in the aftermath of World War II.[37]

---

[37] Miriam Camps, *Britain and the European Community, 1955–1963* (Princeton, N.J.: Princeton University Press, 1964).

The circles represented the Continent, the Commonwealth, and North Atlantic relations; and his image of Britain's unique position had considerable influence in keeping Britain from joining in the Treaty of Rome and in the evolving economic relationships on the Continent. The image of falling dominoes has been associated with American foreign policy in the Middle East and in Indochina in justifying the need for the United States to protect foreign governments which came under domestic and international pressure. This image operates to picture coherently the uncertain consequences of the collapse of these governments. Well-known historical episodes (the Versailles Peace Conference; the Munich Conference in 1938) which have come to have simple meanings (the harsh peace and political failure of ideals; the policy of appeasement) have provided organizing concepts for analysis of subsequent policies and for subsequent decisions. To the cognitive theorist, these images and analogies provide internal anchors around which inference mechanisms of the mind can structure ambiguous information. The beliefs thus anchored have strength independent of direct evidence, a strength which derives from the simplicity and coherence of the inference structure they embody and the role they play in organizing a great deal of ambiguous information.

Inferences of Transformation (Wishful Thinking)

One of the critical characteristics of a belief structure is the time frame in which it is organized. It can be readily seen that the operations of the reality constraint, weakened under conditions of uncertainty, will have a natural tendency to produce beliefs limited to a very short time span of the present and immediate future. This observation is reflected in the emphasis given by writings falling loosely under the cybernetic paradigm to the "incremental" nature of decision processes. The mental framework of decision makers is believed to be generally limited to short-term projections, and this is upheld by many impressions of business executives, for example, who are often found to be focused in a narrow time frame.[38]

Though this tendency is powerful, it is not absolutely powerful, for we do observe men engaged in long-range projections and taking them seriously in their decision processes. Many of

[38] Yair Aharoni, *The Foreign Investment Decision Process* (Boston: Harvard Graduate School of Business Administration, 1966).

116

these projections, of course, follow normal logic and are established on the basis of available evidence and deductive inference. However, there is a class whose strength derives not from objective evidence, but from the role they play in managing complex belief structures. When a set of beliefs is under pressure from inconsistent information being processed in a short time frame, it is possible to maintain consistency without changing the beliefs by casting them in a long-range time frame and adopting the inference of transformation; namely, that the immediate situation will succumb to a favorable trend over time. The many projections by U.S. policy officials about the consequences of U.S. military intervention in Vietnam have sadly become famous examples. In 1963, for example, it was projected that U.S. military operations in support of the floundering Saigon regime would reverse the ill-fortunes of that government and lead to a favorable resolution of the conflict by the end of 1965.[39] Though one cannot be sure these statements were not made purely for political effect, it seems reasonably clear that at least some decision makers genuinely believed them, and the cognitive theorist would suspect the inference of transformation in that case. The strength of transformation beliefs in terms of cognitive theory derives from the fact that they protect the established belief structure from negative evidence and from the necessity which would otherwise arise of undergoing massive restructuring. Massive restructuring, of course, would violate the principles of stability.

Inferences of Impossibility

One of the major burdens on the information-processing system of a decision maker under uncertainty derives from the fact that his problem is logically open. He cannot be sure, objectively seen, that he has the best alternatives in mind or that all the critical components of the situation are known, even in outline form. New information is likely to suggest whole new dimensions to be added to the decision problem, thus threatening a potentially radical revision of previous calculations. In this situation, the analytic paradigm expects the process of lateral and upward expansion to occur, processes which are often associated with the idea of creativity and which at any rate actively promote change in the decision maker's intellectual structure. Cognitive theory, by contrast, emphasizes the need for internal economy and ex-

[39] *New York Times*, October 3, 1963, p. 1.

pects decision makers to ward off sharp changes in belief rather than promoting them. In other words, the analytic notion of iterative cycles of analysis whereby the decision maker holds open the entire range of his calculations to radical revision, is in fundamental tension with the cognitive principles of simplicity and stability.

Given this tension, cognitive theory expects decision makers under complexity to rely heavily on negative logic. In formal systems of logic, an elaborately constructed argument can be invalidated by the discovery of a single contradiction. Thus, an empirical generalization in mathematics, which might be based upon considerable positive evidence, can be destroyed by a single negative instance. There is great economy in this logic of disproof, for a simple argument is used to invalidate an elaborate process of weighing evidence and constructing governing hypotheses. There are famous examples in the history of thought. From the time of Euclid on, mathematicians tried to prove that the fifth postulate of his systematized geometry could be derived from the others as a theorem. Finally, logicians in the nineteenth century succeeded in demonstrating that this could not be done, and the search ended. The mathematician David Hilbert embarked on a very elaborate program for formalizing number theory and certain parts of set theory, and the effort consumed a great deal of mathematical research until Kurt Gödel demonstrated that it could not be done—that the task was, in essence, impossible.[40] The second law of thermodynamics, a cornerstone of physics, is an impossibility argument, as is Einstein's central postulate that it is impossible within a system of uniform motion to detect any change in the velocity of light in a vacuum. Einstein articulated the economy involved in such argumentation quite clearly:

> . . . I despaired of the possibility of discovering the true laws by means of constructive efforts based on known facts. The longer and more despairingly I tried, the more I came to the conviction that only the discovery of a universal formal principle could lead us to assured results. The example I saw before me was thermodynamics. The general principle was there given in the theorem: the laws of nature are such that it is im-

[40] See Stephen Cole Kleene, *Mathematical Logic* (New York: John Wiley and Sons, Inc., 1967).

possible to construct a perpetuum mobile (of the first and second kind).[41]

Impossibility inferences block off whole ranges of calculations and thus allow for obvious simplifications of belief structure, and these have been critically important in the development of that structure of belief which is scientific understanding.

It is an important fact for the cognitive theorist that impossibility arguments have often been adopted in situations where they were less compellingly supported than those which concerned Gödel, Kelvin, and Einstein. R. V. Jones cites numerous examples from scientific research where false arguments of impossibility have retarded progress.[42] Scientists, for example, once held that radio waves could not be transmitted across the Atlantic because of the curvature of the earth and the laws of diffraction. Marconi then proceeded to do it and forced them to consider reflection by the ionosphere. Some of Jones's examples are direct problems of complex policy decisions. The British Air Force early in World War II attempted without success to attack German oil production plants. They concluded that this sort of bombing could not be done and commenced general attacks on German cities—wreaking death and destruction on the German populace without giving any clear aid to the British war effort. It was only very late in the war that they discovered improvements in bombing accuracy did allow oil plants to be destroyed and that this was enormously effective in reducing the capacity of German armies. One can expand Jones's list at will. American military planners believed that a Japanese attack on Pearl Harbor was impossible because of the range of Japanese planes.[43] The fall of Singapore was held to be impossible before it happened. The number of times men can be observed constraining their thought processes by inferences of impossibility when subsequent developments proved them wrong leads the cognitive theorist to posit a source for such beliefs other than direct evidence or clear logical deductions.

Within cognitive theory the use of impossibility arguments is clearly understandable as another of the inference mechanisms

[41] R. V. Jones, "Impotence and Achievement in Physics and Technology," in *Nature*, 207, 4993 (July 1965), p. 122.

[42] Ibid., pp. 120–125.

[43] Robert Wohlstetter, *Pearl Harbor: Warning and Decision* (Stanford, Cal.: Stanford University Press, 1967).

which the mind uses to organize its own internal structure in a world of complexity. The economizing power of impossibility inferences, which set constraints blocking off whole ranges of calculations, is brought to bear when increasing information threatens to add unmanageable complexity to a decision process and to force substantial restructuring of the established set of beliefs by means of which the decision problem is being understood. The economy of the inference lies in the fact that it establishes itself on the basis of a simple argument. Rather than requiring a trek through complexity, it actually licenses a neglect of such a journey, i.e., an elimination of particular dimensions of the decision problem from serious consideration. Such inferences, in the logic of cognitive theory, derive strength from their structural role in the mind of decision makers, independent of their validity.

Negative Images

A variant of the impossibility argument which operates in essentially the same way and which seems to play an important role in decision problems is the negative image. Decision makers who have become committed to one of the alternatives in a given decision problem will experience inconsistency pressure. That is, arguments favoring the competing alternative will put pressure for change on a belief structure which they are seeking to stabilize. In that situation the cognitive theorist expects some decision makers to infer a strongly negative consequence which would result from the adoption of the competing alternative. That inference then serves to block off the competing alternative from serious consideration and thus to eliminate the pressure of inconsistency arising from arguments favorable to that alternative. The presence of uncertainty in the decision problem allows logical leeway for such inferences to be made plausible. The image of impeachment which President Kennedy attached to the alternative of acceding to the Soviet missiles in Cuba may have had this character. One might consider also the cable sent by then-ambassador John Foster Dulles as North Korea invaded South Korea in 1951:

. . . To sit by while Korea is overrun by unprovoked armed attack would start a disastrous chain of events leading most probably to world war. We suggest that Security Council might call for action on behalf of the organization under Article 106 by the five powers or such of them as are willing to respond.[44]

Dulles was an intensely committed man and did not want to weigh the pros and cons of inaction. He advanced in the cable an inference which went well beyond what the sheer weight of evidence would allow, and the cognitive theorist again would strongly suspect the operations of inconsistency management in his vision.

SMALL-GROUP INTERACTIONS

The third set of forces which contribute to belief strength independent of the reality principle are what we might call processes of social corroboration. It is very clear that one of the prime characteristics of human beings under uncertainty is that they bolster their judgments by the concurring opinions of other people.[45] If other individuals impose the same inferences on the same information, it adds to the belief strength of a given decision maker. Studies have indicated that people in highly ambiguous situations converge on the judgments of other people;[46] that even in unambiguous situations people will conform to the erroneous but uniform judgments of a group of peers;[47] that under pressure of inconsistency people will prefer supportive opinions;[48] and that, under strong pressure of inconsistency, beliefs will remain stable only if strong social support is available.[49] The well-known tendency in informal social groupings for individual members to agree on important salient beliefs and even to purge apostates from their midst seems in all likelihood both cause and effect of the cognitive consequences of such social interactions.

[44] Glenn D. Paige, *The Korean Decision* (New York: The Free Press, 1968), p. 112.

[45] Cohen, *Attitude Change*, provides a review, as does H. S. Upshaw, "Cognitive Consistency and the Psychology of Judgment," in Abelson et al., eds., *Theories of Cognitive Consistency*, Chapter 11.

[46] Muzafer Sherif, *The Psychology of Social Norms* (New York: Harper & Row, Publishers, 1936).

[47] S. Asch, "Effects of Group Pressures on the Modification and Position of Judgments," in H. Guetzkow, ed., *Groups, Leadership and Men* (Pittsburgh, Pa.: Carnegie Press, 1951), pp. 117–190.

[48] J. Stacey Adams, "Reduction of Cognitive Dissonance by Seeking Consonant Information," in *Journal of Abnormal and Social Psychology*, vol. 62 (January 1961), pp. 74–78.

[49] Festinger, *A Theory of Cognitive Dissonance*.

The importance of these processes in a policy bureaucracy is well documented and well known to all who have had experience in the policy machinery. Organizational and political groupings form between men in substantial agreement on matters of pertinent policy, and in their day-to-day interactions they mutually reinforce their shared judgments. An intensive study of free-trade legislation in the early 1960s showed that lobbying efforts organized on the various sides of the issue were by and large exchanges of information between Congressmen and lobbyists who agreed with one another.[50] Similarly, social and political relationships in the Navy are organized around weapons systems. The submarine commanders are separate from the others as are the admirals commanding aircraft carriers. Each group had developed strongly held beliefs about the value and importance of its particular form of warfare. There is strong agreement within these groups; a tendency to disagreement between them. In the years before World War II, battleship commanders as a cohesive grouping in the world's navies protected the status of their weapons, in their own minds and in the policies of their countries, as a kingpin of national power despite strong evidence that such ships were so vulnerable to attack as to be virtually useless. In the United States a prominent purge of an apostate might even be found in the court-martial of General William Mitchell.

To the cognitive theorist, these phenomena fit another piece of the pattern. Corroborative judgments by peers is a prime mechanism whereby the inference processes of the mind construct and preserve a stable belief pattern in the presence of uncertainty and under the pressures of inconsistent information.

Summary: Subjective Resolution of Uncertainty in Relation to the Other Paradigms of Decision

With the mechanisms of uncertainty resolution having been laid out, it is clear that cognitive theory provides an analysis of the effects of uncertainty on the decision process which is fundamentally different than that of the analytic and cybernetic paradigms. The arguments of cognitive theory hold, against the analytic paradigm, that uncertainty is not resolved in most instances by probabilistic calculations of alternative outcomes. The implication is that this is done categorically under a single governing set

---

[50] Bauer, Pool, and Dexter, *American Business and Public Policy*.

of beliefs. That implication is very clear in the case where one of the possible outcomes is negatively valued. A negative outcome conceived of as the result of an action favored by the decision maker is psychologically inconsistent. The cognitive theorist expects, according to the consistency principle, that in the processing of information favorable outcomes will be inferred for preferred alternatives and that unfavorable outcomes will be projected for alternatives the decision maker intends to reject. Quite generally, the inferential structures which cognitive operations impose on inherently uncertain situations tend to be simple and coherently organized to present a single-valued problem and a single-preferred alternative to which the decision maker is committed from the outset of the decision process. Under complexity, the mind, in this view, does not match the uncertain structure of the environment in which events might take a number of alternative courses. Rather, it imposes an image and works to preserve that image. A single course of events is projected; evidence for alternative outcomes is manipulated to preserve the expectations. We might call this, then, the *assumption of a single outcome calculation.*

The analytic assumptions of sensitivity to pertinent information is qualified in much the same way by the cognitive theorist as it is by the cybernetic paradigm: Pertinent information may enter the decision process or it may be screened out, depending on how it relates to the existing pattern of belief. Though it may be difficult to predict sensitivity for a single decision, it is clear that the cognitive theory expects to find over a number of decisions and decision makers much more narrowly confined sensitivity to new information than is implied by analytic assumptions. That information which is threatening to established belief patterns is not expected to be processed in a fashion wholly dominated by the reality principle.

In relation to the cybernetic paradigm, cognitive theory offers an important supplementary element: an explanation of how structure occurs other than by imposition from the environment. The simple process of uncertainty control depicted by the cybernetic paradigm is amended, but the underlying problem of eliminating variety is still important to cognitive theory. In cases where the decision problem is highly structured by inherent properties of the environment, where the reality constraint is strong and not problematic, then cognitive analysis might be said

123

to reduce to the cybernetic paradigm. The problems of inventory control and sales decision in a retailing department, which Cyert and March discuss, are plausible examples.[51] Under conditions of full complexity, however, the mechanisms of subjective uncertainty resolution come into play to supplement the simple cybernetic assumptions. In either case, the behavior of the decision maker is fundamentally driven by the need to manage uncertainty. The cognitive paradigm, then, entails the general assumptions; the cybernetic paradigm posits only the more restricted assumptions.

Though there is a great deal of residual vagueness in these derivations from cognitive theory (a condition which cannot be eliminated under the current state of knowledge), enough has been said to provide a basis for addressing the third condition of complexity—the existence of multiple actors. The question at that level is how cognitive principles affect organizational process.

Cognitive Dimensions of Political and Organizational Phenomena

The basis for expanding cognitive theory to the collective level of explanation is provided by the fact that the principles are assumed to hold across the idiosyncratic features of men and cultures. If stable features of the mind encounter stable features of organizational settings, it should produce coherent, recurring patterns of behavior in the organizational decision process, other things being equal. The question then is what characteristics of the organizational setting affect cognitive operations?[52]

Among the more interesting features of the organizational setting for the cognitive theorists are: the natural information channels, the background of the personnel, and the level of organizational hierarchy at which various decision procedures operate. The natural information channels tend to determine the informa-

[51] Cyert and March, *A Behavioral Theory of the Firm*, Chapter 7.

[52] There is a limit, of course, to the power which can be claimed for such analysis, for it does not incorporate substantive variables—the values of an organization, the nature of its business, its peculiar historical experience, etc. —which unquestionably have a great deal to do with its character and behavior. The approach based upon cognitive principles does not counsel a neglect of these substantive considerations, however, and in fact it promises an analytic framework within which such specific information can be more systematically applied.

tion input for the decision maker. His personal background gives some hint as to how his memory is structured. The level of organizational hierarchy determines the range of decision problems which the decision maker encounters, and the scope of those problems. All these factors affect the nature of cognitive experience men will have in an organization; and, as experience accumulates, they determine the structure of the minds which process information and make decisions.

A systematic approach to the problem would take these and other pertinent dimensions of organization and identify the important distinctions within each dimension. Thus, for example, personnel backgrounds could be broken down by distinguishing professionals, substantive experts, and politicians. The intersection of the various dimensions with their internal distinctions could then be used, as in the familiar contingency table, to produce a categorization scheme. Such a project would extend beyond the scope of the current analysis, however, for the point here is not the full development of the theory of organization but rather an application of some of its principles to decision problems of special concern. Accordingly, a more limited approach is adopted. Three modes of thinking are presented below, each of which represents a different resolution of the conflicting principles of cognitive processing and each of which seems clearly associated with a certain kind of organizational situation. These determinants are useful in the subsequent analysis of the nuclear sharing issue and ought to be useful in the analysis of other complex problems. It is not necessary to claim that these thought patterns are the only ones of interest or that the variables associated with them in the discussion are the only operative variables.

Grooved Thinking

The first of the three patterns of thought is essentially the simple cybernetic process discussed in Chapter 3. It is the operative mechanism of organizational routine. A person or organizational entity in such a mode attends to a small number of variables pertinent to the decision problem. Typically, the categories or concepts which the decision maker in this mode uses are determined by ranges of values on the critical variables; and his decisions are programed so that once he determines which category obtains, the decision follows without further question. The police patrolman, for example, regularly faces situations where he is called upon to handle disputes between individuals or alleged disruptive behavior in order to maintain public order. His legal mandate in such situations is exceedingly ambiguous, as is the nature of the threat to order which he encounters. He is therefore a decision maker under uncertainty. Studies of the way police handle these situations indicate that they tend to develop such concepts as "bad actor," "hothead," "liquored up," to distinguish between individuals they encounter and that variables such as race, sex, age, physical appearance, and tone of speech tend to determine which category is applied.[53] A person judged to be a "bad actor" is treated harshly, and the patrolman is quick to use force with him. Persons judged to fall in the other categories receive less hostile, less coercive treatment. A person who readily submits to the authority of the police receives much more circumspect treatment than the person who verbally challenges the authority (which as a legal matter is often subject to challenge). The latter is likely to be seen as a "wise guy," and there are rather tough routines for handling wise guys.

Grooved thinking characteristically occurs in organizations which are well established in the sense that they have been in existence for some period of time and have been conceded competence over a certain range of tasks. They have a regular load of business which repeatedly presents problems similar in character—the production line in a factory, the management of a sales department, the medical clinic, the traffic court, the small-loan department of a bank, the patrolman on his beat, etc. Grooved thinking occurs at an organizational level where the range of problems is narrow in the sense that the decision maker does not often encounter problems which do not readily fall into a small number of basic types.

It will be clear that this process is characteristic of the common bureaucrat who never seems to understand the special problem which the supplicant citizen sees in all its many dimensions. A casually selected newspaper story provides an example: A young, unwed mother gave her baby up for adoption. The adoption agency, following established procedure, matched the baby with a set of new parents on certain characteristics and initiated adoption proceedings. The young, unwed natural father of the child then petitioned to adopt his own child, arguing that he had a job,

[53] J. Wilson, *Varieties of Police Behavior* (Cambridge, Mass.: Harvard University Press, 1968).

126

that his parents would provide shelter and a home atmosphere, and that he had, in fact, cared for the child for several months already. The agency found him unacceptable—he was a man, he was too young, he was unmarried, his job did not pay enough. The young father, the press, and several politicians were outraged. The father struck those who knew him as mature, responsible, devoted to the child and—the critical point—he was the *natural* father. The agency, however, would not budge. They had made a long sequence of such decisions, and their thought processes were well established. Moreover, they did not recognize a preeminent claim of natural parenthood; their business was adoption.

This sort of situation is repeated many times in everyday events. Those decision makers who repeatedly encounter complex decision problems and have the inescapable responsibility of taking some action develop these highly stable patterns of reaction. The fabled frustration of those who experience the results and find them inadequate to their special needs is a consequence of the fact that the decisions are actually taken on very narrow grounds and are determined by the execution of well-established decision rules. Rarely does this provide an outcome finely tuned to the particular needs of an individual case.

In cognitive terms the chief characteristic of a grooved decision process is that its stability is well established by long exercise over an extended sequence of decisions. This experience, recorded and weighted in memory, offers powerful analogues for new decisions and protection against the variance of new decision problems. The burdens of responsibility—uncertainty, political pressure, heavy workloads, potential controversy over the outcome—are handled unusually well by this sort of thought process, precisely because of the ready-made, well-anchored structure to which new problems can be fitted. The fact that this mode of thinking arises with repeatedly presented problems means that it is strongly determined by the reality principle. The variables which provide the focus of the process are likely to be the obviously pertinent, observable features of the situation—the apparent characteristics and immediate behavior patterns of those he encounters on the street, in the example of the policeman. This means that the grooved decision process operates in a very short-range time frame and with only a very low level of abstraction. The simplicity of such structures is preserved by this

127

short time-horizon and by the narrowly limited sensitivity to information—a few variables out of hundreds of variables contained in the true state of the world. Moreover, there is a strong supposition that simplicity will also tend to produce problem conceptions organized around a single value.

It is clear that these features of the grooved thought process operate in such a way as to break a particular, short-range component out of a complex policy problem and to make decisions solely in that context. The result of this, repeated over many organizational entities (be they individuals or low-level offices and bureaus), is a fragmentation of a complex decision problem into small pieces which are essentially independently treated. This phenomenon becomes particularly important when high-level decisions are filtered through the low levels of a policy bureaucracy for implementation.

Uncommitted Thinking

A second cognitive syndrome which operates in an organizational setting is what can be called uncommitted thinking. It appears in response to the problems of decisions at high levels in an organizational hierarchy. The natural information channels at the apex of an organizational hierarchy carry relatively abstracted, aggregated information. Since the apex of an organization represents the intersection of a number of different information channels, both the range of problems presented and the scope of individual problems is much greater than is the case at lower organizational levels. As a consequence, the decision maker experiences pressure to deal with problems more abstractly, and the decision process tends to operate in a more extended time frame. The decision maker will be much less able to adapt the short-term, highly specific focus of the grooved thinker. Moreover, this situation is further compounded by the intense workloads which are characteristic of high-level positions in the public sector. The sophisticated information processing which his position tends to demand takes time, and high-level officials experience many competing claims for their time.

The behavior of high-level officials is further affected by their backgrounds. In public-sector organizations, many high officials come to their jobs through political channels, and at any rate they are often reasonably unfamiliar with the organization and its business when they assume office. As a consequence, their beliefs are not stabilized by the weight of past experience. They are particularly vulnerable to uncertainty; and, for many of the problems which face them, they quite literally do not know what to think. Such officials naturally come to depend upon the problem structuring done by their personal staff, the organizations which they head, and/or outside experts. At any rate, the information channels to which they attend provide structured, generalized arguments, and coping with these—for a wide variety of problems—is their daily business.

The pattern of uncommitted thinking which tends to occur in this organizational situation has a number of notable features. First, the decision makers do adopt generalized concepts which are embedded in larger, theoretical belief structures and are not simply determined by a small number of specific variables, as in the case of grooved thinking. Such decision makers, in other words, will associate theoretical considerations about the state of the world with particular alternatives, and they will attempt to calculate the outcome which would result from each alternative. Second, for these non-expert high-level officials, their belief structures (relating an alternative and an outcome via a causal theory) will be associated with a sponsor (a utilization of the principle of social reinforcement to bolster belief strength). And finally, the critical point, the high-level policy maker, beset with uncertainty and sitting at the intersection of a number of information channels, will tend at different times to adopt *different* belief patterns for the same decision problem. Since his own experience does not commit him to a particular belief pattern, he will adopt several competing patterns, not at once, but in sequence.

The cognitive theorist lays out the principles involved in uncommitted thinking. Because of the organizational setting, the reality principle forces a more abstract intellectual framework than the highly specific focus of the grooved thinker. Abstraction, however, involving a set of interacting and reasonably extensive inferences cast in at least a medium time frame, is made difficult by uncertainty. The decision maker thus has difficulty in establishing his beliefs and protecting them against the pressures of inconsistent information. The use of social reinforcement provides some of the belief strength required, but does not eliminate inconsistency because of the normal structure of coherent belief patterns—i.e., their tendency to be organized around a sin-

129

gle value and to project but a single favorable outcome. Such general belief patterns are prone to inconsistency because of the trade-off relationship of the two-value problem and because a complex environment is generally capable of producing a number of possible outcomes. The pressure of inconsistency then produces an oscillation over time between a number of belief patterns, each of which represents a psychologically coherent and consistent segment of the overall problem. The cognitive principles of consistency and simplicity prevent an overall integration of the separate patterns—that is, that inference mechanisms of the mind operate to keep them separate. However, new information and new argument received in organizational channels is not likely to allow any one pattern to dominate without some independent source of belief strength, because of the intrinsic complexity of the environment. And a principal source of independent belief strength—the corroborative judgment of other people —will not allow a dominant pattern either, because, at the intersection of organizational channels, "sponsors" are diverse and likely to disagree. The overall effect, then, is an oscillation between competing belief patterns, a process which compromises stability to some degree, but not completely. The separate patterns of belief will be internally stable, and oscillation may occur only over two or three different patterns. Such is the syndrome of the uncommitted thinker.

The syndrome of the uncommitted thinker is one which the cognitive theorist readily observes in the behavior of Presidents. The common quip about Roosevelt—that he was of the mind of the last person he talked to—is an exaggeration which seems to reflect the process, as Arthur Schlesinger suggests in his description of the President in the winter of 1934–1935. With economic affairs still in a critical state and with growing radical political movements, Roosevelt faced policy choices between apparently conflicting demands of economic reform on one hand and recovery on the other. Schlesinger reports him vacillating between prescriptions for tightly controlled national planning, for economic orthodoxy to restore the confidence of business, for economic reform inspired by the antitrust sentiments of Brandeis, and for the use of public spending as a recovery device. Each position had its advocates, who at various times thought they had elicited favorable responses from the President.

Schlesinger in hindsight detects a gradual drift in one direction, but his qualifications are more significant:

> Unconsciously, he was drawn in the new directions urged on him by Frankfurter, Corcoran, Cohen, and Eccles. But, as usual, he avoided ideological commitment. As usual, he even avoided intellectual clarity.
>
> Thus his decision to send the holding companies' message to Congress in March did not necessarily mean full acceptance of the neo-Brandeisian analysis, any more than his support to the Eccles banking bill through the late winter and spring meant that he advocated (or even understood) the bold use of fiscal policy.[54]

In fact, Roosevelt did not even resolve the situation on his own. The second New Deal emerged when the Supreme Court imposed an outside constraint on him by striking down the National Recovery Act, thus closing off a range of alternatives and the analysis associated with them. The pattern Roosevelt displayed of oscillating between groups of advisers—siding with one on one issue and with another on the next and then back again—is the signature of the uncommitted thinker.

Theoretical Thinking

The final syndrome clearly suggested by cognitive theory is a mode of thinking in which the decision maker adopts very abstract and extensive belief patterns, patterns which are internally consistent and stable over time and to which he displays a great deal of commitment. One might label this pattern theoretical thinking, to reflect the generalized, highly deductive belief system which is its prime characteristic. The theoretical decision maker is an aggressive thinker who is very active in imposing an extensive pattern of meaning on immediate events. In the decision situation this means that he will connect concrete alternatives to an extensive pattern of calculations about the environment. Typically he is committed to one alternative which he invests with substantial significance in terms of very general values. In accord with the general cognitive pattern, his beliefs are organized around a single value, but in this case it tends

[54] Arthur Schlesinger, Jr., *The Politics of Upheaval* (Boston: Houghton Mifflin Co., 1960), p. 263.

rather clearly to be a dimension of value in which very general values ("peace" and "world progress") are connected by a chain of inference to quite specific objectives (increased aid for Panama or additional conventional forces for Europe). The justification of the decision taken by a theoretical thinker is made in terms of the entire chain of inference and not simply its most specific component.

The characteristics of theoretical thinkers are most striking under conditions of uncertainty, since typically such a man has buffered himself from the impact of uncertainty by establishing his belief system on grounds relatively independent of the reality principle. Since the beliefs in question tend to extend well beyond what can be held on the weight of available information, some other basis of belief strength must be operative. (He is often called a "theologian" in bureaucratic vernacular, to reflect the act of faith involved in his world view.) With his beliefs established in a long-range framework and well anchored, his inference management mechanisms are able to handle the pressure of inconsistency in any short-term situation. Inferences of transformation and impossibility, the selective use of information, and other inconsistency management mechanisms are brought to bear for this purpose. Since the theoretical thought process is strongly deductive and thus relatively less dependent upon incoming information in order to *establish* coherent beliefs, incoming information can be molded and even ignored or denied with greater ease than is the case with other thought patterns. The theoretical thinker thus can act quickly and with great confidence in those fluid, chaotic situations of short duration which cause a great deal of distress to others operating in different modes of thought. Over longer durations, however, precisely because of the relative independence from incoming information and because of the tendency to structure beliefs around only a part of the complex policy problem, the theoretical thinker is likely to have trouble.

A particularly interesting example of theoretical thinking is provided by a prominent British staff officer at the outbreak of the First World War. Brigadier General Henry Wilson (later a field marshal) undertook, beginning in 1910, to formulate plans with the French Army for a British Expeditionary Force to aid the French in case of a German attack.[55] Wilson had become con-

[55] Samuel R. Williamson, *The Politics of Grand Strategy* (Cambridge, Mass.: Harvard University Press, 1969), pp. 168–172.

vinced of the necessity of British intervention by a set of calculations which foresaw a German attempt to dominate the Continent and which articulated the threat such domination would pose to the British world position and to the cause of British civilization. He constructed a military argument to show that a six-division British force would be a decisive factor in a French-German battle, a logic woven around assumptions that the German Army would attack through Belgium but without crossing the River Meuse. The limited number of roads in that area would limit the number of German divisions and allow the battle to be swayed by the British six-division force. Wilson's plans were elaborately laid out in close coordination with French plans; and in 1914, despite a great deal of reluctance in the British Cabinet regarding not only the wisdom of ground intervention but also Wilson's particular deployment, the plans determined the action which the British did in fact take. In the actual event, the German Army did cross the Meuse and swung wide on the British-French left flank. Though Wilson had available a fair amount of evidence that this was the way the battle would develop, he rigidly stuck to his original plan and managed to convince the British government. Wilson in the 1914 crisis is a clear case of the theoretical thinker. He connected his specific deployment plan to very general conceptions of value (British world position, the preservation of the empire) and overlooked specific evidence (of the wide German sweep) which represented grave difficulties for his conceptions.

The cognitive theorist is naturally interested in the particular way in which the extensive generalized belief system of the theoretical thinker comes about. Though this is particularly an area where a great deal is yet to be learned, cognitive theory is reasonably clear about two points: (1) that the development of such belief patterns takes time; and, (2) that even independent of duration the basic patterns must be established early in a person's maturational process. Regardless of whether belief strength is established by mechanisms of reinforcement or simply by the weight of stored information, it is clear that time must elapse during which the mind processes and stores information. Strong beliefs are thus the result of a gradual process of strengthening. The importance of early experience in a system biased toward stability is obvious, and it is established as an empirical matter that fundamental attitudes appear early and tend to persist

133

throughout the life cycle. Established belief patterns cannot be uprooted without massive disruption to the highly interactive, well-structured system of memory characteristic of the mature mind.

There is, to be sure, a dispute as to what point in the biological life cycle is "early" in cognitive terms. As is well known, Sigmund Freud, who saw strong connections between beliefs and the biologically based sex drive, conceived "early" to mean early childhood—up to six. To the cognitive theorist, however, "early" might well occur much later in the biological life cycle. Indeed, this would seem to be the first hypothesis to adopt, for the beliefs of concern involve the interactions of men, peoples, and governments in the general area of public affairs—not directly the central issues of early childhood. The most direct proposition is that the foundations of a theoretical belief system are laid down early in a person's professional training, or at that point in his career when he first becomes seriously concerned with the affairs of policy. The suspicion is that powerful, formative experiences of the young person in his twenties or early thirties or perhaps highly structured professional training (such as engineering or theoretical economics) are the sources of operative ideology. These "early" attitudes, strengthened and reinforced through subsequent experience, provide the first grounds for the cognitive theorist to build his explanation.

It is also well to recognize immediately that early experience strengthened over time is not likely to be the only basis for theoretical thinking. The principles of cognitive theory underscore the proposition that the mind is a generalizing, inference-drawing machine in all its operations. A seminal historical event, a particularly compelling image, another man of great persuasive power are all capable of causing a given decision maker to adopt a large-scale, generalized conception of his situation and to act upon it. Undoubtedly, there are other critical factors as well. The important argument of cognitive theory asserts that when highly generalized conceptions do become established, they provide the mind (with its inference-management mechanisms maintaining stability and holding inconsistency below some criterion) with a basis for handling the uncertainty of the immediate decision problem. It is when operating in the theoretical mode that decision makers produce strong resolutions of the intrinsic uncertainty which provided the puzzle addressed at the beginning of the chapter.

It is also important to note that to the cognitive theorist the theoretical mode is not solely characteristic of wild-eyed intellectuals, fanatics of various hues, or even of exuberant, aggressive, and inevitably unusual thinkers such as Henry Wilson. One evokes dramatic examples for the sake of clarity, but the syndrome also operates on a more mundane, day-to-day basis. Virtually every decision maker will find himself in some situations where he displays the pattern. Indeed, it is a basic proposition of the cognitive theorist that any normally functioning person is capable of strong, highly generalized belief which he takes seriously enough to affect his decisions.

The organizational context which contributes to the theoretical thought patterns is primarily one which affords enough time for such patterns to become operative. Whether they must be created or merely connected with preferences for specific alternatives, theoretical patterns are not developed over short durations. Thus, a person who enters public service from a background closely related to his new responsibilities is more likely than others to display the pattern. So is the staff officer who remains in his job for some time and whose mandate concerns a rather specific area of policy. Unless some issue seizes high-level policy makers over a considerable period of time, theoretical thinking is likely to be removed from these positions at the intersection of channels and to be located within a particular information channel in an organizational unit, formal or informal, which has a restricted scope of concern. Moreover, theoretical thinkers are particularly likely to be found in small, closely knit groups which interact with one another about the issues of concern on a regular basis. This provides a stable source of social reinforcement to bolster their strong belief systems. Military officers and bureau chiefs are clearly prone to the syndrome on the issues which concern them. It is less likely to occur with Presidents and Cabinet officers.

THESE three patterns of cognitive operations in organizational settings—grooved thinking, uncommitted thinking, and theoretical thinking—provide the most direct and most immediately usable contribution of cognitive theory to the analysis of complex policy problems. As noted at the outset, the syndromes are sketched in general outline and become much more powerful when they can be used to structure data regarding specific situations—as they will be in the analysis of the nuclear sharing question. The three cognitive syndromes state in the most concrete terms the general argument of cognitive theory as to how basic structure comes to be established for the complex decision problem. That argument holds that the inference mechanisms of the mind impose structure on uncertain situations in systematic ways under given organizational conditions, and that the cybernetic decision process operates within the structure thus established.

Some precautions need to be restated. First, the cognitive principles utilized are not idiosyncratic to individuals, as has been repeatedly emphasized. As a result, the three cognitive syndromes identified cannot be assumed to refer to personality types. It is reasonably clear that every person at different times and, most critically, *in different decision problems*, is likely to operate according to different syndromes. Many decision makers doubtless could be observed fitting all three patterns at one time or another. Second, in any actual organizational situation the various positions of power are likely to be held by people operating in different modes of thinking. Awareness of this fact is likely to aid analysis when details of the specific context can be supplied, but it is difficult at the moment to provide general propositions of any power. One cannot say with complete confidence what the consequences will be if an "uncommitted" thinker with a "theoretical" staff directs a "grooved" bureau chief or division commander.

COGNITIVE LEARNING

It should be clear from the preceding discussion that cognitive modes of thinking are not likely to produce the laterally and upwardly expanding process of causal learning which the analytic paradigm expects. All of the cognitive syndromes dissect the complex problem and operate upon segments of it, and the learning process produced by the operation of these syndromes is limited as a consequence. The strong tendency for the segmental patterns to stabilize themselves means that after some period of time of operating in a certain issue area both individuals and organizational entities will have learned to structure their decisions in a particular way, and changes in the established structure will

136

be unlikely, short of substantial changes in personnel. This is the pattern of rigidity and resistance to change so familiar both to serious students of bureaucratic organization and to those who in one way or another have had to do business with them.

The cognitive theorist might call this process *constrained learning*. Clearly, more conceptualization is involved than in the instrumental learning process, but it does not entail the full process of causal learning. In constrained learning, new information and new decision problems are fit into already established conceptual structures without causing any general adjustment of the structure. New ideas, new inferences, new perceptions are formed at lower levels of generality, and thus a belief system in a process of constrained learning is not static. However, the general structure of conceptualization remains both stable and partial even over very extended periods.

Apparent examples of such a learning process are readily found in the annals of medicine. Doctors, of course, are decision makers under complexity. The human body is a highly interactive, very imperfectly known system, and its medical treatments regularly present trade-off problems and unexpected outcomes. Medical history provides many examples in which a therapeutic procedure successful within a very limited context (or even only apparently successful) has persisted over an extended period of time despite very negative consequences. One might cite the use of bloodletting in earlier times. One might cite the use of certain drugs in contemporary medicine. The case of chloramphenicol provides a contemporary example.[56] The drug was marketed in 1949 as a broad-spectrum antibiotic with established utility against typhus and typhoid fever. The drug also works against a number of minor ailments including common respiratory diseases, and it quickly came into such extensive use that it is clear that many physicians have been prescribing it for such minor ailments. Unfortunately, the drug also can have damaging and, in several dramatic cases, fatal side effects. In one documented case a doctor's son died of a reaction to the drug, which was administered for a minor urinary tract infection. Despite government

[56] The case of chloramphenicol (chloromycetin) is developed in hearings conducted by Senator Gaylord Nelson (U.S. Senate, Select Committee on Small Business, Subcommittee on Monopoly, *Competitive Problems in the Drug Industry*, Part 6, 90th Congress, 2nd Session, February 1968). I am indebted to Susan Lutzker for research on this case.

hearings and reported warnings to the medical profession, widespread prescription of the drug continued at least into the late 1960s and may well continue today. To the cognitive theorist this persistent misapplication of the drug reflects constrained learning. Doctors, with a ready conception of what broad-spectrum antibiotics do, find that conception confirmed by a number of successful applications for minor infections. The negative consequences are subtle, bizarre, and unexplained; and they do not occur in every instance. The learning process of many practicing doctors is not sufficiently flexible to adjust to the cumulating evidence, which yields a clear analytic case for sharply restricted application.

The term "constrained learning" gives a connotation of potential trouble which the case of chloramphenicol dramatizes. Given the nature of complexity, the implicit warning is well taken, but the entire thrust of cognitive analysis is to suggest the inevitability of such limitations when one is considering the decision process in general. (A more analytic standard can be achieved, of course, under special circumstances, but not for all decisions, according to cognitive analysis.) Constrained learning.could be a virtual synonym for "stability" or "consistency," and cognitive theory argues at length that these are necessary qualities of the mind. The term "constrained learning" cannot be properly considered pejorative within the framework of cognitive analysis.

SUMMARY

The principles of cognitive theory which have been introduced into the analysis of the complex policy problem provide a set of arguments as to how the mind produces a decomposition of such problems in the absence of stable environmental decompositions. These arguments suggest general tendencies to set up decision problems conceptualized in terms of a single value, to associate but a single outcome with the available alternatives, and to restrict information utilized to a relatively limited number of variables. Thus, the propositions of the analytic paradigm—the idea of value integration; the conceptualization of a range of outcomes; the broad sensitivity to information—are all doubted by the core principles of cognitive theory. The central idea of the cybernetic paradigm—uncertainty control—is also adjusted by the more general picture of the mental operations which emerges from cognitive theory. To the cognitive theorist, the mind active-ly but subjectively resolves uncertainty because of its universal tendency to generalize. It does so, however, without confronting the full thrust of variety inherent in any complex problem. In sketching the way in which subjective uncertainty resolution occurs—that is, by resort to sources of belief strength independ-ent of evidence from the empirical world—the principles of cog-nitive theory explain how problem structures are set up within which cybernetic mechanisms can operate. The assertion is that the cybernetic paradigm needs to be supplemented with cogni-tive theory when complex policy problems are under analysis.

The picture of the organizational process which emerged from these considerations is partial, but clear enough to challenge the conceptions of the learning process which emerge from the ana-lytic and the cybernetic paradigms. Cognitive principles have been used to derive three coherent and non-idiosyncratic thought patterns which, it can be argued, emerge in organizational deci-sion process. Though the nature of the interactions between these processes in the overall decision process is far from completely clear, and perhaps cannot be made clear at this level of abstrac-tion, nonetheless there is a strong implication that learning will proceed not as the process of instrumental learning pictured by the cybernetic paradigm. Rather, cognitive theory expects a con-strained learning process which develops partial but general models of the environment as required by the analytic paradigm, but which does not evolve in the manner predicted by that paradigm.

In the language of the study used henceforth, the cognitive paradigm refers to the assumptions of cybernetics as amended by cognitive theory. The cybernetic paradigm refers to the more restricted set of assumptions of Chapter 3.

CHAPTER 5

Politics and Policy

MISSING IN the discussion to this point is any immediate sense of energy. The everyday events of government decision making are suffused with frequent crises and constant strain that the detailed paradigms of the decision process do not capture. For example, treating U.S. policy in Indochina or the phenomena of poverty and urban decay as problems of high uncertainty and of delicate balances of competing values would illuminate critical dimensions of those issues, but it alone would not give appreciation of the political convolutions which they produced in the United States. One must blend conflict, sharp disagreement, and maneuvers for power into the conception of the complex policy problem in order to reflect the realities of policy making. Harry Truman, as one who should know, coined one of the more appropriate metaphors: "Those who cannot stand the heat," he once declared, "should stay out of the kitchen."[1] Heat, he realized, was an integral part of doing the Presidential business.

In trying to understand why heat is associated with the decision process, theorists have generated a set of assumptions about that process and about the outcomes which emerge from it which stand outside the paradigms developed in previous chapters. The point of departure is the existence of a number of actors, each with some power to affect the other actors and thus the ultimate decision. For the decision process as a whole, this means simply that there is a dispersion of power to affect the outcome—one of the identified characteristics of complexity. The actors are assumed (or found) to be in disagreement on the issues being explained and, more importantly, to stand in quite general competition with one another over a much broader range of issues. They are seen to engage in a variety of bargaining and coercive maneuvers to exert their will, and the "pulling and hauling" which results is seen as the essential characteristic of the decision process. Outcomes occur in this view as consequences of an elaborate bargaining game which spins them out, as often as not, as a by-

[1] John Bartlett, *Familiar Quotations*, Emily Morison Beck, ed. (Boston: Little, Brown & Co., 1968), p. 983a.

140

product of action taken in the course of play. What happens is rarely intended and even more rarely preferred by any one of the actors individually. The stakes of the game are high, and the play is commensurately rough. It generates the heat which Presidents and others feel.

This political view of the decision process has been documented by those who have watched it, in particular instances, in the detail required to see the pattern. Richard Neustadt in his study of the Presidency examined several cases of Presidential decisions in order to lay out the forces involved in the bargaining games in which Presidents engage.[2] He analyzes the techniques which must be used by a President to marshal enough power to effect his will. In his analysis, Neustadt emphasizes that effective power is not conferred by the office in and of itself. More recently Neustadt has carried his sensitivities to an examination of two major diplomatic crises between the United States and Great Britain.[3] He has shown how both the Suez crisis of 1956 and the Skybolt controversy of 1962 were fundamentally shaped and determined by the domestic political games in which the two heads of state were necessarily engaged at the time. Foreign policy outcomes in both these cases were in many ways by-products of other concerns.

Neustadt's presentation of the decision process can be bolstered from a wide variety of other sources. Ralph Huitt, in studying hearings before the Senate Banking and Currency committee in 1946, saw the decision process of the committee in terms he associated with David Truman's classic treatise on the governmental process.[4] The members were all partisans of some special interest, and the committee's product emerged as the result of a series of clashes between the partisans—reflecting no overall design. Roger Hilsman has supplied similar testimony as a knowledgeable observer who experienced the foreign policy decision-making process from the inside.[5] Morton Halperin has

[2] Richard E. Neustadt, *Presidential Power* (New York: John Wiley and Sons, Inc., 1960).

[3] Richard E. Neustadt, *Alliance Politics* (New York: Columbia University Press, 1970).

[4] Ralph K. Huitt, "The Congressional Committee: A Case Study," in *American Political Science Review*, vol. 48 (June 1954), pp. 340–365.

[5] Roger Hilsman, *To Move a Nation* (New York: Doubleday & Company, Inc., 1967).

141

done the same.[6] Warner Schilling[7] and Samuel Huntington[8] have documented such a process in shaping defense policy, and Robert Dahl[9] and Edward Banfield[10] have done the same for decision making at the level of municipal government. Charles Lindblom[11] has extensively articulated the theory of this sort of process. Graham Allison[12] has aggregated this literature as a means of explaining policy outcomes by specifying the concepts, assumptions, and major propositions of this sort of analysis.

What emerges from this work is a conception of the decision process more supplementary than competitive to the analytic and cognitive paradigms. The maneuvers whereby political actors seek to convince, bargain with, cajole, and coerce each other are inherent features of major public issues. In order to address themselves to complex policy problems, the other decision paradigms must operate within such a setting. Politics is thus a critical element of the context, but the basic conception of the *decision* process is still provided by either the analytic or the cognitive paradigms.[13]

In particular, the fact that theories of bargaining concern themselves with the overall effects of a number of partially pow-

[6] Morton Halperin, *Bureaucratic Politics and Foreign Policy* (Washington: Brookings Institution, forthcoming).

[7] W. Schilling, P. Hammond, and R. Snyder, *Strategy, Politics and Budgets* (New York: Columbia University Press, 1952).

[8] Samuel Huntington, *The Common Defense* (New York: Columbia University Press, 1961).

[9] Robert Dahl, *Who Governs? Democracy and Power in an American City* (New Haven, Conn.: Yale University Press, 1961).

[10] Edward C. Banfield, *Political Influence* (New York: The Free Press of Glencoe, 1961).

[11] Charles E. Lindblom, *The Intelligence of Democracy* (New York: The Free Press, 1965).

[12] Graham T. Allison, *Essence of Decision* (Boston: Little, Brown and Company, 1971).

[13] The process of bureaucratic politics is frequently conceived by analogy to force vectors in physics. In that framework a resultant vector often tends in a direction quite different from the component forces, and by analogy political outcomes might be produced by opposing political forces each of which had something quite different in mind. This process might well qualify the political perspective as a separate paradigm since it does suggest a conception not captured within the other paradigms. However, it seems better to treat such occurrences as part of the set of general causal forces whereby outcomes are determined and to continue to restrict the notion of decision to situations where intention or purpose, somehow conceived, is plausibly imputed.

erful actors immediately establishes such analysis on the collective level of explanation, and hence the political analysis is clearly open to any set of assumptions about that particular decision process in which each of the separate actors is engaged. Again, the most developed body of theory assumes that the individual actors operate in accord with the analytic paradigm and their various game strategies, and bargaining maneuvers are often understood on that basis.[14] Though this is a useful device, it is clear from the preceding discussion that this is not the only assumption which can be made. Cybernetic and/or broader cognitive processes can be assumed on the individual level, and the implication for the overall process of bargaining can then be analyzed at the collective level.

POLITICS WITH ANALYTIC ACTORS

A major proposition of many bargaining theories holds that individual actors are driven by motives extraneous to any reasonable conception of national objectives and public purpose. Narrow consideration of personal career and the power position of organizational subunits supply many of these objectives, but often, substantively unrelated issues are also tied together in the process of political maneuvering. When the Navy bitterly attacked the worthiness of the B-36 as a weapons system, many strongly suspected that their conviction was generated not only by matters of ground strategy but also by calculations which related expansion of the Navy inversely to that of the Air Force.[15] When President Kennedy sought to deal with Soviet missiles in Cuba he found that United States missiles, long implanted and tolerated in Turkey and Italy, had become part of the issue. It is not unusual for a Senator who wants a bill providing federal support for education to discover that a higher tariff for shoes is the price of doing business because of the dispersion of power in Congress.

A great deal of general political analysis proceeds by specifying the kinds of outside objectives which are introduced to substantive policy decisions. The pursuit of power, fame, and/or fortune is often depicted as the essential motives of the game, with

[14] See A. Downs, *Inside Bureaucracy* (Boston: Little, Brown and Company, 1967).

[15] D. Hammond, *Super Carriers and B-36 Bombers: Appropriations, Strategy and Politics*, Interuniversity Case Program #97 (New York: The Bobbs-Merrill Company, 1963).

arguments about national interest serving as appropriate screening devices. As just noted, however, if the argument is to be held at the same theoretical level as that of the other paradigms, such distinctions regarding the kinds of values typically pursued by political actors arise after it has been decided which paradigm will be used as the basis for analysis. The prior question is whether the political process serves to integrate conflicting objectives of any number and character, or whether objectives are bundled in some other fashion. Essentially it is a question as to which of the two paradigms identified provides the proper base for understanding the political process.

The most frequently used theories of collective decision in a political context are based upon analytic assumptions. These theories disaggregate the decision process into separate and conflicting actors and then trace out the consequences of each actor operating analytically in terms of his own internal logic. Mancur Olson is an articulate spokesman of that position. The products of government activity, he notes, are not only benefits to the collective as a whole—public goods in the economist's sense. Government activity also produces private benefits for certain individuals. A person's "share" of a collective benefit, Olson argues, is rather diffuse, weak, and ill-defined typically, and hence to the cool, analytic actor is valued less than the private benefits which, for the lucky person who gets them, are often substantial. Consequently, those who find substantial private interests to be at stake in an issue will be dominated by those considerations, and they will tend to dominate the decision process because they are more intensely motivated and can analytically justify greater effort. Thus, the manufacturer of shoes who cannot compete with foreign products will reliably act to preserve his business by promoting import restrictions—even if the overall interest of the United States economy, in which he participates, is thereby damaged. Historically this sort of actor has been relatively successful.

In a collective decision process of this character, public objectives will be determined by compromises and other power maneuvers undertaken because of their private effects. For the two-value problem (where the values are public-good objectives) two major propositions emerge: First, one expects that substantively remote objectives reflecting the special interests of important actors will be integrated into the decision process; and second, that relative balancing of public benefits can be expected to be a by-product of equilibrium between these special objectives.

The first proposition (which can be called value extension) asserts that in the political process of decision, private values will be added to the set or objective, whether as constraints upon the outcome or as demands for inclusion. To distinguish, one might speak of positive value extension (adding additional costly elements to the outcome) and negative value extension (setting constraints on the outcome). This idea of value *extension* is a very different process than the concept of expansion as conceived by the causal learning process of the analytic paradigm. Upward expansion as a component of causal learning implies higher-order integrations of the public values involved in the decision problems. The proposition of value extension, by contrast, asserts a process whereby substantively extraneous, private values are integrated into the decision process.

The second proposition asserts that the outcome for the public values will be systematically dominated by private values in the decision process. Some mix of benefits will be delivered to the public values, but not by a direct weighing as entailed in the concept of utility. Rather, by a process which can be labeled extraneous value integration, public benefits are determined as a by-product of bargaining dominated by private values. The propositions of value extension and extraneous value integration are, then, central propositions of political analysis using the analytic paradigm.

Many apparent examples of these propositions can be found in history. The confrontation between the United States and the Soviet Union over missiles in Cuba in 1962, though often treated as a classic of analytic response, was powerfully affected by the personal political stakes of President Kennedy.[16] Given the constellation of domestic politics of the time, the Soviet missiles in Cuba were a far more serious and compelling threat to the political career of the President than they were to the strategic objectives of the United States as a whole. Hence the significant risk of war entailed in their removal under the threat of force is more readily understood as a somewhat indirect result of the position taken by the politically threatened President than as the expected analytic reaction of a strategically threatened nation. Similarly,

[16] Allison, *Essence of Decision.*

145

the enormous resources devoted by the United States to the preservation of a rather inept government in South Vietnam seems more readily explained as the unfortunate consequence of decisions taken under the duress of American politics than as a cool, analytic calculation of American strategic interests in Asia. On a less dramatic level, the system of oil import quotas maintained for many years by the United States at a cost to the economy of approximately $4 billion per year is more readily explained as the effect of the actions taken on behalf of oil producers than as a protection of domestic supply necessary for purposes of national defense.[17]

POLITICS WITH COGNITIVE ACTORS

If political analysis is conducted on the basis of the cognitive paradigm rather than utilizing analytic assumptions, the central theoretical focus shifts from the problem of value trade-offs to the problem of uncertainty. This shift in focus produces some important changes in the analysis of political events, but it leaves the proposition of value extension intact. The fact that payoffs to private values are simpler, narrower in scope, and more immediate renders them more understandable and less prone to uncertainty than payoffs to public value. The latter involve complicated social effects hard to predict, explain, or even observe. The focus of a cognitive decision process thus can be expected to center on the clearer, more compelling dimensions of private value. This is particularly reinforced by the utilization of social judgments in cognitive operations as an uncertainty-reducing mechanism. It is natural that political demands would act as information channels; and, in providing a focus for decisions, they would function as a means of handling uncertainty. High policy officials, such as Presidents and Cabinet officials, who must face a number of different issues, each with substantial uncertainty regarding the effects for public objectives, are very likely to rely heavily on the pattern of reaction from the press, Congress, the public, various parts of the executive bureaucracy, and foreign governments to get a sense of the issue. These are very likely to become the operative information channels upon which cognitive decision

[17] Cabinet Task Force on Oil Import Control, *The Oil Import Question: A Report on the Relationship of Oil Imports to the National Security* (Washington: U.S. Government Printing Office, 1970).

processes operate. If what is conveyed in these channels is support and opposition for various options determined largely on private grounds, then the process of value extension is likely to be the result even if all individual actors are operating not as analytic calculators, but rather as cognitive processors.

A change in the paradigm base of political analysis does sharply change, however, the assumed handling of value trade-offs, with dramatic effects on traditional views of politics. If cognitive actors are engaged in politics, the natural presumption is that the role of bargaining as traditionally understood will be sharply diminished. Bargaining implies a willingness and capacity on the part of actors to adjust their conflicting objectives in a process of reaching an accommodation—a clear form of value integration. It is natural to suppose, by contrast, that cognitive actors will not display the same degree of deliberate accommodation, will act more independently, and will by-pass bargains which under analytic assumptions would appear to be obvious. The limited outcome calculations, the single-value focus, and the dependence on selected feedback channels, should all retard the process of accommodation. If, because of the peculiarities of a given decision problem, conflict among the separate actors is relatively intense, then the overall decision process should display less coherence than that produced by mutual accommodations among analytic actors.

Consider, for example, the game of Chicken, long a favorite of theorists of bargaining as a simple model of political conflict. In one of its more dramatic forms, the game consists of two players each of whom drives directly at the other at 60 mph down the center of a deserted highway with an audience of peers looking on. The first player to swerve to avoid collision loses, is labeled a chicken, and suffers the contempt of his peers. The game poses a classic value trade-off problem—survival on the one hand, preservation of honor on the other. Thomas Schelling has provided an analysis of the game under the assumption that both players are analytic decision makers.[18] The first player to establish clearly an irreversible commitment to the center of the road (such as by tying the wheel and climbing in the back seat) will win the

[18] Thomas C. Schelling, *The Strategy of Conflict* (Cambridge, Mass.: Harvard University Press, 1960), and *Arms and Influence* (New Haven, Conn.: Yale University Press, 1966). See especially Chapters 2 and 3 of *Arms and Influence*.

game. The other player, still retaining control, faces a certainty of death as against a finite loss of honor, and everyone knows how an analytic actor will resolve that choice. The scenario, which Schelling labels "compellence," is played out daily, usually for lesser stakes, on street intersections throughout the nation.

One's sense of this game changes drastically if a cognitive decision maker is inserted into the scenario. There are at least two good reasons why such a decision maker might not yield to a cleverly established commitment by the opposing player: first, while focusing on other things, he may not notice the commitment; second, he may simply fail to engage in a value trade-off while carrying out his prior intention. Rather than compellence, with such a player involved, one readily imagines disaster. Viewed from the assumptions of the cognitive paradigm, moreover, it is not a disaster which emerges from an error in calculation, but rather it is the consequence of the normally functioning decision process.

Such profound differences in political analyses generated by the two paradigms can also be seen in less bizarre and more directly relevant circumstances. In some large cities in recent years, to illustrate, attempts have been made to adjust police deployment to better correspond to the incidence of crime. These attempts have sometimes met with fierce resistance from police patrolmen and their representatives, and this resistance has strongly limited the impact of the effort. With crime increasingly a serious issue for governments of large cities, and with police deployment inevitably one of the major mechanisms used to control it, the question of deployment adjustments has become a serious policy question, and the resistance of police has become a matter which city officials must necessarily understand. Some assumptions must be brought to bear in arriving at such an understanding, and it matters a great deal which paradigm holds sway.

The cognitive paradigm would readily generate an understanding of police resistance in terms of routine police operations. Decisions about police deployments must be made daily at various levels of the organization, and over time these decisions have become highly programed and encrusted by tradition. They involve the working out of seniority, of career incentives, of the patterns of thousands of individual daily lives. When the police organization and its daily routines are studied in all their complexity, it is no wonder that the police do not respond rapidly to high-level policy decisions regarding deployment. Police resistance can be understood as the inertial resistance of a large organization, inertia resulting from the operation of a multitude of interacting, essentially cybernetic decision processes.

An all-too-plausible and sharply different understanding of such resistance can also be generated by application of the analytic paradigm. It is known that large-city police departments are prone to corruption as an inevitably human consequence of the nature of their business. Police are paid modest salaries to perform in the service of a diffuse public interest. In doing so they must remain in constant contact with a criminal subculture whose members have it in their power to make the policemen's work less dangerous and/or more remunerative. For those who succumb to the inherent temptation, a trade-off is established between their private arrangements and the public objectives to which they are legally responsible. The important point is that it would seem to require analytic actors, capable of subtle balances between their competing claims and of sophisticated outcome calculations, to establish and preserve an organized network of corruption operating systematically and at various levels in a police department hierarchy.[19] Such a network and the business it conducts would be threatened by more flexible deployment decisions made at the top levels of the department, and this could explain resistance to redeployment. Needless to say, this is a diagnosis which would lead to very different corrective efforts by city officials than those indicated by the other paradigm. An official seriously facing the issue of police deployment would be intensely interested in learning which picture of the situation was the more accurate.

PERSPECTIVE

Though the paradigms which provide a coherent view of the decision process appear to be necessary components of any political

[19] The actual existence of such a network in a particular police department is not an allegation to be made lightly. There is some evidence to be found, both in historical and in current situations, but, for illustrative purposes, the reality of the example is less important than its plausibility. Hence only plausibility is claimed. Wherever it does exist, organized corruption is presumably capable of more sustained operation, higher volume, and hence greater consequences than the petty extraction of small sums by individual policemen on their beats. The latter is perfectly imaginable for cognitive decision makers. The former is less so.

analysis, obviously neither of them offers a complete theory of politics. It is well established that many attributes of a society—its political culture, the structure of its government, its class and ethnic composition, the personality of its leaders, etc.—affect its political events. Any actual analysis of a complex decision problem necessarily involves a weaving in of these basic political forces which remain exogenous to the theory of decision. For these reasons the process of linking the abstractly articulated paradigms of decision to the specifics of a complex problem is a critically important element in any analysis. It is a process which can be done well or badly, and it is probably true that the ultimate quality of the analysis hangs even more on this question than on the care taken in the articulation of theoretical assumptions.

Because the business of establishing the connection between theoretical assumptions and an actual decision is a process of particularization (inevitably a matter of setting up *ad hoc* assumptions), there are few generally applicable rules to follow. The standard rules of scientific method apply, of course, but they, too, need interpretation for any given situation, especially in that the pertinent data are largely non-quantitative. One relies ultimately on the judgment and care of the analysts.

It can be said, however, that very high standards ought to obtain, particularly in that an attempt is being made to establish the importance of the paradigm distinctions which have been outlined. This means that in actual application of the paradigms, the important dimensions of complexity must be laid forth, facts must be well documented, and care must be taken to apply the separate perspectives fairly and independently. The illustrations of the theoretical arguments to this point, it must be conceded, have been too casual to be commensurate with the importance of issues so fundamental to the conduct of political analysis. Accordingly, the analysis of the nuclear sharing episode which follows is developed in detail.

PART TWO

THE POLITICS OF

NUCLEAR SHARING:

1956–1964

CHAPTER 6

Strains in the Alliance: Genesis
of a Two-Value Problem

IN DECEMBER of 1960 the NATO foreign ministers met in Paris for their regular semiannual meeting, and Christian A. Herter, the outgoing Secretary of State, used the occasion for a diplomatic initiative. The United States, he announced, would commit to the alliance before the end of 1963 five nuclear submarines with eighty Polaris missiles in all, provided that the Europeans could agree on some mechanism for controlling the weapons. He also suggested that the Allies purchase one hundred medium-range ballistic missiles (MRBM's), to be deployed at sea along with the Polaris boats. As a footnote, but with emphasis, Herter warned that the Allies would have to relieve the United States of some of the financial burden of NATO programs. The conjunction of the themes suggested a redirection of NATO effort, and the ministers were quick to recognize that Herter's initiative posed serious business. It was the debut of an idea which was to become a concrete proposal, a multilateral nuclear strike force for NATO.

On the surface there was an illogic to Herter's timing. The Secretary was to leave office in a month, and President-elect Kennedy, though agreeing in principle to Herter's announcement, would not be committed to the details of any proposal, not even one as carefully wrapped in vagueness as this one was. This apparent anomaly of timing was due in part to the long-established schedule of NATO meetings, but it is indicative of the nature of the issue that the United States could not let the December meeting slip by uneventfully to await the new President. The problem of nuclear sharing had gained momentum imparted over a substantial period of time, and though the President would powerfully affect it, he was not the only force. Indeed, the status of the issue independent of the new President is precisely what must first be understood.

In essence, the issue of nuclear sharing threw two major values of American foreign policy into fundamental conflict—that is, in-

153

to a trade-off relationship. On one hand was the pursuit of political and economic integration in Europe emerging from the post-war economic resurgence of the European states. On the other was the defense of Europe in the nuclear era, a problem which imposed strong requirements concerning the control of nuclear weapons. Neither these values nor the specific policy objectives which they generated were the invention of any group of decision makers subject to definition and redefinition at their discretion. The objectives were deeply rooted in historical experiences and in the whole posture of Western political institutions. In broad terms they stood as given, even for a strong-willed President. One cannot review all of postwar history in order to grasp the force which the central values of the problem had achieved by 1960, but it is important to recall some of the highlights.

THE POLITICS AND ECONOMICS OF EUROPEAN RECOVERY

Postwar Germany began its existence in spectacular economic and social chaos, and that provided the background against which foreign policy of the period was played.[1] German cities were in ruins, and housing was critically scarce. Its agricultural production was insufficient to feed a population artificially swollen from the westward influx of millions of refugees. Starvation was a serious threat, and industrial production was at a fraction of the best prewar levels. Moreover, France, England—Europe in general—shared in the chaos. Economies throughout Europe were logjammed.

The chaos, however, turned out to be exceedingly transient. By 1952 European economies had reachieved the point of self-sustaining growth. Industrial production at that point was up 25 to 35 percent over prewar levels, and agricultural production was up approximately 10 percent. In all the countries of the future European Economic Community (EEC) except Belgium, the growth rate of Gross Domestic Product for the decade 1949–1959 exceeded that of both the United States and Great Britain.[2] West Germany's GNP for the decade led all Western

[1] John W. Spanier, *American Foreign Policy Since World War II*, 2nd ed. rev. (New York: Frederick A. Praeger, 1965), provides a general review.

[2] United Nations, Secretariat of the Economic Commission for Europe, *Some Factors in Economic Growth in Europe During the 1950's*, New York, 1965, Chapter III.

economies at an impressive 7.4 percent, yielding a per capita increase of 6.3 percent. When the first Sputnik sent its shock through Western societies in 1957, West German GNP, at 50 billion U.S. dollars, was the fourth greatest in the world.[3] Combined GNP for the six EEC countries approached 150 billion U.S. dollars—greater than that of the Soviet Union and second only to that of the United States.[4] By 1960 the six core countries of continental Western Europe, led in many respects by the West German economy, constituted the second largest and most important industrial complex in the world. Moreover, these partially integrated European economies seemed distinctly more dynamic than that of the United States.

The fact that World War II imposed such a breaking point in modern history affected the way in which these events were understood in the minds of men. The defeat of Germany and Japan, the advent of nuclear power, the crumbling of empires, and the massive changes in world political relationships all served to close old episodes (and indeed eras) of history and to open new ones. As a result, prewar and postwar trends were separated rather than integrated. Economic trends of the first half of the century which might have smoothed the curves of postwar change were disassociated from postwar events. The battered, exhausted, stagnating Europe of the immediate postwar years stood in stark contrast to the booming Europe of the 1950s, and the recovery seemed miraculous—and still does. In Germany, where 1945 imposed unquestionably the sharpest break, the expression *Wirtschaftswunder* became a household word.

Closely associated with European recovery in the minds of all involved—and especially in the minds of U.S. policy makers—was the Marshall Plan, which had provided the catalyst. In a dramatic turn away from an isolationist foreign policy, the United States had accepted clear and substantial responsibility for postwar Europe in 1947, one of the darkest hours. The Truman administration assumed the British burden in Greece and Turkey and pronounced the Truman Doctrine—the United States would protect friendly nations against attack from what had come to be understood generally as "the other side," the Communist bloc. The Marshall Plan followed, bringing massive economic aid for

[3] Bruce M. Russet et al., *World Handbook of Political and Social Indicators* (New Haven, Conn.: Yale University Press, 1964), Table 43, p. 152.
[4] Ibid.

the Western European countries. Formerly isolationist Republican Senator Vandenburg joined in the initiatives, thus symbolizing a shift in the foreign policy consensus of the United States. It was a moment of high political drama in Washington, and it was very gratifying to see it all turn out so well. Greece and Turkey were preserved in the orbit of what U.S. citizens came to know as the Free World, and the miraculous economic recovery in Europe ensued. The Marshall Plan was recorded as a resounding success—by most accounts the greatest success in modern American foreign policy.

Intimately associated with the Marshall Plan and the economic reemergence of Western Europe during the 1950s were a series of arrangements for cooperation among the many countries.[5] The Economic Cooperation Act of 1948, the legislative vehicle for European aid, required cooperative arrangements among the several European nations for disbursing grant funds. The Act clearly announced the objective of creating a larger market in Europe by removing trade barriers. The Organization of European Economic Cooperation (OEEC) was founded in 1948 to meet these conditions, and its experience soon revealed an impetus in continental Europe for much more intense cooperation. There was a revulsion against the nationalism associated with the two world wars. There was a recognition of the inconvenience of putting a strong international boundary between the coal fields of Alsace-Lorraine and the industrial complex of the Ruhr district. There was the cool calculation of the advantages of large markets in running modern economies and of the size and importance of the Soviet Union, at the very least a threat to be hedged against. Based upon traditional principles of intergovernmental cooperation and unable to transform itself into a more extensive set of arrangements, the OEEC soon yielded leadership to a series of initiatives establishing functionally specific European agencies with some supranational authority.

NATO itself was one such institution. Born in 1949, it embodied some measure of authority in its international commander (SACEUR) and in his international staff (SHAPE). A serious proposal for a European Defense Community (EDC) followed in 1954, presenting more extensive arrangements for an interna-

[5] L. N. Lindberg, *The Political Dynamics of European Economic Integration* (Stanford, Calif.: Stanford University Press, 1963).

tional authority with competence over defense matters. Despite its ultimate defeat, the EDC proposal enjoyed enough success to leave a distinct impression of the potential of European institutions on those intimately involved in European affairs. In economic matters, the European Coal and Steel Community (ECSC) established an international authority for administering and developing a system for pooling Europe's coal and steel production and resources. The High Authority of the ECSC took office in August of 1952, headed by the foremost advocate of political unity in Europe, Jean Monnet of France.

Broader-based economic arrangements were provided in 1957 by the Treaty of Rome and the subsequent creation of two new functionally based "supranational" institutions. Euratom forged cooperation in nuclear energy at the frontiers of technology, and the European Economic Community (EEC) cast it throughout the broad range of economic activity. Nuclear energy was to be jointly developed and regulated, tariff barriers internal to the six EEC members were to be dismantled, monetary and labor policies were to be harmonized, and all these things were to be built upon the explicit assumption of unified political purpose.

To these concrete moves for cooperation in Europe was attached an image of Europe's future as a gradual process of integration whereby the murderous and myopic national states of recent history would give way to a broader community, building upon common interests in the emerging bipolar world. Principal leaders of the recovery effort—Robert Schuman, Paul Henri Spaak, and Jean Monnet—articulated aspirations for political unity in Europe as a culmination of cooperation in functional areas, and social and political theorists set to work propounding and analyzing the idea. Fueled by the sharp, incisive success of recovery, the contrasting horrors of the past, and the concrete steps already taken, the theories of Monnet and his associates called into being a political movement for European integration. It was an idea of clear appeal—uniting the moral with the economic, the mundane detail of trade and tariffs with grand conceptions of European civilization, and providing a hopefully permanent escape from the bloodletting of the past. Moreover, it gave both the Europeans and the Americans, with their new global responsibilities, something to *create*. Europe was not simply a line to be held, malevolent opponents to be thwarted, a *status quo* to be maintained. For those setting their sights on historic purposes, it was a constructive cause.

The NATO foreign ministers in 1960 were molded by the recovery their societies had made in the previous fifteen years, and by the institutions and ideas through which they had come to be associated with each other. They were far from monolithic on the meaning of the experience or on the proper course for the future, but they all were deeply affected by the events which had occurred.

DEFENSE ISSUES

The NATO foreign ministers in December of 1960 met in a context also shaped by conflict. The allies of the war against Hitler had split and were at each other's throats. The foreign ministers in 1960 were still working out the consequences. NATO, by the nature of the institution, was seized with the concrete military threat to Western Europe. In the late 1940s this had consisted largely of the Soviet Army in Europe, which had not demobilized after World War II to the extent that the American Army had. Though the Soviets exploded their first atomic device shortly after the NATO treaty was signed in 1949, the ground forces of the Soviet Army defined the threat during the formative years of the organization. The counterthreat was wielded by the American strategic forces armed with nuclear weapons which were at least theoretically capable of striking the Soviet Union in response to aggression in Europe. Frightened by the Korean War, the Western allies had upgraded the alliance to something more than an American guarantee. Meeting at Lisbon in 1951, they had provided for a military organization with substantial forces in being—35 divisions on the ground in Europe was the official (but unmet) aspiration.[6]

In 1954 significant quantities of long-range bombers began to appear in the Soviet forces, and in August of that year the Soviets exploded two thermonuclear devices. These events heralded coming Soviet strategic power of global consequence, and the point was driven home in 1957. In August the Soviet ICBM was tested; on October 4 it was given a gala premier as the launch

[6] Robert E. Osgood, *NATO, the Entangling Alliance* (Chicago: The University of Chicago Press, 1962).

vehicle for Sputnik I. If the coming of Soviet strategic power was no surprise to serious analysts of American strategy and force structure, it was a distinct shock to the nation as a whole and to the European allies. Those who had not learned the intricate details of weapons technology, which spelled out probable proliferation and exceedingly rapid technical change, were inevitably staggered by the transformation of the Soviet threat from the "howling Tartar horde" which had invaded Berlin in 1945[7] to a technically avant-garde military power.

As the 1950s ended, Europe looked eastward down an apparent gun barrel. The Soviet Army in Europe was recognized as about the most modern in the world—highly mobile and equipped with weapons from the postwar technical era. Overall Soviet Army strength was still estimated in most places in 1960 at 150 to 175 divisions and was generally conceded overwhelming superiority on the ground. Moreover, there were now totally new dimensions to the threat. The Soviet ICBM program seemed to be distinctly ahead of the American program. A debate raged in the United States as to whether a "missile gap" was opening to the Soviet advantage, and the realization spread in Europe that the core of European security—the American strategic force— had come under threat of direct attack for the first time. Moreover, intercontinental missiles coupled with the hydrogen bomb produced a threat of unprecedentedly swift and destructive character. Western analysts might discount whether this new vehicle could yet reach the United States in very large numbers, but they could not gainsay very impressive Soviet strength against Europe. Hundreds of MRBM's were recognized in the Soviet forces, all capable of striking targets in Europe.[8] They constituted a force capable of saturating all of Western Europe with the various effects of nuclear explosions. In all, the Soviet Union was conceded the capability of inflicting staggering damage on any or all Western societies, and no responsible analyst promised a program to eliminate this capability. This, in substantial part, was the defense problem.

[7] An account of the Red Army during its initial occupation of Berlin in April 1946 can be found in Cornelius Ryan, *The Last Battle* (New York: Simon and Schuster, Inc., 1966).

[8] Public knowledge of strategic force balances has been summarized by the Institute for Strategic Studies (ISS), *The Military Balance, 1962–63*, London, 1962.

By 1960 there was already a substantial legacy of policy which guided responses to the problem. The response to the Soviet threat and to the changing technology of war was well underway, NATO members had already begun to tread different paths, and many seeds of discord sown in the early days of the Cold War had begun to bear fruit.

American Strategic Thought

The United States was quick to affirm that exceedingly rapid development of military technology had become a fixed element of the postwar world. Such familiar objects as radar, jet aircraft, plutonium and hydrogen bombs, nuclear-powered submarines, high-speed digital computers, and ballistic missiles were added to national arsenals during the fifteen years following the close of World War II. To U.S. military planning, this succession of technical achievements imposed sharp changes in the nature of war, which in turn occasioned rapid change in military strategy. In reaction, American military thought underwent a series of changes.

The rapid American demobilization after World War II and the early monopoly over nuclear weapons led to a reliance in the early postwar years on a strategy of bombing in response to attack. The perceived threat, as noted, was the Soviet Army in Europe. In the wake of the experience in Korea, an attempt was made, in the famous doctrine of massive retaliation, to apply the threat of strategic nuclear retaliation against the (Soviet) enemy's homeland to a range of potential military provocations occurring both within and without Europe and including attacks of moderate scale. As Soviet thermonuclear capacity became a reality, however, the concept of deterrence as the core of strategic doctrine was forced to undergo considerable sophistication. The threat of massive destruction from U.S. strategic retaliation was advanced as a means to prevent strategic nuclear attack upon the United States or its NATO allies, but, with a Soviet counterthreat in being, it became a matter of great contention under what circumstances and in what manner U.S. retaliation should occur.

In the process of technical development, war became so destructive that it was soon impossible to imagine any legitimate purposes which it might promote. Nuclear weapons in the U.S.

160

arsenal came to be seen essentially as a means of preventing the enemy from using the ones in his arsenal and of limiting damage to the United States if their use became inevitable. The one clear case where all could agree that a rational man would choose to attack with such weapons was that in which (a) he had become convinced that the other side was unalterably committed to an attack and (b) he had the capability to strike first and thus blunt the attack. Strategic analysts wanted to avoid putting the Soviet Union in that situation. They wanted to avoid getting the United States into it, and above all they wanted to avoid the most extreme variant of it—where the United States could be disarmed if the Soviets attacked first. The conclusion was that the United States forces must be capable of threatening very extensive retaliatory destruction even after absorbing the worst attack the Soviets could muster. The overall incentive was to avoid war to the greatest extent possible—better no attacks at all, and if they should occur, better to make them as small as possible. This counseled delaying massive retaliation to the last possible moment, certainly not unloading it with the first small attack. It also counseled announcing these intentions as broadly and as believably as possible.

This logic made anomaly of the massive retaliation notion as applied to conventional war in Europe. It was very unclear how much of an attack would have to be tolerated or met with other means. Some low-level attacks, however, would have to be suffered without resort to strategic retaliation, and for many the logic seemed to apply to anything short of a full strategic nuclear attack by the Soviet forces. The alliance faced very severe difficulties in coping with the problem. Isolating the threat of strategic nuclear retaliation seemed to expose individual members to low-level attacks. Generalizing that threat seemed to expose the entire alliance to a greater danger of war and therefore a greater danger of unprecedented destruction. There were difficulties in deciding the proper balance internally; there were difficulties in the signals given to the Soviet Union.

The strategic logic affected quite directly the treatment of ground forces in Europe. From the beginning of NATO, it had been politically impossible to admit the ultimate implications of the *de facto* defense strategy; namely, that the Soviet Army would be conceded the ground conquest of Western Europe,

161

while strategic retaliation by the U.S. Air Force was directed against the Soviet Union. Especially the Germans, who viewed the Rhine as an all-too-tempting line of defense, were nervous about the prospect of a conquest and "liberation." The "forward strategy" committing NATO to a ground defense of Germany had been a declared doctrine of NATO from the beginning, although the failure to meet the Lisbon force goals had given it an element of bravado.[9]

When low-yield nuclear weapons became available for use by field armies, the prospect for a real ground defense of Western Europe was apparently opened. Tactical nuclear weapons greatly increased the fire power which a small army could deliver. It was thought that the use of such weapons would enable the outnumbered NATO troops in Europe to prevent offensive concentrations of Soviet troops and thus hold off the horde while the strategic retaliatory attack was being delivered. At its 1956 ministerial meeting, NATO adopted the plan of using tactical nuclear weapons to defend Western Europe—even against a conventional attack. After this decision, tactical forces in Europe were in fact equipped with nuclear weapons. In the case of non-American troops (especially the German Army), the nuclear warheads were controlled by U.S. troops and the delivery vehicles by Allied troops. In the case of war, the warhead would be released by the American President and fired under the orders of the military commander (SACEUR)—by tradition and political reality an American. By the early 1960s, these nuclear-armed tactical forces in Europe had reached very substantial proportions.

This strategy and force structure, featuring tactical nuclear ground defense in Europe and strategic nuclear retaliation against the Soviet Union, was unanimously adopted as official NATO doctrine. Under the leadership of the Supreme Allied Commander, the doctrine of tactical nuclear defense was embodied in NATO force goals and in NATO war plans. As soon as this conception had been promulgated, however, it began to chafe against the changing strategic conceptions which were responding to the new Soviet threat. It was especially significant that the various members of the alliance began to resolve the central dilemmas of the new situation quite differently.

American analysts recognized that the U.S. bomber bases were now vulnerable to sudden attack and that if the Soviets launched

---

[9] Osgood, NATO.

such an attack first, the resulting damage to U.S. forces would greatly hamper the effectiveness of retaliation. It might even bring about the worst case situation—the forces might be so severely damaged that no retaliation at all would be possible. Under the impetus of the first-strike threat, steps were taken to make the U.S. strategic retaliatory forces less vulnerable to damage by such an attack. The difficulties encountered in trying to achieve invulnerability, however, and some of the measures adopted raised with renewed seriousness the question as to what would happen if deterrence failed. The possibilities of a calculated first strike or of accidental war resulting from high-readiness measures made a failure of deterrence a possibility serious enough to worry about.

The adjustment of American strategy was a highly compelling matter. Possessing an intimate knowledge of weapons effects, the Americans began calculating damage to be expected from various types of possible attack. It became clear that levels of damage in terms of lives lost were highly sensitive to total megatonnage which the enemy could deliver and the way in which he delivered it.

If they struck first with a countervalue attack (cities, people, industrial capacity), the Soviets could kill over one hundred million Americans. If they could not deliver a full first strike before retaliation, and if they avoided urban industrial targets and concentrated on U.S. forces, damage might be held under fifty million deaths—still an enormous figure, but also enormously lower than the first.[10] By such calculations, it seemed that millions upon millions of lives depended upon the way in which strategic forces were handled both in peace and in war. The imperfections of protective measures and the incentive to retaliate quickly in some circumstances forced a high state of readiness of strategic forces, but accidental or miscalculated release had to be prevented. Above all, one did not want automatic retaliation, for one desperately wanted to utilize any chance of avoiding destruction by mutual forbearance from attack. This meant that the actual conduct of strategic strikes had to be carefully controlled in the difficult wartime environment. In order to give the Soviets incentive to avoid hitting U.S. cities, the United States had to avoid theirs.

[10] Alain C. Enthoven and K. Wayne Smith, *How Much Is Enough? Shaping the Defense Program, 1961–1969* (New York: Harper & Row, Publishers, 1971), Table 9, p. 189.

Strategy therefore shifted decisively away from massive retaliation against urban-industrial targets in favor of carefully (and centrally) controlled counterforce strikes. The shift posed immense technical difficulties for command/control systems, but the stakes in achieving it appeared to be so high as to stagger the imagination.

Concomitant with the shift in strategic retaliatory strategy was a change in perspective regarding the ground defense of Europe. By 1960, as the shift in American strategy in favor of post-attack, damage-limiting objectives was occurring, the strategy of escalation in Europe was looked upon with increasing disfavor. In the first place, the Soviet Army also had tactical nuclear weapons. War games such as Operation Carte Blanche, played under the assumption that both sides would use such weapons, revealed the very high destructiveness of the sort of war in which both sides used tactical nuclear weapons. It threatened the virtual annihilation of European populations.[11] Moreover, because of the premium on first strike and because of the co-location of Soviet ICBM's and IRBM's, such a war seemed all too likely to escalate to general war. The European arrangements, therefore, seemed accident-prone, and they were not at all what Americans would want if an accident did occur. To the Americans, who had been analyzing the intricate details of nuclear weapons for a decade or more and whose homeland had not been directly attacked in the previous wars of the century (and could not be attacked by the means of similar wars), the possibility that the established NATO strategy might precipitate a general war was conclusive evidence against that strategy. American analysts by 1960 were very interested in the possibility of a conventional defense of Europe, were very skeptical about the value of tactical nuclear weapons, and were very desirous of isolating nuclear weapons in alliance strategy.

European Strategic Thought

In Europe the views differed considerably. The European allies were vulnerable to conventional attack and even to a nuclear strike in a way in which the United States was not. They still had vivid memories of World War II; and the conventional weapons of that war, if less by large multiples than the nuclear weapons of 1960, were quite destructive enough to kill, to maim, and to

[11] Osgood, NATO, p. 126.

164

destroy cities. The subtleties of the nuclear age and the images of horror which it generated were more blurred against this backdrop than they were across the Atlantic. Moreover, the Europeans had had less experience with nuclear weapons, in significant part because of the way in which security on nuclear information had been handled within the alliance as a matter of U.S. policy. The combined effect was that the Europeans weighed the dilemma posed by the Soviet threat quite differently than did the Americans.

With the post-Hitler Germans still necessarily in a low profile in foreign policy and especially in defense matters, and with the British tied by a special history to the United States, European reactions were given their sharpest reflection in France. Of all the profound resonances which the experience of France in World War II and thereafter created in the Paris of 1960, the one which resounded most at the NATO conference was their relation with Britain and the United States regarding their nuclear weapons program and their views on strategic doctrine. The French began their work on nuclear weapons in close cooperation with the British and, under their sponsorship, with the United States. When the Manhattan Project was set up in the United States to pursue with ultimate success the technology of an energy-conversion weapon, a number of French physicists participated, having been brought in by the British team. These French physicists quite naturally had close connection with the prewar leader of atomic research in France, M. Joliot-Curie, and many of them were enlisted by him to join a French atomic energy project beginning in 1945. Joliot-Curie, it turns out, was a member of the French Communist Party and a strong sympathizer with the Soviet Union, and this put relations with the Americans into difficulty right from the start. Though all the allies participating in the Manhattan Project were excluded from its theoretical, technological, and concrete products as American security provisions were clamped down hard, there was a special insistence on it in the case of the French—inspired by the Joliot-Curie connection and promoted by many other irritants as well.[12]

The French began a weapons program on their own in 1945, and with substantial investments after 1954, they had produced a fission bomb by 1960. They had some expectation that once they

[12] Harold L. Nieburg, *Nuclear Secrecy and Foreign Policy* (Washington: Public Affairs Press, 1964), pp. 61–62.

had demonstrated a capacity to produce atomic weapons on their own, they would be readmitted to partnership with the United States for the more advanced stages of weapons technology, including thermonuclear devices. This had been the British experience, and that stood for them as a precedent. In 1958 the Secretary of State, John Foster Dulles, offered to provide information on nuclear submarine propulsion along with the requisite fuel, and that appeared to be the beginning of the process. The Dulles proposal was vitiated, however, by opposition in the United States from the Joint Committee on Atomic Energy, the Congressional watchdog which had set itself astride the road to any agreements for international cooperation. In 1959 the French ambassador in Washington was forewarned that the explosion of a few atomic bombs would not remove U.S. restriction on information.[13] In the same year a contract with a U.S. firm to build a jet engine for the Mirage bomber was canceled, and detailed talks between the French and an American firm regarding solid fuels for missiles were discontinued, in at least the latter case as the result of a U.S. government decision.[14] As the French weapons program came to fruition, the Americans made it clear that the French could not play in the same league as the British.

On its part, France soon refused to cooperate with American programs which had a NATO-wide context. In the same year, 1959, the French refused an American proposal advanced through SACEUR to station IRBM's on French soil with warheads under U.S. control. The French condition—that they be given warheads under their own control—was unacceptable to the United States. Similarly, the French refused to allow the stockpiling of tactical nuclear weapons on French soil. Cycles of intensifying distrust had begun by 1960.

The irritations regarding practical questions of cooperation were exacerbated by growing differences in strategic doctrine. The French took alarm at the development of a Soviet threat to the United States, and proclaimed that never again could the United States guarantee be completely reliable to Europeans. Their thesis, repeatedly articulated, was that the United States would not take risks to defend Europe if its own homeland were at stake. In response to American strategic calculations which

[13] Leonard Beaton and John Maddox, *The Spread of Nuclear Weapons* (New York: Frederick A. Praeger, 1962), p. 88.
[14] Ibid., p. 93f.

pointed out the effects of a relative balance of forces on vulnerability of force components, the French advanced the principle of proportional deterrence. A small force could be made partially invulnerable, they held, and the amount of retaliatory destruction it must assure in order to achieve deterrence would only have to be proportional to the value of the country as an objective.[15] Implicit was the idea that a country which could only afford a small force would naturally be only a small objective to its enemy and that somehow a properly proportioned relationship would be achieved by that level of forces which the country could afford.

The prime element of the French doctrine of deterrence was the principle that the decision to retaliate must be guaranteed by an implacable will to do so. They held that only a national government defending its own territory could exhibit such will.[16] This doctrine was quite distinct from the American view, which analyzed deterrence to be a function of capacity to retaliate after first strike and saw the will to retaliate to be rather directly related to capacity. Since capacity depended very much on relative force levels and on technical characteristics which were expensive, the French view did not fare well in American eyes.

This clash of practical purpose and strategic doctrine between the United States and France had become embedded in a broader conflict of political purpose by 1960. The United States was the natural leader of the alliance, given that its overall strategic strength was the fundamental element in Western security. France, under the leadership of General de Gaulle, resented this preeminence and clearly aspired to equal status within Europe. De Gaulle, in a famous letter to Eisenhower in 1958, had suggested the formation of a tripartite executive committee consisting of France, Great Britain, and the United States. After this initiative was politely rejected, he gradually established an independent course in opposition to the United States and Great Britain, not only on core questions of strategy but also on the full range of foreign policy issues. This raised the possibility that de Gaulle's France would lead continental Europe, especially including the resurgent Germany, into some independent status or

[15] For an exposition of the French view, see Beaton and Maddox, *The Spread of Nuclear Weapons*, and Pierre Gallois, *The Balance of Terror: Strategy for the Nuclear Age* (Boston: Houghton Mifflin Company, 1961).
[16] See especially Gallois, *The Balance of Terror*, for this view.

perhaps into a resurgence of nationalism. Either eventuality would too closely resemble patterns of the past to be acceptable in Washington or London.

Trend Toward Sharing

A third major dimension of the defense problem was the fact that within the United States by 1960 the restrictive policies regarding nuclear technology, which seemed to be a core element in difficulties with the French, were in the midst of a liberalizing trend. From the very beginning of the Manhattan Project there was a strong and quite natural tendency to treat the theoretical and technical knowledge which conferred such enormous destructive power as a matter of the greatest secrecy. The first weapon projects had been exceedingly difficult, and there was hope that these difficulties would stand as substantial barriers against the spread of nuclear technology to potential enemies and/or unreliable states. The desire to prevent the widespread possession of nuclear weapons was universal, and for many that translated quite simply into very tight security. The pertinent knowledge was to be trusted to as few people as possible, and they were to be trustworthy people. Unprecedented destructive capacity required unprecedented caution. In Congress and within the military this view predominated, and virtually everyone concerned had this as a natural instinct.

For some prominent scientists and policy officials concerned with the American nuclear program, however, the issue of secrecy had a second, troublesome dimension. For them, the attempt to control knowledge appeared virtually hopeless in the long run. They saw an inevitability to the diffusion of knowledge; it was in the nature of modern science. They felt that faced with the inevitable it was better not to engage in divisive efforts to prevent it. Rather, it was better to control the application of knowledge to the actual production of destructive weapons. Proponents of this latter view recognized constructive potential in nuclear energy and sought to utilize that as a means of cementing cooperation on the prevention of weapons programs. It was, to say the least, a difficult question, prone to sharp disagreement and productive of emotional, even explosive, politics.[17]

[17] Thomas W. Wilson, Jr., *The Great Weapons Heresy* (Boston: Houghton Mifflin Company, 1970); Philip M. Stern, *The Oppenheimer Case: Security on Trial* (New York: Harper & Row, Publishers, 1969).

The strain toward restrictiveness in handling the nuclear technology was primarily embodied in the McMahon Act of 1946. Nuclear research and development programs, the production and deployment of weapons, and the custody of existing theory, data, and technical knowledge were all given to a special civilian authority, the Atomic Energy Commission, and placed under very restrictive security regulations. Canada and Britain, original partners in the Manhattan Project, were denied access to the knowledge and materials which it produced. The weapons themselves were locked up under AEC control in a central depot and were not distributed to military commanders.

The restrictive strand of atomic energy policy soon came under pressure from scientists and policy officials who feared the consequences of an inevitable process of diffusion. David Lilienthal, first chairman of the AEC, and J. Robert Oppenheimer, director and chief scientist of the Manhattan Project, argued vehemently that international cooperation involving exchange of information on peaceful uses of atomic energy should be sought as an urgent matter. Their views were embodied in the Baruch Plan, which was advanced to the fledgling United Nations. The plan called for an international agency to monopolize nuclear materials and information. The Soviet opposition, which summarily ended the career of the Baruch Plan in 1945, was by most accounts a natural consequence of the U.S. monopoly over the most potent political and military force in the world. That opposition was inevitable enough to render the plan more a gesture for the record than a serious initiative. More consequential reflection of the liberalizing thrust soon appeared, however, in early AEC programs for making radioisotopes and other materials available to worldwide research laboratories and in a series of declassification conferences between the United States, Britain, and Canada.

During the fifties, the restrictive spirit of the McMahon Act was gradually eroded by the liberalizing trend. The restrictive policy reached its zenith early in the decade as the Cold War developed full momentum in the wake of Korea. In 1950 the AEC announced that no information on individual uses of atomic energy would be exchanged with other nations until international control was achieved. This made explicit the desire to prevent even allies from developing nuclear production capabilities. The McCarthy era in the United States followed, as did the celebrated purge of Oppenheimer from high councils of nuclear policy. By

1954, however, Eisenhower announced his Atoms for Peace proposal, reflecting the main ideas of building international cooperation by dissemination of nuclear technology for peaceful purposes. The McMahon Act was revised that year to allow for bilateral agreements of cooperation in order to facilitate the implementation of the Atoms for Peace program. Fissionable materials were allowed to be exported under a system of controls designed to prevent production of weapons material. At first, very tight technical control provisions were established which gave high reliability of catching any diversion of weapons-grade material from peaceful reactors. As the program developed, however, these control measures were eroded because of the political irritation entailed. In negotiating its agreement for cooperation under the program, for example, the European consortium, Euratom, successfully insisted on operating its own inspection system. As the Atoms for Peace program became widespread, and as its tight control procedures were loosened by the pressures of international politics, the amount of nuclear material being processed internationally and the leeway allowed by the control system combined to disseminate, as a practical matter, the capacity to produce weapons-grade material. Thus the restrictive spirit of the McMahon Act was breached not only by the diffusion of information, but very concretely by the diffusion of the material for weapons production.

More extensive consequences soon began to occur as allied nations successfully demonstrated their nuclear capacities by exploding weapons of their own manufacture. The British, the closest ally and the only nation willing to integrate their strategic forces with those of the United States, tested a hydrogen bomb in 1957. In 1958 the McMahon Act was again revised to allow an extensive exchange of information in aid of the British weapons program. This set a precedent, even though the British were at pains to construct their U.S. ties in defense matters as a "special relationship." Beyond that, there was erosion internally as well. The development of long-range striking power in the Soviet Union put great pressure on the U.S. forces to develop a rapid response capability. As a consequence, the dispersions of nuclear warheads from the centralized depots in which they were stored in the early fifties became a virtual necessity. The resulting system, whereby bombs were loaded on planes standing ready for take-off and warheads were attached to missiles ready for firing, is inherently less conservative, from the viewpoint of security, than the earlier system of depots.[18] Though the permissive action link was developed to give positive physical control to the President or some other qualified official, this could not be the same as physical separation of warheads from the weapons which would carry them and the men who would command those weapons.

THE CENTRAL TRADE-OFFS

As NATO ministers met in December of 1960, the legacies of the postwar experience were woven into the political fabric of the institution, yielding a complex pattern still very much under development. The corrosive effects of nuclear arsenals on alliance relationships were apparent. Nations which had long dominated world politics had been eased into subordinate relationships and no longer controlled the forces upon which the defense of their people and sovereign territory rested. Not only did they not control the new weapons, but they did not even understand them very well, even on a relative scale. This was in part the consequence of the U.S. security policies, which withheld from the allies theory, data, and the critical opportunity to think through the central issues at length and in penetrating detail. This arrangement did not square with the tradition of Europe and its historical sense of identity—intangibles easily translated, it was feared, into the concrete forces of internal politics. It did not square either with the new sense of destiny which economic recovery under the aegis of supranational cooperation had inspired. It did not square with the fact that nuclear technology, as some had predicted from the outset, was indeed spreading, and thereby conferring the capacity to make weapons, given the will to do so. The incongruities reflected the existence of underlying trade-offs which had not found an harmonious balance.

Though trade-offs were everywhere in the issues of European defense in 1960, none was so central as the fact that the evolving logic of deterrence, read differently on the two sides of the English Channel, strained those links which the proponents of economic, and ultimately political, cooperation sought to forge. The strong control which the United States sought to impose on its

[18] Irving C. Bupp, a former staff member of the AEC, provides a detailed argument on this point in his unpublished paper, "Nuclear Proliferation," Harvard University, 1967.

own forces and the financial burdens of assuming responsibility for the defense of Europe led all too plausibly to a division of labor which would leave the nuclear deterrent to the United States and conventional forces to the Europeans. Nearly everyone sensed this to be a politically unacceptable solution. Pressure for nationally controlled nuclear forces on the pattern of the British and the French was a development many expected and all feared. To grant the Europeans some control over nuclear weapons was the politically indicated course of action; to deny any dispersion of control was the militarily indicated course. This was the core of the problem which called forth the Herter proposal and which remained the central dilemma of nuclear sharing proposals over the next several years. It was this problem—energized by a fear that miscalculation in either of the subtle dimensions might ultimately bring the terrible consequences of nuclear war—which tangled the foreign policy machinery of the United States government in complexity as we have defined it.

These brief historical sketches give the picture in broad outline —enough to see that the problem confronted is of the variety described above as complex. This can be appreciated in finer detail as we examine the evolution of policy and apply the analysis prepared in theoretical discussions.

CHAPTER 7

The Development of Nuclear Sharing
Proposals: 1956–1960

THE BROAD historical forces which framed the nuclear sharing problem began to generate serious policy proposals and serious occasion for decision after the Suez crisis of 1956. That crisis shook the Western alliance to its foundations and augmented those forces for a revision of defense arrangements which European recovery had spawned. The orbiting of the Soviet Sputnik a year later provided more acceleration, and by the end of Eisenhower's tenure concrete policies had gained impressive momentum. Understanding of the Herter initiative and the subsequent developments requires a look in some detail at the post-Suez period, for it was in those years that the general, historical themes of policy were translated into a concrete set of action proposals. After 1956 political stakes became tangibly real, and the day-to-day interests of the policy machinery became more directly engaged. This means that a more fine-grained analysis is required to understand what was occurring.

At Suez, Britain and France consorted to use force against Egypt, and out of their sense of necessity they acted independently and without the knowledge of the United States. Eisenhower's government, they calculated, would have vetoed the project if given advance notice. The military capacities of the two European allies were such that they could not pull off an occupation of the Suez Canal without U.S. backing. What was to have been a *fait accompli* became a political fumble; the swift and decisive move envisaged was executed in slow motion and exposed to countermoves while still short of its objective. The Soviet Union, while smashing the Hungarian uprising with one hand, threatened the British and French with nuclear reprisal on the other. With the chips down, the United States, rather than screening the ineptly exposed Suez operation, quietly strangled it by bringing severe financial pressure to bear on the British pound. In all, the Soviets played very tough and won, both in Eastern Europe and in Suez. The British and the French tried to play tough and

173

demonstrated weakness instead. In the brutal world of international politics they lost badly, and each learned in the process to mistrust the other. The United States, the powerful ally who might have rescued them, rather let them stew in their own mischief. In the aftermath, the Western alliance was split, and rancor was high on both sides of the Atlantic and of the Channel.

The general significance of the crisis was understood thereafter in various ways. To some, notably the French, there was a renewed insistence on national independence, and this translated quickly into the demands for strategic weapons. Within the State Department there was a strong feeling that precisely this could not be allowed to happen. At high levels of the American and the politically altered British governments, chagrin was dominated by a cool realization that a reconciliation was necessary, that the alliance would have to be knit back together. All these reactions set major forces in motion which subsequently concentrated on the question of who would control the nuclear weapons protecting the alliance.

THE MAJOR POLICY THEMES

The French came to the NATO meeting in December of 1956 proclaiming the necessity of possessing their own deterrent forces and issuing strong demands that they be given control over nuclear weapons—with General de Gaulle more than a year away from power. The main business of the meeting was the adoption of a NATO political directive prescribing a strategy of using nuclear retaliation at the outset of any attack, rather than yielding European territory. The French, angry in the aftermath of Suez and chafing under the discrimination they had experienced all along, demanded national control as the only means of assuring that such retaliation would in fact occur.

The American reply, delivered through General Lauris Norstad, the newly appointed SACEUR, affirmed the principle of nuclear sharing within the alliance. In Washington, in discussions predating the crisis, there had been concern regarding the growing Soviet missile threat, and a need was felt to arm the alliance in similar fashion. The United States weapons program was already producing weapons with a wide range of explosive power, thereby diversifying the potential military uses. In the "new look" policy which the Eisenhower administration had been develop-

ing, there was an emphasis on utilizing these new weapons designs to reap economic gains in the defense effort. Nuclear fire
power was to be substituted for conventional fire power in the
general-purpose forces, thus, it was argued, reducing manpower
requirements and allowing the United States to match Soviet
conventional strength, as then calculated, on economically acceptable terms. The corollary was that NATO forces would become much more involved with nuclear weapons; and, with the
Soviet missile threat developing against Europe, it was logical to
envisage NATO arrangements covering weapons of strategic
range. All this made it easy in the post-Suez situation to advance
the principle of nuclear sharing as a path to reconciliation within
the alliance. This Norstad did in a speech to the NATO Council:

> Our thinking . . . for the 1960–1965 period calls for broaden-
> ing considerably the base of our atomic capability. That means
> we would like an atomic delivery capacity available to more
> types of commands and to the forces of more countries.[1]

The concrete idea which stood behind the Norstad presentation was that of a nuclear weapons stockpile in Europe. Under
the arrangements of the stockpile, allied troops would be given
delivery systems capable of firing nuclear weapons. The United
States would stockpile the appropriate warheads in Europe and
would deliver the warheads to allied troops "in time of emer-
gency."[2] This notion was the result of compromise on the American side. Military planners had seriously considered directly providing the allies with both missiles and warheads as a logical
extension of liberalization of weapons control in the United
States. The Joint Committee on Atomic Energy, however, was already pulling in the reins after the McMahon Act revision of
1954. The previous year (1955) members of the committee had
attempted to block an agreement with the British to provide information on nuclear propulsion for submarines and had been
outmaneuvered by the executive branch. Desirous of reexerting
their control, they promised political trouble over any sharing arrangements, and Suez strengthened their hand. The stockpile
concept was the compromise.[3] It put delivery systems into the

[1] Lauris M. Norstad, speech, *NATO Letter*, December 1956, p. 37.
[2] Ibid.
[3] See the article by Jack Raymond, *New York Times*, February 16, 1957,
p. 1.

hands of allies and still retained U.S. custody over nuclear warheads by means of a "dual key" arrangement. Under its provisions, the United States would retain a veto over the firing of any
weapon supplied to an ally.

The nuclear stockpile idea was swift in execution. By early
1957 the British and American defense ministers had worked out
an agreement embodying the concept.[4] In March of 1957 Eisenhower and Macmillan agreed to the sale by the United States to
Britain of sixty Thor missiles (1500-mile range), to be operated
by the RAF and fired by means of a dual key mechanism.[5] That
was in itself a sign that policy on sharing was evolving, and a further sign was soon available—the original concept began to be
elaborated.

For his part, Norstad, representing the NATO machinery, soon
transcended the original stockpile idea. Surveying NATO defense needs in 1957, he articulated the thesis that NATO required
a force of medium-range ballistic missiles (MRBM's), a delivery
system not envisaged in the stockpile compromise. His argument
was twofold. In part he reached back to the old military concept
of a "theater balance." Pointing to the growing force of Soviet
missiles capable of hitting Europe but not the United States, he
argued that NATO must have an offsetting missile force in Europe. Simultaneously, he argued the need for modernization of
the already existing NATO forces. He expressed the fear that
NATO tactical interdiction forces were becoming obsolete in the
face of developing Soviet technology, and he repeatedly emphasized that these forces would have to be replaced with ballistic
missiles. Missiles, he argued, would be required in the very near
future (1961–1965) in order to penetrate to the important interdiction targets; that is, the forces under his command would have
to be equipped with missiles in the future if they were to continue to perform the mission already assigned. The conjunction
of arguments made it very clear that Norstad wanted effective
control as NATO commander over weapons of strategic range
which would be based in Europe. Thus the MRBM requirement

[4] Ibid.
[5] Raymond Dawson and Richard Rosecrance, "Theory and Reality in the
Anglo-American Alliance," in *World Politics*, vol. 19 (October 1966), p. 42.
See also *New York Times*, February 16, 1957, p. 1, and December 11, 1957,
p. 1.

projected a reasonably concrete plan for nuclear sharing with the NATO organization.

Norstad's position was a natural one for a military commander. Faced with responsibility for the defense of Europe, he wanted all the forces necessary to conduct that defense to be at his disposal. His was also a weighty opinion. In his role as commander of the American forces, he could call upon the established tradition in the American military that a theater commander be given what he says he needs, if at all possible. The traditional autonomy of the theater commander was strengthened in his case by his simultaneous status, his "second hat," as an international officer and by the close ties to European governments which that brought as a practical matter. The American government, though heavily invested, did not wholly own SACEUR, and that made him all the more valuable and popular in European capitals. His proposal for a NATO MRBM system was destined to give serious impetus to the business of nuclear sharing.

A separate line of development on the diplomatic side soon added a new dimension and gave different emphasis to the nuclear stockpile idea, again as an evolutionary extension of the original compromise. In July of 1957 Secretary of State Dulles advanced the stockpile concept as a political matter. Even if there should be an agreement to cease production of fissionable material, he argued, there would have to be a deterrent force in Europe based upon nuclear weapons:

> We do not ourselves want to be in a position where our allies are wholly dependent upon us. We don't think this is a healthy relationship. Therefore, we are studying ways whereby through perhaps a NATO stockpile of weapons and various arrangements of that sort, there can be assurances to our allies that if they are attacked, if war comes, they will not be in a position of suppliants, as far as we are concerned, for the use of atomic weapons.[6]

Dulles further elaborated that he thought the proposed stockpile "would be an act of confidence which would strengthen the fellowship of the North Atlantic Community." On the following day President Eisenhower corroborated the sentiments of his Secre-

[6] Transcript of news conference, *New York Times*, July 17, 1957, p. 6.

tary. What Dulles was saying was that the nuclear stockpile idea was to be a mechanism of policy responsive to political objectives. Leaving Norstad to make the military argument for the same proposed arrangements, Dulles saw in the NATO stockpile a means of unifying an organization beset by the divisive effects of dependent relationships.

The nuclear stockpile concept came to fruition at the NATO Council meeting in December of 1957, attended not only by the foreign ministers but by the heads of government as well. The communiqué of the meeting, which revealed a stockpile agreement, reflected General Norstad's calculus:

> The Soviet leaders . . . have made it clear that the most modern and destructive weapons including missiles of all kinds are being introduced into the Soviet armed forces. . . .
>
> . . . We are . . . resolved to achieve the most effective pattern of NATO military offensive strength, taking into account the most recent development in weapons and techniques.
>
> To this end NATO has established stocks of nuclear warheads which will be readily available for the defense of the allies in case of need. In view of the present Soviet policies in the field of new weapons, the Council has also decided that intermediate range ballistic missiles will have to be put at the disposal of the Supreme Allied Commander, Europe.[7]

As SACEUR, General Norstad was given the responsibility for working out details.

But again the Council was meeting in the wake of a major international event, this time the orbiting of two Soviet earth satellites, the first in history, in October of 1957. The resulting dramatization of Soviet military progress and of the fact that the United States itself was soon to be vulnerable to attack caused further discomfiture among the allies and renewed their demands for nuclear weapons of their own. In the United States, where Sputnik had an even greater effect than in Europe, there was increased responsiveness to these demands. Under these conditions of political pressure, Dulles and Eisenhower apparently expanded their political calculus to cover not only the nuclear stockpile but also the second aspect of Norstad's program—namely, the MRBM. As noted in the communiqué above, the heads of government agreed to make medium-range missiles

[7] *New York Times*, December 20, 1957, p. 8.

available to SACEUR. President Eisenhower offered to give the allies technical information on ballistic missiles and nuclear-powered submarines.

There was an undeniable military element in this move, for Sputnik had convinced the Americans of the need to bolster the deterrent forces. Since the only available U.S. missiles were IRBM's, they would have to be stationed in Europe to reach the Soviet Union, and the heads of government meeting paved the way for such missile emplacements. However, they also mixed this with a response to political demands. Dulles talked vaguely of a second-generation system to follow the IRBM in Europe, even though by then the American ICBM and Polaris systems would be available, thus removing the military need for European placements. The Eisenhower-Dulles views were also reflected in the December 1957 communiqué:

> As regards defense production we have decided in view of the progress already made to take further measures within NATO to promote coordination of research, development and manufacture of modern weapons, including intermediate range ballistic missiles.
> . . . Those NATO countries whose programs have already reached a very advanced state have offered to share with their allies significant production techniques and results of their research work in order to stimulate a truly productive effort in the defense production field.[8]

Thus, major themes were introduced into the continuing deliberation within the alliance. The control over nuclear weapons, meaning both warheads and missile delivery systems, was to be devolved in some fashion within the alliance in response both to military requirements as conceived by the NATO commander and to political requirements as conceived by Eisenhower's Secretary of State. The dramatics of Suez and Sputnik had set policy in motion, and a decision process began to wind through various choice points.

THE GENESIS OF PROPOSALS

The proposals made within the NATO machinery in December of 1957 clearly enough implied that the allies would be given the

[8] Ibid.

capacity to produce weapons, that there was no longer any question of avoiding an attempt to amend the McMahon Act, as had been hoped the year before. In January of 1958 the administration submitted proposals to Congress for new authority to transmit to the European allies information and materials pertinent to nuclear weapons. The proposals were to authorize, among other things, the transmission of weapons design information, of information regarding nuclear ship propulsion, and of fuels for ship propulsion reactors. Robert Murphy, in testifying for the administration at the Congressional hearings, connected these arrangements to the policy themes articulated earlier:

> . . . I am advised that under the Atomic Energy Act as presently written it is not possible to attain full effectiveness in the training and operational planning necessary for full NATO readiness and effectiveness. I wish to emphasize the *political* importance of improving this situation. It is of major importance to the security of the United States and to the unity and resolution of the free world that our allies have confidence in their ability to meet aggression swiftly and effectively. To have this confidence they must have not only modern military equipment but also the full knowledge and training which are requisite for effective action. [emphasis added][9]

Again the administration argument held that it was of political importance to the United States to meet demands which the allies advanced on military grounds. This time there was elaboration of the argument revealing the workings of American fears which had been jangled in the Suez and Sputnik crises. The essential political calculus, Murphy explained, held that "if NATO is furnished a nuclear capacity on a cooperative basis, there will be less incentive to additional countries to enter the atomic weapons field."

The main military purpose of the proposals advanced by the Eisenhower administration was the strengthening of NATO "shield" forces—i.e., those forces stationed in Europe whose theoretical mission was to hold the line in Europe while the strategic retaliatory forces of the United States were providing the mechanism of victory. Under the official strategic concept approved in May 1957, NATO war plans featured immediate reliance on nu-

[9] U.S. Congress, Joint Committee on Atomic Energy, *Hearings Amending the Atomic Energy Act of 1954*, 85th Congress, 2nd Session, 1958, p. 93.

clear weapons even in response to conventional attack. The nuclear weapons were intended for use on the battlefield against short-range interdiction targets. The nuclear stockpile was meant to be an American-controlled system of supply for allied troops equipped to handle such weapons. These weapons were "tactical" in the military lexicon. Eisenhower and Dulles at the Paris Council meeting, however, had also evidenced a willingness to cooperate with allied interests in strategic weapons systems. The proffered information on nuclear submarines was, at the time, the most concrete exemplification; but vague references were also made to a second-generation missile replacing the original IRBM. It was consistent with the political doctrine of reducing European dependence that the allies also be given a role in the main business of defense—the strategic weapons which formed the NATO "sword."

As might be expected, the moves toward liberalized sharing provisions in 1957 were opposed again by those who had opposed them in 1956, and in fact the thrust of the administration's position in 1958 was blunted by opposition from the JCAE. The members of the Joint Committee still adhered with vehemence to their accustomed policy of tight security, and they sought to inhibit the dissemination of nuclear technology. There was a revision of the McMahon Act in 1958, but the provisions for the nuclear weapons stockpile for NATO were granted only under tight, exclusively American control. The information authorized for transmission to the allies was of minimal nature, enough to allow troops to fit the warheads on their delivery vehicles and to fire the weapons. The only authorization for transmission of substantial information, including some aspects of weapons design, was applied exclusively to Britain; and the committee, in exerting power of review over executive implementation, virtually guaranteed that Britain would continue to be the sole benefactor. Bowing to the inevitable, Dulles' offer to the French regarding information on nuclear ship propulsion was dropped.

Congress, however, as a chronically distracted institution, had considerable difficulty keeping up with executive machinery once it was put in motion. Enough was done on the nuclear stockpile in 1958 to provide a mandate for that machinery to begin implementation, and this process in subsequent years gradually provided allied troops assigned to NATO, particularly the Germans, with a large number of weapons systems—largely tactical aircraft and short-range missiles equipped with American-controlled nuclear warheads. The details of control varied, but it is clear that the American control was very tenuous for some of the weapons. When members of the JCAE went to Europe to inspect the arrangements in 1960, they found fighter aircraft loaded with nuclear bombs sitting on the edge of runways with German pilots inside the cockpits and starter plugs inserted. The embodiment of control was an American officer somewhere in the vicinity with a revolver. The enraged committee precipitated the installation of radio locks called permissive action links (PAL's). Thereafter it required the deliberate act of the President to arm the weapons. Even with this provision, however, it is clear that the stockpile agreement put a large, nuclear-armed force with enormous explosive power in the hands of the allies. Thus, though the committee blocked some of Eisenhower's offers relating to weapons systems of strategic range, and though it continued sharp restrictions on the degree to which the allies could be informed about nuclear weapons systems, it acquiesced in provisions which eventually provided NATO allies with large forces of "tactical" range systems.

There was motion in Europe as well. The pressures of domestic opposition which induced restraint on the tendencies of the Eisenhower administration toward sharing of weapons systems did not operate to the same extent on General Norstad and his planning staff at SHAPE. Given prime responsibility for working out the details of the 1957 communiqué, Norstad soon was working from a three-part proposal. The first aspect involved the placement of Thor and Jupiter IRBM's in NATO countries under some variation of the "dual key" arrangement. This arrangement was the subject of a U.S.–U.K. agreement in February of 1958 and was carried by Norstad as a proposal to other allied countries, including France, but apparently not including West Germany.[10]

[10] At this point and others below an obvious question of evidence arises. The problem of documenting the facts needed to conduct a penetrating analysis of critical decisions on nuclear sharing is obviously complicated by the fact that a great deal of the pertinent information remains under security classification. In conducting research, I was not given and did not request authorization for direct access to the classified record. It was impossible to do the research from the public record alone, however, even though the public record was indispensable. I approached the problem, as other scholars have, through interviews with persons who did have access to the critical policy documents and were willing to talk about them. The price of such a

When the French demanded aid to their independent national force as a condition for even allowing weapons stockpiles on French soil, Norstad refused to cooperate and dropped the idea of putting IRBM's in France. Eventually he secured placements in Italy and Turkey as well as in Britain, but the British would not agree to assign their missiles to SACEUR, arguing significant-

---

procedure is that the persons providing accurate information invariably did not want to be known as a source and agreed to provide information only if that condition were granted. In order to make this procedure as responsive as I could to the ideal of pure, open scholarship, I have adopted the following rules:

1) I have asserted something as fact only if it has been corroborated by more than one source and not contradicted by any.

2) I have referenced the public record whenever it was accurate and pertinent in the light of the information I had available.

3) In conducting interviews I went to some effort to establish in general terms the content of critical policy documents, their authors, and the approximate date of their preparation. The discussion at this point and elsewhere repeatedly refers to such documents and gives a précis of their arguments as best I could ascertain them. Hence when the classified record eventually becomes available, the account of events developed here can be checked against what these documents actually say.

Fortunately, the questions which were important for the current analysis concerned matters of general policy and political judgment whose public discussion after the event does not compromise national security, and hence officials with access to the record were generally quite willing to make it known. The detailed characteristics of weapons systems and of military operations which are germane to the current discussion were taken entirely from the public record.

There is good reason to believe that the account here and elsewhere of classified proceedings internal to the government is accurate. Obviously it must be qualified, however, according to whatever degree of belief the reader is willing to ascribe in the light of the procedure. Since such qualification is implicit in the entire discussion, I have avoided constant repetition of such phrases as "apparently," "reportedly," "according to reliable sources," "it is generally alleged," etc. Where such phrases have been included it is not a sign that my own confidence in the facts is relatively less, but rather a means of suggesting that the most naturally imputed (and therefore most obviously reliable) sources for the information are not necessarily the ones actually used. At points in the narrative where I judged the actual situation to be quite uncertain, I have stated that fact directly.

Henceforth reference will be made simply to "interview material." A memorandum on the interview material for this book has been deposited in the John F. Kennedy Library in Waltham, Massachusetts. It will be made available to any person with a legitimate scholarly interest in checking the sources.

ly that this was inappropriate, given that the weapons had a strategic role. These missiles were the relatively primitive first-generation weapons, vulnerable to sabotage and direct attack, which subsequently came to fame in the Cuban crisis of 1962. They were not acceptable to Norstad as fulfillment of his MRBM requirement—even for the 1960–1965 period.

Hence the second part of the proposals called for the United States to give blueprints for missile delivery systems to an agency designated and controlled by NATO, probably a consortium of the major allies. The weapons, to be produced in Europe, would presumably relieve the United States of some of the costs of arming NATO. More important, however, the proposal was understood as a first step toward giving the allies a nuclear capability by arming not the individual countries but the NATO military apparatus. As seen at SHAPE at the time, where all nuclear planning was done by British and American officers, this proposal was "anticipatory" of the requirements (and demands) of the Europeans.

The third part of the plan envisaged the design and development of subsequent-generation delivery systems by the established consortium. Taken as a whole, the proposals outlined a plan for the controlled dissemination of the technology of advanced delivery systems. NATO as such would be the recipient, though it is unclear the degree to which NATO could dominate national interests, should the third phase come about.

Having secured the Jupiter and Thor placements as a temporary measure, SHAPE planners focused their interest on the Polaris system as an acceptable answer to the MRBM requirement during the early sixties. During 1959 negotiations were conducted at SHAPE between the United States, the United Kingdom, France, and Germany. In June of that year a "compromise" proposal was circulated which would allow interested NATO countries to develop and to produce an IRBM to NATO specifications. Warheads for such missiles were to be supplied under the stockpile arrangement, and operational control would be assigned to SACEUR. After NATO needs had been met, participating countries under this plan were to be allowed to continue production for their own purposes, and the United States would still be committed to supplying warheads. This plan apparently had both French and German approval.

Then, in August, in the United States, the President's Committee to Study the United States Military Assistance Program (known as the Draper Committee after its chairman, U.S. NATO Ambassador William Draper) argued in its report that it was of "strategic significance" that the NATO allies have at their disposal mobile, solid-propellant IRBM's. What the committee had in mind was Polaris, and most of its members supported the idea of European production. Polaris was a premium weapon of the developing American arsenal. The characteristics which made it a good weapon for submarines would also allow land mobility. Its range was sufficient to reach deep into the Soviet Union from Western Europe. If deployed in Western Europe, Polaris would go far toward making NATO a first-order nuclear power. With this in mind, plans were derived in SHAPE for a mobile, land-based Polaris system which would be camouflaged in trucks and railroad cars, and would be able to fire from the roadside on reasonably short notice. This proposal to place Polaris on the Continent was then made to the allies at the NATO Council meeting in December of 1959.

During 1960, designs for the land-mobile Polaris system were taken to Europe and shown to the allies. The discussions, which stimulated considerable interest, centered on the idea of European production, and the impression was conveyed that the consortium under NATO which Norstad had proposed would manufacture the land-mobile Polaris in accordance with the design specifications developed in the United States. The consortium would be allowed to manufacture enough weapons to meet SACEUR's requirement.[11] The complete details of control over the system were not specified, but it was clear that the intentions were that SACEUR would operate the force, target it as an integral element of NATO war plans, and probably give the immediate firing command, under Presidential authorization. The idea was presented to the NATO defense ministers in April of 1960.

This proposal that the allies manufacture the land-mobile

[11] This requirement is variously given at from 300 to 700 missiles. Charles Murphy gives the top figure in his authoritative account, "NATO at a Nuclear Crossroads," in *Fortune*, vol. 66 (December 1962), pp. 85–88. C. L. Sulzberger in the *New York Times*, June 25, 1960, p. 20, gives the low figure. Norstad himself apparently used the range 300 to 600.

Polaris—and the design for the Polaris which accompanied the proposal—apparently raised a good deal of interest among the Europeans, including the Germans. The French, however, imposed a similar condition to that imposed on the stockpile and the 1959 compromise plan; namely, that some part of the weapons be given to them for their national requirements.[12] Although this condition by virtue of its unacceptability to the American administration stalled the proposal, discussions and staff work at low levels were still in progress when the Kennedy administration took office.[13]

On the political side, there was a continuing debate over the role of the allied governments in defense arrangements. The French kept this topic alive with a series of difficult demands, beginning especially with the accession of de Gaulle to power in 1958. De Gaulle, meeting Dulles in July of that year, complained about the discrimination against France implicit in the Anglo-American arrangements, and he let it be known that France would not accept the IRBM's or the weapons stockpiles on French soil unless there was direct aid to the independent French deterrent force.[14] The French President delivered a sequel to this in the form of his famous letter to Eisenhower and Macmillan suggesting a three-nation directorate for NATO with expanded powers of policy review, thus demanding in effect French political equality with the "Anglo-Saxon" nations in the determination of Western policies.[15] Germany, pointedly, was not to be included. Again de Gaulle demanded aid to the French national force as a condition for participation in the proposed production consortium for the land-mobile Polaris.

Though French demands were refused both by the Eisenhower administration and by Norstad as SACEUR, they were not tendered without effect. The administration again began discussions about giving nuclear weapons into allied control. The JCAE were sufficiently alarmed in February of 1960 that they had called in representatives of State, Defense, and the AEC to testify on plans to provide the allies with nuclear weapons.[16] On

---

[12] *New York Times*, June 25, 1960, p. 20.
[13] Interview material.
[14] *New York Times*, July 5, 1958, p. 1, and July 6, 1958, p. 1.
[15] *New York Times*, October 26, 1958, p. 40.
[16] *New York Times*, February 3, 1960, p. 1.

the very next day, Eisenhower stated at a press conference that he favored a revision in the McMahon Act to enable the allies to receive weapons of U.S. manufacture. He commented:

> But when the Soviets have the information and know-how to do things, it is pretty hard for me to understand why we don't do something with our allies, as long as they are with us in defending against the probably aggressive intent of Communism.[17]

Again picking up the political concerns of 1957, those activated by Suez and Sputnik, he said:

> . . . we want allies to be treated as partners and allies and not as junior members of a firm who are to be seen and not heard.[18]

Eisenhower's comments generated a domestic political squall highlighted by JCAE chairman Holifield's threat of massive and obstructive opposition,[19] and administration spokesmen quickly fled the exposed position. Herter denied any concrete intentions for sharing of weapons, and Eisenhower himself backed off from his position in a note to Soviet Premier Nikita Khrushchev sent in April. However, Norstad kept a variant of the idea alive from his outpost in Europe. When he testified before the JCAE in March of 1960, he raised as an "idea for discussion rather than a firm proposal" the alternative of making NATO a "multilateral fourth nuclear power."[20]

Events in Europe would not let the discussion die under JCAE opposition. In the summer of 1960 de Gaulle shocked West German Chancellor Adenauer during regularly scheduled discussions by opposing integration within NATO. Integration within NATO was at the time the prescriptive policy rubric under which nearly all German disaffections with Western military arrangements had been gathered. Most German grievances were to be solved either as a result of, or together with, further integration in the alliance. De Gaulle's remark thus cut to the core of the German position. In September Adenauer met with Norstad, Paul Henri Spaak of Belgium, and Dirk Stikker, NATO General

---

[17] *New York Times*, February 4, 1960, p. 1.
[18] Ibid.
[19] *New York Times*, February 10, 1960, p. 4.
[20] *New York Times*, March 11, 1960, p. 1.

Secretary, to register his alarm, and the four proposed to push the NATO stockpile (undoubtedly understood in its expanded sense) as a means of reviving integration.[21] They agreed to send Spaak to Washington to argue the case; but by the time he arrived, the State Department, beginning to surface the fears it harbored, had entered the discussion.

THE BOWIE REPORT

The development of the proposal for meeting SACEUR's MRBM requirement with the Polaris, especially the variation under which Polaris would be manufactured in Europe, had provoked some furrowed brows in the Policy Planning Council at the State Department. Gerard Smith, Assistant Secretary of State for Policy Planning, did not approve of the degree of access to weapons already granted the Germans with the introduction of "tactical" nuclear weapons into the NATO forces.[22] If the French were becoming insistent about national control of strategic nuclear weapons, the Germans, it seemed, would soon follow. When the projected Polaris arrangement resulted in allied desires to use production facilities in part for national requirements, and especially when the Germans displayed interest in the proposals, the State Department planners began to see a distinct threat.[23]

In the spring of 1960 Smith contracted a study of NATO defense arrangements from his predecessor in office, Robert Bowie. Bowie addressed the study to the defense needs of the alliance, and the resulting report featured two major proposals.[24] The first recommended strengthening the conventional forces within NATO. The purpose was to enable an adequate response to medium-level conventional attacks on Europe, a response which would not automatically require nuclear weapons. The second proposal advocated the creation of a NATO strategic nuclear force consisting of submarines with Polaris missiles, to be placed under direct NATO command.

The first of these proposals directed itself at the question of what to do in Europe with an attack in which the enemy used only conventional weapons. An all-out conventional attack was still felt to be a proper occasion for nuclear retaliation. However,

[21] Article by C. L. Sulzberger, *New York Times*, November 23, 1960, p. 28.
[22] Interview material.　　　　[23] Interview material.
[24] Interview material.

it was felt that the threat of strategic nuclear retaliation would not reliably deter such attacks, given the rough parity in strategic weapons then perceived between the U.S.S.R. and the United States. Thus, greater conventional forces were required to meet such attacks in their own terms. Similarly, parity between the superpowers was seen as reducing the willingness of European nations to rely completely on the U.S. strategic deterrent forces. As long as the United States itself was vulnerable to attack, European nations would not count on the United States to retaliate for attacks directed solely at Europe. Bowie foresaw two possible responses to these fears: (1) independent, nationally controlled strategic weapons of the sort that the British and the French were constructing, and (2) a collective force controlled by the European allies as a whole. He rejected the former as dangerous and unproductive in military terms, and he recommended the latter.

The collective force envisaged in Bowie's report was to be created in the first instance by assigning a substantial number of U.S. strategic weapons, such as the Polaris submarine, to SACEUR with advance authorization to fire the weapons in case of a "major" nuclear attack on Europe (i.e., on an alliance member). In more ambiguous cases of attack, the North Atlantic Council would authorize firing and the United States would commit itself to concur. In the event that the European nations desired more active control of forces, Bowie recommended the subsequent creation of a multilateral strategic force as a follow-on to the forces of American submarines, should the Europeans desire it. As preconditions, the units of this force were to be manned by elements of the armed forces of at least three nations to prevent a single nation from confiscating them for a national force. Also as a precondition, the participating nations would have to agree on a mechanism of control—how to decide to fire the weapons—if it should come to that. This second-phase arrangement, explicitly conceived of as a favor to the Europeans, was the first form of the multilateral force idea.

The argument for the collective force and the original elements in the Bowie study made it rather clear that it was in substantial part directed against the liberalization of weapons control. The major argument was that the collective force would prevent the development of national nuclear weapons programs, and it was specifically stated that such a force would be a more effective safeguard against national forces than the land-based Polaris program which Norstad had developed for his MRBM requirements. The risks which the collective force entailed—primarily those arising from a relinquishing of sole Presidential command authority through national channels—were thought to be less than those entailed in putting weapons in "host" countries with only SACEUR to stop undesirable and unauthorized uses of the weapons. To shore up the argument, a further precondition to creation of the force was established. NATO would simultaneously have to have upgraded its conventional forces so that its overall posture would not commit it to any earlier use of nuclear forces than the United States was committed to.

It was not hard to read behind the language, which spoke of national nuclear forces and confiscation of weapons by host countries, to reach the State Department's fear of arrangements under which nuclear weapons came under German command. The nuclear stockpile arrangements had already done this for weapons of "tactical" range, and SACEUR's MRBM requirement promised to do it for weapons of strategic range, capable of striking the Soviet Union. In providing a substitute for SACEUR's plans, Bowie gave his former colleagues in the Department of State a constructive position from which to do battle against the trend. That was the prime need of the moment, that was the purpose of the summer study in State's eyes, that was what Secretary Herter took to the NATO Council in December. His initiative preempted that planned by Norstad, Adenauer, Spaak, and Stikker, and it gave the collective force idea an official diplomatic status. Whether acting from his own conviction or under the impetus of the planning apparatus underneath him, Herter delivered in his December speech the first counterattack, from within the executive, in what was forming up as a classic bureaucratic battle over policy on weapons control.

Insufficiently noticed at the time was the fact that Bowie delivered a much larger package than the proposal which Herter used. His collective force idea was embedded in a broad context of policy. Emphasis was given to the role of the dynamic European nations in fostering worldwide development, and images were sketched portraying political unity in Europe as a necessary means of strengthening Europe for the burdens of world leadership. Bowie was an established figure in the movement for

European integration. In the early 1950s he had been General Counsel and Special Adviser to the United States High Commissioner for Germany, and in this capacity he had been influential in mediating between the negotiators of the Schuman Plan (the European Coal and Steel Community) and the leaders of German industry. In 1952 he had participated in a study commission set up by Paul Henri Spaak to examine the idea of a European constitution. These events had a great deal to do with setting the character of his career and forging the assumptions he brought to bear on European issues. The collective force idea was enmeshed, therefore, in this context. Prudently sensitive to the demands of his clients in giving them something concrete, Bowie was nonetheless operating far beyond the needs of the moment. One notices such things in hindsight as early hints of how the issue was to be transformed.

THEORETICAL PERSPECTIVES

Though properly doubtful that the full significance of the Bowie report could have been grasped at the time, one nonetheless may aspire to some general understanding which would systematize the wisdom of hindsight and allow the penetration of subtle clues in subsequent situations. Since this is the central purpose of the study, it is fair to interrupt the historical narrative for a moment to note the diverging explanations for the course of events up to December of 1960 and the conflict in expectations which would have emerged, had the various analytic perspectives been applied at that point to predict what would happen thereafter.

When John Kennedy assumed the Presidency in January of 1961, the decision process on the sharing of control over strategic nuclear weapons had long since begun; but it had not yet produced a major resolution, a coherent policy, or a stable program. It was up to Kennedy to produce that resolution if he could, and precisely therein lies the analytic utility of the situation. The development of the issue within the alliance after 1956 allows an initial reading of the forces engaged in the problem. The turnover in the policy machinery which Kennedy produced—a new set of actors, a new set of assumptions and predictions at the top of government—provided the sort of break in the decision sequence which an experimenting scientist would like to produce,

191

had he the capacity to do so. Failing (inevitably) the capacity to run serious policy-making processes in a laboratory, the analyst looks to naturally occurring situations of this sort which approximate experimental conditions. Given that such conditions seem to have existed with the transition from Eisenhower to Kennedy, the evolution of policy on strategic sharing after 1960 can be treated as data for testing and analyzing the hypothesis which could have been advanced at the point of transition. Though, because of the use of hindsight, the exercise is not truly an experiment, at a minimum the careful analysis of the sequence of events which the experimental logic demands is likely to drive historical understanding deeper than it would otherwise go. Even the very rough approximations to the experimental method which can be achieved in these "natural experiments" promise to be useful.

The analytic paradigm sees in the situation facing Kennedy a classic two-value trade-off problem. On the one hand, the sovereign dignity of European nations seemed to require that they have some control over the means of their own defense and over policies which exposed them to potentially annihilating dangers. However, the exigencies of war in the nuclear age seemed to require sophistication of weapons design and deployment, and meticulous operational control. Only the United States could afford forces of the size and character required, and only the United States could make and execute the central operational decision within the exceedingly narrow time constraints believed to be entailed in war. This presented a central output trade-off. One objective dictated a devolution of operational control over nuclear weapons; the other just as clearly mandated a centralization of control in the hands of the United States. Though individual actors might define other values affected by the issue, none would have the force of these two, both of which were anchored in deep histories and intractable features of the European situation.

The analytic paradigm expects a balancing of these competing objectives and, over time, a rather searching evaluation of the central features of the calculations. Before risking a loss of control of nuclear forces in a serious crisis, a decision maker operating analytically would want to be very sure of the political stakes involved. Any change in the political situation which degraded the payoff gained from nuclear sharing could be expected to produce shifts in support away from that option. The strong expectation of the analytic paradigm would be that the United States decision makers would take actions well short of an actual devolution of operational control, the point at which the military risks presumably begin to increase sharply.

This analysis would see some sense in Bowie's initial proposal, understood in restrictive terms. A force of weapons assigned from the U.S. strategic forces and still under U.S. operational control would nominally belong to NATO. The possibility of actual sharing of control would be dangled before those who desired it, but it would be promised at a future date and surrounded by conditions not likely to be fulfilled. (The Europeans would first have to agree on a mechanism of common control, and they would first have to deploy stronger conventional forces.) The United States could reap the political benefit from a generous offer and count upon disagreements among the Europeans and budgetary pressures to prevent the situation from occurring where the United States in accord with its promise would have to relinquish operational control of strategic weapons to the allies. The two-stage proposal thus defined direct political benefits and served to test the strength of European demands before actually devolving control. For these reasons, Bowie's idea looked like an attractive balancing of the competing objectives. Unless the Europeans lined up strongly behind SACEUR's proposal and brought strong pressures to bear, the analytic perspective would have expected in 1960 to find the United States adapting the first stage of Bowie's collective force and delaying indefinitely the follow-on stage, which was much more costly in terms of the competing objective.

The MRBM system for Europe which Norstad proposed would not be expected as the product of an analytic decision process. It was a weapon vulnerable to attack and whose mission was readily performed by less vulnerable strategic systems. The procedure of basing Polaris on land would only reduce its main benefit—the invulnerability which comes with undersea mobility—and would tempt the Soviets in serious crisis to undertake a massive attack on Europe. Also, the proximity to civilian populations in Europe compounded security problems, especially the danger (and consequence) of an accident. Presumably the MRBM would deliver more benefit to the political objective, but

193

at such substantial loss to the military objective that even completely intuitive analytic judgments could be expected to weigh the two-stage collective force as better, on balance.

The situation in 1960 would have been understood very differently by a theorist informed by the cognitive paradigm and sensitive to organizational context. From that perspective the MRBM system would appear much stronger.

First, the traditional autonomy of the theater commander had cognitive as well as purely organizational implications. It allows a natural segmentation of the problem of overall defense posture into a narrower context; and, if that does not accord with an actual environmental decomposition, it is nonetheless very natural to think it so. Thus the cognitive theorist would expect to find Norstad's problems of theater posture factored out and treated separately, especially since this accords with traditions in the organization. Second, within such a segmented structure there is a natural information focus on the posture of the enemy's theater forces and a natural tendency to match the enemy's deployment unit for unit, weapons type for weapons type. The Soviets were visibly in the process of deploying a large intermediate-range missile force with a capacity against Europe, but not the United States, and Norstad's MRBM was the obvious matching response. Third, according to established routines, Norstad was operating in established channels for demanding new weapons deployments, and officials at all levels of government were disposed to receive and understand such demands from him as legitimate and expected activity.

By contrast, the collective force proposal looked very weak in terms of the cognitive paradigm operating in organizational context. To say the least, it was not routine for the State Department to be in the business of promoting a weapons system. Though it was legitimate in terms of standard organizational arrangements for State to concern itself with the political effects of weapons deployments, the Joint Chiefs of Staff were not disposed to cede to State competence to judge the military utility of weapons programs. The cognitive expectation that decision problems are set up in reference to a single value means that the military objectives tend to dominate for a weapons deployment. In order to gain access to the issue, State would have to force the trade-off structure; otherwise, their special input—information and argument on the political forces in Europe—would not become relevant. The cognitive theorist clearly would predict that State would be unsuccessful in achieving such a structure. In effect then, the Chiefs, whose appetites for new weapons chronically exceeded what realistic budgets could provide, would not be expected to spend money on a weapons system which was not promoted from within the military hierarchy. The Policy Planning Staff of the State Department was just not in a position from which one could lay serious claim on the Joint Chiefs of Staff, and without the Chiefs it would seem to be next to impossible to produce an operating weapons system costing in excess of two billion dollars. Though the cognitive paradigm might expect State to get from Bowie's recommendations some nominal assignment of U.S. strategic forces to NATO, it would appear exceedingly unlikely that State would be able to deflect U.S. deployment from what it would otherwise have been.

For the actual control of the projected forces, the same logic applies even more strongly. Command and control (i.e., authority over military operations) affected the very integrity of the military organizations, and it would appear very unlikely that State would achieve any real adjustment in that by appealing to the political sensitivities of the European allies. Command authority was not set up to respond to such input. Moreover, Norstad had been able to associate Adenauer, Spaak, and Stikker with his plan, and this would provide simple convenient grounds for refuting the State Department claims.

Thus the most straightforward use of the cognitive paradigm would probably have bet on Norstad, if forced to make predictions at the end of 1960. The State Department's attempt to tie an organizationally extraneous, competing objective into strategic weapons problems cut against the whole tendency to separate such objectives which the theory argues. The Bowie argument could not be expected to crack established organizational procedures, and an appeal to higher authority would be of no avail. The White House would be expected to keep the political and military problems separate as well, deal with them sequentially, and give dominant influence in issues concerning weapons to the military hierarchy. The natural evolution of the sharing arrangement for tactical weapons could be expected to provide Norstad with an MRBM system.

An analyst sensitive to politics within and without the policy bureaucracy would be swayed by the analysis of the cognitive paradigm but would harbor some important doubts. Apart from changes which the new administration would bring, there were good reasons for hedging any bet on Norstad's MRBM. Norstad was an intellectual general, more concerned with the subtleties of international politics and less categorical about the use of nuclear weapons in warfare than those on the Air Force staff. Given that he was not a militant proponent of approved Air Force doctrine, the support he could claim among his colleagues was accordingly modified. Even more important, the program he proposed, given limited budgets, was a natural competitor of the weapons programs of the powerful Strategic Air Command. Though up to the point of Presidential transition SAC had not displayed any open jealousy, the enthusiasm of their representative on a strategy review board in 1960 was of distinctly moderate proportions, and this was a sign of trouble to come for the MRBM. The military bureaucracy on top of Norstad—the Air Force staff and the JCS—could perhaps be counted upon to give the MRBM requirement polite, formal approval, but the careful analyst would have doubted that that could supply real political muscle. Given the aroused suspicions of the Joint Committee on Atomic Energy, it may well have appeared to the political analyst in 1960 that formal support by the JCS would not be enough.

As for the Bowie proposal, there were some obvious political debilities. Even without intimate knowledge of how Kennedy would react to the Presidency, one could foresee his not wanting to relinquish Presidential authority over the firing of nuclear weapons. If Presidents could be counted on to hold any decision for themselves, it would be that one, and Bowie's suggestion that real authority be shared with the alliance was a clear candidate for amendment at the White House level. Also, British and French opposition to the collective force ideal could be foreseen, for somewhat different reasons, and this would strengthen Presidential reluctance. Sensitive to the possibilities of a compromise outcome, the political analyst in 1960 might well have bet that the interim proposal of the Bowie report—"assignment" of Polaris boats to NATO—would succeed in derailing any land-based system to fulfill SACEUR's MRBM requirement, but that the devolution of operational authority envisaged in Bowie's follow-on proposal would be removed. The Europeans would get vague language and a nominal strategic arsenal, but in reality no change in the operational control or procurement/deployment patterns would take place. The outcome predicted by this analysis differs from that of the simple analytic paradigm only if European pressures for nuclear sharing developed appreciable strength. In that case the simple analytic analysis, to preserve the benefits of the political objective, would predict that a real measure of control would be devolved to the NATO or some European apparatus.

THE ACTUAL OUTCOMES

The actual course of subsequent events differed significantly though not completely from these simple predictions. The collective force idea flourished in American policy but not under the circumstances which analytic assumptions would have suggested as necessary for its development. During the period from 1960 to 1964 an elaborate strategy was devised for easing the Americans into an actual sharing of control as called for in the second phase of the Bowie plan. The preconditions established in 1960, ostensibly to test the seriousness of European demands, were removed as it became clear that they would not be met. Rather than awaiting strong European pressure to trade off military control for political returns, the United States pushed the sharing plan against substantial European opposition. This was done even after it became clear that the United States had a substantial advantage over the Soviet Union in strategic weapons and therefore did not need to worry as much about the credibility of their alliance guarantee as was feared in 1960.

The Norstad proposal for land-based MRBM's quickly lapsed into a dormant state. Officially sanctioned but pragmatically ignored, it ceased to function as a serious contender for inclusion in the force posture of the alliance. Nonetheless, the multilateral force proposal, which had been created apparently to head off the Norstad plan, took on a life of its own; and the normal processes of military procurement, whose operators were expected to keep the proposal at bay, were effectively by-passed. Beyond that, the incoming Kennedy administration worked out explicit analytic calculations from which evolved a new and apparently superior option for handling the sharing issue. This was swamped, however, as momentum developed behind the multilateral force. In the end the United States, with elaborate effort and costly commitment, carried the collective force idea to the brink of fruition and then suddenly dropped it. The anomalous *status quo* of 1960 was allowed to stand as the Johnson administration became preoccupied with Indochina.

It is clear, then, that the simplest applications of the decision paradigms do not suffice to understand the actual flow of history and that valid use of the paradigms requires more sophisticated application. In order to promote greater sophistication in applying the paradigms to actual decision processes, it is necessary to trace the development of the collective force proposal in some detail. It turns out that the simple arguments used to derive the predictions are not wholly wrong about the forces at work on the issue; and with important adjustments made possible by hindsight, some rather good explanations can be advanced for the intuitively surprising course of events.

CHAPTER 8

The Rise of the Multilateral
Force: 1961–1963

NEW PRESIDENTS, in one of the more intriguing images, come to Washington like the head of an occupying army and should expect about as much cooperation, about as much resistance.[1] They may bring some reliably loyal cohorts and establish these in critical positions of power, but most business will have to be conducted through those who conducted it previously. The more permanent residents of the town—in Congress and in the government bureaucracy—form an alien culture inherently hostile to outside power. They are necessarily submissive, but nevertheless vigilant for any opportunity to subvert Presidential power to serve established purposes. The image is overly dramatic, of course, but in its simplicity it catches much of John Kennedy's problem as he sought to exert his authority over American policy.

Kennedy's occupation of the Presidential offices was unusually complicated in most areas by the fact that his victory had been exhausting. His margin at the polls was extraordinarily narrow, and his "outside power" as a consequence was not overwhelmingly imposing. In general this sharply constrained the angle of any new departure which he could realistically plan. Regarding NATO, the inherent fluidity of policy, due to the absence of a coherent legacy from Eisenhower and to the disarray within the bureaucracy, qualified this effect enough that Kennedy could move early in articulating his own conceptions of the alliance. He was a full two years in office, however, before major outcomes in Europe clearly emerged; and when they did, not only did events on the Continent contradict his design, but also American policy was set in tracks which were against his inclinations. Neither the alliance nor the government he headed carried out the policy his administration set forth.

All this became clear on the second anniversary of his inaugural in January of 1963 when Kennedy was presented with a

[1] The image is taken from Richard E. Neustadt in a personal communication.

now famous series of moves by French President Charles de
Gaulle. British entry into the Common Market was blocked for
the indefinite future; U.S. aid to the French nuclear force, and
putative influence over it, was rejected; a formal relationship
which had potential for exclusiveness was formed between
France and Germany. The Western capitals were again badly
divided, and Kennedy found himself and the American government lined up behind the collective force idea as a prime means
for recouping diplomatic defeat.

In tracing in retrospect the evolution of NATO policy during
Kennedy's first two years as President, it becomes clear that he
and the policy machinery he inherited were grappling with three
alternative courses of action. On one hand there was a program
for alliance defense and especially for nuclear arrangements
which developed out of the increasingly sophisticated logic of
strategic analysis under the strong leadership of Kennedy's Defense Secretary, Robert McNamara. Simultaneously there was a
constant temptation in dealing with de Gaulle, reinforced by
some officials within the American government, to acquiesce in
the apparently inevitable and give the French the sort of
advanced military aid already granted to the British. Finally,
there was the multilateral force (MLF in bureaucratic vernacular) as an elaboration of Bowie's idea of a collective force, which
not only gave expression to residual fears of German militarism
but also (and more constructively) connected to a mainstay of
postwar policy—support for political and economic integration
in Europe. Each of these options had deep roots in American
postwar experience, and it is no accident that they came to form
the area of discussion. It was in the interplay between them that
policy on nuclear sharing and alliance defense posture was carried through to the interim resolutions of January 1963.

THE ATHENS PROGRAM

Reflecting serious concern about NATO policy, Kennedy, a bare
two weeks into his term, announced the appointment of Dean
Acheson, former Secretary of State and elder statesman of the
Democratic Party, as chairman of a committee to conduct a thorough review of NATO issues and to make policy recommendations. Acheson in turn called upon Albert Wohlstetter, the man
who had done the SAC basing study at the RAND Corporation

and who was recognized by insiders as one of the more prestigious of the new military analysts, to address the questions of
defense policy. Wohlstetter, as spokesman for a number of prominent civilian analysts at RAND, had just published a pivotal
article on strategic policy.[2] In it he had strongly contested the
view that nuclear weapons, by their very existence, had abolished
large-scale war as a human enterprise and that threats of massive
retaliation would guarantee without difficulty the defense of Europe. Deterrence, he had warned, did not flow automatically
from the existence of nuclear weapons. It would be difficult to
achieve, at best, and could not realistically be guaranteed. The
degree of stability, he had argued, depended upon the details of
the Soviet threat and upon the structure, deployment, and operations of our own forces. Even with best efforts, disastrous war remained possible. While doing everything possible to prevent it,
the United States needed to think about what to do if it did happen. In joining the Acheson group, Wohlstetter gained an
opportunity to carry these concerns to high policy councils in
the new administration.

The analysts Wohlstetter represented, seriously worried that
war could occur, and scrambling to minimize the chances, had
produced some prescriptions which were simple in conception
if difficult in execution. In the first place, they argued, the United
States should develop a posture of second-strike retaliation,
meaning that its deterrent forces be able to absorb a full attack
and still retaliate, massively, against the enemy. This required
forces of such size and sophistication relative to the Soviet Union
that only an economy of comparable size could afford them. The
American economy was the only one of that size organized under
a single governmental structure. Second, the analysts, aware of
the full destructive potential of nuclear warfare, wanted to hold
any war which started as far below its full potential as possible.
That meant that they expected deterrence to continue beyond the
first attacks. The analysts counseled U.S. decision makers not to
respond to attack with full-scale destruction of enemy cities and
populations. Rather, they argued, U.S. decision makers should
concentrate on destroying the enemy's offensive weapons and
should avoid as much damage to enemy cities and populations as
possible. Such a policy would leave room for bargaining moves

[2] See Albert Wohlstetter, "The Delicate Balance of Terror," in *Foreign
Affairs*, vol. 37 (January 1959), pp. 211–235.

to end a war short of the utter destruction of which both sides were capable. This requirement necessitated making nuclear forces responsive in the post-attack environment to direction by political authorities. One did not want parts of the armed forces of the alliance responding according to some established program and unresponsive to attempts to end nuclear exchanges early. As a third prescription, the analysts sought to restrict the applicability of nuclear retaliation to attacks of major proportions, in order to prevent nuclear wars from developing out of battles fought at lower levels of violence.

These notions which were carried into the Acheson review contained some distinct departures from earlier policy. NATO was officially committed to an early use of nuclear weapons by the strategic agreements adopted in 1957. NATO war plans called for rapid nuclear response to major attack (even conventional attack) and thereby built escalation into both strategic doctrine and organizational procedure. Moreover, French theories of deterrence, which emphasized guaranteed response to attack, reinforced the NATO posture and clashed directly with the ideas of post-attack deterrence/bargaining and of early war termination which the American analysts propounded. There was some danger that NATO, whose planning was all predicated on a sudden massive strike from the East, would turn even a modest attack into general nuclear war. The autonomy of SACEUR and the dominance of this office in the NATO organization compounded the danger. In the analysts' view, one did not want to encourage modest attacks, to be sure, but even less did one want to risk a fully destructive nuclear exchange. The Acheson review found much in need of revision.

The report which the Acheson group submitted in March of 1961 made a number of recommendations.[3] NATO planning was to be diverted from its extensive focus on massive attack by Warsaw Pact forces and was to plan for more likely contingencies involving lesser provocations. NATO was to emphasize its conventional weapons and to strengthen itself so as to be able to meet a conventional attack exclusively with conventional means. Conventional forces rather than nuclear ones were to be the objects of marginal investments in the years to come. Stronger operational controls over the nuclear weapons deployed under SACEUR were to be instituted. These desired changes were sum-

[3] Interview material.

marized by the strategic doctrine of "flexible response," expressing the underlying desire to have reliable non-nuclear options for coping with a wide range of security problems which might arise in Europe.

Concerning strategic nuclear deterrence, the Acheson review determined that the major part of U.S. forces were not to be subjected to a European veto (i.e., capacity to prevent their use), though those deployed in Europe might be. The report suggested, however, that the United States should gain a veto over nuclear weapons deployed by the European powers. There was, in other words, to be a frank asymmetry in the alliance on the operational control of strategic nuclear weapons. To soften the effect of asymmetry, the United States was to encourage the development of new and more explicit NATO guidelines on nuclear weapons usage and to abide by them unless they conflicted with larger strategic purposes. The United States was to commit five Polaris submarines to the alliance, in line with the Herter proposal, though retaining the right to use them for defense of the United States alone if need be. Britain was to be encouraged to abandon its national nuclear weapons program, and the Skybolt missile, under development in the United States for joint United States–United Kingdom purposes, was to be discontinued if not justified by U.S. needs alone. The French were to get no assistance in procuring a nuclear arsenal. The collective force mentioned by Herter was to be held open for discussions, but *no* devolution of operational control was to be contemplated, and the force was not to be procured until there first had been a buildup of conventional forces. European national nuclear forces were not to be encouraged, regardless of their relationship to SACEUR.

The logic of the strategic analysts which stood behind these proposals won an early and easy victory within the new administration. In April of 1961 the recommendations of the Acheson report (subsequently known as the Green Book) were promulgated by the President as a policy directive of the National Security Council. With this, the Green Book became official United States policy, and its principles remained the dominant strategic doctrine of the Kennedy administration.

The policy of the Green Book, however, was anything but self-executing. In moving away from NATO policy, it cut against the grain of established attitudes and expectations in European capitals, and a strong hint of trouble over the new principles had preceded the policy directive (which remained officially secret). In February, a letter from Secretary of State Dean Rusk to Defense Secretary McNamara was reported in press stories which provided some flavor of the logic governing the Acheson review.[4] The letter proportedly emphasized the importance of increasing NATO's conventional forces and suggested that the response to attack in Europe should not automatically involve nuclear weapons. The press accounts caused a great din of concern in Europe; and, whether intended or not, it served as a trial balloon indicating some rough political weather to come for the new policy line. Since political cohesion within the alliance was an established objective whose interests would be protected by parts of the American bureaucracy, European opposition to the recommendations of the Acheson report was not only an inconvenience but a distinct political threat.

The response of the strategic analysts was to attempt persuasion. They noted the long history of secrecy whereby the allies had been precluded from knowing details of nuclear weapons and their operation—often details which the Soviets already knew. They argued that if the secrecy policies were relaxed, thus enabling the allies to be educated in the exigencies of the nuclear age, then the allies would eventually accede to American views. The analysts felt that the problems of vulnerability, the dangers of presenting only first-strike threats, the dangers of escalation, the need for protected and highly responsive command and communication channels, and the urgency of arms control all provided compelling logic against having small nuclear forces which were not thoroughly integrated into the main deterrent force (i.e., into the nationally controlled forces of the United States). In some of the scenarios which supplied the basis for strategic calculations, the difference between poor performance of strategic forces and better than poor was measured in terms of millions of lives that could be saved.[5] This, not unreasonably, was held to be a persuasive argument no matter what the politics of the moment might be. The argument was strengthened, moreover, by an intelligence breakthrough during 1961 which re-

[4] *New York Times*, February 28, 1961, p. 5.
[5] Alain C. Enthoven and K. Wayne Smith, *How Much Is Enough? Shaping the Defense Program, 1961–1969* (New York: Harper & Row, Publishers, 1971), Table 9, p. 189.

vealed the size and character of the strategic forces of the Soviet Union.[6] The latter were far less numerous and far more vulnerable than previous intelligence estimates had suggested. The performance of the United States strategic forces suddenly looked, if not exactly encouraging (as too positive a word for such grisly business), then nevertheless better than previously feared. The military need for a European supplement faded accordingly, and it was hoped that the Europeans, once apprised in detail of the situation, would draw conclusions compatible with the Green Book.

The issue of secrecy was thus joined in the fall of 1961 as part of the campaign of persuasion. Roswell Gilpatrick, Undersecretary of Defense, revealed in a public speech in October the knowledge of the actual strategic balance which the United States had gained over the previous year.[7] More important, a thorough briefing on relative force levels (United States–U.S.S.R.; NATO–Warsaw Pact) and on the reduced estimate of U.S. vulnerability which the new intelligence indicated was prepared for Chancellor Konrad Adenauer when he visited Washington in November. Fighting back opponents of more liberal information policies, analysts from the Office of the Secretary of Defense delivered a lengthy briefing to an intensely interested Adenauer, and McNamara followed up with a repeat performance before the NATO Council in December.[8] To a greater degree than ever before, McNamara revealed to the allies what was known about the Soviet forces and the relative vulnerability of the United States strategic forces.

By early 1962 civilian defense officials of the office of International Security Affairs (ISA), who were responsible for alliance problems, had extended the aspirations regarding persuasion of the allies. Encouraged by the response to their revelations, they developed a briefing not only on relative force levels but on strategic concepts, and this they embodied in a now famous speech which McNamara delivered to the NATO Council meeting at Athens in May.[9] In his Athens speech McNamara outlined the characteristics of forces required to minimize the damage of nu-

[6] William Kaufmann, *The McNamara Strategy* (New York: Harper & Row, Publishers, 1964), pp. 65–66.

[7] Ibid.   [8] Interview material.

[9] Declassified version given at University of Michigan in June 1962, printed in the *New York Times*, June 7, 1962, p. 1.

clear war, and he pointed out that the range of damage to Europe in a general nuclear war varied from under 25 million dead to over 115 million, depending on how the forces of the combatants were handled. He analyzed the role of relatively small independent forces (such as the French were planning) in a nuclear crisis and he strongly discounted their utility, summarizing in an oft-quoted phrase: "In short, limited nuclear capacities operating independently are dangerous, expensive, prone to obsolescence, and lacking in credibility as a deterrent."[10] In nuclear war, McNamara stated with deliberate emphasis, the target system of the enemy is indivisible. No part of it can rationally be attacked without attacking all of it, and it was intolerable to contemplate a theater commander such as SACEUR or a single ally such as France striking independently of the main deterrent forces. Centralized planning, centralized force operations, and centralized strategic control in crisis and in early stages of war were held to be essential if maximally damaging wars were to be avoided. The logic was tough; but, as long as nuclear weapons existed in the arsenals of mutually hostile nations, it was a harsh world indeed, and sovereign dignities would have to be adjusted.

By contrast, McNamara's speech at Athens emphasized the utility of conventional weapons for the alliance. Comparisons of relative strength between NATO and the Warsaw Pact in manpower, readiness, flexibility, mobility, air support, etc. largely favored NATO and indicated that a conventional defense was wholly feasible. In response to the crisis over Berlin, which had begun in the previous August, the alliance had increased its conventional forces; and the detailed contingency planning which accompanied the crisis had emphasized the importance of conventional options. Citing this most recent experience, McNamara called for the alliance to meet the official force goals of thirty combat division equivalents. The increase would have to come from Germany and France, and within realistic budget levels for those countries it would preempt any serious nuclear program.

The Athens speech bluntly stated to the allies the policy position promulgated in Acheson's Green Book together with its surrounding argument. It was a request for NATO to adopt the strategy which the United States had adopted at the highest levels of the Kennedy administration; and, if anyone in Europe cared to look for it, there were plenty of signs that McNamara was

[10] Ibid.

deeply serious. He underscored his position directly by announcing the "assignment" of five Polaris submarines to NATO with the promise of five more to come as they were available.[11] The boats, which were the total Polaris force at the time, were to be under the operational control not, significantly, of SACEUR (Supreme Allied Commander, Europe) but rather SACLANT (Supreme Allied Commander, Atlantic). The latter, Admiral Dennison at the time, was stationed in Norfolk, Virginia, and doubled as the American commander in the Atlantic. He was much more reliably American than was SACEUR. The implication was clear: The strategic forces of the United States and those of the alliance were to be the same thing.

Further confirmation of the American position was soon to follow as the United States moved quickly to deal with the MRBM question. It was implicit in McNamara's Athens speech that an MRBM force for NATO was not an urgent military need. In June U.S. Ambassador to NATO, Thomas Finletter, stated that directly to the NATO Council.[12] Reiterating McNamara's point that there could be but a single, world-wide theater in nuclear war, Finletter argued that the U.S. strategic forces already programed would provide the proper mix for covering Soviet targets and that there was no need to put expensive MRBM's in Europe. Finletter did not directly preclude this possibility, but having sharply discounted the rationale which Norstad had offered for the MRBM requirement, he then surrounded any fulfillment of the requirement with very difficult conditions: (1) the allies would have to bear a substantial part of the cost (estimated by Finletter at $2 billion for a 200–250 missile force) and (2) the allies would first have to achieve a substantial buildup of conventional forces. The possibility of both a conventional buildup and an MRBM deployment being accomplished, given limited European defense budgets, was very slim indeed. It was readily perceived in the Council that the Finletter briefing was a strong attack on the MRBM requirement. What may not have been appreciated was the fact that Finletter had been directly instructed by President Kennedy himself. The Athens program had gained active concurrence by the Chief Executive.

The policy thinking outlined in the Athens speech was also apparent in issues of American strategic deployment decided in

[11] *New York Times*, May 6, 1962, p. 1.
[12] Interview material.

1962. McNamara's insistence that strategic logic govern the procurement of the deterrent forces was displayed throughout the year in bitter, protracted battles with the United States armed services. The cherished program of the Air Force, the B-70 bomber, was scrapped as an inefficient program in terms of the strategic analysis.[13] The bomber would spend large sums of money to extend its speed and cruising altitude, whereas the outcome of any bombing campaign, analysis indicated, depended much more on its ability to carry special electronic equipment to aid penetration. Moreover, the bomber as a weapon was inherently vulnerable, and therefore not the ideal weapon for McNamara's second-strike strategy. The program had gained substantial momentum through an expensive development effort and through the devotion of Congress to American preparedness. McNamara's decision to cancel it was difficult politically and served as a good gauge of his sense of strategic purpose. Similarly, an early anti-missile defense system, the Nike-Zeus, was not put into production, and the Skybolt missile was canceled. Throughout all of these episodes, McNamara displayed intentions to make the logic propounded at Athens connect to the concrete details of force posture and to prevail in this even over vehement opposition.

By most accounts, McNamara's speech at Athens was well received—primarily, it seems, because the obvious increase in American candor was very welcome to the allies. Since the speech was read rapidly, however, and since the recipients had no time to prepare responses, the official policy reactions did not come in until later. In fact, official European reactions were not apparent until after Finletter's presentation to the NATO Council and after a declassified version of the speech was delivered publicly by McNamara at his commencement address at the University of Michigan in June 1962.[14] Whether the result of more reflection or of the decision to publicize the argument, reactions in Europe to the Ann Arbor speech were sharp and negative. The British reaffirmed their intention to maintain an independent deterrent, and McNamara felt constrained to explain that he did not have the British force in mind when attacking independent deterrent forces. Other allied reaction concurred more with the

13 Enthoven and Smith, *How Much Is Enough?* Chapters 2 and 7.
14 *New York Times*, June 7, 1962, p. 1.

British than with the Ann Arbor presentation. A debate immediately developed regarding the commanding officer of the committed Polaris submarines, the Europeans making it clear that they preferred Norstad (SACEUR) to Dennison (SACLANT). NATO Secretary General Stikker told Finletter that the Germans were disturbed by the political dominance of Europe implicit in the American position.

The essential means by which the Athens program sought to deal with new allied disenchantment was to redouble the efforts at persuasion. Civilian analysts at ISA reasoned that part of the problem with the allies was that they had been asked up to that point simply to listen passively to enlightenment by the Americans. It seemed much more in the interests of persuasion to encourage the allies to conduct strategic analysis for themselves, thus testing American logic against their own. Moreover, in addition to greater persuasion, this promised to prepare them for a resolution of the sharing issue which involved planning rather than military hardware. Britain's Alastair Buchan had developed the planning approach by clever appeal to a difference in meaning between the French word *contrôle* and the English word "control." *Contrôle*, he had argued, connotes planning and political direction, whereas "control" implies physical possession.[15] The proponents of the Athens program liked the distinction. The sharing of planning decisions with the allies was relatively easy and gave greater scope for actual influence. The sharing of operational control was hard, and the desire for national influence cut against the necessity of discipline in the military chain of command.

To achieve more effective persuasion and to prepare for effective consultation on planning, the civilian analysts in ISA sought to establish a course on strategy for the allies. Extensive data was to be made available, and the allies were to conduct continuing analysis of the Soviet threat and the allied options for response. A framework for this had been provided in April by a report of the NATO Secretary General.[16] This report suggested guidelines to be established regarding consultation over the use of nuclear weapons and affirmed the establishment of a NATO Nuclear

[15] Alastair Buchan, "The Reform of NATO," in *Foreign Affairs*, vol. 40 (January 1962), pp. 165–185.
[16] *New York Times*, May 6, 1962, p. 1.

Committee to receive information from the United States and to perform any other functions assigned to it. The committee was an obvious forum for the strategy seminar, and a proposal which called for very liberal sharing of information with the committee was prepared in ISA.

Independent of the politics of persuasion, the logic of the Athens program was strengthened in the eyes of its proponents by several events of the summer and fall of 1962; notably, a reassessment of the conventional weapons balance in Europe, the decision to cancel the Skybolt missile development program, and a favorable outcome to the first strategic nuclear confrontation. Each in its way added an important component to the overall policy posture.

All through the postwar period the Western allies had assumed the Soviets to have conventional superiority in Europe. The basis for the assumption were estimates which counted up to 175 Soviet divisions as against 20 actually deployed in Europe by the allies.[17] Taking account of the different size of a Soviet division, the overall manpower figures, and budget support levels, calculations were done in 1962 which pulled the estimate of Soviet divisions down to 50 or 60. This was a figure which made a conventional defense of Europe look very promising. With only those NATO forces programed in the contemporary force goals—i.e., 30 divisions—a defensive line could be held against a 50–60 division Soviet threat. In arguing for a conventional buildup, the United States could assert, they were not asking the impossible, but rather for relatively small steps to realize conventional strength which was close at hand.

The cancellation of Skybolt, for its part, affected the status of individual nuclear forces within the alliance.[18] The missile was designed to be hung under bombers to enable the planes to cruise outside the Soviet air defense network and shoot into it. It was under development in the United States, and the British had an agreement for joint procurement of the missile if development proved successful. The significance of the missile resided in the fact that the British depended upon it to extend the useful life of

[17] Enthoven and Smith, *How Much Is Enough?* Table 2, p. 135.

[18] The story of the cancellation of the Skybolt program and the negotiations attending its demise are recounted in Richard E. Neustadt, *Alliance Politics* (New York: Columbia University Press, 1970), Chapter 3. The account here rests on this source.

their bomber force, the weapon which gave them a nominally independent deterrent. Without it the British would not have a credible strike force of their own and from the perspective of the Athens program this would be a favorable development. If the British went out of the nuclear business, moreover, it should set a very convenient precedent for the French, who had followed them into the business, and for the Germans, who might be tempted.

The Skybolt program was canceled in line with the policy directive of April 1961 promulgating Acheson's recommendations.[19] It was a wasteful expenditure from the American point of view. As the development program strung out, plagued with technical difficulties, analytic studies made it clear that the mission of the missile could be done better by the land-based missiles which were a mainstay of the force. Under the directive, it was to be canceled if not useful for U.S. purposes alone. The British, under the joint procurement agreement, were free to continue development, but no one believed they would do it on their own. Thus, the cancellation of Skybolt was a concrete decision giving apparent momentum to the Athens program and promising a significant consolidation of the nuclear deterrent forces.

The crisis in Cuba in October of 1962, graced with a favorable outcome, enhanced the credibility of the American deterrent forces and thereby strengthened the American claim to competence for nuclear defense of the alliance. In the aftermath, the Americans could now claim not only a grasp of the abstract numbers of strategic analysis, but also some pertinent experience with strategic confrontation. Whatever horrors may have been aroused in European hearts, the alliance in fact held together rather well during the crisis, and the success of the American stand was at least publicly conceded. The Americans felt more confident in the aftermath, and their detractors, if not converted, were nonetheless more subdued.

The campaign of persuasion, however, was not able to reap whatever benefit was to be found in these natural advantages. The strategic seminar idea encountered both organizational and political difficulties within the United States, to which it had largely succumbed by late 1962. The idea could not be implemented through a speech or two by a high official; it needed to be established as routine business. This meant that existing rou-

19 Interview material.

tine procedures, notably security regulations, had to be adjusted, and that in turn meant trouble. For one thing a great deal of delay was encountered in trying to set up an approved security system for the NATO machinery, and underlying that was the feeling, widespread in the Pentagon, that NATO was inherently leaky and not to be trusted with serious information. For another thing, severe political cross-pressures sapped the will of the policy machinery. If, for example, discussions were encouraged which went much beyond what McNamara had already said at Athens, there was a risk of opening up for stark review the vulnerability of Europe to Soviet IRBM's. The Soviet MRBM/IRBM force was approaching 500 missiles in the fall of 1962; and, although these ultimately would be covered by American forces, not all of those forces had been procured and deployed. If U.S. officials insisted on dwelling in gruesome detail on what the Soviet IRBM's could do to Europe—without having fully deployed coverage from American forces—they ran a risk of stimulating more pressure for a fulfillment of the MRBM requirement. This made candor delicate business, even for the most avid of its proponents.

In addition there was outright opposition to the idea of a strategy seminar. The State Department was not anxious to have relatively junior Defense officials conducting propaganda against established NATO policy. That meant a great deal of embarrassment for them in diplomatic channels. Moreover, parts of the State Department were not in agreement with the policy which would be defended in the seminar. The JCS was naturally jealous of its own competence to give military briefings, and the Chiefs were in disagreement with McNamara and the civilian analysts on the MRBM issue. The result was that the JCS gained control of the idea and watered it down from a strategic seminar to a one-day briefing which was made to square with established NATO policy and which still withheld important detailed information. In this compromise the campaign of persuasion faltered, and no one moved seriously to rescue it.

The demise of the program of persuasion proved to be a consequential one, but that was difficult to foresee in 1962. As Kennedy's second year in office drew to a close, the Athens program was still the established position in American policy and was doing well in the main. A number of concrete decisions about the American force posture had been made to give effect to the strategic logic, and NATO had been put on clear authoritative notice that it, too, would have to adopt new policies. The President and his powerful Secretary of Defense seemed thoroughly committed, and events seemed to be running in their favor. The natural expectation was that the dominant member of the alliance, following the hard logic of modern weapons, would ultimately prevail and that NATO and the European allies would adjust. Since it did not turn out so neatly, however, it is important to examine the counterthemes in American policy as a lead to other forces affecting the situation.

The long struggle concerning relationships on nuclear matters between the original partners in the Manhattan Project, which was bequeathed to the Kennedy administration in a fully active state, was not wholly resolved by the momentum developed behind the Acheson review and the Athens program. Though the policy directive which followed the Acheson study explicitly stated the undesirability of aiding either the British or the French in their efforts to build nationally controlled nuclear forces, not all that had been accomplished in the last years of the Eisenhower administration could be undone. In the 1958 agreements on the deployment of Thor missiles in Britain under joint control, the British explicitly refused to have their missiles assigned to SACEUR, pointedly preserving the principle of their national competence over strategic weapons. Later in the same year, as noted above, the British received specific technical assistance for their weapons program by means of a revision of the McMahon Act. By 1961 substantial exchanges of information had taken place, and knowledge once granted could not be withdrawn.

In the spring of 1960 the United States and the British deepened their nuclear relationship with the agreement for joint procurement of the Skybolt missile and an agreement to grant the United States bases for servicing Polaris submarines at Holy Loch, Scotland. In these agreements the British again resisted the idea of assigning the Skybolt force to SACEUR, and their insistence on independence from even a nominal multilateral framework was all the more intense since they canceled their troublesome ICBM program as a concomitant of the Skybolt arrangements. Skybolt became the sole follow-on weapon for the British deterrence force, and all the more were they insistent that it remain independent. This point faded in American minds with the change in administrations, but it remained vivid within the British government. It had been a key element of their policy all along, and with all due politeness to the alliance they had always insisted on it quite directly. Thus a process of entanglement had occurred between the United States and the British, outside of the NATO framework, and it would take a great deal more than a policy directive to sever the elaborate relationship. No contemporary President would lightly disrupt established arrangements with Britain, and Kennedy in particular could not welsh on Eisenhower commitments.

These relations with the British, who for their own reasons insisted on constructing the U.S. tie quite plausibly as a "special relationship," exacerbated the long-festering relations between the United States and France. After the 1958 revisions of the McMahon Act, not even diplomatic cosmetics could hide outright discrimination against the French. Given the existence of the French nuclear weapons program and the emphasis which de Gaulle brought to it, it was clear to all that the first[20] truly independent nuclear force operated by an ally was but a few years away. This tended to cast U.S. policy as a fight against the inevitable, whose main fruit would foreseeably be more independence and more bitterness. It also raised the question as to whether the Germans would be next.

Since coming into NATO in 1954, the Germans had been loyal to the renunciation of nuclear weapons production, which had been a condition of their entrance. Their interest in Euratom, however, did reflect distinct interest in nuclear technology; and Euratom's vehement insistence on its own independence provided some reading on the attitudes of its members for those who were concerned. Early in 1958, France, Germany, and Italy initiated a scheme for pooling "all efforts towards development and production of modern weapons."[21] This did not specifically in-

[20] The independence of British strategic nuclear forces has always been more a matter of principle than fact. The British forces are so well integrated with the U.S. forces that it is very difficult to conceive of their undertaking independent operations. This was the other side of the special aid which they were given.

[21] C. Kelleher, "German Nuclear Dilemmas," unpublished doctoral dissertation, Massachusetts Institute of Technology, 1967, Chapter 5.

clude nuclear weapons, but the implication was clear. C. L. Sulzberger subsequently claimed that there had been a secret agreement by which the Germans would acquire French nuclear weapons in exchange for financial aid and that this had been vetoed by de Gaulle when he came to power.[22] The Sulzberger story is at least accurate in reflecting a widespread sense that German public discretion with regard to nuclear weapons was not an infallible guide to German desires.

In alliance discussions the Germans made no particular attempt to hide their perceived requirement of tactical delivery systems with a pipeline to American-controlled warheads. In June of 1959, via Defense Minister Franz Josef Strauss, they had announced their eagerness to participate with the allies in the production of MRBM's (i.e., Polaris) to replace fighter-bombers.[23] When the control they maintained over nuclear-armed and highly alert tactical delivery systems was attenuated somewhat in 1961 by the introduction of permissive action links, they had registered distinct and clear displeasure. Moreover, they showed a good deal of responsiveness to British and French doubts about the American guarantee, and they had joined the chorus of concern when the American press uncovered the Rusk letter to McNamara heralding a change in American strategy. In all, by 1961 it had become apparent the Germans were ready to register official concern, however discreetly.

Fundamental realities began to exert their effect. Having been in bed with the British, the United States found it quite difficult to protect its virtue when the French came to court and the Germans began to flirt. Within the United States the past was an embarrassment to those who wanted to stand firm against proliferation, and an entering wedge for those for whom virtue regarding proliferation was not a cherished value. A number of Air Force officers fell in the latter category. They felt that nuclear weapons were inevitably the means of modern warfare and that political restriction on their use constituted an inconvenient or even dangerous impediment to military operations. These men welcomed France to nuclear status as a step toward legitimizing nuclear weapons. Moreover, for them, American aid to the French force was desirable as an opportunity to relieve American balance of payments difficulties arising from heavy defense expenditures in

[22] See C. L. Sulzberger in the *New York Times*, July 4, 1962, p. 20.
[23] Kelleher, "German Nuclear Dilemmas."

Europe and to induce the French to allow tropospheric scatter facilities (important for NATO communications) to be located in their country.[24] Many officers of the United States armed services were willing, in other words, to do business with France on nuclear weapons.

The military views were augmented by diplomats and civilian officials who rued the deterioration in relations with France and who saw great depth to the French commitment to have a nuclear force. The French commitment was not only imputed to the person of Charles de Gaulle, but widely understood as something which extended throughout the French government. Bowing to what they perceived as inevitable, these men felt that it was better to buy some influence over de Gaulle. They argued that American aid might be valuable enough to de Gaulle that he could be induced to assign the resulting force to SACEUR as the United States had done (with the same rights of withdrawal for national use) and perhaps to join a collective force to satisfy German demands.

De Gaulle for his part was careful not to risk issuing a personal, formal request for aid that might be rejected. He preferred to raise the issue indirectly—through the American Ambassador in Paris, through his own military, through the French liaison officer to General Norstad. A concrete overture of this sort came early in 1962, when the French General Gaston Lavaud came to Washington with a list of military needs.[25] The items on the list were largely requirements of the French nuclear force, and especially included items relating to delivery systems. Lavaud came

[24] The French refused to agree to these installations, and the reason widely imputed in the United States was that permission was being withheld as a bargaining ploy.

[25] There is some confusion about the total amount of Lavaud's "shopping list." Charles Murphy says that General de Gaulle did not approve of Lavaud's mission, but his Ministry of Defense insisted and Lavaud was "authorized to commit up to $300 million on military purchases" (Charles Murphy, "NATO at a Nuclear Crossroads," in *Fortune*, vol. 66 [December 1962], p. 222). John Newhouse, on the other hand, makes a point of Washington's surprise at the total of only $50 million worth of military goods asked of them instead of the large-volume request they had hoped for and anticipated. (John Newhouse, *De Gaulle and the Anglo-Saxons* [New York: The Viking Press, 1970], p. 156). It is possible that the $300 million figure represented the French Ministry of Defense's desires and the $50 million the maximum that de Gaulle was willing to let Lavaud ask for.

216

with a recommendation from the U.S. Ambassador to Paris, General James M. Gavin, who urged that his requests be honored, pleading the need to repair relations with France. His case was carried within the administration by Paul Nitze, Assistant Secretary of Defense for International Security Affairs, who had long felt that bilateral relations with the European countries had been too submerged in doctrines of European cooperation and Atlantic partnership. Nitze could count on support for serious consideration of some aid to the French from General Maxwell Taylor, the military assistant on the White House staff, from Undersecretary of Defense Roswell Gilpatric, and from McNamara himself. This was ample to force the issue to the Presidential level.

Kennedy's consideration of the problem came in April of 1962 in a context which quite directly involved the British relationship as well. British negotiators were beginning to sense trouble in their application for entrance into the Common Market, and the idea arose that Britain might gain French acquiescence in exchange for British aid for the French nuclear program. Since the British program was deeply bound to the United States under the sharing arrangements instituted after 1958, American approval for any serious British aid to the French would be required. The possibility of a British deal with the French, as well as the Lavaud request for specific items of aid, forced some Presidential judgment. The disagreement within the government reached the President in the uncomfortable form of a split between his two major advisers—the Secretaries of Defense and State.

From McNamara, Kennedy heard the military argument. In return for nuclear help, McNamara suggested, the French might agree to greater cooperation on conventional force goals, aid on American balance of payments problems, and cooperation on the NATO MRBM question. Reflecting his department's wishes, McNamara wanted to pursue the question to discover whether the French would respond to terms of that sort.

Rusk disagreed with a more elaborate argument. Reflecting State's position, he held that a *démarche* to the French would disrupt alliance relationships and would produce a series of problems involving first the Germans, then the Italians, then others. Financial burdens, Rusk argued, had become the major barrier to the proliferation of independent nuclear capacities,

and the United States could not act to reduce the price for anyone without setting precedent. Rather than strengthening the
British precedent by adding France, the United States should
seek to induce the British out of the nuclear arms competition. At
any rate, Rusk argued, the government of France would not be,
in the long run, as nationalistic as de Gaulle himself, nor would
it be as trustworthy as the British. Moreover, Rusk pointed out,
the official signals from Europe did not favor a strong move,
since neither de Gaulle nor his Foreign Minister had formally
requested aid. This meant that President Kennedy could not go
to Congress or the public with official French demands. The idea
of British aid to France was putative, and any British pressure
behind the idea was so discreet as to be imperceptible. The Germans had expressed alarm through the NATO machinery about
the possibility of national aid to France; and Jean Monnet, as a
Frenchman and a prestigious figure in Europe, quietly argued
against aid to the French national force. The diffusion of nuclear
weapons was practically and morally wrong to Monnet in that it
operated against the designs for a unified, cooperative Europe.
Rusk passed on Monnet's advice with approval: Be strong with
de Gaulle; the General would accept what he could not change.

Faced with this array of pressures, Kennedy declined to
change the established policy and thus decided against giving aid
to the French force. The only rationale attributed to him directly
was an answer to McNamara's argument—de Gaulle, he believed, would not yield on key principles of his policy in return
for aid. Lavaud's requests were denied, and McNamara's hard
presentation at Athens and Ann Arbor followed.

The pressures which raised the issue in the first place did not
abate, however, with the negative decision of April. In late May
the White House circulated a list of questions which challenged
the main arguments against aid to the French and requested reasoned replies: Would such action really create a demand in Germany or elsewhere? Did the competitive ideas (the Athens program, the collective force) have real prospects for success or
were they fine but unachievable principles? The answers to the
questions followed established positions and produced no new
ideas, but the exercise served to point out that the White House
was still in motion on the subject. By early fall the April decision
had been amended. Some of the items which had been on Lavaud's list were approved for delivery to France—notably jet

tankers (enabling French bombers to fly long-range missions) and parts for nuclear submarines.[26]

As the debate raged over aid to the French nuclear force, State Department proponents of the collective force idea sought to curtail the special nuclear aid which the British enjoyed. The opportunity was provided by the difficulties of the Skybolt program. If this were canceled the British would have no "need-to-know," and the information exchange could be stopped under formal rules. Moreover, that would render the British bomber force virtually incapable of penetrating Soviet air space. Under these conditions, Britain could no longer claim either an independent deterrent or a special relationship in nuclear matters, and that would greatly relieve the pressure for aid to national forces—or so the calculations went. Through Secretary Rusk, the State Department planners urged Defense to avoid any expansion of British arrangements and to hold to the policy directive of 1961 not to continue Skybolt if U.S. needs alone did not justify it. State expected that a cancellation of Skybolt would lead the British to ask for Polaris. Recognizing that that would drive the question of aid to national forces into another, more serious round, they sought to block the path.

When the Skybolt issue did in fact arise in the fall of 1962, however, State did not control the action. Defense Secretary McNamara, whose decision terminated the American Skybolt program, assumed the responsibility of consulting with the British on the American decision and of arranging a resolution of their interests. Under the original agreement, the British could continue Skybolt development at their own expense, and this was one option—with obvious possibilities for greater American generosity. However, given the crucial political importance of Skybolt to the British, and the financial burdens which continuation of the development program would entail, the Defense Department began to study other possibilities. Despite the State Department warning, despite the official injunction in the Green Book, and despite the whole thrust of the Athens program, Polaris emerged in the Defense Department review as a substitute for Skybolt. Defense officials, well aware that British independence was largely nominal, were willing to contemplate giving them Polaris if British protest at Skybolt cancellation were sufficiently strong. Hence, when McNamara went to London in De-

[26] Newhouse, *De Gaulle and the Anglo-Saxons*, pp. 155–159.

cember to consult with the British Minister of Defense, he was prepared to deal in terms of the Polaris option if that was what the British said they wanted.

For reasons well related elsewhere,[27] McNamara's negotiations in London did not go well, and the task of resolving the issue was forwarded to the British and American heads of government. The President and the Prime Minister were scheduled to meet on December 18, 1962, at Nassau in the Bahamas; and, with the failure of McNamara's negotiations, that meeting became the natural occasion for decision.

There was one clear result of McNamara's consultations, however: the clarification of British intentions. McNamara learned in stormy London discussions that the essence of the matter for the British was their insistence on the principle of independence (on the realities of operational control they had long since conceded American predominance). This focused attention all the more on Polaris as the prestige weapon of the Western arsenal. The Hound Dog Missile, which was the closest available variant of Skybolt and which had been put on the list of options by Defense analysts, was not acceptable to the British. Its name, and the fact that its performance characteristics were less impressive than those projected for Skybolt, made it in British minds a poor carrier of the principle of independence. It is significant that by the time McNamara's talks in London concluded, most American officials were conceding a British veto of the Hound Dog option.

Thus the policy conflict between the Athens program and the program of national aid to major allies came into stark focus at the Nassau conference and forced a consequential decision from the American government. That was not the full extent of the problem, however, for by December of 1962 American policy had developed not two major vectors but three. The idea of a collective force for NATO, by then a much-expanded notion, had become a major theme of American policy.

Atlantic Partnership and the Multilateral Force

The Athens program was naturally hostile to the collective force idea which Robert Bowie had advanced and which Christian Herter had proposed. The unification of operational control over the deterrent forces of the alliance was a central canon of stra-

[27] Neustadt, *Alliance Politics*, Chapter 3.

tegic logic and the collective force proposal seemed to be a violation of that canon. To the extent that Bowie and Herter meant to share anything more than what the Athens program intended—information and planning calculations—it would have to be genuine operational control. In the estimate of Athens program proponents, European officials were smart enough to perceive that point and would not spend good money on a weapons system which would give them nothing that they could not get through the envisaged consultation process alone. Hence the collective force idea was deemed either unnecessary if it did not devolve control, or dangerous if it did, and therefore undesirable.

But again logic, even with official sanction, did not automatically wrench policy out of organizational and political grooves. The same pressures within the alliance which kept aid to national forces as a recurring temptation also provided the collective force idea with plausible pertinence. Moreover, there was a continuity across the Eisenhower and Kennedy administrations in some critical staff positions. These two elements sufficed to sustain life—and more. Both the concrete proposal itself and the grand concepts of policy in which it had been embedded in the Bowie report underwent extensive development in the first two years of Kennedy's term.

It began with the Acheson review. Albert Wohlstetter did not represent the sole influence over Dean Acheson's group. With the Herter initiative of the previous December firmly placed on the NATO agenda, Robert Bowie and Henry Owen also joined the study. Owen had been a major contributor to the Bowie report from his position on the Policy Planning Council of the State Department. In the new administration not only did he work closely with Acheson in conducting the policy review, but he was also recruited into loose association with the White House staff by Kennedy's Special Assistant for National Security Affairs, McGeorge Bundy.[28] Together, Bowie and Owen provided channels for their ideas to the high policy councils of the new administration.

Some responsiveness to those ideas was guaranteed by the character of the New Frontier. Kennedy was an activist President by strong inclination, and in line with the country's mood in 1960

[28] Bundy, desiring to keep his own staff small, supplemented the manpower available to him by claiming the services of various officials in the bureaucracy whom he considered bright and responsive to White House leadership. This enabled him to penetrate the bureaucracy—and vice versa.

he looked outward to define his objectives. The status of Berlin, the end of imperial rule in Africa, the aspirations of non-European peoples were the seminal events of the day. Martin Luther King, Birmingham, Selma, and the Northern ghettos still lay at the edges of the nation's consciousness. Desiring to lead the United States into a constructive, progressive world role—indeed, having run his campaign on that promise—Kennedy needed something more positive, more hopeful, more human than the grim logic of deterrence. The concepts of integration in Europe and partnership across the Atlantic which played off the successes of the past had natural appeal. That appeal was enhanced by the fact that Bowie, Owen, and their colleagues in the State Department soon began connecting these themes to the general tasks of social and economic development of the Third World. This effected not only a channel from State's planners to the White House, but an interested listener on the other end.

Well before the Acheson review was completed and the resulting policy directive set forth, Kennedy had begun to articulate broad principles of alliance policy which were strongly resonant with those which had informed the Bowie report. In the press conference at which he announced Acheson's appointment, for example, the President advanced an expansive view of the alliance:

> This is our central and most important defensive alliance but in a larger sense much more. Members of NATO must be leaders also in and out of NATO itself and in such great causes as the integration of Europe and the cooperative development of new nations.[29]

A few days later, he underscored the point in more binding fashion by incorporating it in a special message to the NATO Council:

> Effective collective defense is the first mission of ... NATO ... but the interests of the community as a whole are not military alone. . . . Through its various instruments the Atlantic community must equip itself to respond with speed and unity of purpose on every front—by improving the process of consultation, by expanding the idea of our cooperation to include common problems of trade and money and by uniting in the effort

[29] *New York Times*, February 9, 1961, p. 1.

to construct a sound growing economy in the entire non-Communist world.[30]

This was strong encouragement for Bowie and his colleagues.

The underlying logic was simple: Together, the nations of Western Europe, including Britain, represented the world's second-largest power concentration calculated in terms of people, productive capacity, and the intangibles of national competence. If the plans for European unity should come to full fruition, if not only a common market but a common political structure could be achieved, the United States would have a sympathetic partner of comparable size and power capable of comparable responsibility. Together, a unified Western Europe and the United States could shoulder the formidable tasks of constructive world leadership and exercise a great deal more influence and capacity than could either alone, or the United States in loose concert with the European national states taken separately. "European integration" and "Atlantic partnership" were the phrases which summarized these images.[31]

Even given early White House interest, the prime institutional base for the Atlantic partnership idea was the Policy Planning Council of the State Department. Bowie, as its former chief, was a consultant there, and Henry Owen a principal staff member. The Chairman of the Council, Walt Rostow, was as committed as Bowie to the basic premises, and quickly moved into a primary role in developing the idea of partnership. Robert Schaetzel, as Deputy Assistant Secretary in the Bureau of European Affairs, was a close and active collaborator. All were assured of high-level sympathy by the presence of George Ball, long an activist for the European cause, as Undersecretary of State. If Kennedy, both by the nature of the man and by the pressures of his office, was a coy sympathizer who would not carry interest and responsiveness into passionate advocacy, Ball provided a source of deep, solid commitment, and even passion, in a critical position of power. Throughout 1961, State's policy planners, granted occasional and politically important access to the White House for briefings, worked on the idea of partnership as the central theme in European policy.

[30] *New York Times*, February 6, 1961, p. 2.

[31] The ideas were repeated often enough by major figures of the administration that some perplexity arose in Europe at what was felt to be an American confusion between NATO and the OECD.

The essential problem in developing the idea was its connections to the immediate problems of alliance relations. The stirring abstractions of unity and cooperation, and the image of the dominant, constructive power which was to result, were extremely vague when it came down to daily business, especially in the economic and social dimensions. Not even the most unabashed enthusiasts thought the economic communities would move quickly into political union, and in the meantime there were decisions to be made. Ironically, on questions of immediate policy the advocates of European unity and Atlantic partnership often found themselves in a negative stance.

There was constant friction with de Gaulle, for example, whose devotion to the restoration of the power and stability of the French national state made him a thorn in the side of the European movement. The American proponents of partnership were often caught in the uncomfortable position of engaging in vehement and even bitter debate with the French President in the name of greater harmony in the Western community. It was similar, if more subtle, on questions of trade. The Trade Expansion Act of 1962, a prime piece of Kennedy legislation, was, in the minds of its designers, a step toward the ultimate integration of the Western economies.[32] Unfortunately, the paramount problem of getting such legislation enacted and operating over the opposition of a broad-based protectionist coalition required that the Common Market be constructed in the domestic debate as a general threat to American trade. Politically the Kennedy administration had to counter the cries of private doom, which arose as tariff protection was diminished, with threats of general doom if progressive trade arrangements were not established. This and the fact that some unpleasant compromises with private American interests had to be conceded (to the chagrin of the Europeans) made trade expansion a poor vehicle for the grander conceptions of partnership. By contrast, the compelling problems of defense policy offered a context for achieving a symbol of partnership which to the public mood of the early 1960s might seem progressive and inspiring. In the minds of his State Department colleagues Bowie's collective force rapidly developed as the primary vehicle of partnership.

[32] R. Bauer, I. Pool, and L. Dexter, *American Business and Public Policy* (New York: Atherton Press, 1963).

By all testimony, Kennedy was not prepared in his own mind to weaken Presidential command authority over nuclear weapons, and accordingly he was less responsive to the collective force idea than to the overarching concepts of Atlantic partnership and European unity. He was nonetheless willing to give some scope to his State Department advisers. At their suggestion he made Herter's proposal his own in a speech to the Canadian Parliament in May of 1961:

> To make clear our intentions and commitments to the defense of Western Europe, the United States will commit to the NATO command five—and subsequently still more—Polaris atomic missile submarines . . . subject to any agreed guidelines on their control and use and responsiveness to the needs of all members but still credible in an emergency. Beyond this we look to the possibility of eventually establishing a NATO seaborne force which would be truly multilateral in ownership and control, if this should be desired and found feasible by the allies, once NATO's non-nuclear goals have been achieved.[33]

The preconditions—the Europeans must first agree that they want the force and must first effect a conventional buildup—reflected the fact that Kennedy's approval was qualified. The reservations did not affect the main result, however: The collective force idea was officially placed on the list of alternatives for NATO nuclear defense arrangements.

The first serious point of decision on the collective force idea arrived in April of 1962. The pace of events was forced by the development of the Athens program and of the proposals for aiding the French force, both of which themselves required decisions prior to the NATO meetings in May. The State Department planners opposed both lines of policy and sought to promote the collective force as a substitute.

The Athens program, designed to withhold actual control of weapons from the allies, would not work in the estimation of the State Department planners. The outcome of this hard line in the eyes of Bowie, Owen, and their colleagues would be nuclear forces procured and operated independently by the European allies either separately or in some combination. Ultimately they felt the Germans would take this path; and, though they esti-

[33] *New York Times*, May 18, 1961, p. 12.

mated it would take ten years for real pressures to develop in Germany, their fears of the consequences demanded immediate action to foreclose the possibility. In their estimation, aid to the French force was a capitulation to de Gaulle and his anti-integrationist policies and would produce the same result sooner. Thus, either the hard Athens line or the extension of aid to national programs would entail severe dangers to the political cohesion of Europe. The historically based fears and hatreds of the Germans would likely be reactivated; politics would be polluted with distrust, and the separate countries would withdraw again within their national shells. A collective force, by contrast, would not only offer the best means of blocking this development, since its mixed-manning principle prevented the withdrawal of force components for national use, but it would also offer something positive as well—new supranational arrangements to bolster those already in existence. At the far reaches of foreseeable success, the collective force would add a defense institution to the economic communities—the critical component missing since France scuttled the European Defense Community in 1954.

Looking to the decisions impending in 1962, State Department planners prepared a number of papers supporting their position. The critical one, drafted by Henry Owen, attached the collective force idea to the program for sharing information advocated by proponents of the Athens program.[34] Using the same mechanisms which Herter had introduced two years earlier, the paper suggested first that the United States assign Polaris submarines to NATO on a schedule adjusted upward as more submarines were produced, and second that the United States indicate its willingness to join in a multilateral force (hereafter MLF). The description of the MLF constituted the bulk of the paper. It was presented as a 200-missile sea-based force whose components would be manned by a mixture of nationalties sufficient to deny anyone effective operational control. The costs of the force were to be borne primarily by the allies, and participation would have to be broad enough that it would not be, in effect, a United States–German operation.

On the critical question of control—how such a force would be fired—Owen's paper was subtly vague. It affirmed the control principles of the Athens program; notably, it required that the MLF be fully integrated with the United States strategic deter-

---

[34] Interview material.

rent forces. At the same time it tried to suggest leeway for sharing of control with the allies. This was to be achieved by indicating to the allies flexibility on the control question and by engaging in discussions about proper formulae. The paper suggested guidelines for force use which would authorize firing by the operational commander in the case of a clear, large nuclear attack on NATO and would provide for a vote by the North Atlantic Council in more ambiguous situations. The Athens guidelines eventually evolved from this suggestion.

The Owen paper was politically adept in several ways. By attaching the MLF idea to a major part of the Athens program, it obscured the natural conflict between the two. By including a suggestion that the United States be willing to share control of the Polaris force assigned to NATO—in order to meet an interim *political* need for sharing of control over an MRBM force—it drew off natural and inevitable opposition. It was predictable that strong opposition to sharing control of Polaris would arise in the JCS. The Chiefs were extremely protective of the Polaris force as a prime element of the American deterrent, and they did in fact direct their wrath at the idea that control of Polaris submarines be shared. This left the MLF standing as an apparently moderate compromise.

In handling the control issue in the MLF proposal, Owen was mainly concerned with forestalling a clear United States decision *not* to share control. In alliance with the Athens program proponents, he argued that the European allies would be convinced over time of the wisdom of control centralized in the United States Presidency, or at least including a United States veto, *if* the United States did not insist on it in advance of all discussion. Also, though this was not a stated U.S. policy, not to foreclose the sharing of control would allow time for a coalition to build in Europe around the MLF, with the possibility of real sharing of control dangled as bait wherever necessary. Finally, the formulation allowed leeway for an argument to be used in Europe which was most interesting to the proponents of integration; namely, that the United States would share operational control with a Europe united, as the United States was, behind a single executive.

Moving astutely within the bureaucracy, Owen cleared his paper through the civilian staff in the Pentagon and State Department hierarchy. His timing was superb. When Kennedy, Rusk, McNamara, and McGeorge Bundy met in April 1962 to decide on the question of aiding the French nuclear force, the MLF proposal was also on the agenda, and Owen's paper was the basis for discussion. While withholding aid to the French national force, Kennedy approved the Owen paper with a single change. The suggestion that the United States might share control of Polaris submarines assigned to NATO was specifically rejected, respecting the JCS position. With this change the paper was issued as National Security Action Memorandum (NSAM) 147, giving official status within the United States government to the MLF concept. Though Kennedy remained very reluctant to share control, an attitude expressed at the April meeting, he agreed to dangle the possibility as Owen had argued that he should.

Owen's skillful presentation of the MLF idea was supplemented conceptually by a series of papers by Walt Rostow and Foy Kohler, both of which were influenced by Bowie as a consultant.[35] Rostow quite directly connected the ideas of European unity and Atlantic partnership with the nuclear sharing issue. He sketched the dangers of independent European programs which he thought would result from United States recalcitrance on the issue and argued that the United States should pursue the collective force idea as prime means of building a unified Europe strongly allied with the United States, a means potentially even more important than tariff arrangements. He argued strongly against continuing the special relationship with Britain on nuclear matters because of its disruptive effects for Western Europe as a whole. He urged that the special relationship be dissolved in collective arrangements for NATO. Kohler supported the argument by presenting an extensive case against allowing the British to bargain their way into the EEC by offering nuclear information to France in exchange. Since the British did not propose such a bargain with France, neither Rostow's nor Kohler's arguments required decisions, but they did explicitly articulate the policy context for Owen's MLF concept.

The effect of NSAM 147 was to authorize the beginning of staff work within the Navy. Since the MLF was projected as a sea-based force it was clear that the Navy would have to take a position, and for those promoting the idea it was important that the Navy's position not be a veto. Admiral John M. Lee, director of the ISA Policy Planning Staff under Paul Nitze, seized the initia-

[35] Interview material.

tive. He drafted a memo which went to the Navy over Nitze's signature urging them to examine the idea. It is not completely clear whether Lee at the time was in close connection with the policy planners at State,[36] but without question his action was not only friendly to their purpose but also bore their signature of bureaucratic adeptness. Lee's question, in the first place, was adroitly phrased. Knowing that the Navy was not destined to be enthusiastic about an idea which was generated in the State Department and which contemplated foreigners on ships' crews, he did not inquire as to whether the Navy thought the MLF a wise idea. Appealing rather to Navy pride and to traditional subordination to civilian direction, he posed the question: If ordered to create the MLF (implicitly, for political reasons) can the Navy do it? Lee was also careful to arrange adequate sponsorship for the study. With his prodding, the study was set up in the summer of 1962 under Rear Admiral Frederick H. Michaelis with the blessing of the Deputy Chief of Naval Operations, Admiral Claude N. Ricketts. Significantly, both were not submarine, but surface-fleet commanders.

With the Navy study adroitly structured as a feasibility inquiry, the more dangerous comparative question—whether the MLF was the best approach to the problem among available alternatives—did not arise. The burden of proof was thereby shifted to the opponents, and it was up to anyone who wished to exercise a veto on absolute grounds to come forward. The first to do so was Admiral Hyman Rickover, a man who had established by then unchallengeable authority over critical components of the nuclear submarine program: the nuclear reactor itself and the selection and training of crews to operate it. Rickover's power rested very significantly on the Joint Committee on Atomic Energy, which had sponsored his career. Since the JCAE would have to approve a revision of the McMahon Act for the MLF to be possible, and since Rickover's branch of the Navy would have to run the program, his veto was one which promised to be lethal. It was delivered on the argument that crews of mixed nationality

[36] Some interaction between the policy planning staff of State and ISA is virtually guaranteed by their overlapping concerns, and Lee certainly knew of his counterparts' activity. Within six months he was working closely with Owen, Bowie, Schaetzel, and others on developing and proposing the MLF idea. Some interviewees state flatly that Owen inspired Lee's initiative, but opinion on that question is divided.

speaking different languages could not achieve the near-perfect timing required to operate a nuclear submarine effectively. This could be convincingly defended in public if need be. Behind that argument lay the clincher which could not be argued in polite diplomatic exchange: Foreign crews were not to be allowed access to certain aspects of nuclear submarine technology which the Soviets were apparently having difficulty in mastering.

Rickover's veto was painful for MLF proponents. The Polaris submarine, as the premier American weapon, was commensurate with the European sense of identity and national integrity. The alternative of a surface-ship configuration was much more problematic in this regard. In March of 1961 President Kennedy had sent a message to Congress announcing the cancellation of a plan to install a Polaris system on the cruiser *Long Beach*. The President had argued that the money would be "far better spent on the less vulnerable Polaris submarine," and this was a matter of public record.[37] One could not have high confidence that the Europeans would accept something for their defense which the United States had rejected for its own.

The problem drove the Navy study into its only piece of comparative analysis: an assessment of the relative advantages of submarine and surface fleet configurations of the force. A cost/effectiveness comparison was prepared which argued that the surface-ship configuration was in fact a desirable option. The central problem was vulnerability. The compelling property of nuclear submarines was that they could cruise for long periods beneath the surface of the ocean, where electronic surveillance technology was relatively ineffective. On the surface of the ocean the game was a great deal easier for the hunter, and the surface force appeared vulnerable to preemptive attack. The Michaelis report[38] argued that the problem of vulnerability could be handled, for a twenty-five-ship force, by a variety of measures designed to confound continuous surveillance of all the ships. With this done, the same mission could be accomplished more cheaply than it could by the submarine force, and the surface force would be available at an earlier date. This was clearly a useful argument. The only way to prevent Rickover from stopping the MLF was to remove it from his jurisdiction. Hence a surface configura-

[37] John F. Kennedy, *Public Papers of the President* (Washington: U.S. Government Printing Office, 1961), p. 239.
[38] Interview material.

tion for the MLF was necessary. If the Europeans could be convinced of the validity of the comparative analysis, one might appeal to their natural interests in economy to gain an acceptance of the switch to surface vessels.

Another challenge to the feasibility of the MLF idea came from the Office of International Logistics Negotiations, then headed by Henry Kuss, which conducted most of the United States world arms trade. Strong testimony to the Michaelis group from Leonard Alne of that office argued the difficulty of coordinating a project such as the MLF through the national bureaucracies of allied governments. Alne cited bitter experience in trying to run NATO military operations through a multitude of bureaucracies. To the main figures of the study, however, Alne's warning was as much a strength as a weakness. Precisely the problem of coordinating national bureaucracies would necessitate in their estimation a common, highly autonomous supranational organization to run the force. This meshed nicely with State's overall concept of integration in Europe. As one of the Navy men put it: A little Navy requires a little Navy Department; and a little Navy Department requires a little government.[39]

Thus, the Michaelis report, while noting that the MLF was quite expensive and that it would require massive support from the governments involved, pronounced the MLF feasible and specifically included in this judgment the surface-ship configuration. That meant that as a matter of official record the Navy could manage a multilateral operation which would make a military contribution. The significance was that the Navy as a whole would not, for the moment, deliver a veto.

The choice of Admirals Michaelis, Ricketts, and Lee as the central figures in the Navy's studies was very significant. Ricketts and Lee had risen to flag rank through command positions in the fleet, Michaelis through the aircraft carrier force. The fleet commands and the carrier commands are separate specialties within the Navy. Since an officer's career is generally pursued along one such channel, subcultures form and political interests coalesce around fleet escort vessels, carriers, and submarines respectively. These subcultures deeply affect the politics of weapons acquisition within the Navy.[40] Though fleet commanders and carrier

[39] Interview material.
[40] Morton Halperin, *Bureaucratic Politics and Foreign Policy* (Washington: Brookings Institution, forthcoming).

commanders are not infrequently at odds on issues of weapons policy, they would form a natural alliance on a question which turned essentially on the vulnerability of surface vessels. The fact that the surface-ship commanders sponsored the MLF feasibility study destined in advance that no viable submarine option could emerge from it. But, given Rickover, that was not to be had in any case. The two fleet admirals and the carrier man did virtually guarantee a live surface-ship option, for they were not likely to develop calculations about vulnerability which might erode the core interests of the Navy units to which they belonged.

Whether the sponsorship of the Navy studies was a conscious design or a consequential accident is a matter of sheer speculation. The natural presumption must favor the latter interpretation in the absence of direct evidence, even though the sophistication entailed in the conscious design would not have been out of character for the MLF proponents. However, once Rickover's veto was delivered and the surface-force option advanced, the MLF proponents were quick to consolidate their organizational position. Beginning simultaneously with the Michaelis study and continuing after it, substantial staff work was done in ISA on technical details of the surface force concept. Under a civilian analyst, Timothy Stanley, and Captain John Cotten of the Navy, such things as design specifications for the surface ships, command arrangements, missile control procedures, and language training were worked out in detail. This developing body of plans gave the proposal serious organizational stature. The scope and detail of the staff work signaled within the bureaucracy that the matter was reasonably serious, and as the work proceeded it gave proponents confidence that the ideas they were propounding had been examined in some depth. Moreover, the product of the staff work provided a basis for diplomatic discussions, and that in fact was the next major development.

At Henry Owen's suggestion, Gerard Smith, former head of the State's Policy Planning staff, and the man who had commissioned the Bowie report, was engaged as a consultant in August of 1962 to develop a briefing for the allies on the MLF idea as developed by the Michaelis study and by the staff work in ISA. Labeling the proposal the "Ottawa force" to reference President Kennedy's public endorsement of the idea in his speech before the Canadian Parliament, Smith, together with Admiral Lee, briefed European officials on the status of the idea in various trips to Europe during the fall of 1962. The force they described to allied governments was the surface-ship configuration of the MLF, a force of 200 Polaris A-3 missiles to be placed on twenty-five surface ships. The fleet was to be jointly owned and operated and was to have a governing body. Individual ships of the fleet were to be manned by various nationalities, so that no single national contingent could control any given ship. The provisions for joint ownership and control were so to intertwine the participating governments that withdrawal of any component of the force for national purposes would be out of the question.

The critical question of control was handled much as Henry Owen had argued that it should be earlier in the spring. The United States position was interpreted as flexible on devolving control, particularly if there should be progress toward political integration in Europe. The Smith/Lee briefings made it clear that at the outset United States as well as allied consent would be required in giving firing orders to the force. By the fall of 1962, however, a number of public statements had been made indicating that the United States might be willing to relinquish a veto if the Europeans could achieve unified political arrangements. McGeorge Bundy suggested this possibility in a speech in Copenhagen in September of 1962.[41] George Ball repeated it in a major address to the alliance following the Cuban missile crisis,[42] and Secretaries Rusk and McNamara both reiterated the theme at the December meeting of the NATO Council.[43]

Through NSAM 147 and the ensuing studies, the MLF had gained enough momentum by the fall of 1962 to make the Secretary of Defense distinctly nervous. Seeking to maintain policy control, he promoted two high-level defense policy conferences at which he and the Secretary of State and the top officials of their two departments would meet to review outstanding NATO issues. McNamara used the second of these conferences to challenge directly the developing MLF idea. Questioning Admiral Lee very sharply, he voiced doubts as to whether the Smith/Lee briefings had made the preconditions for an MLF clear to the allies; namely, that they bear the cost and that they first achieve

[41] *Department of State Bulletin* (*DOSB*), October 22, 1962, pp. 604–605.
[42] *DOSB*, December 3, 1962, pp. 831–835.
[43] *New York Times*, December 15, 1962, p. 1.

an increase in conventional forces.[44] McNamara was confident that if these preconditions were made clear the MLF idea would be quickly discarded. To him the fact that some interest had been generated in Europe was a sign that the briefing had been more sanguine than he desired. Beyond that, he attacked and successfully derailed a plan which had arisen to have a small MLF instituted in the Mediterranean (known as the Mediterranean Pilot Force or MPF) as a substitute for the Thor and Jupiter missiles in Turkey and Italy upon which the Cuban crisis had focused so much attention. McNamara labeled this idea unworkable and gained State's acquiescence in dropping all discussion of the proposal.

Both Secretary of State Rusk and McGeorge Bundy came to the rescue of Smith and Lee in the wake of McNamara's attack, expressing confidence that the two emissaries had not exceeded instructions. In doing so, however, Rusk made clear his own assessment that the Europeans would not take up the MLF as serious business. Thus, to all appearances, McNamara substantially won his point. He did not like the MLF, and he did not want it to record any real progress. The MPF, as an early step to the MLF, had been scuttled; and the Smith/Lee presentation had been toned down. The stage was set for the events of December.

THE OUTCOMES

The two-year jostling among the Athens program, aid to national nuclear forces, and the MLF came to a head in December of 1962 as the American decision not to continue the Skybolt missile program precipitated a crisis in British-American relations. Robert McNamara, who had assumed the responsibility for working out the British interest in Skybolt, was not aware (as others were not) that British politics hung on the Americans making a generous offer to substitute for Skybolt and that they awaited his initiative. He assumed rather that they would enter negotiations with a proposal of their own; and on this impasse in assumptions his negotiations failed. This had the effect of forcing the issue to the head-of-state level. Since President Kennedy and Prime Minister Macmillan were independently scheduled to meet on December 19 at Nassau in the Bahamas, that meeting became an unavoidable forum for negotiations of the issue.

[44] Interview material.

This unexpected twist left American timing badly awry.[45] Secretary McNamara had to proceed from his negotiations in London to the NATO Council meeting in Paris and could not fully prepare the American position. Secretary of State Rusk had scheduled a diplomatic dinner and could not even attend the conference.[46] President Kennedy, unaware of some dimensions of the problem until he boarded the plane for Nassau, had prejudiced the negotiations by previous public comments deprecating the Skybolt missile. The President's comments were designed to justify, to a domestic audience, his administration's decision to cancel the program, but they also had the effect of convincing the British Prime Minister that any arrangement involving Skybolt was unacceptable. En route, Kennedy devised a deal whereby the United States would share half of the financial burden of continuing the Skybolt program solely for the British forces. This was more generous than the original agreement at Camp David and would leave the British little scope for credible outrage. When he arrived at Nassau, however, Kennedy found Harold Macmillan firmly unwilling to accept Skybolt on any terms and McNamara equally, if more reservedly, negative. His own preferences were soon awash in crosscutting political tides.

The British position was simple and direct. Macmillan demanded an American commitment to an independent British deterrent, a commitment concretely symbolized by a weapons agreement. Skybolt, he maintained, had been destroyed as a symbol by the American decision to cancel it and by the resulting public discussions. The closest military substitute, the Hound Dog missile, was too infelicitously named, too prone to British satire, too much a consolation prize to be a political substitute. Supplying Polaris to the British forces was the only acceptable substitute. Failing that, Macmillan intimated he would excoriate the United States and consort with the French in order to remain

[45] The account here follows Neustadt, *Alliance Politics*.

[46] As with many points in the story, there is an opening here for intriguing speculation. Why could a diplomatic dinner not be rescheduled under such conditions? It would have been awkward, but not impossible. Why could the Secretary not commute to the dinner from Nassau? It is plausible that Rusk, a well-known Anglophile, would welcome an excuse to be absent from the Nassau negotiations. If Nassau produced British-American rancor, he would have been in a good position to play the mediator. If the British got satisfaction at Nassau at American expense, he could not be accused of having arranged a sellout.

the champion of British independence and thus stave off a collapse of his government. Macmillan portrayed collective force arrangements as a separate issue, to be decided after the symbol of independence was firmly in hand. As a substitute for Skybolt, any British Polaris at least at the outset would *not* be assigned to SACEUR.

The State Department was represented by George Ball and staffed from Washington by Bowie, Owen, Schaetzel, and Rostow. To them the British demands were anathema. They constituted a steep and very slippery slope which, if granted, would lead directly to a crisis first with the French, then with the Germans, and then on down the line within NATO. The only wise solution in their view was the MLF, a dissolution of the independent British force into a collective deterrent. At any rate, no arrangement with the British was to be made which was not firmly enmeshed in a multilateral, NATO-wide context. Ball argued, with Bowie's strong concurrence, that the British threats could be faced down with American resolve and diplomatic finesse. Macmillan would be constrained, in civilized Britain, by the need to appear reasonable, and the United States could deny him a reasonable anti-American position. The obvious countermove was to offer the generous Skybolt deal Kennedy had devised or the Hound Dog substitute or perhaps to delay the whole business with an extended study, any of which would give Macmillan some difficulty in arguing American perfidy to the House of Commons. Faced with that prospect, State's planners felt the Prime Minister would most likely accept the multilateral arrangement they preferred.

McNamara was accompanied by Paul Nitze at the Nassau meeting, and this staff arrangement reinforced his tendency to acquiesce in the British demands for Polaris. He had been convinced of the inevitability of this resolution after his London negotiations, and the tight integration of United States and British forces made opposition based on the Athens program principles unnecessary. McNamara apparently was willing even to include France in the arrangements in the hope that the French force would thereby be brought into the same closely integrated relationship to the American forces that had been achieved with the British. He also had hopes of obtaining French support for an increase in NATO conventional forces. Both results would have represented net gains in the immediate situation to the objective of unifying the alliance deterrent forces even if the extended consequences might look more problematic. The idea of sharing the costs of continuing Skybolt solely for the British was distasteful to McNamara because it sacrificed half the budget savings he had achieved with his decision to cancel the program and because it appeared to be an unworkable arrangement for the British to deal with American industry on a missile system which was bound to recede in priority. Beyond that, McNamara had been under the impression all along that the original Skybolt agreement entailed a clear relationship to NATO which could be transferred to the substitute system. It is not clear that he had been disabused of this notion until just before the conference actually began. This lingering impression reinforced his basic hostility to the MLF idea.

Kennedy responded to the immediate pressures. Against his own wishes and intentions, he acceded to Macmillan's demands and McNamara's inclination. He agreed to sell Polaris missiles to the British under an arrangement whereby they would provide the warheads. The British could expect all the help they required on weapons design through the information exchange program. To George Ball, Kennedy gave mostly rhetoric. The forces created by the agreement "would be made available in a NATO multilateral force" and would be used for the defense of the alliance in all circumstances "except where Her Majesty's Government may decided that supreme national interests are at stake."[47] As Kennedy himself pointed out in a subsequent background briefing for the press,[48] the only time that the use of nuclear weapons is considered is when supreme national interests are at stake. There was enough general language in the communiqué to enable Ball and his State Department colleagues to claim subsequently that the principle of a mixed-manned collective force had been affirmed in the Nassau agreement, but behind the language was the fact that Macmillan was given what he requested, and that contradicted the MLF design.

To the proponents of the Athens program, for whom McNamara was a wavering advocate at the conference, there was also a bit of rhetoric to soothe the hard fact of the decision. The indivisibility of alliance defense was proclaimed—a diplomatic phrase which had come to signify both the need for centralized

[47] *New York Times*, December 22, 1962, p. 3.
[48] Ibid.

command/control over deterrent forces and the reliability of the American forces for European defense. There was also an exhortation for increases in conventional forces and a reversal of some traditional NATO images. Conventional forces were referred to as the NATO "sword"—the prime means of military action—and the nuclear forces were portrayed as the NATO "shield."[49] The decision, however, was to extend a substantial new form of aid to a national nuclear force. Thus, the conference communiqué, which recorded policy governing the agreement, simply rolled all the conflicting positions into one document, giving a separate paragraph to each and ignoring the contradictions.

One consequence of the decision came due immediately: something had to be done for de Gaulle. Macmillan had met with de Gaulle just before coming to Nassau to discuss the British application to the EEC. De Gaulle had been so discouraging that at least the professional British diplomats began to anticipate the failure of the negotiations. This point had not come through to the Americans, however, and they were distinctly worried about the General's reaction to a striking new Anglo-American deal. Having taken the first step, therefore, Kennedy immediately agreed to the second. The Polaris offer was extended to France, and a letter was improvised to inform the General. It was obviously makeshift diplomacy with no staff work, no prior conversations, and with de Gaulle not even a partner in the improvised negotiations. The President and his Cabinet members, however, resolved to compensate with good intentions. The French would be given scope to negotiate a full measure of aid for their nuclear weapons program, and they would be given the same escape clause the British had received, allowing use of the force for national purposes.

In the wake of the Nassau agreements there was puzzlement in the Pentagon and deep gloom in the State Department. American policy had made a sharp turn with very little warning. Earlier decisions against aid to national forces had been reversed. Both the basic tenets and the critical policy documents of the Athens program had been directly contradicted. The demoraliza-

---

[49] This reversed the nuclear sword/conventional shield imagery to which Norstad still held and which reflected much more clearly the reality of NATO war plans. Norstad, though scheduled to be replaced, remained as SACEUR because the Cuban missile crisis precluded a change in major commands.

tion deepened as de Gaulle made his moves—rejecting the Polaris offer without negotiations, terminating EEC negotiations with Britain, signing a treaty of cooperation with the Germans, and in general demonstrating commanding influence over the course of European events. Unified deterrence, Atlantic partnership, and European integration were suddenly all in eclipse; and a split between the Anglo-Saxon and the Continental powers seemed imminent. Moreover, consequences accrued which could not be changed for a significant period of time: Britain was excluded from European economic communities; the French national force was set on an independent course of development. NATO strategy and force posture remained as before, with French participation very much a matter of doubt. None of the three American options had achieved its objectives.[50]

THEORETICAL PERSPECTIVES

The fate of the predictions which were charged to the separate paradigms at the point of December 1960 gives good entrée to the problem of providing a theoretical account both of the decision process in which the Kennedy administration engaged and of the outcomes which resulted. The relative success of the predictions made gives some clue as to the power of the central assumptions of each paradigm and the accompanying logic in illuminating the events of the period. It is at once true that the events provide some test of the paradigms and that the paradigms provide a means of understanding the events.

It can be argued that the major drift of *policy* corresponded reasonably well to the expectations of the analytic paradigm. The

---

[50] Students of de Gaulle are insistent that the General would have acted as he did regardless of what happened at the Nassau conference, and they strongly suggest that nothing the United States could have done could have turned a man of his will and sense of direction. It seems quite clear that de Gaulle had in fact decided on his veto of the British EEC application before the Nassau conference and that his rejection of the Nassau offer followed quite readily from the same underlying logic. It is also clear that the United States would have had trouble with de Gaulle in pursuing any of the policies outlined. De Gaulle, however, for all his sense of history, was not the sole arbiter of its forces. It is conceivable that other outcomes could have occurred in Europe. The way in which the United States acted had some effect on the course of events. For the argument regarding de Gaulle's undeflectable will, see Newhouse, *De Gaulle and the Anglo-Saxons*.

policy directive which emerged from the Acheson study placed primary emphasis on unified deterrent forces and on conventional force capacity in order to diminish NATO's reliance on escalation. The sharing of control within the alliance was not foreclosed, but hedged with a number of difficult preconditions. The implicit message was that it would not be done unless there were very intense European pressure and no alternative. This was a plausible analytic balance of the competing objectives. The well-rehearsed dangers of nuclear war seemed clearly to dictate the emphasis on centralized command and control. Though it was clear as well that control of the deterrent and possession of nuclear weapons were sensitive political issues, a number of reactions in Europe were possible, and hence there were a number of plausible policies. If the political issues could be handled without having to compromise on unified operational control of the nuclear forces of the alliance, that would be an efficient solution in analytic terms—a gain on the political objective with no loss to the defense objective. The analytic paradigm would expect the United States to seek such an outcome, and that is what the officially dominant Athens program was trying to accomplish.

To the chagrin of the analytic theorist, however, decisions did not always follow established policy, and the flow of events did not neatly accord with any of the various intentions displayed at various points in time. If American behavior of the period is understood as an analytic balancing of competing objectives, for example, the failure to follow through on the campaign of persuasion emerges as a serious anomaly. This was the major feature of the Athens program, designed to enable an efficient resolution of the problem, and yet it was allowed to lapse. Close examination reveals it to have been largely the special, accident-prone project of a small number of analysts in ISA and not the widely shared commitment analytic theory would expect.

It is difficult, moreover, for the analytic paradigm to account for the support which developed behind the second-phase MLF —the mixed-manned, jointly owned and operated NATO fleet with Polaris missiles. The first phase of Bowie's 1960 plan—the assignment of United States forces to NATO—sufficed for the immediate purpose. Without strong political pressure from the European allies (which did not develop) there was little apparent justification for pursuing the second-phase idea. To do so was action in the absence of new information. The MLF was a complicated idea with major risks, such as the possibility of stimulating and legitimizing rather than preempting a German weapons program, or the possibility of losing the conventional force precondition and driving European defense allocations redundantly into nuclear weapons. United States activity, in developing the idea and in seeking European comment, was premature to the analytic theorist.[51]

The major anomaly for the analytic perspective, however, is the outcome of the Nassau conference. Both the sudden shift to aiding national forces after a series of negative decisions and the vehicle of the aid—the prime weapons system of the American forces—are hard to fathom within the logic of the paradigm. The arguments of the Athens program against national aid had become stronger rather than weaker during the eight months intervening between the decisions of April, which were negative on the question, and the forcefully positive decision of December. Obvious and available countermoves to British pressure in December were not attempted. The agreement of the conference was accepted in direct contradiction to the President's clearly stated preferences of the day before the conference opened. The opening left for de Gaulle was damaging by any assessment and disastrous by many. It is a distinct strain on analytic logic to account for such decisions.

In terms of the basic propositions of the paradigm, value integration appears to have held plausibly well in the limited context of defining abstract policy. It was seriously compromised, however, in the flow of concrete decisions over the period. The shift in Presidential decisions and policy-setting actions back and forth between the three contending options is hard to reconcile with stable preferences. One could assume that Kennedy's underlying analytically integrated preferences were shifting, but this would

[51] This is not to deny that the program could be made to conform to assumptions of the analytic paradigm if a sufficiently long time frame is ascribed to the decision makers and if strong assumptions about the beneficial effect of the proposal in soothing European fears are granted. Since such assumptions would be quite visionary in the highly uncertain situation of the. time, however, one would still find the analytic paradigm strained in accounting for the pattern of argument which developed. It should be recalled also that by the restricted definition of the paradigm adopted here it would be perfectly possible for the arguments in question to be perfectly correct in an empirical sense (i.e., come "true" in time) and still violate analytic assumptions.

be a rather blatant *post hoc* manipulation of the theory, robbing it of any predictive power. Regarding utilization of information, similar difficulties are experienced. The Nassau solution and the development of the second-phase MLF idea occurred against a trend whose natural tendency would have been to strengthen the Athens program. The utilization of new information to update probability assessments would hardly have produced the Nassau results. An assessment of whether alternative outcomes were projected requires a more fine-grained analysis such as developed in the next chapter, but such evidence as exists suggests that the judgments made were categorical rather than integrative. To those proposing aid to the French, an independent French force was seen as inevitable. To MLF proponents, the Germans over the long run categorically would not accept a status less than that of a strategic nuclear power. All these judgments could be reconciled to the analytic paradigm with some ingenuity in the application of *ad hoc* assumptions, but however that may be, the point is made: an analytic interpretation, though by no means inapplicable, does have serious difficulty in explaining what occurred.

The prediction charged to the cognitive paradigm at the end of 1960 held only weakly in the ensuing two years. Norstad's MRBM proposal was still officially supported by the Joint Chiefs in December of 1962 and appeared in their planning documents. The life, however, had clearly gone out of it. After the pronunciations of McNamara at Athens, the MRBM system became a *pro forma* requirement both within the alliance and within the American government, and there was never again any very substantial possibility of the "requirement" being met by a program of the sort Norstad had envisaged in 1960. The logic behind the prediction had some validity, but the forces to which the prediction was sensitive clearly did not dominate the outcomes.

One can do somewhat better by using the cognitive paradigm as a framework for retrospective analysis. Organizational analysis based on simple cybernetic assumptions, for example, helps explain the demise of the program for working the allies into the strategic planning process (the campaign of persuasion). The failure of the attempt to mount a serious campaign of persuasion was in a large part the result of organizational routines inimical to the program's being too powerfully established to be overcome by policy decisions won by the Athens program proponents. The grounds for this result are discovered within the paradigm: the inertial resistance to change of established organizational procedures. It may have been hard to predict this turn of events from the vantage point of 1960, but the paradigm readily explains what was happening as the episode began to evolve.

If not simple cybernetic assumptions, but rather the full cognitive paradigm is applied, the retrospective explanation becomes even more powerful. Indeed, the cognitive paradigm handles rather well those events which the analytic perspective finds puzzling. The behavior of the President, which is anomalous to analytic theory, fits quite well with the pattern of uncommitted thinking which the cognitive theory expects of a man of a political background in an office which imposes responsibility overarching all major issues. The shift in President Kennedy's position back and forth between the three separate lines of policy urged on him by separate sets of advisers is a direct reflection of this pattern. In his policy directive of April 1961 and in his personally worded instructions to NATO Ambassador Finletter in June 1962 (delivered to the NATO Council), Kennedy backed the Athens program. His rejection of aid to the French in April of 1962 was in that spirit as well. In different contexts, however, he gave the MLF his own authorization in the Ottawa speech of May 1961[52] and endorsed the governing concepts of Atlantic partnership and European unity throughout the period.[53] In April of 1962 he authorized staff work on the second-phase MLF despite the clear implications of his instructions to Finletter, which were subsequently produced. Finally, though denying aid to France in April of 1962, he immediately had the White House staff elaborately challenging the negative arguments, thus delivering a clear signal within the American bureaucracy of his continued interest in bilateral nuclear aid. Then, at Nassau, he supplied the British with a form of aid directly against the arguments of the Athens program and his own policy directives, and opened up the full range of aid for negotiations with France. His decisions in each case were highly responsive to the immediate context, and never at any point was a clear, stable policy line established.

All this is as expected from the perspective of the cognitive

[52] *New York Times*, May 18, 1961, p. 12.

[53] See for example his July Fourth speech in Philadelphia in 1962 in the *New York Times*, July 5, 1962, p. 1.

paradigm. In a man who had pursued a political career—always confronting a variety of issues and never having the occasion to work into any one area of policy in great depth—the paradigm would not look for the deeply rooted generalized belief structure characteristic of the theoretical thinker, who might have set a single, firm policy. Many informed characterizations of Kennedy as President confirm this expectation.[54] As a man who clearly valued intellect and reasoned policy positions, Kennedy would naturally be swayed by the policy arguments of the contending advisers. The pattern of decisions and policy pronouncements leaves clear indication that Kennedy did indeed shift back and forth in his mind between the three sets of arguments. The analysis of the paradigm holds that he made decisions following one line of argument without trying to reconcile them with the alternative policies. In each case the particular policy framework which was evoked and supported would be determined by what the President was receiving on his natural information channels —the demands and opinions of key political actors.

This offers a straightforward interpretation of the decision at Nassau. The demands of Macmillan dominated what in terms of the paradigm would be understood as the President's feedback channels, and these demands provided the natural focus for his decision process. The arguments in favor of aid to national forces which Kennedy had heard for two years provided an intellectual framework for Macmillan's demands. This was evoked in the situation, and Kennedy's decision followed accordingly. What is

[54] His aide and his historian, Schlesinger and Sorenson, both testify that Kennedy's attitude toward the alliance was what they call pragmatic. As Sorensen puts it, "The truth is that Kennedy himself did not look upon either the Alliance or Atlantic harmony as an end in itself. He cared about the concrete problems which the Alliance faced, such as Berlin, trade negotiations, and the American balance of payments. But he felt that State Department tradition had led us to think of every problem of foreign policy in terms of the Western Alliance when it was no longer as central to all our problems as it once had been and when Europe's own strength had caused it to assert its views more independently. He tended to look upon the rest of the Alliance in somewhat the same light as he looked upon Congress—as a necessary but not always welcome partner, whose cooperation he could not always obtain, whose opinions he could not always accept, and with whom an uneasy relationship seemed inevitable. As the Cuban missile crisis illustrated, he was at his best when his responsibilities did not have to be shared." See Theodore Sorenson, *Kennedy* (New York: Harper & Row, Publishers, 1965), pp. 562–563.

astounding to the analytic perspective is perfectly natural to the cognitive paradigm. Kennedy acted as an uncommitted thinker.

The explanation applies to some extent to Defense Secretary McNamara as well. Though he was, in the public mind, the champion of the Athens program and was seen as anything but an uncommitted man, McNamara was much more consistent in his support of a conventional arms buildup among the European allies than he was for other parts of the program which the professional defense analysts devised. The program of persuasion withered under McNamara without drawing his attention, and he was directly instrumental in promoting the Polaris deal with the British in preference to any sharing arrangement which would keep Skybolt alive. Under pressure from the Joint Chiefs he funded a research and development program for the MRBM far beyond the point where the analysts who worked for him had written it off. In these decisions he, too, reflected a strong responsiveness to immediate political pressures, to the content of short-term feedback channels. His handling of the Skybolt issue also accords with this view. Skybolt represented a major and immediate budget saving which was a prime focus of McNamara's decisions, and in his calculations the longer term considerations—i.e., the consequences of risking centralized control of the deterrent by extending Polaris to Britain and France—paled in comparison to this. The dominance of the immediate budget saving and the wavering on central principles of the Athens program is puzzling to the analytic theorist but quite understandable within the framework of the cognitive paradigm.

In terms of the basic propositions of the cognitive paradigm, it seems clear that the way in which the three alternatives were structured does reflect a separation rather than an integration of the competing objectives. Certainly the national aid proposals and the MLF were directed at specific problems having to do with political objectives—repairing bilateral relations in one case and bolstering the integration movement in the other. The structure of the Navy's feasibility study reflects this. All of the questions in the MLF proposal as to how the MLF compared to other options, which would have been raised if the integrative analytic process had been the one utilized, were defined out of the study. The result was a study which promoted the MLF cause but did not balance competing claims of other objectives and other alternatives. The fact that both the MLF and national aid posed serious problems in compromising the control of forces was generally handled by positing that the objective of centralized control could not be achieved—a variant of the inference of impossibility. Especially the MLF argument, as will be seen in some detail in the next chapter, displayed rather clearly the use of inference management mechanisms to block off the claims of the competing objective. The Athens program also was pursued with the critical balancing component essentially vitiated—that is, the information exchange and the seminar on strategy. Each of the contending programs, then, was essentially a response to one of the contending objectives. With Kennedy adopting the separate perspectives in sequence, there is a good case to be made that nowhere in the decision process did value integration occur.

There are also some dimensions of the story which clearly require a political perspective for anything approaching complete elucidation. For one thing, the focus of the feedback mechanisms discussed above is provided by the demands of other political actors. In terms of direct outcomes a prime example is provided by the fading of Norstad's MRBM proposal as a major force in the issue. The lapse of the idea into a formal and essentially meaningless paragraph in planning documents and a relatively inexpensive research and development program was quintessentially a political result.[55] The predicted political weakness of Norstad's position seems to provide a decent explanation of what happened. When he forced a confrontation on the issue in early 1963, he lost. He was replaced as SACEUR by General Lyman Lemnitzer, who moved from the Army Chief of Staff position and who could be counted on not to be an intolerable enthusiast of the land-based MRBM.

A political perspective is important also in understanding the development of the second-phase MLF as a serious contender. Though the intellectual structure of its proponents is critical in understanding why they were in motion on that proposal, the degree of success achieved is in significant part attributable also to skill at political maneuvering within the bureaucracy. The MLF advocates could not match the strong intellectual momentum which stood behind the Athens program, momentum built up with long years of analysis of basic problems of defense policy. Nor could they play off of immediate political forces comparable

[55] Analytic theory would predict a clear negative decision.

to the pressure exerted by the British and French governments for national aid. Their substitute was a strong commitment relatively impervious to uncertainty *and* a great deal of skill in operating the machinery of the American government. Both dimensions of strength require further analysis.

The account thus provided by applying the separate paradigms is a first rough assessment of the relative power of the paradigms and the first resolution of some of the MLF puzzles. It is easy to see that it would be hard to do without any of the paradigms in explaining the story, for in some respects reality was a blend of forces illuminated by all three perspectives. That, however, does not license the assumption that a true account can be achieved simply by adding the paradigms together. A key insight seems to be that, contrary to the expectations of analytic theory, the central trade-off between military and political values was being broken up and that the two dimensions were not being integrated. Moreover, outcome calculations appear to have been rather truncated, and the overall process looked more like one of the cognitive variety than anything else. It is too early for any theoretical conclusion, but it seems established that holding the separate paradigms in direct competition is a useful thing to do, despite good indication that in some limited sense they are simultaneously valid.

CHAPTER 9

Ascendancy and Sudden Death of the
Multilateral Force: 1963–1964

THE CONSEQUENCES of the Nassau conference and the actions of
Charles de Gaulle propelled the MLF proposal to ascendancy in
American policy toward Europe. This happened, however, without resolving major anomalies inherent in the concept. The President remained unwilling to relinquish his veto over the firing of
any NATO force, and yet a sharing of control remained the essence of the proposal. The project would cost between $2.3 and
$5 billion, depending on the time frame used, and by calculations
available at the time it would contribute for that cost far less to
the defense posture of the alliance than could be gained with
other expenditures. With distinct British and French opposition,
the proposal promised to divide rather than to unite Europe and
to force the German government, intended to be the major bene-
ficiary, into precisely that situation Bonn desired above all to
avoid: a choice between Paris and Washington. There was very
little evidence suggesting the imminence of the major problem
the MLF was to answer: pressure within Germany for the control of nuclear weapons. Speculation about long-term development of such pressure could affirm or deny it with roughly equal
plausibility. Within the United States government the proposal
was supported primarily in the Policy Planning Council of the
State Department, normally a relatively weak subunit of the foreign policy machinery and not at all an advantageous place from
which to promote a new weapons deployment. The proposal was
opposed, moreover, by the powerful Secretary of Defense, and
it did not have active support of any of the armed services. In all,
with both the weight of substantive argument and the national
tendencies of bureaucratic politics tilted against the MLF, one
would expect its prominence to have been short-lived. To the intuitive observer of 1963 the proposal would have been readily
interpreted as a brief resting place during the shuffle caused by
de Gaulle's maneuvers, a useful haven for the moment, but hardly the basis for American policy of the ensuing period.

248

A casual glance at the last half of Kennedy's term might see a confirmation of those expectations. Shortly after President Johnson was elected in his own right in 1964, he scuttled the MLF idea and shifted his focus of attention away from Europe to Indochina. In this perspective the intervening two years, with all the turmoil of Kennedy's assassination, might seem a perfectly natural duration for the MLF to strangle on its inherent contradictions. Our intuitive observer might find no reason to pause and wonder.

This casual view, however, misreads the phenomenon. During 1963 and 1964 the MLF became far more than a temporary expedient for dealing with the policy crisis created by de Gaulle. For these two years the United States waged a diplomatic campaign on behalf of the proposal which very nearly brought the force into being, and which inevitably created a test of American leadership and prestige in Europe. A draft treaty was prepared via extensive negotiations with allied representatives. The British and German governments were maneuvered into position, and the requisite acquiescence of various components of the American bureaucracy was achieved. President Johnson's name was publicly attached to the proposal. His intentions to secure an agreement were officially expressed to the alliance, and the election in November of 1964 gave him sufficient political mandate. The demise of the proposal in December of 1964, therefore, was not the gradual and inevitable fading of an expedient but rather the abrupt, unexpected, and costly reversal of a commitment.

This makes the episode somewhat puzzling and worthy of more careful analysis. Both the making and the breaking of a major alliance commitment by the American government are interesting topics, particularly so during the period in question. Thus, there are two major problems of explanation: Why did the United States become committed to the MLF in the first place, given the inherent difficulties of the proposal? And, given that the United States did become committed, why was that commitment reversed just as the conditions for achieving the established objective appeared to be in hand?

THE MLF COALITION

Organizational Position

The Nassau agreement and the de Gaulle press conference which followed were near-calamities in the logic of those who sup-

249

ported the MLF and/or the concepts of European integration and Atlantic partnership. In their view, instead of gracefully terminating the inherently troublesome special defense relationship with Great Britain, the United States had given it another decade of life. Instead of achieving a broadening of the European communities through British membership, a step which it was felt would promote Atlantic as well as European cooperation, there was an explicit exclusion of Britain. De Gaulle's more nationalistic policies had apparently gained the ascendancy in Europe. State's Europeanists feared a dead halt, if not a reversal, in the progress of integration. To them the events of December and January had all the proportions of a tidal wave with the additional agony that their own government had had a distinct hand in wielding the destructive force.

But, for all that, disaster carried also the seeds of strength, and the MLF proponents were extremely quick to nourish those seeds. First, the extemporized Nassau agreement presented enough ambiguities, inconsistencies, and loose ends to give ample scope to use the staff work which inevitably followed to control the implications for aid to national nuclear forces. Second, MLF proponents were well positioned within the State Department to use that opportunity. The conference made Undersecretary George Ball a champion of the multilateral concept and put Secretary Rusk somewhat on the sidelines. Hence, to Ball went the task of directing the post-Nassau planning exercise and conducting the necessary discussions in European capitals. That helped solidify the position within the State Department of the MLF proponents, and the de Gaulle press conference added more strength. Walt Rostow was stirred by the turmoil to give personal attention and support to the MLF proposal. Robert Schaetzel, a very aggressive Deputy Assistant Secretary for European affairs, became an active worker on behalf of the MLF when his main cause—British entrance into the EEC—was stymied. Both the individuals and the positions they held were important supplements to the MLF coalition centered around Henry Owen, Robert Bowie, Gerard Smith, and Admiral John Lee.

Third, the course of the MLF was significantly strengthened by the fact that the Nassau agreement and de Gaulle's riposte neutralized the opposition of Robert McNamara. McNamara had handled the Skybolt negotiations with unusual independence for a Secretary of Defense, since negotiations are normally considered a State Department problem. As the negotiations went sour and produced an outcome which the President had not intended and did not prefer, McNamara was left in an exposed position. When de Gaulle destroyed a key element of the Nassau solution, McNamara's exposed position dictated retrenchment. The sequence left him far less able to shackle the MLF than had been the case in November when, at the State-DOD Defense Policy Conference, he had rather clearly signaled his desire to do so. Moreover, his tardy realization that the original Skybolt agreement with the British had not mandated assignment to SACEUR created a problem which he himself recognized as difficult. With the British obviously interested in parading independence, the connection of the Nassau agreement to NATO was an unanswered question. By the end of January McNamara's skepticism regarding the MLF had been substantially silenced, and the vehement opposition of Athens program proponents was thereby bottled up within the Pentagon.

A fourth source of strength to MLF proponents lay in the fact that to all concerned the Nassau formula had plausibly created a German problem as one of its glaring loose ends. Though wise enough to be subtle and reasonably quiet about their feelings, the Germans had insisted for some time that they should not be subjected to discrimination within the alliance, and they reiterated that theme with emphasis in post-Nassau discussions. Bilateral nuclear aid to Britain and France without including Germany seemed in context all too clear a case of discrimination, all too clear a message that Germany could only overcome it by becoming a nuclear power in her own right. The MLF provided the only available answer to the problem within the constraints everyone wished to impose. Falling well short of the all but unthinkable step of extending the Nassau offer to Adenauer, it was a way of broadening the German relationship to the United States on problems of nuclear defense. At the same time it suggested a NATO-wide framework within which, everyone could imagine, the British and French forces might ultimately be subsumed. If the proposal was hardly compelling, it nonetheless was the only one which did not have to be improvised on the spot. The fact that Smith and Lee had already briefed Europe on the MLF was very convenient. Indeed the proposal they had prepared fit too well the immediate needs of the post-Nassau situation not to be used.

251

The main themes of the argument which connected the MLF to post-Nassau problems did not change with de Gaulle's press conference or with the Franco-German treaty of cooperation signed a week later. If anything, the argument was strengthened as a chilling alternative appeared for those prone to imagine the worst; namely, a Franco-German nuclear program. That would mean an open split between the Atlantic powers and continental Europe on the issues of deterrence. The anomalies of the MLF paled somewhat by comparison.

A fifth break for the MLF came from an accident of timing. The aftermath of the Cuban missile crisis left the Kennedy administration strongly committed to removing the Jupiter and Thor intermediate-range missiles which had been placed in Italy and Turkey under Eisenhower. Kennedy had ordered their removal before the Cuban affair and was angered that they had not been removed and that they became a factor in the crisis. However, the same complexities of alliance politics which held up their removal before continued to operate after the crisis and the task remained difficult. Inevitably, there was a question as to how to cover the mission to which the missiles had been assigned. The only available substitutes were American Polaris submarines, assigned to NATO and operating in the Mediterranean. Since these were controlled solely through American command channels, both Italy and Turkey in effect were being eased out of a nuclear sharing arrangement. In this context, it was convenient to be able to advance the MLF as the mechanism whereby the sharing arrangement would be reconstituted. Reflecting the fact that this connection had been made in diplomatic conversations, the Italian government, at the same time that they announced the removal of their Jupiter missiles in favor of a sea-based Polaris force, announced approval of a multilateral force for NATO, "in which Italy would play a minor role."[1]

In the weeks following the Nassau conference the MLF proponents used the tactical advantages which the unfolding situation provided to build a strategic position within the policy machinery. Immediately after the conference, Jeffrey Kitchen, head of State's Office of General Political and Military Affairs, was assigned overall staff responsibility for the post-Nassau planning studies. Kitchen was not in the MLF coalition and Seymour

[1] *New York Times*, January 25, 1963, p. 1.

252

Weiss, his deputy, was known to be vehemently opposed. Kitchen also reported up through U. Alexis Johnson, State's Second Undersecretary, and thus was somewhat independent of George Ball. Ball, however, controlled the alliance discussions immediately following the conference and, most critically, he briefed the Germans on what had been said. Ball told Adenauer that the language of the Nassau communiqué referred to the force that Smith and Lee had outlined the previous fall, and he reported that the German Chancellor had been pleased by this information. As planning within State proceeded, Henry Owen and Robert Schaetzel were added to Kitchen's group as chairmen of the critical subcommittees on the MLF and France respectively. Owen produced a paper[2] arguing that the basic course for the American government should be the pursuit of the MLF, and he emphasized its advantages as a solution to the immediate issues which the Nassau agreement raised. Kitchen allowed the paper to go through normal clearance and thus circulate around the bureaucracy.

By the end of January 1963 both the Germans and the American government had been told that the Nassau agreement implied progress on the MLF as a major emphasis; de Gaulle had removed the major contradiction to the interpretation which national aid to France would have entailed; and in the White House it was conceded that at least for the moment the MLF had official priority. Seizing the favorable moment, the MLF proponents consolidated their position. As advanced by Henry Owen's paper, the MLF proposal was brought before the President, and his approval was gained for proceeding with negotiations within the alliance to establish the force. Moreover, as urged by the Owen paper, the President removed the conditions he had previously imposed. The MLF negotiations were not to be hindered with requirements that the Europeans pay for the force in full or that they first achieve conventional force goals. The approval of negotiations and the removal of preconditions were officially recorded in National Security Action Memorandum 218.[3] Finally, and most significantly, a special organizational apparatus was established within the State Department to control the MLF negotiations. Livingston Merchant, a former ambassador to NATO, a former Assistant Secretary of State for European Affairs, and a former

[2] Interview material.   [3] Interview material.

Undersecretary of State, was appointed Special Ambassador to coordinate the negotiations with NATO Ambassador Thomas Finletter. Merchant was an old colleague of Robert Bowie's from the Eisenhower period when both had been among Secretary of State Dulles' most trusted advisers. Merchant was a committed proponent of the MLF, as was Finletter.

The creation of Merchant's office within State allowed MLF proponents to control the routine business pertaining to the proposal, including conversations in Europe and cable traffic with Finletter. This short-circuited other parts of the State bureaucracy which were either unreliable advocates of the proposal or direct opponents. This was particularly important in the case of Jeffrey Kitchen, who still had staff responsibility, who was not an MLF proponent, and who would be inclined against it to the extent that he listened to his deputy. It was also important in dealing with the Assistant Secretary of State for European Affairs, William Tyler, who was also not a clear MLF advocate. Schaetzel was Tyler's deputy and this was enough to prevent a veto from the regional bureau. Tyler's distance from the proposal meant, however, that the regional bureau would not be a good base of operations. This organizational base is what Merchant's office provided.

A mechanism for circumventing Kitchen was found in an ambiguity in the Nassau agreement. The communiqué had used two words to refer to collective NATO arrangements which were to follow the British-American deal. The word "multinational" occurring in Paragraph 6 implied forces owned, manned, and controlled by national governments (i.e., the United States, Britain, and potentially France) but "assigned" to NATO missions and bearing some relationship to SACEUR.[4] Such forces clearly afforded the right of withdrawal in instances of "supreme national peril," and that arrangement was what the British had insisted upon. The second word, "multilateral," which occurred in Paragraph 7 of the communiqué implied the mixed-manned arrangement of the MLF proposal which was designed, of course, to prevent withdrawal of force components for national purposes. Paragraph 6 and the multinational concept was the basis for negotiations with the British for implementing the sales agreement concerning Polaris. Paragraph 7 and the multilateral concept was

[4] *New York Times*, December 22, 1962, p. 3.

the basis for developing the MLF. The appointment of Merchant established Paragraph 7 as the basis for negotiations with the rest of the alliance and took these negotiations essentially out of Kitchen's hands.[5]

In seizing the action from Kitchen and providing a channel which was not absolutely dependent on Tyler, Merchant's office delivered operational power to the seat of MLF advocacy—the Policy Planning Council headed by Walt Rostow, energized by Henry Owen and Robert Bowie, and protected in high councils by George Ball. The MLF coalition already forged by Nassau and the aftermath thus gained both a mandate and usable authority as Kennedy entered his third year in office.

Structure of the MLF Argument

Though the creation of Merchant's office provided necessary conditions for serious pursuit of the MLF, it cannot by itself explain the diplomatic campaign which followed. Even with tactical advantages and its newly acquired operational arm, the Policy Planning Council remained a relatively weak organizational position from which to mount a major, highly controversial initiative. Natural enemies in the Pentagon had far greater resources in terms of the classic components of bureaucratic power. Despite this, the MLF proposal continued to gain momentum even as the tactical advantages of January faded and as immediate political conditions in Europe created a number of barriers to agreement. This anomaly compels the serious analyst to broaden his base of inquiry, and the cognitive paradigm suggests where to look for help: at the structure of the argument made for the MLF.

The proposal which Merchant inherited envisaged a fleet of twenty-five surface[6] ships each carrying eight Polaris A-3 mis-

[5] Kitchen maintained nominal responsibility, but it was explicitly acknowledged that Merchant would handle the MLF negotiations.

[6] The general confusion of the Nassau agreement temporarily clouded the issue of whether the ships would be submarines or surface ships. Since the British were being provided with missiles for a *submarine* force, the original MLF idea of a mixed-manned submarine force was the natural framework to adopt. The submarine configuration was distinctly preferred by both the Germans and the Italians, and that made it tempting to resurrect the submarine option in the wake of Nassau. Admiral Rickover, however, stood as a barrier, and he reminded all concerned of the fact with a visit to the President in February (see Arthur M. Schlesinger, Jr., *A Thousand Days: John F. Kennedy in the White House* [Boston: Houghton Mifflin

siles. The A-3 would have a range of 2500 miles with a warhead of approximately one megaton, and it would be capable of enough precision to be used against some counterforce targets. The ships were to be manned using both officers and men from at least three nations, with no single nation supplying enough to control the ship by itself. As frequently noted, that was the crux of the idea—the mechanism whereby the Germans were to be given, and yet not given, strategic nuclear weapons. The ships were to have hulls resembling those of merchant ships, and other design features whose purpose was to complicate long-range surveillance and thus reduce their vulnerability to attack. Though required by international law to be marked clearly as warships, the intended markings were to be apparent only at short range. Cost projections to build the force in five years and to operate it for another five years envisaged $500 million per year (or $5 billion for the decade planned).

Regarding the critical question of control, the instructions given to Merchant in the National Security Action Memorandum issued in January mandated him to open negotiations by suggesting a formula which would require unanimity to authorize firing of the missiles. Tacitly, however, the record written in the previous year still held. The possibility of an eventual elimination of the U.S. veto, should the Europeans desire it and should they develop common political mechanisms, was to be held out as an incentive. As before, public statements by American officials served to keep this possibility alive. Operational control, it was perceived, would be given to SACEUR with the possibility of a powerful force commander or special nuclear deputy established under him.[7] The details of operational control, with a host of other critical issues such as ownership specifications, the financial contributions of participants, logistics and supply, routine political control, etc., were to be worked out in the course of negotiations.

Perhaps more important than the specific details of the pro-

Company, 1965], p. 874). The surface-ship configuration was realistically adopted by the Merchant mission as the basis for negotiation.

[7] General Lemnitzer, as he assumed the office from General Norstad, was worried enough about this not being the case, however, to warn specifically against separating the MLF from his command (see the *New York Times*, June 8, 1963, p. 1). To separate the force from SACEUR would virtually establish a new alliance.

posal, however, was the general framework of policy in which the MLF idea was embedded. It was becoming increasingly clear by 1963 that the driving force of the proposal and the core of the MLF argument was provided by American conceptions of the future of Europe and its appropriate political structure. In 1960 fears of the Soviet strategic threat and of Norstad's MRBM requirement had also been palpable in the MLF idea, but the intervening years had strongly attenuated these fears without drawing energy from the MLF. What remained in 1963 were the conceptions of Atlantic partnership and European integration drawn from the powerful experiences of World War II, the Marshall Plan, and European recovery. These events had dominated the early professional careers of the MLF proponents and the intellectual derivatives suffused their thinking. Robert Bowie, as a parent of the proposal and a prime theoretician of its significance, exemplified both the intellectual and the personal connections.

As already noted, Bowie was a longstanding advocate of European integration, with associations which went back not only to the beginnings of the movement but also to the beginnings of his career. This experience gave him a clear sense of the issues in Europe. He saw it as a focal point of the Soviet threat and thus a defense problem; he also saw it as a political and economic opportunity to be developed. The issues of nuclear sharing, he observed, involved both questions in competing claims.

> Any serious discussion of nuclear control within NATO must recognize that no solution will fully satisfy all the desirable criteria. As in most foreign policy questions each course has its advantages and weaknesses. The problem is to compare the merits and defects of the alternatives in order to make the best choice.[8]

Bowie saw, in other words, the presence of two values in the decision problem, and he perceived conflicts between the two values. The arrangement for nuclear control within NATO, he said,

> (1) . . . should reinforce Western unity. The growth of the European Community and the steady move toward Atlantic partnership have been the most significant developments since

[8] Robert R. Bowie, "Strategy and the Atlantic Alliance," in *International Organization*, vol. 17 (Summer 1963), p. 720.

the end of World War II. In the last year they have suffered serious setbacks. Whatever is done in the nuclear field should foster the progress and vitality of European integration and Atlantic partnership and should not undermine or weaken these constructive trends.

(2) The solution should also assure responsible political control over the weapons and unify the deterrent. It should be designed to take full account of the integral character of the defense of the NATO area. It would be foolhardy to suppose that a separate defense of either the United States or Europe is feasible. But this need not mean a monopoly of control in a single hand.[9]

With the trade-off problem thus set, Bowie examined the established policy alternatives. Nuclear arrangements in Europe, he said, could take three possible forms: continued reliance on the U.S. deterrent with shared planning (in essence, the Athens program); support for national programs loosely integrated into NATO (the Nassau solution); and the MLF. His immediate argument for the MLF consisted, then, in eliminating each of its competitors as an acceptable option.

Regarding the Athens program, he conceded a central piece of the argument: "In strict military terms it is probably true that the alliance would be best served by such a unified control in the United States' hands."[10] He neutralized the effect of this prescription, however, in two ways. First, he heavily discounted the possibility of deterrence failure: "If NATO has adequate and secure strategic nuclear forces, there seems virtually no risk that the Soviets would actually contemplate a massive assault on NATO."[11] The intended implication was that such forces were largely in hand and that there was no need to take strong steps to hedge against deterrence failure. Second, and most important, Bowie asserted that the continued reliance on the U.S. deterrent was not possible because the allies would not accept it. Though he uses qualified public language, his words reflect what he asserted in the councils of government as a categorical judgment:[12]

[9] Ibid.   [10] Ibid.

[11] Ibid., p. 715. Though this statement does not cover all possibilities of deterrence failure, Bowie showed little concern for this elsewhere. This element of his belief structure is corroborated by associates in interviews with the author.

[12] Again, corroborated through interviews.

But continuing monopoly by the United States does not seem feasible any longer. For one thing Britain and France have launched their own programs. . . . But the problem really goes deeper.

The debate over strategy and nuclear control partly reflects discontent over the position of Europe in the NATO alliance. With their enhanced confidence and revived strength, many European members inevitably desire a larger part in the planning of NATO strategy and the control over forces for its defense, especially nuclear. Thus, many Europeans now feel that a virtual monopoly in United States hands is no longer appropriate or acceptable for the long term. This feeling is mainly political, but it must be recognized and treated as genuine and real.[13]

On the same principle, Bowie rejected the proposal for having the Europeans share planning arrangements rather than the physical control of weapons.

The desire . . . for a role in nuclear control is not likely to be satisfied solely by measures for sharing knowledge and planning. As has been said, such steps are overdue and should be valuable in solidifying the alliance and mitigating some types of doubts or concern. But they fall short of offering the Europeans a position as real partners, even for the future. They are likely, in the long run, to feel that they remain wards of the United States, if the real power of decision rests indefinitely with the United States.[14]

This was explicitly a political argument: the military desideratum of centralized control was not to be achieved because of European political demands.

Reflected in this argument were widely held judgments about basic political forces. The economic resurgence of Europe had made them too strong politically to accept secondary status on the most important issue of their own defense. The hard logic of deterrence made it inevitable that they would distrust the American guarantee, inevitable that they would harbor doubts as to whether an American President might abandon them in a crisis in order to save American lives. In this view, the disagreements on

[13] Bowie, "Strategy and the Atlantic Alliance," p. 722.
[14] Ibid.

strategy between the United States and Europe derived from stable differences in national interest and were not to be reconciled by rigorous logical analysis and reasoned discourse.

In rejecting the other alternative to the MLF—i.e., direct aid to national nuclear forces—Bowie reversed his logic. Here he allied with the strong condemnation of national forces which McNamara had issued at Athens and subsequently at Ann Arbor. The thrust of the argument was that given the facts of the nuclear age, small, nationally controlled forces were not in the true national interest of the European nations and that promoting such forces was not in the interest of the United States. Despite the fact that Bowie appealed to intractable political demands to reject McNamara's hard line against sharing of operational control, he saw no difficulty in simply rejecting the strong demands of the British and French for national aid.

The more troublesome argument for Bowie came from a variant of the national aid proposals which the Nassau solution had buttressed: namely, the *multinational* force idea favored by the British. An MNF as opposed to an MLF would be comprised of national units loosely integrated into a collective command structure. As a practical matter, the national units in such a force could be withdrawn for national use. Indeed, if the Nassau formulation governed, that would be allowed as a matter of policy. Such an arrangement, Bowie argued with implied emphasis, was not an acceptable answer for Germany.

> The German leaders have repeatedly stated that the Federal Republic cannot indefinitely accept a second class status or discrimination. . . . Over the long pull, the 1954 WEU limitation can hardly keep Germany from demanding equal nuclear status with the United Kingdom and France. If Germany is not treated as an equal, this discrimination will produce friction and discord. Aversion to a German national nuclear force would create tensions and cleavages within the alliance which the Soviets would certainly seek to exploit. In either case the unity of the alliance will be seriously jeopardized.[15]
>
> . . . given the reasons advanced for such national forces, any . . . British-French force, even if agreed to, would certainly leave intact the national forces under some façade as has been done in the so-called inter-allied nuclear force recently set up by

[15] Ibid, p. 725.

NATO, to which the British have "assigned" their V-bombers while retaining the national command structure and the right to withdraw for national purposes. This would be a far cry from an integrated European or NATO force. Any such truly integrated force would have to be set up so that the Germans and others could take part in it as equals, and to be reliable it would need to be so organized that it could not be pulled apart into national components. Otherwise it could be a source of jockeying and bargaining rather than unity. Half measures will hardly satisfy a German aspiration for equality. Germany and other European nations would certainly not be content with merely taking part in a "control group" for French and British national forces. . . . In the quest for equality, the Germans would be led to press for their own national force, whether by removal of the United States joint control of nuclear warheads, by French assistance, or some other way.[16]

Bowie and others were fully aware that there was no immediate threat of a German national nuclear program. Although the Germans were conceded a technical capacity to conduct such a program, prohibitive political costs were too readily imaginable for an immediate German scare to get much of a hearing. It was too apparent that a German nuclear program would rip open the scars of World War II in both Western and Eastern Europe. It was too clear that the German economy, its state security, and the entire balance of its domestic politics was too dependent on international good will to allow credible pressures for a nuclear program to develop in the short term. Both internal intelligence reports and independent research by American scholars confirmed this strong, general impression.[17] Thus the fears which Bowie's language reflected were concerned not with immediate circumstances, but with the long-range, slow-moving macroscopic forces of world politics. Memories of German reaction to the harsh peace of World War I and memories of the role German resentment had played in the rise of Hitler were still vivid. Faint echoes of such resentment were perceived in Bonn's polite but persistent and repeatedly articulated complaints about dis-

[16] Ibid., pp. 725-726.
[17] Karl W. Deutsch, *Arms Control and the Atlantic Alliance* (New York: John Wiley and Sons, Inc., 1966), Chapter 6; Deutsch et al., *France, Germany and the Western Alliance* (New York: Charles Scribner's Sons, 1967).

crimination within the alliance. Though no one thought the past would simply repeat itself, there was a widespread sense that this was an issue to be treated with considerable caution. Bowie and his colleagues privately continued to estimate that it would be a decade before real trouble over nuclear arrangements could be expected in Germany, but they wanted preemptive action to begin immediately. Few senior officials in the United States were prepared to dismiss this argument easily.

For Bowie and for many others as well, the mechanism for solving the German problem was the movement for European integration. Fifteen years after being physically devastated, conquered, and bisected, the German state was in many ways the strongest nation of Western Europe, and it was the one with the greatest inherent claims against the *status quo*. Its eventual dominance in Europe was not a comfortable prospect, but that could be avoided only by direct discrimination (i.e., an anti-German coalition) as long as national states and national economies remained the basis of organization. Integration among the separate European nations was to break the dilemma by changing the basis of economic, political, and ultimately military organization. Given that de Gaulle was hardly cooperating in the grand strategy and that the British were still struggling with their European identity, a slow festering of resentment in Germany would be dangerous to the progress of integration. Should overt nationalist politics emerge in Germany, it could be fatal. To control that risk, Bowie thought it essential that a defense component be added to the integrated arrangements in Europe, a component missing since the defeat of the EDC proposal in 1954. Thus, he insisted that the central issue of deterrence had to be addressed in a "truly integrated" collective framework.

This flow of logic left the MLF standing in Bowie's mind as the only viable alternative among the possible nuclear arrangements, the only one which fit the larger design for integration. In his own words:

> In summary, a multilateral force offers a constructive means for handling the issue of nuclear control within the alliance. In its initial form, it is no final or perfect solution. As has . . . been stated, however, there is no perfect solution under existing conditions. The alternatives are clearly less constructive and offer less hope for the future.

An Anglo-French force would hamper real European integration. Assisting the national programs would solidify the commitment of France and Britain to national forces, encourage de Gaulle's concept of a Europe based on nation-states, push the Germans and the Italians ultimately to a national nuclear effort and fragment the alliance.

In contrast . . . a multilateral force would not fragment the alliance but would tend to pull it together. Such a force would also enable the Federal Republic and Italy to have a proper part in nuclear defense without raising the spectre of a separate German strategic force. . . . The cost of such a force would be materially less for the members. By combining their efforts they could create a respectable nuclear force without unduly diverting resources from more adequate conventional forces. The multilateral force should foster European integration by bringing together the Five and the British into an integrated nuclear effort open to France when she is ready to join.[18]

The imperfections in the MLF proposal, which Bowie conceded, included the fact of French and British opposition, the paradoxes of the control problem, and the vulnerability of the surface force. These difficulties were not presented as incorrigible impediments, however, as European opposition was held to be for the Athens program, as German dissatisfaction was for the MNF, and as vulnerability, expense, and interalliance imbalance were for independent national forces. To the difficulties of the MLF, rather, Bowie applied a transformational principle:

. . . Any solution should take account of the fact that the situation is still evolving and evolving rapidly. The shape of Europe is not yet finally determined. Obviously, various tendencies are contending for the ultimate outcome. And the relation between the emerging Europe and the United States also continues to develop. Hence one should not assume that it will be feasible to strike off a definitive answer now. What is needed is to lay the basis for a constructive solution which can be worked toward over a period of time.[19]

[18] Bowie, "Strategy and the Atlantic Alliance," pp. 729-730.
[19] Ibid., p. 720.

This reflected the underlying assessment that major difficulties of the MLF proposal would be transcended as the force and its decision-making mechanisms were caught up in the process of integration. Britain and France, it was felt, would ultimately give up burdensome national programs and join the common enterprise. The control issue would be eased by the emergence of a European executive or at least a central policy body with some authority. A unified Europe could ultimately build submarines.

In general outline, then, Bowie's case for the MLF revolved essentially around the conceptions of European integration and the allied notion of Atlantic partnership. The essential argument was that the MLF alone of the available options fit this larger design. The entire argument, in other words, was focused on the political objective.

Other members of the MLF coalition shared with Bowie both his involvement in the early events of European recovery and economic cooperation and the basic structure of his thinking which connected the commitments thereby developed to the MLF. George Ball was an old associate of Jean Monnet's, a consultant to the three European communities, and an important lobbyist for the cause of integrated Europe throughout this period. Walt Rostow had served on the Economic Commission for Europe. Livingston Merchant was the Assistant Secretary for European Affairs in the early 1950s. The others, Gerard Smith and Henry Owen, were associated with Bowie on the Policy Planning Council, with Smith succeeding Bowie as head of the Council. Merchant, Bowie, Smith, Owen, and Schaetzel were all longtime associates in the State Department. Ball, who was relatively new to the Department and who, by virtue of his position, was somewhat removed from the day-to-day development of the pertinent ideas, was independently a committed proponent of European integration.

The public statements of these major figures generally follow the pattern noted with respect to Bowie's. George Ball in a speech to Princeton University Alumni presented Bowie's argument directly.[20] Henry Owen provided a close variant in an article published in the *European Review*, where he arrayed four objectives relevant to the force:

[20] George Ball, in *Department of State Bulletin* (DOSB), May 13, 1963, pp. 736–739; also *New York Times*, April 27, 1963, p. 3.

Atlantic Partnership: to ensure that the atom was a force for fusion in the alliance—that it increased, rather than diminished ties between the United States and Europe.

European Unity: to meet the concerns of major European non-nuclear countries, narrow the gap between these countries and the nuclear powers, and otherwise enhance cohesion within Western Europe.

Military: to enhance NATO's defense and to resolve in some measure the issue arising out of the Supreme Commander's proposal that medium range missiles be deployed to NATO forces.

Non-proliferation: to avert or reduce any future pressures for national nuclear proliferation and to do so in a way that would not in itself contribute to national nuclear proliferation.[21]

In addressing the military objective, Owen made the argument which had been prepared in the Michaelis study in 1962. He asserted that the projected force would make a military contribution without raising its relative merits against other options and without raising the issue of a compromise of command/control integrity and the consequences in case of deterrence failure. In support of his contention he cited a statement by Defense Secretary McNamara that the MLF if constructed would substitute for forces which otherwise would have to be added to the United States forces.[22] Owen thus argued that the MLF would contribute both to military and to political objectives of the alliance. He did not discuss the trade-off between them.

Other members of the coalition such as Gerard Smith and Walt Rostow affirmed the central role of the MLF in promoting Euro-

[21] Henry Owen, "What the Multilateral Force Could Achieve," in *European Review*, vol. 14 (Autumn 1964), p. 12.

[22] Ibid. Whether this use of McNamara's statement by Owen was disingenuous or not, it is highly likely that McNamara meant it as a subtle roadblock. It was a signal to the Joint Chiefs that the MLF might mean a lost opportunity to add Minuteman missiles or even a cutback. This was virtually assured of cooling whatever enthusiasm might be generated for the MLF among the services.

pean unity while fending off the claims of competing objectives. Smith was concerned with arms control:

> The MLF is a new concept. It is designed to meet a new need: closer integration within the alliance in the strategic nuclear field, accomplished in *a way that will not hinder progress towards arms control* [emphasis added].[23]

As the MLF proposal gained momentum and public exposure, the Soviet Union began to voice vehement objections. The Soviets labeled it a device to arm the Germans. In an elaborate propaganda barrage they raised specters of German revanchism and accused the United States of a deliberate plot to proliferate nuclear weapons. The MLF proponents dismissed the Soviet campaign as an enemy's attempt to divide the alliance. They rebutted the charges regarding proliferation by arguing that since an MLF agreement would not add new independent national units to the nuclear club it could not be considered proliferation.[24] Since the MLF proponents believed that they were preventing ultimate proliferation to Germany which would otherwise be inevitable, they maintained in public and private that there was no conflict with non-proliferation objectives. This is the argument which Smith conveyed.

Rostow argued similarly regarding the military objective. The MLF, he argued, would provide a political return without incurring a military loss:

> It has been the policy of our government beginning with the latter days of the Eisenhower administration to look toward arrangements which would increase the effective degree of partnership in nuclear matters within the Atlantic community *without diminishing the effectiveness and unity of our collective security deterrent.*[25]

[23] Gerard C. Smith, "The Nuclear Defense of NATO," in *DOSB*, May 8, 1964, p. 790.

[24] The issue became a matter of contention in negotiating the Nonproliferation Treaty, which was ultimately signed in August of 1963.

[25] This formulation is found in three speeches by Rostow, appearing in *DOSB* on April 15, 1963, pp. 551–557; June 3, 1963, pp. 855–860; and April 16, 1964, pp. 578–587. In his speech before the W.E.U. Assembly on June 24, 1964 (*DOSB*, July 13, 1964, pp. 38–43), Rostow constructs the argument

These public arguments of the MLF proponents, which fit the proposal within the policy framework of the earlier articulated notions of European integration and Atlantic partnership, accurately presented the basic structure of the case they made within the secret councils of the government. To be sure, many politically sensitive nuances were not laid forth in public. Enmeshed in the pursuit of the MLF was a mistrust of German politics, a deep anger with de Gaulle, a desire to counteract French influence on the Continent, and a contempt for British policies of independence. None of these arguments could be stated either publicly or in official classified documents[26] with the force that they actually had in the minds of the MLF proponents. Even so, although they unquestionably contributed to the energy and resoluteness with which the MLF was pursued, such coarser motives do not seem to provide an independent, contradictory account of the MLF argument as much as a manifestation of the depth of commitment to the European cause. What was presented publicly as a matter of pursuing the good was often conducted, in context, as a fight against evil. The definition of evil and the conception of good were so inextricably bound, however, that a distinction between them would be arbitrary. The MLF coalition was not in business purely to stave off trouble. They sincerely wanted the progress which they felt European integration would bring, and their very conception of what was and what was not serious trouble took its character from that commitment. The possible failure of deterrence, for example, could be discounted; political moods in Europe could not be. Integration was their objective, fixed in clear focus, and their understanding of the problems of policy was organized around that objective.

---

more nearly like formulations of the other MLF proponents: the MLF is needed to make alliance nuclear arrangements work for European unity. There is no mention in that speech of the requisite that the answer not diminish the overall military effectiveness of the deterrent.

26 Just as there is an unwritten but universally recognized code concerning what may and what may not be said in public statements of policy, so is there a code concerning internal memorandums, even though these are classified. Political and personal topics which are totally or partially tabooed in public discussion are also restricted by practice in classified papers, though to a somewhat lesser extent.

The First Cycle

In appointing Livingston Merchant as Special Ambassador in January of 1963, the Kennedy administration was already easing out of the officially passive stance of the previous year, in which the United States awaited, with vaguely promised sympathy, *European* suggestions for nuclear sharing arrangements. It was clear that Merchant would not merely collect European suggestions; he would carry the MLF proposal to Europe. The proposal had already been prepared in sufficient detail to provide the basis for discussions. Strong U.S. leadership to bring about the favorable development of Europe flowed quite naturally from the broad policy assumptions surrounding the MLF. Gerard Smith and Admiral Lee, already experienced in presenting the MLF to European officials, were added to Merchant's delegation, and behind them stood the MLF theorists in State. All this meant that the United States to some degree was moving toward active initiative in seeking a nuclear sharing arrangement and toward assuming the various burdens of being the initiator in highly complicated, highly sensitive international negotiations. The degree of activism, however, was still a matter of some dispute and remained subject to varying interpretation. Merchant's appointment established only broad principles.

Despite his conferral of the appointment, President Kennedy remained reluctant to engage in a strong initiative. In part this simply reflected the natural cautiousness which experience in the Presidency brings. Kennedy had had initiatives fail and had learned to be wary. Beyond that, he remained skeptical concerning the substance of the proposal. He knew he would always be unwilling to relinquish Presidential control over the command channels whereby nuclear weapons are fired. Given that, he could not see how Europeans would gain from the suggested arrangement or any variant acceptable to him. If allowed to follow his own preferences, Kennedy most likely would have heavily constrained the approach to Europe, burdening Merchant with a new round of studies and holding him to restrictive instructions until very clear pressure emerged from allied capitals. Critical, therefore, to the development of a United States initiative was the setting of early deadlines to force the President to points of decision beyond Merchant's appointment.

Such deadlines were soon brought about by the fact that meetings for the Merchant team were scheduled in European capitals for the end of February. Such appointments would not usually be sufficient to force the hand of a reluctant President, but in this case they had that effect because of the reverberating public discussion which had accompanied the diplomatic dramatics of January. The dispute among the Atlantic powers had drawn both public interest and press attention to the alliance conversations which followed Nassau and de Gaulle's response. Similarly, the role the Jupiter missiles had played in the Cuban missile crisis drew press interest in the negotiations with Italy and Turkey regarding their removal. Inevitably, traces of the diplomatic exchanges and of the policy battles within the Kennedy administration began to appear in print. And once the leaks began, they proliferated, as proponents of various policy positions, in attempting to keep their views competitive, briefed friendly newsmen on the United States position. A bewildering variety of news articles resulted which confused the multinational and multilateral concepts and which presented a variety of proposals for phasing one into the other and for packaging forces of both types into an overall NATO force.[27] This familiar process of conflicting press leaks alerted both Congress, particularly the Joint Committee on Atomic Energy, and foreign governments; and from both sources came requests for clarification which could not be ignored. In this context Merchant's appointments in Europe gained enough urgency that the White House felt compelled to face the problem. Two meetings were held in the third week in February to brief the President and to work out Merchant's instructions.

At the first of these meetings President Kennedy underscored his reservations in the presence of Rostow, Merchant, Smith, and Lee, as well as Secretary Rusk.[28] He stated bluntly that he did not want the United States tied too closely to the MLF concept in the event that it failed. Observing that the British were unconvinced, the French opposed, and the Italians lukewarm, Kennedy felt that failure of the proposal was a very real possibility. He

[27] See for example *New York Times* articles January 12, 1963, p. 1 (Robert Doty); January 16, 1963, p. 1 (Wallace Carroll); January 16, 1963, p. 6 (Drew Middleton); January 17, 1963, p. 1 (Hendrick Smith); January 18, 1963, p. 3 (John Finney); January 31, 1963, p. 6 (editorial); and February 1, 1963, p. 1 (news article on U.S. offer to train submarine crews).
[28] Interview material.

also expressed the argument that the Germans would not pay good money for a force arrangement which did not give them operational control. He especially did not want the principle of multilateral nuclear arrangements for NATO to be associated exclusively with the MLF.

As protection he suggested, with Jeffrey Kitchen also present at the meeting, that that principle be associated as well with the British forces established under Paragraph 6 of the Nassau agreement—i.e., with the multinational concept. Kennedy directly suggested that these latter forces might provide an alternative to the MLF.

The State Department group answered the President's concerns with the arguments they had developed: there was a need to counter de Gaulle's influence in Europe; some arrangement for the Germans had to be worked out; and the long-run organization of Europe was at stake. Both the Nassau agreement and the 1957 NATO agreements were cited as earlier commitments to proceed with a multilateral arrangement. To Kennedy's repeated statement that he did not contemplate relinquishing an American veto over any decision to fire the force, the Merchant group replied that they did not expect this to be a central problem for the Germans. The Germans, they asserted, were more concerned with international status than with the fine detail of control. In the end, despite his expressed lack of enthusiasm, Kennedy agreed to issue instructions for Merchant along the lines the latter requested, and a second meeting was set to review and appraise a draft which Merchant was to prepare.

The instructions drafted specifically authorized Merchant, Smith, and Lee to investigate the possibility of an agreement on the MLF and to negotiate a preliminary agreement should two or more governments prove interested.[29] Guidelines were attached, one establishing the surface configuration as the official proposal, another specifying the control formula to be advanced. At the insistence of the President, these guidelines established that the Merchant delegation would offer the concept of a committee controlling the force which could fire the weapons only by unanimous vote. In line with the long-standing argument of the MLF designers, however, the guidelines also included authorization to consider contrary control suggestions from allies and to

[29] Interview material.

point out in dicussions that the control formula could be renego-
tiated after the force was established. This preserved Henry
Owen's formulation of the previous year, the main principle of
which held that a devolution of control over time should not be
explicitly excluded. The overall result allowed Merchant and
others leeway to suggest that political integration in Europe
might soften the American position.

As the draft was being prepared, another issue was interjected
by the Joint Committee on Atomic Energy. Learning of Merchant's impending trip to Europe, the Committee insisted that he
testify on his views in advance, and they used the occasion to grill
him on the fine details of control.[30] The point of the exercise was
to signal both their deep suspicion of the MLF concept and their
intention to play a role in determining any final arrangement.
The testimony brought out the critical fact that new legislation
would be required to implement the MLF, a fact which gave the
JCAE a veto over the agreement. Previous sharing arrangements
had all maintained U.S. control via physical custody of warheads.
In the envisaged MLF, control was to be exercised only at the top
by U.S. veto over the firing command in order to assure equality
of position within the force. Some warheads, therefore, would be
handled by foreign nations, and that would require Congressional authorization.

The fact that he would have to get legislation if the MLF were
approved and that it promised to be politically difficult legislation did not become clear to the President until he met with the
Merchant delegation for the second time to review their instructions. The realization again awakened strong reservations on his
part, but he acceded to Merchant's and Smith's strong arguments
that the political effectiveness of the proposal depended upon establishing symmetry of control. After revising the guidelines to
mandate a firm defense of the unanimous control formula, Kennedy approved the instructions drafted for Merchant's delegation. The change excluded any concrete *promise* of a devolution
of control after the MLF was established, but authorization for
raising the possibility still remained.

The outcome of the February meetings with the President gave
distinct if not uncontested impetus to a United States initiative
on behalf of the MLF. Though the President in his own mind

[30] Interview material.

271

gave but partial and tentative approval to the MLF concept, he nonetheless gave specific authorization for an aggressive, committed negotiating team to proceed to Europe, feeling deeply about their general cause and convinced of the need for strong U.S. leadership in the midst of the turmoil which they felt de Gaulle had brought about. Merchant had ample authority to carry a proposal to European governments which had been prepared in considerable detail and to argue its merits. It was clear that he would do so vigorously, backed by the MLF coalition in State, and that the enterprise would strike the European governments as something distinctly more forceful than a polite inquiry as to whether they might have an interest. Solicitations for European ideas on nuclear sharing had circulated before; the MLF idea had been floated before. In context, Merchant's mission was destined to be read as American pressure on them, regardless of Kennedy's desire not to assume the role of salesman.[31]

On the other hand, Merchant and the MLF group departed the February meetings with some real impediments. Whether by conscious design or not, Kennedy had also given some continuing life to the competing (and, to the MLF advocates, contradictory) idea of a NATO force organized according to the multinational concept (or MNF).[32] Under this concept, strategic strike forces operating through national command channels would be assigned to NATO under SACEUR but would also remain available for missions of national interest not related to the alliance. The prime case was provided by the British V-bombers, which were to be assigned to NATO as a way of providing an alliance-wide framework to balance the arrangement they had made at Nassau. True to their policy of independence, the British during the post-Nassau negotiations had firmly resisted United States attempts to make the NATO assignment binding. Preempting the negotiations, Macmillan shortly after Nassau had publicly committed himself to assigning the entire British V-bomber force to NATO, and he had then insisted at the negotiating table that the

[31] Arthur Schlesinger reports that the Merchant mission toured Europe in a chartered plane with a party of 32 and an elaborate itinerary, thus conveying a strong impression of activism. See Schlesinger, *A Thousand Days*, p. 874.

[32] This was paragraph 6 of the Nassau agreement. It was also called at various times the Atlantic Nuclear Force (ANF) and the Interallied Nuclear Force (IANF).

right of withdrawal be even less restrictive than the "supreme national interest" language applied to the Polaris forces at Nassau,
since Britain had national missions outside the NATO area. With
Nitze and Kitchen acting as central figures in these negotiations
and with Britain arguing that the multinational concept was the
most popular stance in Europe they could advance, this British
position had already been conceded by the time of the February
meetings on Merchant's instructions.

To the MLF advocates the MNF concept was heresy. The arrangement could not be extended to the Germans without granting them precisely the national nuclear capability the whole
MLF concept was designed to prevent, and such nationally organized forces could hardly carry the cause of European integration. The heresy, moreover, was dangerous. The British, aware
that they had incurred an obligation at Nassau to cooperate with
an alliance sharing arrangement, were clearly maneuvering to
establish a nuclear force for NATO on a multinational basis, thus
completely preempting the MLF they distrusted.

The British plan entailed that strike aircraft, already deployed
in Germany and manned by Germans, would be included in a
NATO nuclear force, an arrangement easily extended to all other
allies. A central committee would be formed in the alliance to
handle policy. This plan did not require new weapons deployments, did not give the Germans missiles, and could be implemented immediately. British intentions were to seek to establish
such a force as a major, dramatic move at the regular NATO
Council meeting in May. With Kennedy ready to consider the
MNF as an acceptable collective arrangement, the British plan,
labeled originally the Atlantic Nuclear Force (ANF), threatened
to derail the MLF before Merchant had a chance to use his mandate.

The threat to the MLF by the British initiative was vitiated
through the combined efforts of William Tyler, the Assistant Secretary of State for European Affairs and, ironically, of Charles de
Gaulle. Tyler, working with the other American negotiators, was
able to get the British to withhold a proposal for establishing a
Nuclear Trusteeship Group comprised of contributors to the projected force. Such a group would have given a political component and a new European institution to the multinational concept and would have made it a rather clear substitute for the
MLF. The deletion from the British plan was accomplished ex-

plicitly to afford Merchant an opportunity to pursue his proposal. This move was complemented by General de Gaulle, who provided his second major assist to the MLF cause by also taking pains to dilute the British plans. Doubtlessly irritated by press reports that the British sought to have French aircraft included in the ANF whether or not France consented, the General threatened vehement opposition if the British tried to achieve anything like the dramatic initiatives they had planned.[33] When it finally came down to the NATO mettings in Ottawa in May, the Council "noted and accepted"[34] the force assignments without fanfare and without attaching any name to suggest that the weapons constituted anything more than a normal organizational adjustment within the alliance. The arrangements made at Ottawa were far from insignificant, but they were not constructed as an alternative to the MLF. The force assignments were consistent with the kind of first phase to the MLF which Herter had envisaged in the initial suggestion and which had been discussed in the Bowie report.

With the MNF threat fading, the Merchant team spent three weeks during late February and March explaining the United States proposal to NATO officials and to the governments of Britain, Germany, Italy, and Belgium. The reactions they encountered were too qualified to count as support, too polite to count as opposition. The qualifications centered around the surface-ship configuration, the control formula, and the relative financial burdens to be carried. The Germans and the Italians both preferred the submarine configuration and were skeptical about surface ships. The Germans reportedly were also worried about the unanimity rule as a mechanism of control, fearing not so much a U.S. veto as a veto exercised by one of the other European participants. Even without getting down to the divisive business of discussing specific instances (they had Britain and Italy in mind), there was an argument which concerned the Germans that a reasonably large committee could not in principle display to the Warsaw Pact the firm resolve necessary for a credible deterrent. The British for their part shared similar reservations but were especially concerned about financial burdens. Press reaction in Europe during Merchant's trip was distinctly negative, a

[33] *New York Times*, May 7, 1963, p. 12, and an article by Max Frankel, May 19, 1963, p. 1.
[34] Text of communiqué in *New York Times*, May 5, 1963, p. 2.

fact which was interpreted by him as a failure on their part to understand the proposal.

Despite these clouds, Merchant detected enough interest to recommend in late March that the United States give unqualified support to the proposal and seek its enactment. He urged the President to move vigorously to achieve a preliminary agreement which would establish the force as a mixed-manned surface fleet controlled by a provision assuring a United States veto, financed jointly by participants, and not prejudicing conventional options. He estimated that vigorous United States action could produce a preliminary agreement to be initialed during the President's trip to Europe which had been scheduled for June. A preparatory commission to draft a full treaty establishing the force would follow the preliminary agreement and would be composed of those who had signed it.

At the White House, Merchant's recommendation appeared too strong for the degree of European interest it recorded. Several times in February and March the President had taken care to point out in press conferences that the MLF was not something that the United States wished for its own security but rather an arrangement we were willing to give to the Europeans upon demand.[35] Within the government, he had frequently voiced doubts that the Europeans would really want it. What Merchant brought back was hardly pressure from European governments, and Kennedy reacted with commensurate caution. He agreed to write Italian Premier Fanfani and German Chancellor Adenauer affirming his support for a surface force and for a control formula (not necessarily the unanimity proposal) which preserved the United States veto. He agreed to make the surface-fleet configuration more attractive by advancing the suggestion that missile-carrying submarines might be added to the force at some future date. But he also made further progress on the proposal contingent upon the German response and prohibited any contacts with the Congress on the matter until that response was in hand.

Merchant was strongly disappointed to receive authorization well short of what he had desired, but the resolve of the MLF group was undiminished. Rostow produced a paper arguing that after bungling a long series of opportunities to assume leadership

[35] See article by Max Frankel in the *New York Times*, March 7, 1963, p. 12, and report of JFK news conference, March 21, 1963, p. 1.

in Europe, Britain faced a last chance in the MLF.[36] For Britain to forgo it, he argued, would be a step into irrelevance. Schaetzel produced a paper arguing for resolve and commitment to the cause of integration during a period of drift.[37] Tyler went to Europe to talk with the Germans and Italians, and while he was in Europe there arrived a cable from Bonn over U.N. Ambassador Stevenson's name reporting a comment from a high German official to the effect that Germany would seek parity with France and Britain if the MLF failed.[38] The cable was brought to the President's attention, and he quickly noted its usefulness in dealing with Congress. Finally, the President's approval was gained for sending Admiral Ricketts to Bonn to try to convince the doubting German military that the surface-force configuration was militarily useful. With authorization to report the results of the Navy studies of the previous year, Ricketts was persuasive enough that German political officials were able to get acceptance of the MLF from their military officers.[39] Ricketts and Tyler both told the Germans that the eventual evolution of the MLF to include submarines was entirely possible.

Pressure built on the President during April. The MLF advocates, fully aware of the great importance of deadlines in gaining Presidential action, pushed hard to utilize Kennedy's major trip to Europe as a deadline-setting event. It would give dramatic impetus to the MLF to have the President initial a preliminary agreement in London, Bonn, and Rome; and the MLF proponents hoped to tempt the President with visions of such an achievement as a solid result of his trip, a dashing counterthrust to de Gaulle. The President, however, was more concerned with fears of having just such an image floating in the public mind while the promised initiative foundered on alliance politics. The

[36] Interview material.　　　　　[37] Interview material.

[38] Whether this was an instance or not, many sources reported that favorable cables were inspired by MLF advocates in the sense that American embassies were apprised as to what information would be useful (i.e., supportive of the MLF) and were encouraged to send it if they had it.

[39] American military officers subsequently argued in interviews that the German military had not been convinced and had agreed to the surface-ship configuration only under political orders. This was consistent with impressions gained at the Ricketts discussions. At the first day of the Ricketts briefing, the German military officers were clearly negative. On the second day they withheld their objections and formally accepted the surface-ship configuration (interview material).

same conditions which promised opportunity for a clear and ringing success carried also the risk of an obvious failure. Since de Gaulle had deftly skewered his last initiative, making Nassau look like an amateurish performance, it was important to avoid another failure. Thus, though moving with the pressure, Kennedy was preoccupied with preparing a fallback position. He recognized that he could not fully disavow having made an initiative, and in that light he concluded that if the MLF encountered an insurmountable snag it should be allowed to fade from view gradually in hopefully imperceptible increments.

At the end of April Chancellor Adenauer replied to the letter Kennedy had sent in March in response to Merchant's recommendations. Speaking officially for the German Federal Government, Adenauer accepted the two central provisions of the MLF proposal which Kennedy's letter had specified—the surface-ship configuration and the control principle. He specifically reserved the right to reopen both issues once the force had been established and there had been some actual experience in operating it. Moreover, Adenauer requested that a provisional agreement on the MLF be prepared for signature in June while Kennedy was in Europe.[40]

By all accounts Kennedy was surprised, since such acquiescence violated his conception of German interest. Nonetheless, given the German decision, the major condition which he had attached to Merchant's recommendations was achieved, and this undeniably moved the proposal toward agreement. There was a sense in the White House that the President stood close to a binding commitment, that the MLF stood on the brink of enactment.

With momentum thus regained, the MLF proponents again sought to launch the broad-scale initiative which had been denied to Merchant in March. This time they brought their case to the White House with their position somewhat bolstered within the government. The Joint Chiefs of Staff had prepared a memorandum asserting that the MLF was feasible, would be militarily useful, and was desirable.[41] The language provided important political cover even if it betrayed a distinct lack of enthusiasm among the Chiefs.[42] Also the AEC had certified that the

[40] Interview material.   [41] Interview material.
[42] Members of the Joint Chiefs of Staff were highly suspicious of the

physical control arrangements required in the MLF proposal could be made consistent with security requirements, and this certification also would help in approaching Congress. On the basis of all the developments, George Ball requested authorization to begin Congressional consultations and urged that the President plan to initial the preliminary agreement, renamed "terms of reference" to mollify the JCAE, during his European trip. A specific negotiating schedule was laid out which would produce a final agreement by September.

Meeting with both State and DOD officials in early May, Kennedy again demurred on the full initiative. He said that a German-American MLF was not sufficiently broad to be politically viable and imposed the further condition on the project that British participation be assured. He withheld authorization for an approach to Congress until British participation had been negotiated. He agreed to help with that, however, by writing Macmillan; and, though he insisted on at least a 10 percent financial contribution from the British, he was willing to ease the burden somewhat by compensation within the context of other agreements. He also wrote Premier Fanfani. Italian participation was also seen as an important broadening element, but the judgment was made that the Italians would follow the British. Finally, Kennedy agreed to respond to Adenauer accepting his formulation, notably that the issue of control over the MLF be held open to revision in the light of experience. The question of the negotiating schedule was left open, awaiting the British response.

The meeting with the President precipitated a new series of moves by the MLF coalition to ease the project over the new hurdle which had been imposed. George Ball and Admiral Ricketts left immediately for London. A member of Merchant's staff suggested to an Associated Press reporter the possibility of Kennedy's signing an agreement on his European trip. Finletter sent a cable detailing numerous official British statements since Nas-

---

MLF and furious with the State Department for what they considered biased promotion of the project. There was no strong support for the alternative land-based MRBM, however, and the MLF did not appear serious enough to threaten major weapons programs. Given this, the established tradition of comity within the JCS prevailed, and the support of the Navy group under Ricketts and Lee translated directly into tepid JCS approval. No one there would have any regrets if the MLF project were stopped, but they were not about to wield the ax.

sau which acknowledged their commitment to give material support to the MLF. Elaborate maneuvers were prepared to have German contacts with the British Labour Party put pressure on Harold Wilson, the Parliamentary Party's new leader, not to give Macmillan difficulty on the MLF. A letter was drafted urging Belgium Premier Paul Henri Spaak to give official approval to the project. The Germans were encouraged to start giving background briefings to their press on the surface-force configuration. General memos were prepared for signature by Ball and Rostow reiterating the governing concepts of European integration and Atlantic partnership. These memos detailed the dangers threatened by de Gaulle's policies and by possible German reactions to discrimination, and they again urged firm, resolute United States leadership in a period of drift.[43]

Despite this promotion, however, pressure to take the final steps did not build in anticipation of the deadline, but rather dissipated in the context of larger events. Precisely because the proposal had been pushed to relatively advanced stages, major political forces became engaged and these were not favorable at the time. The NATO conference at Ottawa was held in late May with the British initiative for the MNF (by then called the Inter-Allied Nuclear Force, IANF) at least tacitly the major item of business. Elaborate negotiations between the British, French, and Americans had reduced the British initiative to a relatively routine "assignment" of U.S. Polaris submarines and British V-bombers which was merely "noted and accepted" by the NATO Council.[44] Having been an active party to this blunting of the British thrust in order to placate the French, it was difficult for the United States to follow credibly with an appeal to the British to join a strong initiative of our own, an initiative they distrusted and which the French flatly rejected. Even considered solely within the diplomatic context, the British had good reason to drag their feet.

Domestic politics in Britain made it even more difficult. The Macmillan government was in sight of elections and was suffering among voters from an accumulation of frustration which plagues any government long in power. The Tories had held power since 1950 and Labour was arguing the need for a change with real effect. Moreover, several sexual-political scandals were

[43] Interview material.
[44] Text of communiqué in *New York Times*, May 5, 1963, p. 2.

breaking over the government to lend spice and substance to public disaffection. The most famous of these, the Profumo affair, involved the Defense Ministry and raised issues of security. With strong opposition to the MLF in both the prestigious British Navy, personified by the war hero Lord Mountbatten, and in the Labour Party, Macmillan's government was in a very poor position to join the American cause.

The timing was wrong in Italy as well. For a year the Italian government had been ruled by a minority coalition which depended, in the Italian Chamber of Deputies, on indirect support of left-wing socialists headed by Pietro Nenni.[45] The Nenni socialists abstained on critical votes, allowing the government coalition to prevail. The political arrangement which allowed this gave concessions to Nenni on domestic issues in return for his acceptance of a pro-Western foreign policy. Nenni's party had a strong left wing which was close to the Communists, and the whole business was very tricky. The acceptance of NATO itself was difficult, the MLF all the more so. In late April the Christian Democratic Premier Amintore Fanfani led the government into a general parliamentary election hoping to emerge strong enough to be able to solidify the deal with Nenni, but the maneuver failed. The Christian Democrats slipped 4 percent from the 1958 vote and the Communists gained 3 percent, while Nenni was holding about even.[46] In May the Fanfani government resigned and the assignment to form a new government went to Aldo Moro, a solid NATO supporter who stood somewhat to the right of Fanfani and was therefore more difficult to sell to Nenni's party. The protracted, confusing negotiations to reconstitute the deal with Nenni lasted right up to the eve of Kennedy's visit and ultimately failed.

By the beginning of June it was clear that the President's trip could not produce a preliminary agreement under any title, and the MLF group was preparing a fallback position. They urged the President to reaffirm the April agreements in Germany and to gain commitments to continued progress on the proposal from Britain and Italy. In a revised scenario for negotiations, they proposed that a negotiating group be quietly established to work out

[45] The account here follows Norman Kogan, *A Political History of Postwar Italy* (New York: Frederick A. Praeger, 1966). Susan Lutzker was helpful in researching Italian politics of this period.

[46] Ibid., p. 193.

a draft treaty. The group would be established under the principles set forth by Merchant in March, which were to be incorporated in a preliminary agreement, but it was to be acknowledged that the final position of the government would depend upon the outcome of the negotiations. Thus both Britain and Italy would be able to join the talks without forcing their governments to commitments which they lacked the political authority—or inclination—to make. This provided a means of continuing to move the project under adverse conditions, but it removed a critical element—the action-forcing deadline.

As it turned out, that was essentially the way Kennedy handled the issue. In his critical policy address at the Paulus Kirche in Frankfurt on June 25, Kennedy reaffirmed United States commitment to European political integration and Atlantic partnership, but chose a phrase, "a fully cohesive Europe," designed to minimize French chagrin.[47] He reiterated the central theme that only such a Europe would be capable of full and equal partnership with the United States, and he reaffirmed the doctrine that not national deterrence forces but "a more closely unified Atlantic deterrent, with genuine European participation" was to be encouraged. He set forth the MLF as a means of bringing about such cohesion and reasserted the critical diplomatic phrase which preserved flexibility on the control issue: "As Europe moves towards unity, its role and responsibility here [i.e., in the nuclear force] as elsewhere would and must increase accordingly."[48] When he met with Adenauer, Kennedy made clear the impracticality of trying to proceed immediately with an agreement. Suggesting that the quiet discussions be continued, he stated his hope that the MLF could eventually succeed, but he mentioned the need to prepare other arrangements in case it did not. Adenauer agreed, thus removing the sense of obligation Kennedy had felt upon receiving Adenauer's letter in April. In the communiqué issued, the two heads of government reported agreement "to use their best efforts to bring the MLF into being and to pursue with other interested governments the principal questions involved in the establishment of such a force."[49] The

[47] *New York Times*, June 26, 1963, p. 16.
[48] Ibid. At the time, the German Defense Minister von Hassell was reported through State Department channels to believe that an adjustment of the control formula in the second-phase MLF would be necessary.
[49] Ibid.

same formula was used in the meeting with Macmillan, where it was explicitly acknowledged that the U.K. would join discussions on the MLF "without prejudice to the question of British participation in such a force."[50] In all, the official result of the trip was general affirmation of the MLF concept and its surrounding logic but an agreement to conduct quiet "discussions" without a deadline or target date. Neither of the shaky governments in Britain and Italy was pushed to sign onto the project.

The climax thus passed with a preliminary agreement still unsigned and with the conditions of British participation still to be achieved. This inevitably drained momentum from the MLF project. Its proponents had driven hard for the summit, expending political and organizational resources in the process. Having been forced to retreat to a lower plateau, they faced a period of renewal before another drive could be sustained. Some conditions would have to change and some new forces would have to be marshaled. Moreover, they had suffered real damage as well as political exhaustion. The President had gained a direct impression of European attitudes and had returned with his personal reservations regarding the MLF strengthened. Support for the project in the European capitals was weak to nonexistent, and this he had noted. Adenauer, the only other head of government officially committed, had stated directly that the Germans were doing nothing to promote the agreement. British and Italian leaders were full of skepticism and political caution, and de Gaulle's opposition was firm and potentially explosive.

Catching the President's mood shortly after the trip, his National Security adviser, McGeorge Bundy, in a memorandum for the record, established some summary judgments: If the Europeans did not want the force, it was not worth the effort: the initiative probably should be allowed to fade away.[51] This constituted an apparent resolution, and it ended a cycle of the MLF's career.

The Second Cycle

It can readily be seen in retrospect that the resolution of July 1963 held the ingredients for a new cycle in the cause of the

[50] *New York Times*, July 1, 1963, p. 10.

[51] The existence of this memo is documented in Philip Geyelin, *Lyndon B. Johnson and the World* (New York: Frederick A. Praeger, 1966).

MLF. The President had not taken decisive action to implement the fadeaway option. McGeorge Bundy's memo did not circulate. The machinery which the MLF coalition had forged remained intact within the State Department, and all members of the coalition still held their jobs. Though forced into a narrower context, MLF proponents still had scope for action provided by the agreements of June—i.e., to continue discussions within the alliance. Most critically, their will remained undiminished. Like contemporary versions of Sisyphus, they slowly began to roll the rock back up the hill.

By August, Ambassador Merchant had initiated discussions with representatives of Germany, Italy, Greece, and Turkey to negotiate provisions for institutionalizing the discussions which the President's trip had vaguely authorized. It was agreed that two groups would be established. The first, consisting of the NATO ambassadors of the interested countries, and meeting in Paris, was charged with working out the legal and political dimensions of the force, and the understanding was that the group would prepare a draft treaty. It soon came to be known as the working group. The second group, a subgroup of the first, and meeting in Washington, was set up to discuss technical military issues, ship design, command arrangements, operational tactics, ownership specifications, financial arrangements, etc. Trying to forge the commitment which had eluded them in June, the MLF proponents sought to impose strong ground rules on the working group discussions: Only those governments could participate which had a serious interest in the proposal. The British, however, still resisted. They stayed away from early sessions of the talks and went through several inconclusive Cabinet meetings before finally extracting from both Secretary Rusk and the President a reaffirmation that joining the working group would not entail a commitment to participate in whatever force emerged.[52] With this assurance they did join the working group, giving it the broad representation which was necessary but loosening the discipline of the discussions. Under a similar understanding, Belgium and the Netherlands joined also.

By the end of September a new idea began to emerge through the working-group discussions. The United States representatives, Finletter and Merchant, used the forum of the talks to sug-

[52] *New York Times*, October 4, 1963, p. 2.

gest that demonstration of the MLF concept be undertaken. A single ship would be manned with officers and men from interested nations and would be equipped with an existing missile system complex enough to provide some rough approximation of Polaris. The ship could then be taken on NATO maneuvers and could show its international flag in NATO ports.

The origins of the idea are obscure,[53] but its utility is obvious. To the MLF proponents, it was a way of regaining momentum. It would require some agreement from participating countries. It would be another feasibility demonstration analogous to the U.S. Navy study of 1962. It would provide useful publicity, which might cut through the sarcastic opposition of the European press. It would give an early success, and hopefully some lasting legitimacy, to the working group under whose auspices the full force was to emerge. To Kennedy (and others whose zeal for the MLF was distinctly qualified) the demonstration ship idea was appealing as a concrete product which would give some substance to the diplomatic initiative and which would screen the gradual demise of the larger project. It could be readily achieved with marginal commitments of men and equipment, thus requiring no great expenditure of political capital, and it might even dissipate the energies of MLF proponents.

With MLF sponsors and detractors thus in agreement, the demonstration ship moved quickly. The USS *Biddle* (later renamed the *Ricketts* after the admiral who had worked on the project) was assigned to the mission, and under the auspices of the working group an international crew was assembled in the summer of 1964. The ship was sent on fleet exercises and managed to operate normally with its crew of mixed nationalities. This was cited as support for the larger force, and to carry the point to domestic audiences a tour of the ports of participating nations—the United States, Germany, Britain, Italy, the Netherlands, Greece, and Turkey—was begun in the fall of 1964.

Given the existence of the working group with acceptably broad representation (i.e., including Britain and Italy) and given the emergence of the *Biddle/Ricketts* project as a concrete product, there was palpable movement in MLF affairs by the fall of 1963. The difference in commitment between the President and

[53] Many attribute it to President Kennedy himself, and it is certain that he took a personal interest.

the MLF proponents was neutralized for the moment by the limited context which the working group provided and by the absence of a major deadline. As long as the working-group discussions could be interpreted as a means of screening the failure of the larger project, there was no compulsion for the President to intervene in the process. Moreover, Kennedy became personally interested in the demonstration ship project. He urged it on German Foreign Minister Schroeder when he visited in September and frequently queried the Pentagon bureaucracy on the progress of the idea. In this context he granted what he had denied before. He gave authorization for the MLF group to arrange Congressional briefings on their activities. This gave additional scope to their mandate and was destined, given their strong commitment, to provide an additional test of the President's position. Before that could develop, however, John Kennedy was assassinated.

LYNDON JOHNSON assumed the Presidency uncomfortable with foreign affairs, by all accounts, and at any rate politically committed to the policies of the fallen President whose stature, in death, reached legendary proportions. Many nuances of the MLF situation, in which he had been only marginally involved, were inevitably lost to him. What confronted him was Kennedy's public commitment to the project and the personnel and bureaucratic machinery which gave force to that commitment. When asked, he renewed the mandate, including the authorization for approaches to Congress, and thus effectively cleared the project to proceed under the guidance of the MLF coalition. There were limits to what they could do until the new President had established his own bearings, but the brutal transition definitely left the MLF coalition with more power and a less subtle problem within the American government.

While working-group discussions provided the main context for action on the project after Kennedy's death, there were two external issues of critical importance for the MLF proponents: Congress had to be prepared to accept the treaty which would emerge, and another deadline, appropriately timed, had to be found to force a final Presidential decision.

Congress received immediate attention. A Congressional liaison officer was added to Merchant's staff and plans were prepared to have State, Defense, and AEC officials brief the Joint Committee on Atomic Energy, whose suspicion was profound and whose approval would ultimately be required. Secretary Rusk was to brief the Foreign Relations Committees and Secretary McNamara the Armed Services Committees. For months the Merchant group struggled to implement the plan; but, without the pressure of an impending decision and without the signal of direct White House support, they were unable to break into the crush of immediate government business. One scheduled, full-day session with the JCAE was begun with Rusk testifying, accompanied by Admirals Lee and Ricketts and Commissioner John Palfrey of the AEC, the last mentioned a participant in the Merchant group. The afternoon session was postponed and never rescheduled. Rusk was scheduled to meet with the Senate Foreign Relations Committee. He postponed the meeting once because of scheduling difficulties, a second time because of the death of Prime Minister Nehru of India, and a third meeting could not be arranged in the press of the Committee's foreign aid hearings. The House Foreign Affairs Committee was not interested in the topic. Chairman Vinson of the House Armed Services Committee refused to schedule hearings on the MLF until work on "regular" DOD legislation was completed. Chairman Russell of the Senate Armed Services Committee refused to hear anything before that Committee while the Civil Rights Bill was on the floor—most of the summer of 1964. A great deal of staff energy was devoted to stimulating the Congressional campaign, but the general sense of crisis, which can only accommodate a few issues at a time, had shifted from Europe. Vietnam, the American South, and the Republican Party were commanding attention; and MLF proponents could not get much of a hearing. It thus became clear that until another Presidential decision approached, the Congressional campaign would languish.

The focus thus shifted to the problem of setting a deadline to force binding decisions at authoritative levels of the executive branch. This issue continued to revolve around the British and the Germans and included the impending American elections. Both in Great Britain and in Germany the ruling parties had changed the head of government just a month before Kennedy's death, and the highly unusual circumstance thus arose that the three major allies had experienced non-electoral transfers of power almost simultaneously. It was inevitable that a hiatus

286

would ensue until the new President, Prime Minister, and Chancellor could settle in their offices. Any push for a major alliance initiative would be blatantly unrealistic until that occurred. Effectively that meant that the earliest feasible deadline on the MLF was the late fall of 1964, after British and American elections scheduled for October and November, respectively.

The British were a controlling factor. With France increasingly isolated in NATO affairs and irrevocably opposed to the MLF, Britain remained the only ally of sufficient stature to render the MLF something other than a German-American arrangement. Italy continued to roll through a series of weak, short-lived governments with Pietro Nenni still playing a critical political role. He explicitly tied his position to that of the British, and it was reasonably clear at any rate that Italy would have to follow rather than precede Britain into an MLF arrangement. Thus, in order to get the issue before the President for any major action, a clear arrangement with the British would have to be in hand. In a major political move, the Tories had replaced Prime Minister Harold Macmillan with Alec Douglas-Home, whose Defense Minister, Thorneycroft, opposed the MLF. Even if he had the inclination, Home could not get an agreement through Cabinet until after the election. Since the independent deterrent was a prime component of his election stance, he was certain to resist any pressure until then.

With a pre-election deadline precluded, the focus of attention among MLF proponents shifted to Harold Wilson's shadow government, which they expected to come to power in October. A straightforward reading of Labour's position had its leaders distinctly negative on the MLF. Labour's declared defense policy deprecated the reality and value of the British deterrent and vaguely suggested that a Labour government would divest Britain of an independent strategic nuclear capacity. The Labour policy proclaimed the necessity of unifying the alliance deterrent in American hands, and indeed it had much the cast of McNamara's Athens program. The MLF in that scheme was useless. There were also important political liabilities to the proposal. The MLF to casual but interested observers was unmistakably pro-German and anti-Soviet, and for Labour that was exactly wrong. With a strong left wing in the party, Soviet anger at the proposal, quite vehemently articulated, promised to cause trouble on the back benches, and latent anti-German feelings which

287

were widespread both in the party and throughout the British public promised the left wing an appeal beyond their numbers on the issue. As Prime Minister Wilson predictably would sponsor the deflecting alternatives in which the British bureaucracy specialized and would arrive on board the MLF only if delivered there by an American threat or an American deal.

In Germany, Adenauer had relinquished the Chancellorship, reluctantly, to Ludwig Erhard in October of 1963. Erhard was a man initially less dominated by the relationship to France than Adenauer had been and thus somewhat more willing to pursue the American design. That fact was complicated, however, by his greater weakness as Chancellor. Adenauer, who bitterly opposed him, remained chairman of the party (the CDU) and a powerful senior statesman. Their intense personal rivalry tended to be expressed in terms of issues affecting Franco-German affairs. Moreover, the powerful head of the aligned party (the CSU), Franz Joseph Strauss, was beginning to tie his political future to what was publicly interpreted as a German form of Gaullism, and this tended to buttress Adenauer. This boded trouble for Erhard, who was burdened with strong public expectations as to how a Chancellor should perform: that he lay down a firm policy line; that he brook no opposition within his own party. In backing the MLF as he did, the question of his authority was engaged, and French opposition made it tricky for him. It was an opportunity in some ways, but a risk as well.

In this context the process of bringing about another deadline was begun, naturally enough, by working within the established German and American commitments. Johnson and Erhard were scheduled to meet in June of 1964. In April, Johnson reviewed the project with the negotiating team headed then by Gerard Smith, who had just replaced Livingston Merchant upon the latter's resignation. Three members of the MLF coalition—Ball, Finletter, and Smith—briefed the President on the well-established MLF argument.[54] Ball emphasized the dangers of mishandling a resurgent Germany and found the President responsive to that theme. The MLF group left the meeting with the sense that they

[54] Whether by accident or design, McGeorge Bundy and Robert McNamara were both out of town on the day of the meeting and thus unavailable for skeptical comments. The meeting was originally scheduled as an appointment for Finletter to say good-bye to the President before leaving for his post in Europe.

had received authorization to set up an agreement to be signed by the end of the year.[55] Accordingly, cables were immediately sent to European capitals announcing that the United States would seek agreement under that deadline, and NATO Ambassador Finletter visited Bonn to convey that message to Chancellor Erhard personally. Erhard accepted the time schedule, and when he visited Johnson in June the published communiqué explicitly established the point:

> They [the President and the Chancellor] were agreed that the proposed multilateral force would make a significant contribution to the military and political strength of NATO and that efforts should be continued to ready an agreement for signature by the end of the year.[56]

This commitment gave the possibility of a deadline, but in order to make it effective a draft treaty had to be prepared within the working group. Through Finletter, the MLF advocates sought to bring pressure on the group to speed its work, but British recalcitrance proved to be a major problem. By the summer of 1964 the British had introduced an alternative proposal involving the inclusion of land-based missile systems in a collective force, and they had instituted a study of this option whose effect and probable intention was to delay the negotiations. In order to circumvent this problem the United States and German representatives met separately and unofficially to prepare a draft treaty, resolving in their discussions many of the issues which could not be resolved in the larger context. In neither instance, however, was a final formula for firing the force established; and September came with that critical issue unresolved, with the draft treaty having ambiguous status within the working group, and with the full working group moving too slowly to meet the December deadline.

In order to break this jam, an initiative was taken by the German government, probably but not provably inspired by the

[55] There was a dispute in retrospect as to whether that was what the President intended. Philip Geyelin (*Lyndon B. Johnson and the World*, p. 160) reports the incident and offers two versions of the operative language. If the President's real intention is obscure, the record is not. In public statements in April and June Johnson affirmed what the MLF group thought had been decided. See for example the article by Max Frankel in the *New York Times*, April 27, 1964, p. 13.

[56] *New York Times*, June 13, 1964, p. 1.

MLF proponents within the American government. In early October Erhard wrote Johnson noting the United States position conveyed to him by cable in April and publicly expressed in June. The Chancellor expressed concern that the progress of the working group was not sufficient to prepare a treaty for signature by December, and he emphasized German interest in meeting the established schedule. Erhard pointed out that the United Nations General Assembly was considering a resolution urging a moratorium on all changes in the *status quo* until an agreement on the non-proliferation of nuclear weapons could be negotiated. Should such a resolution pass, a possibility, Erhard argued, which could happen as early as January 1965, German participation in an MLF could be seen as defiance of the resolution, and that would subject them to serious political difficulty—both domestic and international. Moreover, the German NATO Ambassador, Wilhelm Grewe, who carried the letter to Washington, informally suggested another element of German concern. German Parliamentary elections, he pointed out, were scheduled for September of 1965, and the treaty would have to be submitted by January or February in order to be ratified before then. The Chancellor, in other words, wanted it done well before he faced the electorate. In order to circumvent the diplomatic impasse, Erhard's letter suggested that the United States and Germany sign the treaty alone, if need be, with provisions for others to accede later. Implicit was the calculation that this possibility would pressure the British to acquiesce in the German-American draft soon after their elections.

Betraying the fact that he had not fully internalized the maneuver, Erhard uncovered the idea of a German-American agreement at a press conference in Berlin on October 6,[57] before President Johnson had responded to his letter and with Grewe still in Washington.[58] This was a clear mistake, for the ploy, meant for the inner councils of government, would have required much more gestation before it could survive that prominent a public display. Hence American officials fled the idea with obvious haste. The Johnson reply to Erhard's letter was sent on the next day, affirming, as a goal, the time schedule agreed in June but empha-

[57] By inside accounts it was an accident. The Chancellor reportedly had a copy of his letter in a briefcase and pulled it out for reference when surprised by a reporter's question.
[58] *New York Times*, October 7, 1964, p. 1.

sizing the principle of broad participation in the force. Secretary Rusk, faced with a direct question, discounted any bilateral agreement at a press conference on October 8.[59]

By the time the British and American elections delivered their results, the deadline was virtually unavoidable. With Harold Wilson assuming office as the new British Prime Minister and with Lyndon Johnson decisively elected in his own right, an early meeting between the two was the natural course of events. With British participation critical for the MLF and the MLF critical for the Germans, that subject was an expected agenda item. Press attention, the commitment to the Germans, and pressure from the MLF proponents all required the President to make some move, for even an attempt to circumvent the subject would have significant consequences. The necessity of a Presidential decision about what to say to Wilson forced fundamental decisions about the entire project, and the White House staff began to prepare. Once again the MLF project was on its way to the summit.

The Final Phase

Policy Review

The effects of the December deadline worked to shift the context of the MLF project in several important ways. Since imminent Presidential business was involved, the White House staff soon was seized with the issue and began to exercise coordinating functions within the government. This loosened somewhat the tight control over the project which the MLF proponents had gained in the course of its development. It also brought broader political forces to bear on the issue, not only because the Presidency is a unique crossroad of political concern, but also because the impending Presidential decision meant that opponents of the project who had hoped it would quietly fade could no longer count on that. In all of the capitals concerned, opposition became more apparent as expectations of a high-level decision became widespread. The public record had President Johnson already in favor of the MLF, and his impending action forced those who wanted it stopped to show their hand. In all, the already complex MLF proposal generated a labyrinth of immediate problems through which the President would have to wend his way.

[59] *New York Times*, October 9, 1964, p. 9.

At the White House, McGeorge Bundy had been friendly to the MLF idea in its broad context since 1961,[60] and not unreasonably MLF proponents counted him as an ally. There was deep skepticism toward the project at lower levels of his staff, however; and, at any rate, Bundy's reaction was not only substantive but procedural. He was professionally charged with "preserving the President's options," and that role made him naturally wary of the dedicated MLF advocates. He was also sensitive to the fact that the situation had many elements of the Skybolt issue of 1962 when he had notably failed to preserve Presidential options. The British and American governments were again locking horns on the nuclear sharing issue and broader relations with France and Germany were again at stake. Bundy's performance on the second round—both because it was a second round and because he no longer served the President who had originally hired him— would have to be better. Thus Bundy, though an MLF sympathizer, was on guard.

Bundy moved into the MLF issue by setting up an *ad hoc* mechanism for controlling the American government. He pulled together a special group around Undersecretary George Ball to review the issue and to work out a position in which McNamara, Rusk, Ball, and himself all concurred and which the British government could be prevailed upon to accept.[61] To facilitate that process he brought in Richard Neustadt, a Columbia professor, to work full time on the issue as a special consultant. Neustadt, the theorist and advocate of Presidential power, had done a detailed postmortem on the Skybolt affair under direct commission from President Kennedy. In the course of that study he had become intimately acquainted with the politics and organizational procedures, both in Washington and in London, which had driven the Skybolt issue out of the President's control. For the MLF

[60] Bundy had given Henry Owen and Walt Rostow access to Presidential speeches through which the public record had been established, and he had himself given an important speech in Copenhagen in December 1962 in which he had promised flexibility on the control issue (*DOSB*, October 22, 1962, pp. 601–605).

[61] The group was called the Ball/Bundy Committee at State and the Bundy/Ball Committee at the White House with obvious differences in political nuance. It will be labeled the Ball Committee below, reflecting the fact that it met in George Ball's office and that he bore primary responsibility for drafting its final report. It should be remembered, though, that it was considered at the time to be a two-headed committee.

problem Neustadt was given two assignments: predict what Wilson would demand and what the United States could get him to accept; and manage the MLF proponents so that they would not run away with the action. This consolidation of Presidential authority was formalized, at Bundy's recommendation, in the middle of November by National Security Action Memorandum 318, in which the President announced a desire to prepare a coordinated position for the meetings with Wilson. The Ball Committee was given an explicit mandate to prepare the position. Also, in an attempt to minimize the use of press leaks and low-level channels of communication as levers over the issue, the President required that all representations to the press and to foreign governments be cleared and specifically authorized.

The central members of the Ball Committee—McNamara, Rusk, Ball, and Bundy—were in agreement in the immediate post-election situation on some fundamental points. The MLF was held to be the least undesirable means of keeping the Germans integrated into the alliance, and that was taken as the major operational objective. In other words, the basic proposition of the MLF case was affirmed at the outset of the Cabinet-level review. There was also general agreement that compromises should be introduced into the original concept to accommodate the British, if it could be done without a great battle. Preserving the President's options in the judgment of the group, therefore, meant getting what the President had officially said he wanted (the MLF) without precipitating a political crisis, paying an exorbitant price, or exposing him to a major policy failure. This entailed preparing an escape route should the costs or the risks become too great. There would be a yes or no decision before the meetings with Wilson, but essentailly the Ball Committee principals understood the matter to be in a process of implementation.

Beyond these general guidelines, the Ball Committee encountered a thicket of complexities, and the consensus was commensurately more difficult. Was there an achievable balance between British and German requirements? What role was to be accorded the established NATO machinery? What posture was to be taken with the French? What solution could get through Congress? How were expressed Soviet (and UN) concerns about nuclear proliferation to be handled? Since issues such as these required additional staff work, a second level was added to the Ball Committee, pulling together staff representatives from all parts of the bureaucracy which had a substantive interest in the issue. Neustadt, representing both Ball and Bundy, was charged with coordinating this staff work, and this arrangement served a dual purpose. The work of this lower-level group provided substantive detail on a number of questions which the Ball Committee principals raised, and at the same time it provided formal procedures to channel the energies of MLF proponents and to give MLF skeptics and detractors access to the decisions being made.[62] Neustadt, mindful of his two assignments, had both purposes in mind in directing the work.

Complications in Europe and at Home

The central problem remained, of course, that of gaining the participation of a reluctant British government, a problem that had taken new focus after the election. As predicted, Harold Wilson's new Labour government brought into office policies, personnel, and priority difficulties which complemented the anti-MLF disposition of the British civil servants. Labour policy, as noted, followed closely the central themes of the Athens program and thus greatly preferred to meet the nuclear sharing issue through mechanisms of consultation organized in close relation to the main U.S. deterrent forces, rather than through special arrangements for sharing operational control. Since Labour policy was strongly Atlantic in orientation with little enthusiasm for tight integration in Europe, it saw the MLF largely in terms of defense policy and in that context disliked the proposal as a waste of resources. The newly acquired burdens of office reinforced these predispositions. In a time of economic weakness at home, Britain still faced demands for major defense efforts east of Suez and for contributions to a conventional defense of Europe as well as for a contribution to the MLF. These other claims represented hard budget choices which the government would have to decide upon in its first few months in office. The decisions would not be easy. The election had given Wilson a majority of only four votes in the House of Commons and hence virtually no protection

[62] The working group under Neustadt included representatives of the Arms Control and Disarmament Agency, the Atomic Energy Commission, the Office of International Security Affairs from Defense as well as the European regional bureau, the Policy Planning Council and the Bureau of Regional Political and Military Affairs within the State Department. Richard Morse of the State Department Secretariat was its Secretary.

against defection in his party. There was opposition to the MLF in the Cabinet (especially from George Brown, Deputy Chief of the Party), in the Navy, in the press, and in the left wing of the party. The MLF, in other words, was significant political trouble for Harold Wilson.

Since acquiring at Nassau some degree of commitment to deal with the MLF proposal, the British had consistently sought to substitute other arrangements for the mixed-manned surface fleet idea. That had been the main thrust of the Inter-Allied Nuclear Force (IANF) initiative in the spring of 1963 and of the proposals which the British had raised in the working group in July of 1964. That also was Harold Wilson's first move. By means of an authoritative article in the London *Times*,[63] traceable to him but not politically binding, he had set forth an alternative sharing arrangement. The NATO force under his scheme would be much broader than the MLF. It would include a variety of weapons systems, such as the British V-bombers and Polaris submarines and the German Pershing missiles. At least some of its components would be nationally manned. Control over all force components would be exercised by a committee, with the United States having one veto over any firing decision and a second veto being available to a coalition of European participants. The mixed-manned surface fleet would be at most a minimal component—far less than the twenty-five-ship American proposal—and perhaps nonexistent.

This counterproposal, standard procedure for a serious negotiation, was designed to meet some British problems. In terms of internal British politics, the proposal would allow the government to continue the Polaris submarine program and to commit the completed submarines to the force. Though Wilson had hinted in the election campaign that he might divest Britain of the expensive Polaris program, he was aware that the Tories had successfully used that against him and he wanted to take the issue away from them.[64] He also was aware of the severe difficulty involved in disrupting a large program once it had begun. In this

[63] See the London *Times*, October 24, 1964. The article was written by Alan Gwynne-Jones, a confidant of Wilson's who soon thereafter joined the government. It was intended and perceived as a trial balloon for the Labour government's position.

[64] See Andrew Kopkind, "The Special Relationship: The Neustadt Dossier," in *New Left Review*, no. 51 (September–October 1968), p. 3.

case two submarine keels had been laid by the time he assumed office and two more were soon to follow. If he could commit the submarines and the British bombers to the force, that would be an acceptable way of continuing the submarine program, and he could get substantial equity in the NATO force at little or no additional cost beyond that of the submarines. That in turn might then enable him to stay out of the mixed-manned surface fleet. Such an arrangement, combined with a promise that the United States (and perhaps Britain) would always retain a veto over the use of the NATO force, was what he thought he required in order to manage the MLF on his four-vote majority. In terms of alliance politics, moreover, the British proposal served to answer what was becoming the main American argument—that the MLF, despite its flaws, was the only acceptable option anyone had suggested. Wilson could quite cogently point to the fact that the official U.S. position had maintained all along that the MLF was simply a suggestion and that European ideas were encouraged.

After floating the proposal, Wilson developed his position further by making a Cabinet decision in November to procure four of the five submarines planned under the Nassau agreement.[65] The fact that the submarine program was continued was a distinct adjustment of Labour's campaign policy, and the fact that Wilson was able to carry it off smoothly was a significant sign of his personal command in the party and in the Cabinet. Significant in another sense was the fact that the program was continued at four. The originally planned number of five was the minimum required to maintain the established stations at all times, the preferred criterion for deployment. What the Wilson government proposed was to assign three subs to the collective force and keep the fourth in mothballs, hedging against an accident. He could then suggest it would be appropriate for the United States to match the British contribution, thereby bringing the force up to requisite size. This was designed to put more pressure on the surface fleet idea, for it would be distinctly burdensome for the United States to match both British submarines and German surface vessels.

[65] As noted, four submarines were either already under construction or were in advanced stages of preparation for construction. The fifth was planned for 1966 and hence was easier to cancel.

In a final counterthrust, Wilson's Cabinet members, objecting more to the surface fleet than to the idea of mixed-manning, began to talk about the possibility of providing international crews for Minuteman missiles and thus substituting components of the main deterrent force for the marginally effective surface ships. Precisely because this idea had some logical appeal it was an adroit political maneuver. If it was going to be necessary to give the Germans access to nuclear weapons, the British could argue, why not give them access to the real thing? Such a force would certainly be a more effective deterrent. It would be less discriminatory than a special force made of weapons which no single nation acting on its own had bothered to procure. It would tie the Germans even more closely into Atlantic arrangements. Though of course they did not discuss it, one can surmise that the British were aware of the enormously disruptive effect the mixed-manned Minuteman idea might have within the United States. It would force the MLF coalition to deal with a new branch of the services—the Air Force rather than the Navy—and would involve them in proposals having very controversial effects in terms of security and overall consequence for the force posture. The organizational politics of the Minuteman idea would be certain to tie up the MLF proponents for a year or more—well past the deadlines immediately presented—and would in all probability ensure their defeat at the hands of the United States Air Force. From the British point of view, the mixed-manned Minuteman idea was a twist which would give the United States at least as much trouble as the surface fleet gave them. Thus Wilson, the accomplished politician, positioned himself for the confrontation in Washington about as well as he could.

As counterpoint to the main theme of the British negotiations, problematic complications arose in France and Germany as well. The French, while rejecting the MLF for themselves, previously had taken an officially tolerant attitude toward German participation. In 1963, upon conclusion of the Franco-German treaty, they had informed the Germans that they would understand if the Federal Republic took an interest and pursued the project. This tolerance lasted until late October of 1964. Then, whether angered by the overt German initiative or alerted by what seemed to be an approaching decision to establish the force, the French began to oppose the MLF categorically and to put enormous pressure on the Germans to back off their commitment. French spokesmen asserted bluntly that German participation in the force would be considered an act unfriendly to France, and they threatened all manner of retribution including leaving NATO and disrupting the Common Market if their warnings were ignored. Brave souls and strong MLF proponents argued that de Gaulle was merely having his fling and that he would adjust to the MLF as a *fait accompli* once it had actually become that. Others (including a number of Germans) who respected de Gaulle's reputation for resoluteness and knew his distaste for the collective arrangements of the alliance were less sanguine. One thing was certain: With the French having a diplomatic tantrum, the MLF issue had become obviously divisive in Europe.

The French pressure put enormous burdens on Ludwig Erhard since it struck him precisely where he was most vulnerable. Most immediately, it activated Adenauer. The ex-Chancellor traveled to Paris in October to receive a routinely scheduled personal tribute from de Gaulle, and he used the occasion to conduct political discussions. He returned to raise the alarm about French disaffection. A party caucus called to hear Adenauer report on his conversations produced a resolution calling for a delay in the MLF agreement until it could be given a "more European character" and made more acceptable to de Gaulle.[66] This was all too clearly contradictory to what Erhard had said earlier, and the resolution—and Adenauer's activity—left him with a small crisis in leadership within the party. Gerhard Schroeder, the Foreign Minister, Erhard ally, and the strongest of the German MLF supporters, came under very heavy pressure for being too rigid with the French, and rumors of his political demise reached Washington. Pressure on Schroeder, of course, reflected indirectly on the Chancellor as well.

The problem was further compounded for Erhard by the fact that he faced a second deadline in December over a grain price agreement for the Common Market.[67] Establishing common grain prices for EEC members was to be the next step in the development of integrative economic arrangements in Europe. Following the crisis of 1963, Europeanists were very intent on having an agreement as a means of breathing new life into the movement.

[66] *New York Times*, November 12, 1964, p. 1.
[67] Miriam Camps, *European Unification in the Sixties* (New York: McGraw-Hill Book Co., 1966), p. 22.

The problem was that German agriculture was highly priced, highly inefficient, and highly protected. The EEC arrangement on agriculture would remove protection and lower German prices, and this promised to be painful for German farmers, who normally provided important electoral support for the CDU/CSU. Naturally enough, Erhard vastly preferred to get through the impending elections before granting the price concessions, but he was under very strong pressure from the French, who would be the main beneficiaries, to come to terms earlier. He had promised to make some decision by December 15, though not necessarily to grant the concession at that point. The French, with heavy hand, pushed him to be forthcoming. Though Erhard tried to keep the two issues separate, the MLF and the grain price agreement quickly merged in the minds of most observers into a single Franco-German crisis, and indeed a larger European crisis.

By mid-November of 1964 general observers of Europe began to feel that the MLF was out of phase. European leaders seemed to think that a period of consolidation would be required before any major new departure in community building could be undertaken. With the fight over grain prices and de Gaulle's general policies threatening the EEC and thereby riveting attention on economic issues of immediate and direct impact, there was little enthusiasm for a complex institutional arrangement such as the MLF, which involved the esoteric and psychologically distant issues of strategic nuclear deterrence. Added to that were a number of special reservations widely attributed to European leaders: notably, a perception that the MLF was indeed directed against France and would provoke a drastic French reaction, that its expense was unjustified, and that it threatened relations with Eastern Europe and the hope for détente. A general memorandum by the Bureau of Intelligence and Research of the State Department reported these views to the American government in the fall of 1964.

The existence of such opinions was subsequently corroborated by evidence from surveys of elite opinion in Europe collected by independent scholars from Yale University during the 1963–1965 period. Interviews by the Yale team with samples of European leaders in various segments of society found in both Germany and France more opposition than support for the MLF on its intrinsic merits and, as an interesting contrast, definite opposition especially in Germany to the need, usefulness, and desirability of a national nuclear force.[68] The survey showed the MLF supported in Germany only on a conditional basis: that is, if the MLF were to be created, German leaders wanted their country in it. Such views did not always lead to opposition to the MLF. Support, however, derived mainly from perceptions that the United States was committed to the project and from the natural political principle that it was best to give the strongest member of the alliance what it seemed intent on having.

The MLF also developed some domestic complications as the December deadline approached. Congress still remained unprepared for the proposal, and intuitive reactions were negative. A few members of the JCAE had been convinced by personal efforts of the MLF proponents, but Congressman Chet Holifield was publicly skeptical,[69] and the critical members—Senators Russell and Anderson—were privately so. Widespread opposition in the Senate was apparently reported to the White House by Vice President-elect Hubert Humphrey. In response to quiet lobbying efforts by a number of peace and disarmament groups, two letters were sent to the President, one from eight liberal Senators and one from forty Congressmen, expressing strong reservations about the proposal and asking that action be deferred until Congress could hold hearings. This opposition was not argued in depth but reflected simple readings of the mood in Europe and of the probable reaction of domestic constituencies. There were virtually no broad domestic forces behind the idea and a few were at least potentially very negative. As one proponent put it, "New York Jews were not destined to favor the MLF."[70]

New opposition arose within the policy bureaucracy as well. Officials of the Arms Control and Disarmament Agency were privately engaged at the time in pursuing the treaty on non-proliferation of nuclear weapons, and they were anything but enthusiastic about the MLF. They had to deal with the Soviet Union, which was still thundering general disapproval. Indeed, Soviet negotiators at Geneva had bluntly stated that the United States would have to choose between the MLF and a non-proliferation treaty. ACDA officials, politically weak within the government

[68] Deutsch, *Arms Control*.
[69] Holifield gave a speech criticizing the MLF shortly before the Johnson-Wilson visit. See the *New York Times*, December 1, 1964, p. 4.
[70] Interview material.

machinery, were polite to the MLF and publicly held the established line that the MLF would not constitute proliferation and would in fact help prevent it. They argued within the government, however, that Soviet feelings were deep enough and their capacity to make mischief great enough that there was in fact a trade-off. Many concerned with that issue urged the President to choose a non-proliferation treaty over the MLF.

Neither the events in Europe nor the domestic problems presented any absolute barriers to the MLF, but they certainly added to the complexity of the issue. They raised the price of the project in providing additional trade-offs for the President. Political capital would have to be expended in getting Congressional approval. A risk would have to be taken regarding the non-proliferation treaty, possibly necessitating some offsetting concessions to the Soviets. The pro-American, Atlantic-oriented members of the German government were being burdened. Harold Wilson was prepared for some hard bargaining. The anger of the French would have consequences hard to predict. As the Presidential decision approached in a cloud of complications, the Ball Committee prepared its final recommendations.

The Cabinet Recommendation

The staff work which went on underneath the Ball Committee was heavily influenced by the MLF coalition, and they produced their response to the situation through this channel. Their basic approach was to try to incorporate the MLF into a larger package designed in the classic fashion to offer something of interest to all concerned. A paper prepared in the MLF office proposed a ten-point program incorporating economic trade provisions, mechanisms for broad consultation on policy, a non-proliferation declaration, aid to the Third World, and an MLF compromised to meet some of the British proposals.[71] The MLF was to be renamed the Atlantic Deterrent Force, and the surface fleet was to be reduced to seventeen ships. The United States and the European partners collectively would each pay half the cost, thus justifying the double veto control formula which Wilson had suggested and thus reducing German weight in the force. Britain was to be allowed to make national contributions to the force (i.e., the Polaris submarine) and would meet financial obligations by

[71] Interview material.

equity from the assigned subs, housing, and other support facilities, rather than from budgetary contributions. In the overall package the British would receive some direct concessions on the MLF and would get the consultation machinery in which they were interested in return for participation in the renamed MLF. The French for their acquiescence to the MLF would get the grain price agreement from Germany. The Germans in addition to the MLF would get diplomatic machinery for the pursuit of German reunification, but they would have to accede to a non-proliferation declaration designed to soothe East-West relations. Stressing the need for strong U.S. leadership, the paper urged that the program be presented as a whole and with diplomatic emphasis, despite the fact that its various components would have to be pursued on separate schedules. Explicit references were made to the Marshall Plan period and to the New Deal in a reasonably direct attempt to capture the imagination of the newly elected President. The "package of progress" memo, as it was called internally, was a characteristically elaborate piece of work by the MLF proponents. It incorporated their main policy themes and the central features of their proposal while responding to the critical political pressures operating at the moment.

In contrast to earlier papers, however, the memo did not rise to prominence within the government. This difference in fate was effected by the changes in organizational procedures which had been made. The path to the White House was blocked by Bundy's caution, by Neustadt's assignment, and by the fact that the Ball Committee, with higher authority, was actively preparing its own position. The mechanism designed in part to control the promotional activities of the MLF proponents had its effect, and the ten-point plan did not flow up to the President as previous efforts by the same group had done.

In preparing the Ball Committee's detailed recommendation, both Ball and Neustadt carefully canvassed London and Bonn during the last weeks of November. In the process, they were convinced that the central problem for the United States was that of getting British participation, including British sailors, in the mixed-manned surface fleet. In their view, substitution of national force components for the surface fleet, as Wilson desired, would inevitably ascribe second-class status to the Germans and would vitiate the point of the exercise. At least two other issues were also important, if slightly less critical: First, the British

302

wanted a guarantee that a U.S. veto over use of the force would never disappear, whereas the Germans demanded leeway for greater devolution of control after experience with the force. Second, the British wanted a separate command, whereas the Germans wanted SACEUR as the force commander. In both cases the competing demands would have to be balanced. Reportedly, Ball and Neustadt foresaw that Harold Wilson would have to be moved substantially on all three issues and warned that the two governments were "on a collision course."[72] Both American emissaries said as much to Wilson and warned him that a successful outcome of the Washington conversations would depend upon his acceptance of the surface fleet.

As the confrontation approached, Ball, with Neustadt's assistance, prepared a memorandum for the President which outlined Wilson's position, defined those points which the United States could not concede, and suggested a set of marginal changes in the MLF concept designed to mollify Wilson somewhat.[73] The memorandum reflected the loose consensus of Rusk, McNamara, and Bundy as well. It urged the President to hold firm on the surface fleet, to insist on British participation in it, and not to countenance any substitution such as a mixed-manned Minuteman force. The number of ships, it argued, could be reduced somewhat, especially if the three British Polaris subs were put into the force. A Defense Department analysis was referenced which showed that the reduction of the British submarine program from five to three would release much of the manpower required for British participation in a nineteen-surface-ship force, and would provide a means of giving the British a 25 percent financial equity in the force for less than it would cost for a three-ship national submarine program.[74]

The Ball memorandum also suggested the President be open to other nationally commanded force components (that is, the British V-bombers and perhaps American Polaris or Minuteman missiles) as long as that did not dilute the surface fleet too seri-

---

[72] Interview material.   [73] Interview material.

[74] A nineteen-ship MLF together with three British submarines would yield the 200-missile force originally envisaged in the twenty-five-ship proposal. If the British sold the submarines to the force, they could have a 25 percent equity of a $2.7 billion force for approximately $200 million less than it would cost them to contribute three submarines and count the contribution as equity.

ously and as long as the United States did not promise to match the British national contributions. Implicitly this meant that the surface-ship option was not to go below the seventeen-to-nineteen range and that the Germans were to have a veto over the inclusion of nationally controlled forces. If the Germans wished to surround the national force elements with collective symbols such as MLF uniforms, flags, etc., U.S. Polaris and Minuteman forces would not be available. The control formula, the memo argued, could be stiffened to a point short of a refusal to reconsider should a single European executive appear. It suggested that a non-proliferation declaration plus consulting arrangements could be attached to a final agreement, and that the name of the force could be changed. The issue concerning SACEUR's role was to be left open for the moment but subsequently resolved in a fashion meeting German approval.

McGeorge Bundy submitted Ball's recommendations to the President and stated explicitly an underlying judgment: Johnson was strong and Wilson was weak in the immediate situation, and Wilson could therefore be made to accept the arrangements.

If the procedure outlined in the Ball memorandum should fail, the alternative suggested was the fadeaway process President Kennedy had envisaged. A separate memo outlined steps to be taken in the event Wilson stood firm. These were designed to let the proposal die in such a way that responsibility for its demise accrued to the European allies rather than to the United States.[75] McNamara, while remaining loyal to the main proposals of the committee, gave indication that he was more inclined to see this option come about.

The Decision

President Johnson confronted the issue on December 5, two days before the meetings with Harold Wilson were to begin.[76] On that day he met with his central foreign policy advisers to review their recommendations and prepare for dealing with the Prime Minister. As in April, there was every indication that the President took the German problem seriously. Without a collective arrangement, he felt, the Germans would seek national control of nuclear weapons and would do so much sooner than the ten

[75] Interview material.

[76] For a basic account see Geyelin, *Lyndon B. Johnson and the World*, Chapter 7.

years estimated by the Ball Committee principals. Moreover, the President apparently accepted the arguments that the British proposals would not answer German needs and therefore would not suffice to prevent a German nuclear program and all the attendant political turmoil. Despite these convictions, however, his reaction to the MLF was dominated by the immediate politics of the issue. He understood Wilson's problem with the American proposal and concluded that he, in the same situation, would not agree to the surface ships. He noted the vehement opposition of the French, the embarrassment of the Italians, the crosspressure on Erhard, and concluded that he could not present the proposal to Congress as a necessary response to European pressure. That in turn meant trouble on the Hill, where the established principle was to preserve the tightest possible American control over nuclear weapons and defense technology.

According to reports of the December 5 meeting,[77] George Ball, as foremost MLF proponent in the group, conceded that Congress was unprepared for the MLF, which must have been corroborated by informal checks on the Hill. Senator Pastore, a member of the Joint Committee on Atomic Energy, believed that the President would be defeated on an MLF treaty. Richard Russell and Clinton Anderson, the most influential members of that committee, were known to be highly skeptical. Ball argued, however, that a major effort had not yet been made and that Congressional approval would be gained. McNamara supported this argument, promised his full effort, and predicted as well that Congress could be brought into line. Since the Pentagon had done nothing to promote the MLF in Congress, this would presumably give new thrust to the proposal among the legislators. Johnson, however, remained unconvinced and ended the December 5 meeting with some sharp warnings to his advisers: he was still unfamiliar with foreign affairs and dependent upon their advice; they were urging him into a major project with most of the basic political forces arrayed against him; that was a misreading of his political strength.

The December 5 meeting thus left the central issue unresolved and necessitated another meeting the following day when a decision on the stance to be taken with Wilson would have to be made. Between the two meetings, the President, now personally

[77] Ibid. Geyelin gives an account of this meeting and subsequent events that is substantially accurate.

agitated on the subject, began to pursue it on his own; and according to knowledgeable reports he either generated or received some critical new information. First, McGeorge Bundy, in response to Johnson's distaste for what the Ball Committee was urging him to do, conceded that the President had not been exposed to the case *against* the MLF. While professing his continued support for the recommendations, Bundy wrote a memo presenting some of the negative arguments.[78] In it he noted that President Kennedy had cooled on the MLF after his European trip, and he appended the memo written at the time to record Kennedy's reaction. Johnson, who had originally supported the MLF out of loyalty to Kennedy's policies, apparently had not perceived his predecessor's reservations regarding the project and found the news very significant. In addition, on Sunday morning, December 6, a cable arrived from the American embassy in Bonn which reported on a growing body of opinion within the CDU party councils that the MLF should be delayed because of the intense French pressure against it. Both the Defense Minister, Kai Uwe von Hassel, and Ludger Westrick, a close Erhard adviser, were reported to be associated with this trend, and both had been cited in documents submitted to Johnson as important stalwarts of the MLF. Finally, Johnson himself talked with Senator Fulbright and probably other Congressional leaders. Fulbright, who had been to a NATO parliamentarians' meeting in November, where the corridors were full of talk about Europe's problems with the MLF, told the President that the Europeans were against the idea and that there was no need for it and no Congressional support.

His confidence further eroded by the new information, Johnson bluntly told his advisers in the second meeting on the MLF that he would not deliver Wilson and that a fallback position would be necessary. This encountered resistance from Ball, Bundy, and McNamara, who knew the record. They pointed out that the European capitals had been told in April that the United States definitely wanted the MLF, and this had only been corroborated since then. American prestige and alliance leadership had been placed on the line, they argued, and the President could not back down without suffering consequences. Wilson was expecting to have to concede on the surface ships and would be surprised if he were let off the hook. They warned that there would

[78] Ibid.

be a resurgence of support for a land-based MRBM system to meet the officially established NATO requirement. Standing on his Presidential prerogatives, however, Johnson insisted that he did not feel personally committed, and he refused to be bound by the record. Elaborating on his lecture to them the previous day, the President spelled out his own interpretations of his political position. His election, he argued, had been a defeat of Goldwater extremism and not a solid liberal mandate. The swollen Democratic majorities in Congress would pose discipline problems, and public expectations were likely to outrun what he could realistically do. His enemies would be anxious to catch him in a major defeat, as had happened to Wilson in 1919 or to Roosevelt in 1937. His immediate problem was avoiding such traps, and he made it clear that he wanted much more respect for his problems from his advisers than he felt he was getting.

In the end it was decided that the administration would listen politely to Wilson's proposals and then reply that the British conception of nuclear arrangements would not handle the German problem and therefore was not viable. Wilson was to be pressured to take German needs seriously and was to be mandated to go negotiate in Bonn as a sympathetic statesman rather than as a shrewd British politician. No commitment to the surface fleet would be required of him.

The British-American meetings began on December 7 with a private conversation between the President and the Prime Minister. The President reportedly interpreted his own political situation to Wilson in much the same terms as he had to his advisers on the previous day. He then complained to Wilson at some length about the difficulties which the Prime Minister's policies on economic and defense matters had created in the United States. Wilson, known to be anxious to solidify a good working relationship with Johnson, backtracked considerably on the MLF question, the lesser priority for him of the two areas of contention. He apparently told the President that he had only expressed firm opposition to a nuclear force operating without a U.S. veto, that he had been noncommittal about the surface fleet. Johnson apparently considered this to be the concession which his advisers had demanded, but he was not inclined to accept the deal.

The decision to delay the MLF question was effectively sealed by that initial meeting between the President and the Prime Minister. In the three sessions which followed, involving the princi-

pal Cabinet members on both sides, the various points of disagreement were discussed without any substantial attempt at
resolution. The Americans emphasized the importance of the
surface fleet in meeting German needs and the importance of
British participation in rendering it nondiscriminatory. The British
reviewed their position on the subject and noted that they wanted
to make an independent assessment of the German position. They
stated their suspicions that the Germans were merely acquiescing
to American pressure. The basic disagreement over the control
formula was discussed at length, with the British refusing to concede the serious leeway for evolution of a European force which
the Americans held to be important. The American formula for
mollifying the French was resisted by the British as discriminatory against them, the British. The only point on which the American side apparently insisted on a well-specified agreement concerned the public interpretation of the meetings. The Americans
did not want Wilson claiming that he had torpedoed the MLF,
nor did they want the lesser suggestion that concrete decisions
had come out of the meetings. The vaguely worded communiqué
reflected this basic concern:

> They [the President and Prime Minister] recognized the im-
> portance of strengthening the unity of the Atlantic Alliance in
> its strategic nuclear defense. They discussed existing proposals
> for this purpose and an outline of some new proposals pre-
> sented by the British government. They agreed that the objec-
> tive in this field is to cooperate in finding the arrangements
> which best meet the legitimate interests of all members of the
> Alliance, while maintaining existing safeguards on the use of
> nuclear weapons, and preventing their further proliferation.
> A number of elements of this problem were considered during
> this *initial exchange of views* as *a preliminary to further dis-
> cussions* among interested members of the Alliance [emphasis
> added].[79]

In the aftermath of the meetings there remained the possibility
that Wilson's conversations in Bonn might actually produce an
Anglo-German agreement on some form of the proposal. Wilson
had some incentive to give it serious effort, not only to forestall
yet another round on the American proposal but because he

[79] *New York Times*, December 9, 1964, p. 16.

seemed to feel under real pressure to find an alliance framework for the British Polaris force. The Germans were not intrinsically as intent on a surface fleet as Ball and others had argued. Though Erhard had maneuvered into a personal political commitment to it, there was a strong possibility that he would agree to the British opting out of the surface fleet as an acceptable compromise. Since the main British dissenter, George Brown, had agreed to a force which included a surface ship component without British sailors, such a solution was readily imaginable. Should it come about, the issue would return to President Johnson in a context which made it much more difficult for him to demur. He would have to renounce the role of alliance leadership in a situation which rather clearly suggested his fear of the American Congress. Given the public record which he had in fact written in support of the MLF, that could pose dangers which might even rival those of an outright defeat.

Since he was worried about the possibility of an Anglo-German agreement, Johnson moved decisively in the latter part of December to put the whole range of proposals in abeyance. He had Bundy prepare a National Security Action Memorandum designed to control the pace of the issue. This document, NSAM 322, reaffirmed the earlier NSAM 318, in which the President had established controls over press briefings and diplomatic conversations. NSAM 322 also went further in explicitly stating that U.S. representatives were not to exert pressure for an agreement either in terms of substance or timing; that the United States could not countenance any agreement which did not have substantial support of Great Britain, Germany, and other interested allies; and that the United States would not seek to act against the direct interests of France and would give careful sympathetic hearing to French views. The draft of NSAM 322 arrived for Johnson's signature as he was talking to James Reston of the *New York Times*. Johnson showed it to Reston; and Reston, obviously with permission, published an account of its substance the next day.[80] Reston's story particularly emphasized the degree to which French sensitivities were to be favored in the further pursuit of nuclear sharing arrangements. The effect, probably intended by Johnson, was to slow the pace of the project considerably; if an Anglo-German agreement was imaginable, French acquiescence

---

[80] *New York Times*, December 21, 1964, p. 1.

was not. Finally, and critically, Johnson dismantled the machinery of the MLF group within the State Department. Simultaneous with the publication of the Reston story, Gerard Smith resigned as MLF coordinator, and his staff was dissolved.[81]

Thus by the end of December the President had rather clearly decided no on the MLF, and the signal was perceived in Europe, though not publicly acknowledged until a year later.[82] Even the fadeaway option and the variant of having European disagreement sink the force had been discarded. In moving against the pro-MLF machinery in the American government, the President made clear his own responsibility for stopping the project.

The story goes on, of course, for the problems engaged in December and the policy themes surrounding them did not die with the demise of the MLF proposal. Those broader ripples, however, belong to another study. For our purposes, December of 1964 produced a final outcome.

Paradigm Perspectives

On the Momentum of the MLF Project

A major reason why the dominance of the MLF project during the 1963–1964 period is posed as a central puzzle is that the most direct application of the analytic paradigm has such difficulty in accounting for it. The falling away in January of 1963 of the critical preconditions of the proposal is difficult to handle because these, in the analytic view, protect the interests of conflicting objectives. The relationship of the proposal to a buildup of conventional forces is an example. Though the circumstances of the January crisis would quite plausibly justify an increase in the weight given to the political objectives, to which the MLF proposal was primarily responsive, one cannot expect within the analytic paradigm the complete separation of the MLF from the question of conventional force deployments. These latter were far too critical for the actual security of Europe. Nonetheless, such a separation did occur and persisted over two years. Moreover, the central rationale of the project was that it was a politically necessary response to European demands. Since there were serious conse-

---

[81] *New York Times*, December 20, 1964, p. 3.

[82] The communiqué from the Johnson-Erhard meetings in December of 1965 officially interred the proposal (*New York Times*, December 22, 1965, p. 10).

quences in devolving control, one would not normally expect to find the United States promoting the project with great vigor against European resistance, indifference, and embarrassment. This nonetheless happened. Finally, the financial aspects were also anomalous to the analytic view. The project was projected to cost $2.7 billion; and, since cost estimates for major weapons systems have regularly been low by a substantial amount, $5 billion was readily imaginable.[83] The U.S. share, projected at various times from one-third to one-half of the total cost, might have run from $.9 billion to $2.5 billion. One would not expect a commitment to a weapons procurement program for political reasons without serious and extensive analysis as to whether, for the range of expenditure involved, alternative means might not be available which would produce an equal political effect and would not involve such serious military problems. Options of this character were simply not developed.

In military terms the projected force had some very severe debilities. The central notion of the MLF was the actual sharing of operational control. Though this was to be limited by a control formula establishing a juridical U.S. veto over firing, by mixed-manning of force components, and by a system of radio locks, none of these elements could be made infallible. *A priori* the construction and development of such a force entailed some possibility that it would to some degree at some point in time begin to operate independently. Though this question was raised by the British, who were against such a possibility, and by the Germans, who favored it, it was not subjected to serious analysis within the United States government. MLF proponents argued that the problem would recede in importance if the force were established and would arise seriously only if Europe united behind a single executive. Military analysts, who tended to view strategic war as an all-out nuclear exchange between the United States and the Soviet Union, generally dismissed the MLF as insignificant in that context regardless of whether it fired or did not fire. If one adopts other scenarios of war, however, an operating MLF begins to look both more significant and more troublesome.

[83] The cost estimates, for example, did not account for modernization of the force, a major, expensive problem in an era of rapidly advancing technology. The implicit assumption that the force could be maintained at its initial technology was an exceedingly questionable political assumption. If it could not, the $5 billion figure would probably be conservative.

If one imagines, for example, a high crisis in which the Soviet Union, though still deterred from full nuclear war, is nonetheless determined to extract some concession from Western nations, and/or in which fighting at a conventional level has already started, then it is not difficult to imagine a Soviet decision-making body looking for strategic targets to attack that would exert strong pressure without necessarily triggering a general nuclear exchange. In such circumstances the surface ships of the MLF, individually vulnerable and deployed at sea, would be very tempting targets. Over some period of time they could be sunk with conventional weapons without spillover effects on European populations. The duration during which they were picked off one by one would exert very severe pressure on the alliance. Such a scenario would put enormous burdens on the control arrangements of the force. It would be impossible to guarantee that the control system would perform in desirable fashion under those circumstances, and some of the imaginable failures would be catastrophic. If the situation seems bizarre, so do all scenarios of nuclear war; and many analysts find circumstances such as that much more likely than the sudden, large, insensate nuclear exchange. The point is that the MLF design, without any penetrating analysis of the military consequences, presented some very great risks in terms of the most critical of strategic variables— force vulnerability.[84] It is a basic strategic maxim that a strike force which is vulnerable to attack invites it in times of crisis. That maxim was treated very lightly indeed.

The benefits to be gained in return for the cost of the force and the risks to be undertaken with it were very difficult to specify. It was conceded by all that neither a German national nuclear force nor political unification in Europe were immediate or even medium-range prospects, whether or not the MLF came into being. To project benefits from the MLF in deflecting the former and promoting the latter required the tracing out of long chains of effects over a considerable period of time—a decade or more.

[84] The vulnerability assessments which were done and which argued that a force of seventeen ships or more was not vulnerable were tied to the general war scenario. This argument was that the force could not be eliminated in one blow with no chance for retaliation. Even granting this argument, there is a substantial difference between a submarine and a surface ship on a one-to-one basis, and for some scenarios that could be important.

In analytic terms this means that the presence of great uncertainty must be acknowledged, and presumably a relatively high discount rate would have to be used in counting the benefits. The vehemence with which the MLF was pursued hardly suggests that such a discount rate was being applied. Similarly, the arguments used publicly and privately to evaluate the proposal did not account for the possibility of unfavorable detours in the long causal chains whereby the benefits were to accrue.

The pattern of learning observed in the case is also difficult to fit with analytic expectations. The positive case would hold that the Merchant mission was an attempt to embody an analytic learning process. Set up in a time of political crisis, the Merchant mission would be understood analytically as a device for testing the political currents of Europe to see whether some compromise with unified control of the deterrent was necessitated. It is very hard to reconcile that view, however, with the actual operation of the mission. The MLF project was run as an exercise in U.S. leadership, and the sharing arrangement was pushed on U.S. initiative rather than conceded under pressure. The argument for the proposal which the MLF group developed was not a matter of adjusting the central trade-offs, weighing options, analyzing the critical uncertainties, and building in effects (such as the implications for East-West détente or alliance ground force posture) which were originally excluded. The MLF argument was designed rather to fend off alternatives and competing objectives, and it remained stable in its essential features throughout. The analytic sophistication which one would expect, given the reasonably extensive staff work over a period of three years or more, did not develop. For example, the rather sharp imbalance in the argument whereby European objections to the Athens program were asserted to be incorrigible, immutable, and absolute impediments, whereas problems with the control formula of the MLF were expected to dissolve over time, was not challenged from start to finish.

One could impute, of course, a pattern of values and probability assessments in the American decision makers which would render the puzzles explicable, but it would have to be a very strange imputation. It would require a very long-range payoff function for the political objectives with a very low rate of discount. At the same time one would have to impose a strikingly short-term view of the military objectives with a very high discount rate. Such a pattern transcends most of the available evidence and strains credulity. It is more in line with the evidence to assume that trade-off objectives were not being integrated, that alternative outcomes were not being projected, that available information was being very selectively used, and that in general the MLF came to dominance in a process contrary to the analytic paradigm.

The general tendency when encountering such trouble in analytic logic is to disaggregate the government and recognize "players in positions"[85] within the policy-making bureaucracy—to engage, in other words, in analytically based political analysis. The assumptions then are generally made: (1) that the individual players are pursuing objectives which are affected by their organizational position and therefore tend to be narrower than broad national interest objectives generally assumed, and (2) that the separate individuals, given their objectives, made decisions in accord with the analytic paradigm. With power dispersed over many separate players, the outcomes are held to be resultants of their separate efforts. Such outcomes are not expected to fit an overall design, but they are expected to result from the analytic calculations of individual players.

It is clear that this set of ideas has some usefulness. It would be hard to explain the dominance of the MLF without understanding the position of its adherents within the State Department, their political astuteness, and the natural advantages which events such as the Nassau conference afforded. The organization of the special office, the access of the MLF proponents to the White House, the critical position of George Ball, and the effects of the Nassau agreement on McNamara made it possible for strong opponents of the MLF to be kept away from the issue. Orthodoxy within the MLF group was vigorously maintained. At least one person who was more sympathetic to the Athens program was forced to leave the Policy Planning Council of the State Department for that reason. Maneuvers within the bureaucracy such as press leaks, the planting of diplomatic cables, the careful management of the naval studies, etc., were important in developing momentum behind the project; countermaneuvers—

[85] Graham T. Allison, *Essence of Decision* (Boston: Little, Brown and Company, 1971).

the Ball Committee and the Neustadt mission—were important in stopping it. The whole story is suffused with bureaucratic politics as should be sufficiently apparent from the narrative.

A political perspective is also necessary in understanding why the surface configuration of the force emerged as the core of the proposal during its dominant phase. Admiral Rickover's powerful guardianship of the nuclear submarine program explains in part why the surface fleet, with such risks of military vulnerability and such obvious political discrimination, was accepted and insisted upon despite the clear displeasure of the Germans and the Italians. Though this enters a realm where it is difficult to obtain any real evidence, it is easy to see in this episode an example of what was called value expansion and extraneous value integration (Chapter 5). In this view Rickover would be understood as chiefly concerned with maintaining his personal influence over the nuclear submarine program. This commitment, extraneous to the broader public objectives, would then have forced very consequential compromises which affected the major objectives at stake. Even without imputing such a motive to Rickover, the fact that he exercised such unassailable authority over the submarine program and that he made his judgment unquestionably on more restricted grounds than those involved in the broader MLF argument helps explain the emphasis on surface ships. What is so anomalous in analytic terms becomes far less so if the political context is understood.

For all that, one cannot simply explain the momentum which developed behind the MLF as the natural consequence of a process whereby the MLF proponents gathered and exercised power within the American bureaucracy. With President Kennedy as reluctant as he was, with Robert McNamara personally opposed, with most of the military bureaucracy either uninterested or negative, the Nassau conference should not have been sufficient to launch the MLF on a two-year career. As suggested at the beginning of the chapter, the position of the MLF group centered in the Policy Planning Council and in a special office was much weaker by any direct political calculus than the opposing forces of the Secretary of Defense, the Joint Chiefs of Staff, and the Joint Committee on Atomic Energy. That the State Department was the chief proponent of this weapon system and that it was able to produce such momentum for deployment is a clear politi-

315

cal anomaly, for the combined resources of opponents and skeptics should have pulled the MLF group up short long before they succeeded in establishing a clear United States commitment.

It is also not as if everyone was simply too distracted to care much. At several points after Nassau McNamara did things which could readily be interpreted as attempts to undermine the MLF. In conversations with the German Defense Minister Kai Uwe von Hassel in February of 1963 for example, McNamara explicitly deprecated the proposal. He emphasized his view that the U.S. support depended on the Europeans establishing valid military reasons for proceeding with the force. Pointing to the U.S. deterrent forces, from which the Germans would receive protection without any payment, he questioned whether there was such a justification. He also questioned how there could be a political justification since the United States would not relinquish its veto over firing. Von Hassel, in response, suggested that the Germans were centrally concerned not with controlling nuclear weapons but rather with tying the United States more firmly into Europe, a thesis which was widely held among MLF opponents in the United States. McNamara then picked up on this at the NATO Council meeting in Ottawa in May of 1963, where he announced a number of provisions for consultation and information exchange. He announced an increase in the amount of strategic military data which would be made available to the alliance. NATO officers, including Germans, were to be stationed at SAC headquarters at Omaha to participate in planning and force operations. A deputy commander for nuclear weapons was to be placed under SACEUR, who would conduct training and operations and greatly increase allied information on these matters.[86] All these provisions would solidify the German-American tie in nuclear weapons areas and presumably speak to von Hassel's concern. As supplements to the British Inter-Allied Nuclear Force (IANF) initiative, which was also announced at the Ottawa meeting, these provisions readily appear as a subtle means of removing thunder from the MLF and of steering alliance concerns along the lines of the Athens program.

In terms of basic political forces it is not clear why the Secretary of Defense did not stop the MLF. It is not clear why such a strong commitment was established by December of 1964 that

[86] *New York Times*, May 23, 1963, p. 1, and May 25, 1963, p. 1.

even McNamara, negatively inclined on its merits, was willing to bow to it even to the point of resisting the President's negative decision.

SOME of these puzzles concerning the flourishing of the MLF against analytic and political adversity can be understood within the framework of the cognitive paradigm. The MLF group in the State Department displayed many of the characteristics of the theoretical syndrome of thinking associated with that paradigm. They argued the proposal in terms of a highly generalized long-term pattern of beliefs organized around the single coherent objective of promoting integration in Europe. There is evidence that the set of images concerning European integration were adopted early in the professional careers of the MLF proponents through experience in the Marshall Plan and the early days of European economic integration. At least, such experience was common in their backgrounds. The main proponents did operate at staff levels, devoting a substantial percentage of their attention to the issue over an extended period of time. They did form a tightly integrated group regularly interacting and providing mutually supportive judgments. They displayed, as well, other of the characteristics expected of the theoretical thinker's syndrome: strong resistance to immediate negative information (e.g., political opposition in Europe, reluctance of the President, military vulnerability of the surface force); the use of internally coherent images (the notions of European integration and Atlantic partnership visualized in terms of a dumbbell); the protection of their belief structure through the use of impossibility inferences (the Athens program was impossible because the Europeans would not accept it); the use of inferences of transformation to protect the preferred option (the anomalies of the control formula would dissolve as the force began to operate). The strange logic whereby the disadvantages of the Athens program were held to be incorrigible whereas the disadvantages of the MLF were asserted to be transient becomes explicable as a pattern of inferences operating to protect the highly generalized belief structure against the pressures of immediate information.

In imposing the assumption that the MLF proponents were indeed operating in terms of the theoretical syndrome, one readily derives an explanation of their aggressive pursuit of the proposal despite its drawbacks. In dissolving the central value trade-offs and focusing on the single political objective of promoting European unity, they remained essentially unconcerned about the effects of the force on damage-limiting objectives in the case of deterrence failure or on the political objective of détente. The issue of vulnerability and its consequences could thus be ignored except as it affected the tactics of getting the proposal accepted, for which the categorical certifications of the Michaelis study sufficed. In these terms it becomes understandable why, though developing the proposal down to details such as the design of mess halls on ships and the uniforms to be worn, the MLF group did not examine the possible consequences of various scenarios of deterrence failure or the possibility of the force actually stimulating a German weapons program. Though critical to anyone trying to weigh the trade-off, these questions were extraneous within the thought structure of proponents focused on the single objective.

In using cognitive assumptions, one also renders understandable why the MLF proponents were so insensitive to European resistance while claiming to be responding to European political demands. The significance of anything being said in Europe as they promoted the proposal was interpreted in terms of how it fit the long-range objective. Thus British resistance was seen as further manifestation of their failure to adjust to the trend of European events and French resistance as a manifestation of reactionary Gaullism. The MLF was never, in the minds of its promoters, a response to immediate demands but rather a critical element in a long-range strategy of institution building.

It is also possible to use the cognitive paradigm to understand the two Presidents and the Secretary of Defense, and this adds to the overall explanation. All three would be expected theoretically to fit the syndrome of the uncommitted thinker. They came to their jobs from backgrounds which had not given them deep and powerful exposure to the substantive issues, and they sat at the top of large policy hierarchies which constantly rushed them from issue to issue with no time to soak in complexities and details. It was much more difficult for them to be dominated by a small group of like-minded associates. Consequently one would expect them to adopt temporarily the intellectual framework of the MLF proposal which its proponents had developed, to make no attempt to resolve the trade-offs which the proponents did not address, and to decide, when required, in the direction indicated by short-term political feedback processes.

This pattern fairly clearly fits the behavior of the two Presidents. Displaying a great deal of reluctance, President Kennedy signed on to the program of the MLF proponents at three critical points: in accepting Merchant's instructions in February of 1963, in responding to Adenauer's commitment in May of 1963, and in giving authorization to approach Congress in November of 1963. In each case he was responding in the context of short-term political pressures and gave authorizations which clearly went beyond his own commitments. This, in the view of the cognitive paradigm, is the normally expected pattern and explains how the highly structured position of the MLF proponents interacted with decision makers operating along different lines. President Johnson's authorization given to the MLF proponents in April of 1964 also fits this pattern.

More striking and more complicated is the case of Robert McNamara. He is usually characterized as the highly committed, highly analytic champion of the Athens program. If that were so, however, one certainly would expect him from his powerful position as Secretary of Defense to bring the MLF under much more stringent control, in effect to prevent such a clear and strong United States initiative. If one posits that McNamara's commitment to the Athens program was less solid than that of the defense analysts who devised it and that he, too, was prone to operate in line with the uncommitted syndrome, his behavior becomes more explicable. In this view he responded to the analytically structured arguments against the MLF, but he did not engage in an analytic decision process himself. Rather he split the trade-off problem into separate military and political segments, and he ceded the political objective to the MLF proposal and its organizational sponsorship to the State Department. Though negative on the merits of the issue, he would concede under short-term political pressure (at Nassau in 1962, in the Ball Committee in 1964) because the central trade-off was not very active in his own mind, to the quiet dismay of his defense analysts. He, too, could conceive of the MLF as exclusively a political problem.

Thus, the cognitive paradigm finds a rather natural explanation for the momentum developed behind the MLF proposal. In the interaction between uncommitted and ideological decision-making syndromes, the decision process of the United States government was not sensitive to those aspects of the proposal which appear anomalous in analytic terms. The power of the United States government within the alliance was sufficient to give the proposal a considerable political momentum. Despite unhappiness in Europe over many substantive aspects of the proposal, the fact that the United States was committed to it weighed heavily in all European capitals except Paris. The importance of continuing the U.S. guarantee was so critical to the Germans that they were willing to buy any mechanism which promised to strengthen that tie, whatever its other merits. The British, with both their American relationship and their general international stature a great deal more secure than the Germans, could afford to be more discriminating in what they would agree to; but they too were in the habit of taking strong American desires seriously, whatever the circumstances. Despite the complex domestic politics which the proposal evoked in Britain, Germany, Italy, and Western Europe as a whole, these underlying factors deriving from basic American strength were sufficient to yield polite, responsive signals in diplomatic channels. On the American side these could be read as positive feedback. The overall interaction in the alliance between the American commitment and the European response can then be seen as a self-amplifying positive feedback system,[87] as in the often-encountered example of the microphone picking up the signal of its own speakers, thus recycling and reamplifying its own output until some natural limit is reached. Such positive feedback systems do not spin out of control forever, but they frequently do take matters far beyond the point where most would have wished to stop.

On the Demise of the MLF

The problem as to why President Johnson reversed his advisers on the MLF and derailed the proposal against a commitment he generated poses a contrasting set of considerations. It is obvious that the very reasons why the strength of the proposal during the 1963–1964 period appears anomalous to analytic expectations help to explain why it would be stopped in December of 1964. If the analytic paradigm has a difficult time explaining the timing of the negative decision and the fact that it occurred after a sub-

[87] Karl W. Deutsch, *Nerves of Government* (New York: The Free Press, 1966).

stantial commitment had been made, thus incurring apparently unnecessary political costs, nonetheless the fact of a negative decision can be readily understood by analytic logic. The proposal was costly, both in budgetary terms and in terms of short-term political capital. It threatened fundamental defense objectives, and it provided very uncertain, very distant political gains in return. This set of considerations undoubtedly had substantial impact, however diffuse and difficult to specify that might be. Impressionistically, for example, such judgments seem to have been important in the very skeptical reactions of the press and of Congress. The proposal, in many people's minds, did not make simple, intuitive sense; and that unquestionably put an enormous drag on the entire project.

A look at such details of President Johnson's decision as are available complicates the issue somewhat. The President gave every indication that he accepted the central argument of MLF proponents regarding the necessity of accommodating the Germans, and indeed he seemed to believe that the danger there was more immediate than the ten-year estimates his advisers provided. Moreover, he did not respond to the military implications of the project at all, and his negative decision was accompanied solely by discussion of the immediate political context—Congressional and European opposition. It is entirely possible that his judgment reflected a different but analytic weighing of the central objectives in the light of these immediate political pressures. Such a process must be imputed, however, in the absence of direct evidence. Interpreting the President in December 1964 as the final arbiter of an analytic calculus of national interest is possible, but hardly compelling.

One can unquestionably add richness to the interpretation of Lyndon Johnson by conducting an analytically based political analysis. In this view he must be seen as the man holding the office of the Presidency—the unique intersection of major forces in domestic and world politics. Because of its political position, the Presidency is likely on any given issue to highlight trade-offs not taken seriously at staff levels of the government. In the case of the MLF there may have been substantively extraneous objectives which were in competition with the MLF objectives because of the limits of Presidential power. If one posits that President Johnson as an individual decision maker acted according to the analytic paradigm but in a complicated political context, then the natural inference is that he weighed the MLF against the prospects for his domestic program and/or against other foreign policy priorities and that he found the trade-offs unfavorable to the MLF.

The thesis that this was the character of his decision and that it was his domestic program which President Johnson sought to protect, gains some direct support from the lectures he gave his advisers at the meetings on December 5 and 6. He made clear in those meetings his wariness about a big defeat in Congress at the beginning of his term, and he established as a major principle that his administration's influence over the Congress was a scarce resource not to be lightly spent. This would suggest that a trade-off with his domestic program was being weighed. He did, in fact, seek his major pieces of domestic legislation in the first session of the 89th Congress.

It is also possible that Johnson could already foresee the major commitment in Vietnam which began to develop just a few months later, and that it was a trade-off between this and the MLF which motivated him to back off the latter. The Vietnam situation was under review at the time. It would not be wholly implausible to assert that the fundamental issue of United States credibility as an ally, which was at the roots of the nuclear sharing problem, was transferred from Europe and the MLF to Indochina. That would account for the timing of the decision and would fit with the justifications subsequently offered for the American effort in Vietnam. One could also note that Walt Rostow, who had been a prime MLF theorist, soon became even more important as a prime theorist of the Asian commitment. All this is speculation, however. The direct evidence of a consciously constructed connection between the issues is very thin, and it would go beyond any evidence short of a laboratory experiment to assert that an unconscious analytic process was at work.

At any rate if one adopts the view that President Johnson was engaged in an analytic decision process weighing some outside objectives in the context of Presidential politics, one can readily explain why he proceeded so decisively. The fadeaway option which he discarded was designed to protect him and the United States from the consequences of suddenly abandoning, under French pressure, an established commitment. Some of those consequences were reasonably serious. The Erhard government, for example, had been maneuvered into a politically difficult commitment to the project by the U.S. initiative, and it was German sensitivities which Johnson seemed to hold as the most serious issue at stake. Though relieving the pressure of the deadline had some immediate conveniences for Bonn, the sudden switch in Washington unmistakably signaled by the Reston story and the dismantling of the special MLF office could only make the Germans more wary of responding to American leadership in the future. Though it is thus hard to see why the President would scuttle the project so openly and so suddenly if he were making calculations relating to the direct substance of the issue, it is quite clear why he would do so if he were making outside trade-offs. The essential fact is that the highly committed MLF group could be counted on to produce yet another decision deadline which would have put even greater pressure on him. Thus the fadeaway option, when seen in political and organizational perspective, entailed a substantial probability of producing the opposite—a new deadline with a new recommendation to proceed and with the American commitment advanced yet another notch. If the President wanted to protect his domestic program or his Vietnam commitment, he would have to stop that before it developed. Disconnecting the machinery of the initiative was necessary if he was to be confident of holding the MLF in abeyance. If we posit that the President was weighing these probabilities, his decisiveness can be explained.

A RATHER different perspective emerges if one posits that President Johnson was engaged not in an analytic decision process, but rather in one resembling the cognitive paradigm; that is, basically a cybernetic process with subjectively imposed structure. In adopting this set of assumptions, one would argue that Johnson, still in the uncommitted thinker syndrome, took the MLF as a single-objective problem (e.g., a response to German political needs) rather than weighing either the central substantive trade-offs or extraneous political ones. This view would argue that he then made the decision as a simple yes/no choice (i.e., push Wilson to accept the surface force or not), based on the immediate flow of information in his natural, i.e., political, channels. The cognitive framework into which he fit the proposal was dominated by the objective of satisfying the Germans and by the fact of Kennedy's earlier commitment. What he got in terms of immediate information—indicating European and Congressional opposition—was negative, and that made him cautious. When he received information between the two critical meetings (the cable from Bonn indicating German unease and the Bundy memo revealing Kennedy's disaffection) which struck at the core of his understanding of the proposal, it became easy for him to follow the immediate political pressures and to decide negatively. The working out of the consequences would then be a matter of staff work with which he need not excessively concern himself. Under such a decision process the President would largely not confront the substantive and political paradoxes of the problem. In cognitive analysis such a process would be the natural one for a man with his background and daily routine confronting a complex problem.

The decisive action which followed the decision of December 6 is more difficult to handle within the cognitive paradigm, but a case can be made. The National Security Action Memorandum prepared by his staff was on his desk for signature while James Reston was in the room. One can imagine the President, on impulse, showing the document to Reston while complaining of the bureaucrats who led him down a rocky path. The resulting story suggesting a French veto could then be laid to Reston's interpretation, and the dissolution of the MLF office to a loss of morale there. Gerard Smith, a man of independent means, not in the foreign service, who was motivated by deep feelings on the issue, had in fact attempted to resign when Richard Neustadt was appointed on his special mission because he felt, correctly, that that signaled a loss of confidence in the White House with his office. The decisions on December 6 and the Reston story could only enhance his wish to leave. The dissolution of his office in this view would appear to be something produced by staff levels at the White House in response to their perception of the President's wishes. This would make the decisiveness of the President's decision less of a conscious design than does the other interpretation.

It should be pointed out that the President's actions if seen in the cognitive framework are far from unsophisticated. Though they do not penetrate the critical substantive issues of the proposal, it is easy to see that as something he could not do. He could not have enough information and background knowledge to exercise his own substantive judgments on the MLF with any degree of assurance, and he knew that dependence upon experts, his major advisers, was inevitable on that issue and many others to come. If one posits that he accepted the inevitability of having to use a cognitive process himself and therefore of being dependent upon expert sponsorship of the ideas he would use in reaching decisions, what he did makes a great deal of sense. His MLF decision disciplined his advisers to be more careful, more penetrating, more protective of him in their judgments, and he went to great lengths in the meetings of December 5 and 6 to articulate that message quite clearly. In an uncertain and distracting world, attempts to tune a cognitive decision process so that it works to advantage may in fact be more beneficial than unsuccessful attempts to achieve some approximation of an analytic process.

THESE interpretations of Johnson's decisions in December are obviously very different and contradictory enough that one would like to be able to decide which account is more accurate. Unhappily, a clear choice cannot be made given direct evidence now available or ever likely to become available. The question has been traced to the detailed workings of a certain individual's mind—precincts very difficult to penetrate indeed. It might have been answered with careful observations taken at the time, but that opportunity is forever gone. It is unlikely that either the complete written record or candid testimony by close advisers of the President would compellingly resolve the issue.

Though this is an uncomfortable result, it does not warrant despair with the exercise. For one thing, the reduction of the problem to a choice between two reasonably coherent explanations is worth a great deal even if the ultimate choice remains problematic. It is better than puzzled confusion; it is better than imposing clarity by arbitrary assertion. For another, the competing explanations provide a basis for approaching subsequent decisions involving the same man. Though not necessary by any logic advanced here, it is nonetheless reasonable to assume that Lyndon Johnson approached the MLF problem with the same sort of decision process he used subsequently.

If one believed in December of 1964 that Lyndon Johnson was an analytic decision maker protecting his plans for the "Great Society" (the most natural analytic interpretation), then the events of the following six months would cause us a rude surprise. In that period the President constructed the essential elements of a commitment to protect the government of South Vietnam, a commitment which had very damaging effects on his domestic program and ultimately on his own political position. Faced with this information, one might wish to shift the imputed objective and still preserve analytic assumptions, thus attributing to Johnson a deep commitment to Vietnam, already operating in December, which caused him to scuttle his European policy. Alternatively, one could shift paradigms and ask why a cognitive pattern which terminated a commitment in December might reaffirm another one the following February. In pursuing that question the career of the MLF prior to December of 1964 would likely offer some useful insight. In other words, the questions raised in the analysis of the MLF and the results achieved have significance beyond the context.

CHAPTER 10

Epilogue: Conclusions and

Implications

THE CORE argument advanced in the foregoing study is reasonably simple. It can be summarized in a few propositions:

1) Decision processes based on fundamental operations of the human mind are critical to understanding the behavior of governments and consequently the determination of political events.

2) There are at least two coherent and logically distinct sets of assumptions as to how such decision processes operate for complex policy problems, and these yield different and in some instances contradictory explanations of the same political events.

3) As the events of the MLF episode illustrate, the analytic paradigm, which currently provides the base decision theory for most political analysis, is not adequate to account for all of the forces which affect the conduct of public affairs. The analytic paradigm encounters serious anomalies in the events of the MLF, and competitive cognitive and cybernetic assumptions provide an attractive supplementary perspective which helps explain these anomalies.

There are a number of implications which can be drawn from the argument.

SUBJECTIVE VS. OBJECTIVE INTERPRETATIONS

The first of the summary propositions—asserting a connection between basic mental processes and the operations of government—is perhaps the most critical and most troublesome element on the list. As stated, it reflects one of those central philosophical ambiguities which have tied analysts in knots for centuries. A subjectivist view of the proposition would hold that the asserted connection is something which arises largely in the mind of the analyst; that is, that the enormously complex processes of government decision making are given coherence in

327

the mind of observers by conceptualizing them in terms of individual acts of decision. An important argument could be built along such lines without trying to confront the question as to whether governmental processes are in fact strongly influenced by simple, fundamental decision processes. The objectivist view of the argument, by contrast, holds that there is an empirical relationship of significant magnitude, that the complex decision processes of large organizations do substantially build upon fundamental processes at the level of single individuals. There is, of course, no point in trying to resolve this time-honored tangle while concluding the study. The issue is raised to sketch out the possible range of interpretation, to point out that the two views of the study are not mutually exclusive, and to suggest that the subjectivist view defines, in effect, a minimum claim.

Thus, for those who are willing to admit nothing else, the study is asserted to be valid as a struggle for the minds of those who analyze government behavior, be they the observers and interpreters of history or participants in on-going issues seeking to make something happen. There can be no doubt that the evidence upon which any person's understanding of the men and institutions of government is based is inherently inadequate. For any issue of much consequence, both the scale of operations and the range of effects which are directly pertinent are simply too great to be gathered together in one mind at one point in time. This means that the framework of assumptions which the analyst brings to his task of forging an understanding is critically important in enabling inferences over wide gaps in evidence and in imposing overall coherence on otherwise confused situations. The study of the MLF points to some of the consequences of adopting different conceptual frameworks for this purpose.

To this subjectivist posture accrue the major benefits of keeping the identified paradigms separate and of insisting on setting up contradictory assumptions. Such procedures bring an element of discipline to the interpretation of the complex events, an enterprise which is difficult to make rigorous. The dilemma in this regard is clear enough: if quantitative precision is demanded it is gained, at the current state of things, only by so reducing the scope of what is analyzed that most of the important problems remain external. If such reduction is resisted then evidence becomes loose and easily bent to the demands of established assumptions. The study supports the argument that if analysts force themselves to use competing assumptions it is less likely that they will reach conclusions which are too firm for the evidence or too limited in scope for the problem. For the subjectivist that is the major conclusion. The study has articulated competing frameworks of assumption, has cited evidence from basic research for taking each framework seriously, and has provided an extended example of how they can be used to unravel problems of understanding actual complex events. If some readers have been sensitized, the point has been made, and some degree of success can be claimed.

For those who wish to reach beyond the minimal subjectivist claim the competing paradigms are an embarrassment. It is, of course, necessary and proper to set up competing hypotheses in the stages of framing the problem and gathering evidence, but that is not a situation one wishes to affirm in the conclusion. The objectivist view demands some resolution. If one paradigm is dominated by another, let the first be rejected; if all obtain under different circumstances, let those circumstances be specified; if complex processes are an aggregate of all the fundamental ones, let the procedure of combination be identified. A coherent view of reality ultimately requires something more definitive than a set of contradictory hypotheses, each partially confirmed.

At the moment there is not much hope that the theoretical disarray will be quickly resolved. At any rate, the question as to how the separate paradigms of individual decision making—the analytic paradigm on one hand and the cognitive on the other—might ultimately fit together in a general model of the mind is wildly beyond the scope of this inquiry. There is a natural argument that analytic procedures are more sophisticated, second-order processes which build upon more primitive cognitive operations. In some sense that must be true, for, as many have pointed out, full analysis of any complex problem is far beyond the capacity one can plausibly attribute to mental operations. Some evidence has been cited, however, that for specific decision problems the two processes can and do operate as substitutes for one another and that they do produce different decisions, other things being equal. While remaining open to the possibility of a general theoretical integration of the separate paradigms, it still seems best, even when adopting an objectivist stance, to focus on the divergent hypotheses they generate and to observe which one seems to accord most closely with actual events.

The clearest and most consequential divergence in theoretical expectations concerns the process of learning. A decision maker proceeding fully in accord with analytic requirements might well begin with such a simple, undifferentiated conception of a complex problem that it would be equally easy to fit his behavior into the cognitive paradigm. If he operates on the problem over time, however, the analytic expectation is that his simple conception will become more sophisticated as separate effects are identified, the objectives they affect articulated, their trade-offs weighed, and a model of operations gradually constructed. The conceptually explicit causal learning process, even in the most complex of situations, will produce some increased differentiation of the problem. Moreover, the analytic decision maker is expected to be reasonably active in pursuing these changes in conception. He thus should distinguish himself by data gathering activities designed not so much to bolster established positions as to test critical assumptions with an eye to change, by arguments more critical than promotional, by reasonably frequent invention of new alternatives and/or adjustment of existing ones. Such a decision maker should be slow to adopt an option wholeheartedly, especially when trade-offs are reasonably harsh. Indeed, given complexity and the inherent inadequacy of his calculus, we would expect to find him relatively indecisive.

By contrast, in the operation of the cognitive paradigm over time one expects to find greater stability. The constrained learning process of that paradigm does not produce the on-going elaboration expected of the analytic decision maker. Information-processing operations within the paradigm do not proceed in active pursuit of conceptual change but rather operate to keep such change within reasonably narrow limits. Especially basic problem conceptions—the defined objective, the major options in basic outline, the image of consequences to accrue—should be much slower to change than in the analytic paradigm and should be driven to it only under considerable pressure.

With all due caution, the best basic judgment that can be made is that the learning process we observe in the MLF case fits much more closely to cognitive expectations than to those of the analytic paradigm. The basic elements of the proposal remained stable except where adjustments were forced by immediate and unmistakable political pressures. Obvious analytic questions were not addressed during the four years the proposal was under development. It was not seriously asked, for example, whether the $3 to $5 billion which the force would have cost could produce a better political return by investing it in an alliance planning system. A categorical judgment was simply imposed, holding that cooperative planning was an insufficient alternative and never addressing the question as to what a $3 billion planning effort might look like. In general the process of development of the MLF was one in which there was a narrowing of the scope of debate rather than a gradual inclusion in the decision calculations of effects originally neglected. As a prominent example, the question of the relationships of the MLF to conventional force increases was essentially eliminated from policy considerations after January of 1963. It was clear that this relationship was direct and immediate under limited European budgets and that it would affect the overall force posture. To have such a major effect eliminated from serious consideration is perfectly natural within the cognitive paradigm.

The objectivist conclusion, then, is that we have observed a constrained learning process in operation and that we have reason to expect it in other instances where government encounters complex policy problems. It should be reemphasized that constrained learning is not a phenomenon which warrants casual condemnation. It is in the cognitive paradigm not an aberration but rather the normally expected consequence of the fact that the decision makers were operating under structural uncertainty and were inevitably reliant on internal mechanisms for structuring and processing information. There are unavoidable normative implications, of course, and we will want to consider these at least briefly. One cannot moralize away the main implication, however: Penetrating understanding of governmental decision making must take seriously the cognitive effects of complexity. Many features of the MLF story will recur in other contexts.

Some Normative Reflections on Leadership

During a White House reception for Harold Wilson in December of 1964, with the fate of the MLF virtually decided, an exchange occurred between Presidential consultants Dean Acheson and Richard Neustadt which concisely captured a central normative problem in the MLF episode. Dean Acheson, called to participate in the final meetings, had sided with George Ball in urging the President to follow through on his commitment to the MLF and thereby to assume his proper role as leader of the alliance. A statesman dealing with issues of a decade, Acheson had argued, could not lose heart at the last moment because of momentary political inconvenience. To Acheson the President personally and the United States as a whole possessed ample power to establish the force which the nation's highest officials had insisted was necessary and had brought to the brink of fruition. Richard Neustadt, by contrast, was fundamentally inclined to protect the political position of the President. He was suspicious of large projects with political liabilities on the order of those which plagued the MLF, and he had recoiled from Ball's strong presentation on December 5. He felt that the Undersecretary of State had overstated the positive case and thereby had clouded the exercise of Presidential judgment. Neustadt had therefore approved of Bundy's memorandum which so effectively presented the negative arguments. As the two special advisers met at the reception, Acheson expressed displeasure at the outcome: "I know your theory," he grumbled to Neustadt. "You think Presidents should be warned. You're wrong. Presidents should be given confidence."[1]

It is most natural in hindsight to side with those who resisted the MLF, to support Neustadt against Acheson. The proposal now seems to have been far too awkward, far too much of a façade to carry the weight which its proponents projected for it. Its dangers were far too casually treated. The collapse of the project was accepted in Germany with relative equanimity, and serious pressures for national nuclear weapons have not developed in the aftermath. SACEUR has come upon lean years and has not generated any momentum to meet the MRBM "requirement" with a weapons system based on the continent. New, more pragmatic perspectives have arisen on European integration as the visions of the early years have adjusted downward with experience. Domestic priorities are everywhere on the rise. Grand international designs are out of favor. The dangers of ill-designed action in world affairs now seem impressive. Thus, to those who were not intimately involved in its creation, the argument for the MLF seems bizarre in retrospect. One intuitively feels that the President should have been warned, indeed even earlier and more vehemently than he was.

[1] As recalled by Richard E. Neustadt in personal communication.

EPILOGUE

There is much support for this position, of course, in the theoretical discussion which has been developed in conjunction with the analysis of the MLF episode. In carefully controlled contexts it has been demonstrated that the human mind, an induction machine of impressive power, operates far beyond the evidence it has available to it. The argument has been extended in this study to suggest that the mechanisms which allow inductions to occur are those by means of which policy leaders develop their conceptions of the national interest and their theories as to how it is best promoted by specific actions. The analysis makes it clear that strong-policy theories are highly vulnerable to error when operating in complex environments without stable decompositions of limited scope. There is a tendency to hold value trade-offs separate, and there will be a limited conception of the effects of any given course of action. The learning process, moreover, may not be proof against serious error, in that established conceptions are likely to be highly buffered against change. Strong-policy advocates, in short, are prone to making big mistakes and to persisting in them. Neustadt's concern for warning Presidents is well taken.

For all that, one cannot dismiss Acheson's argument lightly. In a world of great complexity and poorly developed knowledge, it is inherently easier to develop negative arguments than to advance constructive ones. Uncertainty naturally allies with doubt, hesitation, delay. Fully warned Presidents are likely to vacillate under counteracting pressures; their governments are likely to act incoherently. This, too, has its dangers, for there are some situations in which commitments must be established early, some for which the intrinsic problem is the *timely* discovery and resolute pursuit of larger purposes lying beyond immediate horizons. In these situations the attempt to preserve options beyond the point where events will allow it can destroy the more attractive alternatives and can deliver the decision maker, whether individual or government, over to the control of processes he did not design and cannot direct. Some of the most serious issues generated by modern societies—including especially the handling of nuclear weapons—cannot be effectively addressed if serious action must await the outbreak of a crisis to become compelling.

Precisely because the world is complex, there is a need for men of vision, imagination, boldness, and indefatigable dedication to give the nation concepts of its interest and theories of action when these are far from clear. These are the leaders, the confidence givers, and without them surely no government could manage very well the subtler problems of public policy. Since one cannot guarantee that the most forceful and prominent policy leaders will always be right—again, a point underscored by the analysis of the cognitive paradigm—the price of leadership is the risk of serious error. Despite the dangers, there are indeed times when Presidents should be given confidence.

In this light many of the activities of the MLF proponents which were the cause of outrage in press coverage of the events are not shocking. The MLF proponents were consistently out in front of the President; but that is not such an unusual situation. They actively promoted the project in a reluctant Europe while claiming merely to be responding to European demands, and they made claims for the benefits of the project which could not be justified objectively. Upon reflection, that amount of deception and self-delusion is not obviously beyond the range one must expect to encounter. Though one does not want to approve of such things, to issue a flat condemnation is a bit like the fundamentalist condemning sex as sinful. It is much too close to the core of human affairs to eradicate.

There is, then, a serious dilemma encountered in the tension between the principle of warning and the principle of giving confidence. Both seem to be necessary; presumably neither should be given sole authority over the process of public decision. Since the two principles tend to produce contrasting errors, there is a natural tendency to state the normative issue as a matter of achieving the proper balance between them in the governmental process. That, however, poses the question as to how such a balance is to be achieved, and intuitively that sort of question is not given to an easy or definitive answer. Rather than attempt a grand synthesis, therefore, which at the current state of the art is destined to be impossibly vague and arbitrary, it is better to draw some limited conclusions from each of the contending paradigms.

Normative Arguments of the Analytic Paradigm

The main thrust of the study suggests that the analytic decision process is not the most natural or empirically dominant mechanism of decision under complexity. Though important traces of analytic logic can be found in the MLF story, the conclusion is that an approximation to the analytic process is difficult to achieve and comes about only as the result of conscious and extensive effort. Real investments in time, intellectual effort, information, and political capital are required to work a complex problem such as nuclear sharing into an adequate analytic structure. Despite the fact that the analytic paradigm is theoretically the best understood and most extensively developed, it runs against strong empirical forces and must be cultured with considerable care if it is to survive in harsh political environments.

The argument for expending the effort required to actualize the demands of the analytic paradigm rests in part upon the inherent properties of complexity and the importance of explicitness. The value trade-offs and systemic interactions which form the core of the complex problem seem to be stable features of the human condition, recurring in most of the major problems generated by modern societies. Intuitively, if trade-offs exist they ought to be recognized, for there is little reason to believe that blind decisions will yield better results systematically than those aided with even imperfect vision. For similar reasons decision makers ought to consider alternative outcomes even if only very rough probabilistic assessments are possible. Moreover, the explicit process of calculation, which is a fundamental analytic requirement, seems to be an important means of stimulating the critical process of error correction. Explicitness has been important in the pursuit of scientific knowledge, and it should be important for public policy for many of the same reasons.

These are compelling grounds for normative exhortations. The analytic logic turned back upon itself must concede, however, that costs involved in its actualization produce trade-offs in their own right, and that concession requires the recognition that not every issue of decision can possibly receive analytic treatment. The additional element to the case for the normative use of the analytic paradigm, therefore, is the argument that such issues as nuclear sharing are important enough, by virtue of the stakes to society involved, that they properly command a level of effort and sophistication which cannot be applied universally. Few will have any difficulty granting this assumption regarding the issue of nuclear sharing.

What should have happened, then, in the MLF affair is that a concerted attempt to develop an explicit analytic treatment of the problem should have been made early in the course of events. Surely this should have been well underway before an attempt was made to decide the fate of the Skybolt missile. By the time it came down to either warning or giving confidence to the President in December of 1964, it was far too late to handle the issue on any penetrating analytic basis. Time and effort are required to structure the complex problem along analytic lines in such a way that its major components are all included in the explicit calculus. Pertinent analysis cannot be willed into existence on short notice. Unfortunately, the actual preparation for the decisions made on nuclear sharing was severely truncated. The analysis which underlay the Athens program made considerable headway over a decade or more in connecting specific issues of force structure to the objective of deterrence. That analysis was much less developed, however, in the political dimension—the entire calculus surrounding the campaign of persuasion—where it found much less of a mandate and fewer resources. That dimension of the problem should have received a great deal of analytic structuring after the shock of the Nassau conference. Unfortunately, it did not. The MLF and the Athens program proceeded on separate tracks, mutually suspicious of one another, and there was no systematic, continuing attempt to achieve some integration into an overall alliance posture. The Merchant mission was structured from the outset as a promotional/negotiating operation rather than an analytic learning process.

From the general perspective of the analytic paradigm, the United States government as it operated in the MLF episode was a very primitive mechanism for dealing with an issue of the complexity and importance of nuclear sharing. The penetration of its staff work at specific points of decision was very shallow, as was inevitable since there was no substantial on-going program of analysis with a full mandate over the issue. For the same reason, the capacity of the highest officials of the government was severely overtaxed at those points where their judgments had to be applied. The policy process underneath them was not geared to service judgments of the scope and penetration which the issues required. Hence, in the actual course of decision, the institutional arrangements which provide separate channels within the State Department and the Defense Department for handling issues of interacting political and military dimensions strongly reinforced the natural, psychological tendencies toward fragmentation.

It is impossible to say with any confidence just what difference it would have made had a timely, systematic investment been made to develop an analytic calculus encompassing the full issue of nuclear sharing as it arose in the MLF problem. If there was direct, serious damage done by the actual outcome, it was subtle enough to require another intensive study of the ensuing period. Still it seems unlikely that the government can continue to operate in the manner observed without encountering at some point very serious difficulties. In fact the risks of producing a thorough disaster seem great enough to warrant very serious concern.

It seems clear that the government has not changed its character or radically upgraded its capacity in the period following the MLF episode. It is clear also that the government is not done with the issues which generated the MLF. Those issues are now embedded in a larger context involving arms control discussions between the United States and U.S.S.R., but they linger as before without stable resolution. One can expect another round on this; not a resurrection of the MLF proposal, to be sure, but rather a renewed concern with alliance posture which again poses the central trade-offs involved in strategic deterrence for a loosely knit alliance system. One might hope that the second round will find the government much more prepared than before, but there is little evidence that this will be the case. Again the operations of the cognitive paradigm and of intergovernmental politics are likely to dominate weakly developed analytic approaches.

One can imagine a design for an analytic learning process on issues such as this where high stakes mandate unusual effort. It clearly would involve research and development investment on *policy* issues rather than on technical hardware. It clearly would involve working out institutional arrangements between the suppliers of analysis and officials who carry the burden of decision. All that must await, however, both a reasonably widespread recognition that there are systematic problems in our current mechanisms of government and the development of a political will to do something about it. If the current study contributes to either the recognition or the will, it will have served very well.

Normative Arguments of the Cognitive Paradigm

The arguments and observations of the study have emphasized the importance of cognitive operations, which include cybernetic decision mechanisms, as determinants of the actual behavior of decision makers and of the governments they direct. It is a natural instinct to want to capitalize on this knowledge to improve government performance. This is strengthened by the conclusion that analytic procedures, even in the best of conceivable worlds, cannot be everywhere applied. It is also strengthened by considering the nature of complex decision problems in relation to cognitive operations, a conjunction which suggests that trade-offs and systemic interactions are destined to cause continuous trouble.

Whether or not there is irony to be found in it, however, the cognitive paradigm, though apparently more promising than the analytic paradigm as a framework for interpreting empirical forces, is nonetheless far less developed in an intellectual sense. Notably, far less effort has been devoted to applying the central logic of the cognitive paradigm to issues of decision for public affairs. The long years of effort by means of which the analytic paradigm was applied to issues of defense posture and to federal water programs,[2] to cite prominent examples, have not been matched by any comparable work with cognitive theory. These prototypes of applied analytic logic, which are available to guide efforts on other issues, have yet to be constructed within the cognitive paradigm. As a consequence, the normative implications of the theory are particularly uncertain.

Following cognitive principles, for example, one might seek to distinguish different kinds of individuals and take care to establish a balance of "warners" and "confidence givers" in critical decision channels. In the absence of a reliable procedure for distinguishing, however, this is not a very helpful suggestion. Moreover, even if the argument of the cognitive paradigm is fully accepted, it does not necessarily follow that the syndromes of behavior outlined would be stable for a given individual over a number of issues. The intersection of personnel and institutional position may produce different behavior over a range of issues, notably on issues tangential to the normal flow of business. This would certainly complicate any organizing strategy based on categorization of individuals. Finally, even if this problem proved

[2] See Charles Hitch and Roland McKean, *The Economics of Defense in the Nuclear Age* (Cambridge, Mass.: Harvard University Press, 1960), and Otto Eckstein, *Water-Resource Development* (Cambridge, Mass.: Harvard University Press, 1961).

tractable, it would require long experimentation to develop any confidence that a particular mixture of cognitive tendencies would produce better decisions over a range of problems.

Another possible tack is to assign different institutional sub-units the separate roles of giving confidence and giving warning and to arrange the overall decision process so that each subunit had equal or some proportionate access. This is informally done at the moment in that for issues reaching the President the White House staff is often given the assignment of discovering biases, weak spots, and outright traps in the positions advocated by Cabinet departments. It is possible that if the separate roles were more explicitly conceived and if the question of balance were more consciously addressed there would be an overall benefit in performance. Again, however, deliberate experimentation or commensurate empirical analysis would be required, and one cannot help but note that the normal political process operating within the government is likely to be very corrosive of such stable role arrangements. An organizational subunit which did nothing but probe the fallacies of other people's business would find it very difficult to remain politically viable.

Given these difficulties, the normative role of the cognitive paradigm at the moment is, alas, a negative one—that of challenging the conventional paths to reform. Confronted with complex problems, especially when there is disaffection with the performance of government, men intuitively tend to rely on one of two basic prescriptions. The first concerns itself with fundamental values and seeks reform by reaffirming deeply held values. If there is trouble with the performance of government, it is diagnosed as due to a failure to pursue the right values. The second device lays great expectation on the judgment exercised by experienced men, relying upon them to penetrate problems of great moment. If there is trouble, this approach seeks new leaders of better quality to right the failures of those who have been discredited. Though both devices are time-honored and could hardly be overthrown by any argument derived from the current study, nonetheless the usefulness of both can be seriously questioned from the perspectives herein developed.

Both as a theoretical and as a practical matter, a clear, firm, incorrigible connection between basic values and concrete decisions simply does not exist. Under conditions of intense uncertainty, therefore, a significant part of a decision problem is simply that of forging a credible, logical tie between fundamental values and the particular course of action being contemplated. In the MLF case the idea arose that the project would promote a set of integrative political arrangements in Europe, and this assumption was imposed as the central rationale of the entire effort, despite the fact that it was far from clear in any objective sense that integration would be benefited. Given that men and institutions comprised of men inevitably have grave difficulty understanding the consequences of their actions in a complex environment, devotion to the proper values is not sufficient for good performance of government.

Similarly, cognitive theory emphasizes that there is no guarantee to be found in reliance on seasoned men of good judgment. Though it is comforting to assume that the analytically bewildering complexities of policy problems are ultimately resolved in about the best fashion feasible when the decision process finally comes down to the exercise of judgment by responsible men, there is much in the foregoing argument to indicate that that is a bad assumption. In effect the cognitive paradigm penetrates that often unexamined category called "judgment," and the results constitute a warning. In the exercise of judgment, even by men who are very experienced in their business, there are very strong tendencies for stable simplifications to develop which will render the decision process insensitive to important segments of a complex problem. Over time that is very likely to cause trouble, and such men are likely to be among the last rather than the first to recognize it. Changing leaders might be helpful in a concrete situation, but it will not eliminate the difficulty, for it is endemic in the limitations of the mind. No man can be relied on systematically over a number of issues and points of decision to make intuitive or "experienced" judgments adequate to complex issues.

One can at least conclude that government, increasingly seized with complex problems, ought to recognize that it is profoundly enmeshed in forces which the cognitive paradigm describes. The development of that paradigm ought to be recognized as a serious public purpose and ought to be promoted as a matter of policy. Though there would be a number of practical difficulties in this, which are best explored elsewhere, the stakes appear to be high enough to justify considerable effort.

EPILOGUE

Normative Implications of Political Analysis

The MLF episode was, of course, infused with politics, as any other major issue of public policy is destined to be. As a general matter, conflicts in value and perspective and the dispersion of power over men engaged in such conflicts deeply affect the sensitivities, motives, and intentions of all those who participate in government. The state of personal relationships, official and unofficial coalitions, the maneuvers designed to collect and preserve power constantly have their effects on the outcomes of government activity. No theoretical perspective can usefully be brought to bear on policy problems unless it is able to deal with the political environment in which government is conducted. Both analytic and cognitive perspectives, thus, must adjust to the pervasive presence of politics.

All that would not require special comment were it not for the fact that the effects of intragovernmental politics are not discussed or acknowledged in proportion to their importance. The conduct of policy is supposed to be guided by higher wisdom and a devotion to public interest, and to honor this ethic one avoids discussion of political business in polite society. It is like the problems of sex. Serious discussion is handicapped by social taboos, and explicit discourse is all too dominated by sensationalists who break through the barriers only to give the topic crass and superficial treatment. It seems very clear in the case of politics that the taboos have gone too far and that the damage done to fundamental understanding and the ability to deal with political effects is not outweighed by the service which has been rendered to highmindedness and pure public purpose.

If it is true, as one suspects, that SACEUR's request for MRBM's in the late 1950s had more to do with his need to build a viable organization than with the intrinsic requirements of national defense, then it is unfortunate that the problem was not dealt with more directly. If the alliance organization felt slighted by the promised centralization of command and control over deterrent forces, it would have been far easier to find appropriate compensation if that had been recognized as the main problem than it was under circumstances where the entire issue had to be wrapped in high-order defense requirements. It is conceivable that rampant political hedonism might break out if such taboos

341

were loosened, but the most considered judgment would have to be that the country can stand the strains of more realistic, more complete political debate.

If granted or seized, the freedom to discuss the political details of government should obviously be exercised not to accuse, to vilify, or to drip cynicism on an already corroded public confidence. Rather, more candid discourse should be used to facilitate the hard task of integrating the abstract paradigms of decision theory into the realities of political life. If analytic procedures are to achieve their normative promise, they will have to incorporate much greater sophistication in the political dimensions of government. The prototype applications in strategic defense posture have not been well developed in this area, and we have seen some of the consequences of this in the MLF case. Similarly, the development of the cognitive perspective will require careful analysis as to how the forces it uncovers interrelate with politics in government machinery. The efforts at theoretical development in the service of public policy will have to be supported by greater candor if they are to be productive, and analysts undertaking the development will have to learn to deal with sensitive material responsibly.

IT ALL comes down to a simple plea: let us, as best we can, stop fooling ourselves; let us understand better what we really are about.

Bibliography

Abelson, Robert P. "Computer Simulation of Hot Cognition,"
S. S. Tomkins and S. Messick, eds., *Computer Simulation of
Personality*. New York: John Wiley and Sons, Inc., 1962.

——, and Milton J. Rosenberg. "Symbolic Psycho-logic: A
Model of Attitudinal Cognition," *Behavioral Science*, vol. 3,
1958, pp. 1–13.

——, et al., eds. *Theories of Cognitive Consistency*. Chicago:
Rand McNally and Company, 1968.

Acheson, D. "The Practice of Partnership," *Foreign Affairs*, vol.
41, 1963, p. 247f.

Adams, Jack. *Human Memory*. New York: McGraw-Hill Book
Company, Inc., 1967.

Adams, J. Stacy. "Reduction of Cognitive Dissonance by Seeking
Consonant Information," *Journal of Abnormal and Social
Psychology*, vol. 62, 1961, pp. 74–78.

Aharoni, Yair. *The Foreign Investment Decision Process*. Boston:
Harvard Graduate School of Business Administration, 1966.

Alexander, Christopher. *Notes on the Synthesis of Form*. Cambridge, Mass.: Harvard University Press, 1968.

Allen, H. T. "An Empirical Test of Choice and Decision Postu-
lates in the Cyert and March Behavioral Theory of the
Firm," *Administrative Science Quarterly*, vol. 11, 1966, pp.
405–413.

Allison, Graham T. "Conceptual Models and the Cuban Missile
Crisis," *American Political Science Review*, vol. 63, 1969,
pp. 689–718.

——. *Essence of Decision*. Boston: Little, Brown & Company,
1971.

Allport, F. A. *Theories of Perception and the Concept of Structure*. New York: John Wiley and Sons, Inc., 1955.

Almond, G. *The American People and Foreign Policy*. New
York: Frederick A. Praeger, 1960.

Argyris, C. *Some Causes of Organizational Ineffectiveness Within the Department of State*, Department of State Monograph, Washington, 1967.

Aron, R. *The Great Debate: Theories in Nuclear Strategy*. New
York: Anchor Paperback, 1965.

343

Aronson, E. "The Psychology of Insufficient Justification," S. Feldman, ed., *Cognitive Consistency*. New York: Academic Press, 1966.

Arrow, K. *Social Choice and Individual Values*. New York: John Wiley and Sons, Inc., 1951.

Asch, S. "Effects of Group Pressures on the Modification and Position of Judgments," *Journal of Abnormal and Social Psychology*, vol. 62, 1961, pp. 117–190.

———. "Opinions and Social Pressure," *Scientific American*, vol. 193, November 1955, pp. 31–35.

Ashby, W. Ross. *A Design for a Brain*. New York: John Wiley and Sons, Inc., 1952.

———. *An Introduction to Cybernetics*. London: Chapman & Hall, Ltd., 1970.

Ayer, A. J. *The Problem of Knowledge*. Baltimore: Penguin Books, 1966.

Baldwin, H. "NATO's Uneven Steps Toward Integration," *Reporter*, vol. 32, March 11, 1965, pp. 32–34.

Ball, George. Speech to Princeton University Alumni, *Department of State Bulletin (DOSB)*, May 13, 1963, pp. 736–739.

Banfield, Edward C. *Political Influence*. New York: The Free Press of Glencoe, 1961.

Bartlett, F. C. *Remembering*. Cambridge, Eng.: Cambridge University Press, 1932.

Bartlett, John; Emily Morison Beck, ed. *Familiar Quotations*. Boston: Little, Brown & Company, 1968.

Bauer, R., I. Pool, and L. Dexter. *American Business and Public Policy*. New York: Atherton Press, 1963.

Baumol, William J. *Economic Theory and Operations Research*. Englewood Cliffs, N.J.: Prentice-Hall, Inc., 1965.

———. *Welfare Economics and the Theory of the State*. London: Longmans, Green & Company, 1952.

Beaton, Leonard, and John Maddox. *The Spread of Nuclear Weapons*. New York: Frederick A. Praeger, 1962.

Becker, Gordon M., and Charles G. McClintock. "Value: Behavioral Decision Theory," *Annual Review of Psychology*, vol. 18, 1967, pp. 239–286.

Beer, Stafford. *Cybernetics and Management*. New York: John Wiley and Sons, Inc., 1959.

Begleiter, H., et al. "Evoked Potential Correlates of Expected Stimulus Intensity," *Science*, vol. 179, 1973, pp. 814–816.

344

Beloff, M. *The United States and the Unity of Europe.* New York: Random House, 1963.

Bloomfield, Lincoln P., and Barton Whaley. "The Political-Military Exercise," James N. Rosenau, ed., *International Politics and Foreign Policy*, rev. ed. New York: The Free Press, 1969, pp. 654–663.

Boring, E. J. *The History of Psychology.* New York: Appleton-Century-Crofts, Inc., 1950.

Boulding, K. E. *The Image: Knowledge in Life and Society.* Ann Arbor, Mich.: University of Michigan Press, 1956.

Bower, Joseph L. *Managing the Resource Allocation Process: A Study of Corporate Planning and Investment.* Boston: Harvard Graduate School of Business Administration, 1970.

Bowie, Robert R. *Shaping the Future: Foreign Policy in an Age of Transition.* New York: Columbia University Press, 1964.

———. "Strategy and the Atlantic Alliance," *International Organization*, vol. 17, 1963, pp. 709–732.

———. "Tensions Within the Alliance: Atlantic Policy," *Foreign Affairs*, vol. 42, 1963, pp. 49–69.

———, and C. J. Friedrich. *Studies in Federalism.* Boston: Little, Brown & Company, 1954.

Brehm, J., and A. R. Cohen. *Explorations in Cognitive Dissonance.* New York: John Wiley and Sons, Inc., 1962.

Brodie, B. *Strategy in the Missile Age.* Princeton, N.J.: Princeton University Press, 1959.

Brzezinski, Z. "Moscow and the MLF," *Foreign Affairs*, vol. 43, 1964, pp. 126–136.

Buchan, Alastair. "The Changed Setting of the Atlantic Debate," *Foreign Affairs*, vol. 43, 1965, pp. 547–586.

———. "Control of Western Strategy," *Royal United Service Institute Journal*, vol. 108, 1963, pp. 303–310.

———. "Europe and the Atlantic Alliance: Two Strategies or One?" *Journal of Common Market Studies*, Spring 1963.

———. "The Multilateral Force: A Study in Alliance Politics," *International Affairs* (London), vol. 40, 1964, pp. 619–637.

———. *NATO in the 1960's.* New York: Frederick A. Praeger, 1963.

———. "Partners and Allies," *Foreign Affairs*, vol. 41, 1963, p. 621f.

———. "The Reform of NATO," *Foreign Affairs*, vol. 40, 1962, pp. 165–182.

Bundy, McGeorge. "Responsible Nuclear Policy," *Yale Alumni Magazine*, vol. 29, 1963, pp. 12–16.

Bupp, Irvin C. "Nuclear Proliferation," unpublished paper, Harvard University, 1967.

Cabinet Task Force on Oil Import Control. *The Oil Import Question: A Report on the Relationship of Oil Imports to the National Security*. Washington: U.S. Government Printing Office, 1970.

Camps, Miriam. *Britain and the European Community, 1955–1963*. Princeton, N.J.: Princeton University Press, 1964.

——. *European Unification in the Sixties*. New York: McGraw-Hill Book Company, Inc., 1966.

Chamberlain, J. D. *Legislative Processes: National and State*. New York: Appleton-Century-Crofts, Inc., 1936.

Cherry, C. *On Human Communication*. New York: John Wiley and Sons, Inc., and MIT, 1957.

Chisholm, R. M. *Perceiving: A Philosophical Study*. Ithaca, N.Y.: Cornell University Press, 1957.

Chomsky, Noam. *Aspects of the Theory of Syntax*. Cambridge, Mass.: MIT Press, 1965.

——. *Cartesian Linguistics: A Chapter in the History of Rationalist Thought*. New York: Harper & Row, Publishers, 1966.

——. "Review of B. F. Skinner's *Verbal Behavior*," *Language*, vol. 35, 1959, pp. 26–58.

Cohen, A. R. *Attitude Change and Social Influence*. New York: Basic Books, Inc., 1964.

Crecine, John P. "Defense Budgeting," W. W. Cooper et al., eds., *Studies in Budgeting*. Amsterdam: North Holland, 1971.

——. *Governmental Problem Solving*. Chicago: Rand McNally and Co., 1969.

Cyert, Richard M., and James G. March. *A Behavioral Theory of the Firm*. Englewoods Cliffs, N.J.: Prentice-Hall, Inc., 1963.

Dahl, Robert. *Who Governs? Democracy and Power in an American City*. New Haven, Conn.: Yale University Press, 1961.

Davis, O., M. A. Dempster, and A. Wildavsky. *On the Process of Budgeting: An Empirical Study of Congressional Appropriation*, reprint #252, Graduate School of Public Administration, Carnegie-Mellon University, 1966.

Dawson, Raymond H. "What Kind of NATO Nuclear Force?" *Annals of the American Academy of Political and Social Science*, vol. 351, 1964, pp. 30–39.

———, and Richard Rosecrance. "Theory and Reality in the Anglo-American Alliance," *World Politics*, vol. 19, 1966, pp. 21–51.

Dember, W. N. *The Psychology of Perception*. New York: Holt, Rinehart & Winston, 1960.

de Rivera, Joseph H. *The Psychological Dimension of Foreign Policy*. Columbus, Ohio: Charles E. Merrill Company, 1968.

de Rose, F. "Atlantic Relationships and Nuclear Problems: A French View," *Foreign Affairs*, vol. 41, 1963, pp. 479–490.

Deutsch, Karl W. *Arms Control and the Atlantic Alliance*. New York: John Wiley and Sons, Inc., 1966.

———. *The Nerves of Government*. New York: The Free Press, 1966.

———, et al. *France, Germany and the Western Alliance*. New York: Charles Scribner's Sons, 1967.

Dougherty, J. E. "European Deterrence and Atlantic Unity," *Orbis*, vol. 6, 1962, pp. 371–421.

Downs, A. *Inside Bureaucracy*. Boston: Little, Brown & Company, 1967.

Eckstein, Otto. *Water-Resource Development*. Cambridge, Mass.: Harvard University Press, 1961.

Edwards, Ward. "The Theory of Decision-Making," *Psychological Bulletin*, vol. 51, 1954, pp. 380–417.

Ellis, H. S. *Economics of Freedom*. New York: Harper and Brothers, 1950.

Emmet, C. "The U.S. Plan for a NATO Nuclear Deterrent," *Orbis*, vol. 7, 1963, pp. 265–277.

Enthoven, Alain C., and K. Wayne Smith, *How Much Is Enough? Shaping the Defense Program, 1961–1969*. New York: Harper & Row, Publishers, 1971.

Feldman, S. *Cognitive Consistency*. New York: Academic Press, 1966.

Fellner, William. *Probability and Profit*. Homewood, Ill.: R. D. Irwin, Inc., 1965.

Festinger, L. *A Theory of Cognitive Dissonance*. Evanston, Ill.: Row, Peterson, 1957.

347

Freud, S. *A General Introduction to Psychoanalysis*. New York: Liveright Publishing Corp., 1963.

Gallois, Pierre. *The Balance of Terror: Strategy for the Nuclear Age*. Boston: Houghton Mifflin Company, 1961.

Garner, W. R. *Uncertainty and Structure as Psychological Concepts*. New York: John Wiley and Sons, Inc., 1962.

Geyelin, Philip. *Lyndon B. Johnson and the World*. New York: Frederick A. Praeger, 1966.

Gibson, C., and Ableson, R. P. "The Subjective Use of Inductive Evidence," *Journal of Personal and Social Psychology*, vol. 2, 1965, pp. 301–310.

Giffin, S. S. *The Crisis Game*. New York: Doubleday & Company, Inc., 1965.

Gilpatrick, Roswell. "Our Defense Needs: The Long View," *Foreign Affairs*, vol. 42, 1964, pp. 366–378.

Goodman, N. *Fact, Fiction, and Forecast*. Cambridge, Mass.: Harvard University Press, 1955.

Gore, W. G., and F. S. Silander. "A Bibliographic Essay on Decision-Making," *Administrative Science Quarterly*, vol. 4, 1959, pp. 97–121.

Haas, E. *The Uniting of Europe: Political, Social and Economic Forces, 1950–1957*. Stanford, Cal.: Stanford University Press, 1958.

Hadley, G. *Linear Programming*. Reading, Mass.: Addison-Wesley Publishing Co., 1962.

Hall, Calvin S. *A Primer of Freudian Psychology*. New York: Mentor Books, 1954.

Halperin, Morton. *Bureaucratic Politics and Foreign Policy*. Washington: Brookings Institution, forthcoming.

Hammond, D. *Super Carriers and B-36 Bombers: Appropriations, Strategy and Politics*, Interuniversity Case Program #97. New York: The Bobbs-Merrill Company, 1963.

Haveman, Robert H., and Julius Margolis, eds. *Public Expenditures and Policy Analysis*. Chicago: Markham Publishing Company, 1970.

Heider, Fritz. "Attitudes and Cognitive Organization," *Journal of Psychology*, vol. 21, 1946, pp. 107–112.

Hilsman, Roger. "Congressional-Executive Relations and the Foreign Policy Consensus," *American Political Science Review*, vol. 52, 1958, pp. 725–744.

——. *To Move a Nation*. New York: Doubleday & Company, Inc., 1967.

Hinterhoff, M. "MLF or ANF: An Analysis and Comparison," *NATO's Fifteen Nations*, vol. 10, 1965, pp. 22–29.

Hitch, Charles J. *Decision-Making for Defense*. Berkeley, Cal.: University of California Press, 1966.

——, and Roland McKean. *The Economics of Defense in the Nuclear Age*. New York: Athenaeum Publishers, 1965.

Hoag, M. "Nuclear Policy and French Intransigence," *Foreign Affairs*, vol. 41, 1963, pp. 286–297.

Hochberg, Julian E. *Perception*. Englewood Cliffs, N.J.: Prentice-Hall, Inc., 1964.

Hough, Richard. *The Hunting of Force Z*. London: William Collins Sons & Co., 1963.

Hovland, C. I., I. Janis, and H. H. Kelley. *Communications and Persuasion: Psychological Studies of Opinion Change*. New Haven, Conn.: Yale University Press, 1953.

——, and M. J. Rosenberg, eds. *Attitude Organization and Change*. New Haven, Conn.: Yale University Press, 1953.

Hudson, R. "The *Biddle* and the MLF," *War/Peace Report*, August 1964.

Huitt, Ralph K. "The Congressional Committee: A Case Study," *American Political Science Review*, vol. 48, 1957, pp. 340–365.

Huntington, Samuel, *The Common Defense*. New York: Columbia University Press, 1961.

Iklé, F. C. "Can Nuclear Deterrence Last Out the Century?" *Foreign Affairs*, vol. 51, 1973, pp. 267–285.

——. *How Nations Negotiate*. New York: Harper and Row, Publishers, 1964.

Institute for Strategic Studies (ISS). *The Military Balance, 1962–63*. London, 1962.

Intriligator, Michael D. *Mathematical Optimization and Economic Theory*. Englewood Cliffs, N.J.: Prentice-Hall, Inc., 1971.

Ittleson, W. P., and F. P. Kilpatrick. "Experiments in Perception," *Scientific American*, vol. 185, August 1951, pp. 50–55.

Jackson, John. "Statistical Models of Senate Roll Call Voting," *American Political Science Review*, vol. 65, 1971, pp. 451–470.

Jones, R. V. "Impotence and Achievement in Physics and Technology," *Nature*, vol. 207, 1965, pp. 120–125.

Kahn, Herman. *On Thermonuclear War*. Princeton, N.J.: Princeton University Press, 1961.

———. *Thinking About the Unthinkable*. New York: Avon Paperback, 1962.

———, and Irwin Mann. "Techniques of Systems Analysis," RAND Corporation paper No. RM-1829, 1956.

———, and Irwin Mann. "Ten Common Pitfalls," RAND Corporation paper No. RM-1937, 1957.

Kaplan, A. *The Conduct of Inquiry: A Methodology for Behavioral Science*. San Francisco: Chandler Publishing Co., 1964.

Katz, D. "The Functional Approach to the Study of Attitudes," *Public Opinion Quarterly*, vol. 24, 1960, pp. 163–204.

Kaufmann, William. *The McNamara Strategy*. New York: Harper & Row, Publishers, 1964.

Kelleher, C. "German Nuclear Dilemmas," unpublished doctoral dissertation, MIT, 1967.

Kelley, G. A. "Politics of Nuclear Control," *Military Review*, vol. 43, 1963, pp. 35–48.

Kelman, J. C. *International Behavior: A Social Psychological Analysis*. New York: Holt, Rinehart & Winston, 1965.

Kennedy, John F. *Public Papers of the President*. Washington: U.S. Government Printing Office, 1961.

Kennedy, Robert F. *Thirteen Days*. New York: W. W. Norton & Company, Inc., 1969.

Kenney, E. T. "MLF, the New NATO Sword," U.S. Naval Institute *Proceedings*, vol. 90, 1964, pp. 25–35.

Kilpatrick, F. P., ed. *Explorations in Transactional Psychology*. New York: New York University Press, 1961.

Kimball, Penn. *The Disconnected*. New York: Columbia University Press, 1972.

Kimble, G. A., ed. *Hilgard and Marquis' Conditioning and Learning*, 2nd ed. rev. New York: Appleton-Century-Crofts, Inc., 1961.

King, J. B. "Nuclear Sharing in NATO and the MLF," *Political Science Quarterly*, vol. 80, 1965, pp. 88–109.

Kissinger, Henry. "Coalition Diplomacy in a Nuclear Age," *Foreign Affairs*, vol. 42, 1964, pp. 525–545.

———. "NATO's Nuclear Dilemma," *Reporter*, vol. 28, March 28, 1963, pp. 22–37.

————. *The Necessity for Choice*. New York: Harper & Row, Publishers, 1961.

————. "The Price of German Unity," *Reporter*, vol. 32, April 22, 1965, pp. 12–15.

————. "Strains on the Alliance," *Foreign Affairs*, vol. 41, 1963, pp. 261–285.

————. *The Troubled Partnership: A Reappraisal of the Atlantic Alliance*. New York: McGraw-Hill Book Co., 1965.

————. "The Unsolved Problems of European Defense," *Foreign Affairs*, vol. 40, 1962, pp. 515–541.

Klapper, J. *The Effects of Mass Communication*. Glencoe, Ill.: The Free Press, 1960.

Kleene, Stephen C. *Mathematical Logic*. New York: John Wiley and Sons, Inc., 1967.

Kleiman, R. *The Atlantic Crisis: American Diplomacy Confronts A Resurgent Europe*. New York: W. W. Norton & Company, Inc., 1964.

Knorr, K. "Nuclear Weapons: 'Haves' and 'Have-nots,' " *Foreign Affairs*, vol. 36, 1957, pp. 167–178.

Koch, S. *Psychology: A Study of a Science*, six vols. New York: McGraw-Hill Book Co., 1959.

Koffka, K. *Principles of Gestalt Psychology*. New York: Harcourt, Brace & Company, Inc., 1935.

Kogan, Norman. *A Political History of Postwar Italy*. New York: Frederick A. Praeger, 1966.

Kohl, W. L. "Nuclear Sharing in NATO and the Multilateral Force," *Political Science Quarterly*, vol. 80, 1965, pp. 88–109.

Kohler, Wolfgang. *The Task of Gestalt Psychology*. Princeton, N.J.: Princeton University Press, 1969.

Koopmans, Tjalling C. *Three Essays on the State of Economic Science*. New York: McGraw-Hill Book Co., 1957.

Kraft, J. *The Grand Design: From Common Market to Atlantic Partnership*. New York: Harper & Row, Publishers, 1962.

Krogh, August. "The Language of the Bees," *Scientific American*, vol. 179, August 1948, pp. 18–21.

Kuhn, Thomas S. *The Copernican Revolution*. New York: Vintage Books, 1959.

————. *The Structure of Scientific Revolutions*. Chicago: The University of Chicago Press, 1963.

Lerner, D., and H. Lasswell. *The Policy Sciences*. Stanford, Cal.: Stanford University Press, 1951.

Lewis, C. I. *Mind and the World Order: An Outline of a Theory of Knowledge.* New York: Dover Publications, 1956.

Lindberg, L. N. *The Political Dynamics of European Economic Integration.* Stanford, Cal.: Stanford University Press, 1963.

Lindblom, Charles. *The Intelligence of Democracy.* New York: The Free Press, 1965.

———. "The Science of Muddling Through," *Public Administration Review,* vol. 19, 1959, pp. 79–88.

Lippmann, W. "How Many Drivers at the Nuclear Wheel?" *Atlantic Community Quarterly,* vol. 1, 1963, pp. 37–44.

Llewellyn, R. *Linear Programming.* New York: Holt, Rinehart & Winston, 1964.

Luce, R. D., and H. Raiffa. *Games and Decisions: An Introduction and Critical Survey.* New York: John Wiley and Sons, Inc., 1957.

March, James G. *Handbook of Organizations.* Chicago: Rand McNally & Company, 1965.

———, and Herbert A. Simon. *Organizations.* New York: John Wiley and Sons, Inc., 1958.

McKean, Roland N. *Efficiency in Government Through Systems Analysis, With Emphasis on Water Resources Development.* New York: John Wiley and Sons, Inc., 1958.

Miksche, F. "The Great Nuclear Fallacy," *Atlas,* vol. 7, 1964, pp. 34–36.

Miller, G. A., E. Gallanter, and K. Pribram. *Plans and the Structure of Behavior.* New York: Holt, Rinehart & Winston, 1960.

Moore, G. E. *Principia Ethica.* Cambridge, Eng.: Cambridge University Press, 1960.

Morse, Philip M., and George E. Kimball. *Methods of Operations Research.* Cambridge, Mass.: MIT Press, 1962.

Mosteller, F., and P. Nogee. "An Experimental Measurement of Utility," *Journal of Political Economy,* vol. 59, 1951, pp. 371–404.

Mulley, F. W. "NATO's Nuclear Problems: Control or Confrontation," *Orbis,* vol. 8, 1964, pp. 21–35.

———. *The Politics of Western Defense.* New York: Frederick A. Praeger, 1962.

Murphy, Charles. "NATO at a Nuclear Crossroads," *Fortune,* vol. 66, December 1962, pp. 85–88.

Nagel, E. *The Structure of Science.* New York: Harcourt, Brace & World, Inc., 1961.

Neisser, Ulric. *Cognitive Psychology*. New York: Appleton-Century-Crofts, Inc., 1967.

Neustadt, Richard E. *Alliance Politics*. New York: Columbia University Press, 1970.

————. "The Presidency and Legislation: Planning the President's Program," *American Political Science Review*, vol. 49, 1955, pp. 980–1021.

————. "The Presidency at Mid-Century," *Law and Contemporary Problems*, vol. 21, 1956, pp. 609–645.

————. *Presidential Power: The Politics of Leadership*. New York: John Wiley and Sons, Inc., 1960.

Newcomb, T. *New Directions in Psychology*. New York: Holt, Rinehart & Winston, 1962.

Newhouse, John. *De Gaulle and the Anglo-Saxons*. New York: The Viking Press, 1970.

Nieburg, Harold L. *Nuclear Secrecy and Foreign Policy*. Washington: Public Affairs Press, 1964.

Norstad, Lauris M. *NATO Letter*, December 1956.

n.n. "The Case for the Nuclear Fleet," *War/Peace Report*, October 1964, pp. 8–10.

O'Balance, E. "Multi-National or Multi-Lateral?" *Army Quarterly*, vol. 89, October 1964, pp. 46–52.

Olson, Mancur, Jr. *The Logic of Collective Action*. Cambridge, Mass.: Harvard University Press, 1965.

Osgood, Charles E., and Percy H. Tannenbaum. "The Principle of Congruity and the Prediction of Attitude Change," *Psychological Review*, vol. 62, 1955, pp. 42–55.

Osgood, Robert. *The Case for the MLF: A Critical Evaluation*, Center for Foreign Policy Research Monograph, Washington, 1964.

————. *NATO, the Entangling Alliance*. Chicago: The University of Chicago Press, 1962.

Owen, Henry. "NATO Strategy: What is Past is Prologue," *Foreign Affairs*, vol. 43, 1965, pp. 682–690.

————. "What the Multilateral Force Could Achieve," *European Review*, vol. 14, 1964, p. 12.

Packenham, R. A. "Political Development Doctrines in the American Foreign Aid Program," *World Politics*, vol. 18, 1966, pp. 194–236.

Paige, Glenn D. *The Korean Decision*. New York: The Free Press, 1968.

Pelz, Stephen. *The Race to Pearl Harbor*. Cambridge, Mass.: Harvard University Press, forthcoming.

Pierre, Andrew. *Nuclear Politics: The British Experience With an Independent Strategic Force, 1939–1970*. London: Oxford University Press, 1972.

Pikas, A. *Abstraction and Concept Formation*. Cambridge, Mass.: Harvard University Press, 1966.

Plato. *Thaetetus*.

Pool, Ithiel, and A. Kessler. "The Kaiser, the Tsar, and the Computer: Information-Processing in a Crisis," *American Behavioral Scientist*, vol. 8, 1965, pp. 31–38.

Postman, Leo. *The Psychology of Rumor*. New York: Holt, Rinehart & Winston, 1947.

———. "Toward a General Theory of Cognition," John Rohrer and Muzafer Sherif, eds., *Social Psychology at the Crossroads*. New York: Harper & Row, Publishers, 1951, pp. 242–272.

Pratt, John W., Howard Raiffa, and Robert Schlaifer. *Introduction to Statistical Decision Theory*. New York: McGraw-Hill Book Co., 1965.

Pruitt, D. G. *Problem Solving in the Department of State*, University of Denver Social Science Foundation and Department of International Relations Monograph Series in World Affairs, No. 2, Denver, 1964–65.

Pye, Lucian W., ed. *Communications and Political Development*. Princeton, N.J.: Princeton University Press, 1963.

Quade, E. S. *Analysis for Military Decision*. Chicago: Rand McNally & Company, 1964.

Quester, George H. *Deterrence Before Hiroshima*. New York: John Wiley and Sons, Inc., 1966.

———. *Nuclear Diplomacy*. New York: Dunellen Publishing Co., Inc., 1970.

Raiffa, Howard. *Decision Analysis*. Reading, Mass.: Addison-Wesley Publishing Co., 1968.

Reitman, W. *Cognition and Thought*. New York: John Wiley and Sons, Inc., 1965.

Richardson, J. L. *Germany and the Atlantic Alliance*. Cambridge, Mass.: Harvard University Press, 1965.

Ricketts, C. V. "The Case for the MLF," *European Review*, vol. 13, Summer 1963, pp. 9–11.

Roby, T. B. "Belief States and the Uses of Evidence," *Behavioral Science*, vol. 10, 1965, pp. 255–270.

Rosenberg, Milton J., and Robert P. Abelson. "An Analysis of Cognitive Balancing," *Attitude Organization and Change*. New Haven, Conn.: Yale University Press, 1960.

———, et al. *Attitude Organization and Change*. New Haven, Conn.: Yale University Press, 1960.

Rostow, Walt W. Speeches appearing in the *Department of State Bulletin*, April 15, 1963; June 3, 1963; April 16, 1964; and July 13, 1964.

———. *The United States in the World Arena*. New York: Harper & Row, Publishers, 1960.

Russet, Bruce M., et al. *World Handbook of Political and Social Indicators*. New Haven, Conn.: Yale University Press, 1964.

Ryan, Cornelius. *The Last Battle*. New York: Simon & Schuster, Inc., 1966.

Ryle, G. *The Concept of Mind*. New York: Hutchinson's University Library, 1962.

Samuelson, Paul A. *Economics*. New York: McGraw-Hill Book Company, Inc., 1970.

Sapin, B. M. *The Making of United States Foreign Policy*. Washington: Brookings Institution, 1966.

Savage, L. J. *The Foundations of Statistics*. New York: John Wiley and Sons, Inc., 1959.

Schelling, Thomas C. *Arms and Influence*. New Haven, Conn.: Yale University Press, 1966.

———. *The Strategy of Conflict*. Cambridge, Mass.: Harvard University Press, 1960.

———, and M. Halperin. *Strategy and Arms Control*. New York: 20th Century Fund, 1961.

Schilling, W., P. Hammond, and R. Snyder. *Strategy, Politics and Defense Budgets*. New York: Columbia University Press, 1952.

Schlesinger, Arthur M., Jr. *The Politics of Upheaval*. Boston: Houghton Mifflin Company, 1960.

———. *A Thousand Days: John F. Kennedy in the White House*. Boston: Houghton Mifflin Company, 1965.

Schneirla, T. C., and Gerard Piel. "The Army Ant," *Scientific American*, vol. 178, June 1948, pp. 17–23.

Schramm, W. *On the Science of Human Communications*. Stanford, Cal.: Stanford University Press, 1960.

Schultze, Charles L. *The Politics and Economics of Public Spending*. Washington: Brookings Institution, 1968.

Scott, W. A. "Cognitive Complexity and Cognitive Balance," *Sociometry*, vol. 26, 1963, pp. 66–74.

———. "Cognitive Complexity and Cognitive Flexibility," *Sociometry*, vol. 25, 1962, pp. 405–414.

Sherif, Muzafer. *The Psychology of Social Norms*. New York: Harper & Row, Publishers, 1936.

Simon, Herbert A. *Administrative Behavior*. New York: Free Press paperback, 1965.

———. "The Architecture of Complexity," *The Sciences of the Artificial*. Cambridge, Mass.: MIT Press, 1968.

———. "A Behavioral Model of Rational Choice," *Models of Man: Social and Rational*. New York: John Wiley and Sons, Inc., 1957.

———. "Theories of Decision-Making in Economics," *American Economic Review*, vol. 49, 1959, pp. 253–283.

Simpson, S. *Anatomy of the State Department*. Boston: Houghton Mifflin Company, 1967.

Singh, Jagjit. *Great Ideas in Information Theory, Language and Cybernetics*. New York: Dover Publications, 1966.

Skinner, B. F. *Verbal Behavior*. New York: Appleton-Century-Crofts, Inc., 1957.

Smith, Bruce L. R. *The RAND Corporation*. Cambridge, Mass.: Harvard University Press, 1966.

Smith, Gerard C. "The Nuclear Defense of NATO," *Department of State Bulletin*, May 18, 1964, pp. 783–790.

Snyder, Glenn H. *Deterrence and Defense: Toward a Theory of National Security*. Princeton University Press, 1961.

———, N. W. Bruck, and B. M. Sapin. *Foreign Policy Decision-Making: An Approach to the Study of International Politics*. New York: The Free Press of Glencoe, 1962.

Sorensen, Theodore. *Decision-Making in the White House*. New York: Columbia University Press, 1963.

———. *Kennedy*. New York: Harper & Row, Publishers, 1965.

Spanier, John W. *American Foreign Policy Since World War II*, 2nd ed. rev. New York: Frederick A. Praeger, 1965.

Spence, K. W., and J. T. Spence, eds. *The Psychology of Learning and Motivation*, vols. I & II. New York: Academic Press, 1967 & 1968.

Spinelli, A. "Atlantic Pact or European Unity," *Foreign Affairs*, vol. 40, 1962, pp. 542–552.

Stanley, T. "Decentralizing Nuclear Control in NATO," *Orbis*, vol. 7, 1963, pp. 41–48.

———. *NATO in Transition*. New York: Frederick A. Praeger, 1965.

———. "NATO's Nuclear Debate: Washington's View," *Reporter*, vol. 27, July 5, 1962, pp. 19–21.

Steinbruner, John D. "Some Effects of Decision Procedures on Policy Outcomes," Center for International Studies, MIT, 1970.

Stern, Philip M. *The Oppenheimer Case: Security on Trial*. New York: Harper & Row, Publishers, 1969.

Swets, J. A., W. P. Tanner, and T. G. Birdsall. "Decision Processes in Perception," Ralph N. Haber, ed., *Contemporary Theory and Research in Visual Perception*. New York: Holt, Rinehart & Winston, 1968.

Taylor, M. *The Uncertain Trumpet*. New York: Harper & Row, Publishers, 1959.

Thrall, R. M., C. H. Coombs, and R. L. Davis, eds. *Decision Processes*. New York: John Wiley and Sons, Inc., 1954.

Truman, D. B. *The Governmental Process*. New York: Alfred A. Knopf, Inc., 1951.

United Nations, Secretariat of the Economic Commission for Europe, *Some Factors in Economic Growth in Europe During the 1950's*. New York, 1965.

U.S. Bureau of the Census. *Statistical Abstract of the United States: 1969*. Washington: U.S. Government Printing Office, 1969.

U.S. Congress, Joint Committee on Atomic Energy. *Hearings Amending the Atomic Energy Act of 1954*, 85th Congress, 2nd Session, 1958.

———. *Hearings on Agreement for Cooperation for Mutual Defense Purposes*, 86th Congress, 1st Session, 1959.

———. *Hearings on Agreement for Cooperation for Mutual Defense Purposes with the North Atlantic Treaty Organization*, 88th Congress, 2nd Session, 1964.

———. *Hearings on Agreement for Cooperation for Mutual Defense Purposes with the Republic of France*, 87th Congress, 1st Session, 1961.

BIBLIOGRAPHY

U.S. Congress, Joint Committee on Atomic Energy. *Hearings on Nonproliferation of Nuclear Weapons*, 89th Congress, 2nd Session, 1966.

U.S. Congress, Joint Economic Committee, Subcommittee on Priorities and Economy in Government. *The Analysis and Evaluation of Public Expenditures: The PPB System*, 3 vols., 91st Congress, 1st Session, 1969.

U.S. House of Representatives, Committee on the Armed Services. *Hearings on Military Posture*, 88th Congress, 1st Session, 1963.

U.S. Senate, Committee on Foreign Relations. *Hearings on the Nomination of Robert R. Bowie as Counselor of the U.S. Department of State*, 89th Congress, 2nd Session, 1966.

———. *Hearings on U.S. Policy Toward Europe*, 89th Congress, 2nd Session, 1966.

U.S. Senate, Committee on Government Operations, Subcommittee on National Security and International Operations. *Hearings on the Atlantic Alliance*, 89th Congress, 2nd Session, 1966.

———. *Hearings on the Conduct of National Security Policy*, 4 parts, 89th Congress, 1st Session, 1965.

U.S. Senate, Select Committee on Small Business, Subcommittee on Monopoly. *Competitive Problems in the Drug Industry*, Part 6, 90th Congress, 2nd Session, 1968.

Uphaw, H. S. "Cognitive Consistency and the Psychology of Judgment," Robert P. Abelson et al., eds., *Theories of Cognitive Consistency*. Chicago: Rand McNally & Company, 1968.

Verba, S. "Assumptions of Rationality and Non-Rationality in Models of the International System," *World Politics*, vol. 14, 1961, pp. 93–117.

Vernon, M. D., ed. *Experiments in Visual Perception*. Baltimore: Penguin Books, Inc., 1966.

Verrier, A. "The Multilateral Force Project," *Brassey's Annual*, 1964, p. 81.

Vickers, G. *The Art of Judgment: A Study of Policy-Making*. New York: Basic Books, Inc., 1965.

von Neumann, John, and Oskar Morgenstern. *Theory of Games and Economic Behavior*. New York: John Wiley and Sons, Inc., 1954.

Wald, Abraham. *Statistical Decision Functions*. New York: John Wiley and Sons, Inc., 1950.

Weintal, E., and C. Bartlett. *Facing the Brink: An Intimate Study of Crisis Diplomacy*. New York: Charles Scribner's Sons, 1967.

Whaley, C. "Soviet Strategic Information Processing," unpublished paper, Center for International Studies, MIT, 1967.

Whiting, A. *China Crosses the Yalu: The Decision to Enter the Korean War*. New York: The Macmillan Company, 1960.

Wilcox, F. O., and H. F. Haviland, Jr. *The Atlantic Community: Progress and Prospects*. New York: Frederick A. Praeger, 1963.

Williamson, Samuel R. *The Politics of Grand Strategy*. Cambridge, Mass.: Harvard University Press, 1969.

Wilson, J. *Varieties of Police Behavior*. Cambridge, Mass.: Harvard University Press, 1968.

Wilson, Thomas W., Jr. *The Great Weapons Heresy*. Boston: Houghton Mifflin Company, 1970.

Wohlstetter, Albert. "The Delicate Balance of Terror," *Foreign Affairs*, vol. 37, 1959, pp. 211–235.

———. "NATO and the N+1 Country," *Foreign Affairs*, vol. 39, 1961, pp. 355–387.

———, F. S. Hoffman, R. J. Lutz, and H. S. Rowen. "Selection and Use of Strategic Air Bases," RAND Corporation paper no. R-266, 1954.

Wohlstetter, Roberta. *Pearl Harbor: Warning and Decision*. Stanford, Calif.: Stanford University Press, 1967.

Worshop, R. L. "Reconstruction of NATO," *Editorial Research Reports*, November 1964, pp. 843–859.

Wyburn, G. M., R. W. Pickford, and R. J. Hirst. *Human Senses and Perception*. London: Oliver & Boyd, 1964.

Zalkind, S., and T. W. Costello, "Perception: Some Recent Research and Implications for Administration," *Administrative Science Quarterly*, vol. 7, 1962–63; pp. 218–235.

Index

361

INDEX

France: and European integration,
264; and NATO, 166-68, 174;
nuclear aid to, 203; nuclear program, 165-66, 206, 215, 228, 236,
309; and Suez, 173-74
Franco-German nuclear program,
252
Franco-German treaty of cooperation, 252, 297
Freud, Sigmund, 93, 100-101
Fulbright, (Sen.) William, 306

Gavin, (Gen.) James M., 217
Germany (Federal Republic of), 20;
interest in nuclear weapons, 215,
251, 260-61, 270, 300; politics of,
261-62, 267, 288, 305; reactions to
MLF, 274, 276-77
Gestalt psychology, 101
Gilpatrick, Roswell, 205, 217
Gödel, Kurt, 118-19
Great Britain: and European integration, 264; politics of, 279, 287-
88, 294-97; relationship to Europe,
217; and Skybolt missile, 203, 210-
14 *passim*, 219, 234-37, 245, 250-51,
292; special relationship with U.S.,
214, 219, 228; and Suez, 173-74;
V-bombers,. 272, 279, 295, 303
Green Book, see Acheson Report
Grewe, Wilhelm, 290
grooved thinking, see cognitive
theory

Halperin, Morton, 141
Heider, Fritz, 99
Herter, Christian A., 153, 187, 220
Hilbert, David, 118
Hilsman, Roger, 141
Holifield, (Rep.) Chet, 187, 300
homeostat, 54, 58, 80
Hound Dog missile, 220, 235-36
Huitt, Ralph K., 141
Humphrey, (Sen.) Hubert, 300
Huntington, Samuel, 142

IANF (Interallied Nuclear Force),
272n, 279, 295, 316
incrementalism, 80-81

Jackson, John, 76
Johnson, Lyndon, B., 198, 249, 285,
289-91, 304-7, 309, 319, 321-23
Johnson, U. Alexis, 253
Johnson-Wilson Communiqué, 308
Joint Chiefs of Staff (JCS), see
U.S. Department of Defense
Joint Committee on Atomic Energy
(JCAE), 175, 181, 186-87, 229, 269,
271, 286, 300, 305, 315
Joliot-Curie, M., 165
Jones, R. V., 119
Jupiter missile, 182, 234, 252, 269

Kahn, H., 107
Kelvin, 119
Kennedy, John F., 110, 145-46, 191-
92, 196, 199, 218, 221-23, 225, 227,
234-35, 237-39, 243-46, 249, 252,
255, 268, 270-71, 275-76, 278, 281,
292, 306, 315, 319; quoted, 222-23,
225
Khrushchev, Nikita, 187
Kimball, G. F., 38-39n
Kitchen, Jeffrey, 252, 254, 255, 270
Kohler, Foy, 228
Kuhn, Thomas S., 9-11
Kuss, Henry, 231

lateral expansion, see assumptions
Lavaud, (Gen.) Gaston, 216, 218
law of requisite variety, 68n
learning, 78-80; causal, 40-44, 117,
330; constrained, 136-38, 331; instrumental, 79-80
Lee, (Adm.) John M., 228-29, 231,
234, 250, 253, 268-70, 286. See also
MLF
Lemnitzer, (Gen.) Lyman, 246
Levy, Frank, 81n
Lilienthal, David, 169
limited value integration, see
assumptions
Lindblom, Charles, 80n, 142

Macmillan, Harold, 186, 234-38, 244,
272, 278, 282, 287
Manhattan Project, 165, 168

363

Library of Congress Cataloging in Publication Data

Steinbruner, John D   1941-
  The cybernetic theory of decision.

  Bibliography: p.
  1. Decision-making in political science. 2. Atomic weapons. 3. North
Atlantic Treaty Organization.
  I. Title.
JA74.S68   658.4'03   74-2479
ISBN 0-691-07559-X